D0312866

Praise for *Hungry*

"Who knew that avocado toast was a window to the soul? With substance, style, and a keen eye for data, Eve Turow-Paul uses food to illuminate the psychology of an entire generation. *Hungry* is a deeply insightful book that also happens to be more delicious than dessert."

—Daniel Gilbert, professor of psychology at Harvard and *New York Times* bestselling author author of *Stumbling on Happiness*

"Turow-Paul combines great story-telling with a hard look at many trends and beliefs that are not based on facts. She artfully explains why they pull us in anyway, the psychological needs they fill, and how we can bring order and sanity to one of the most fraught topics today: food."

—Dr. Daniel J. Levitin, neuroscientist and *New York Times* bestselling author of *Successful Aging* and *The Organized Mind*

hungry

Also by Eve Turow-Paul

A Taste of Generation Yum: How the Millennial Generation's Love for Organic Fare, Celebrity Chefs, and Microbrews Will Make or Break the Future of Food

hungry

Avocado Toast, Instagram Influencers, and Our Search for Connection and Meaning

Eve Turow-Paul

BenBella Books, Inc.
Dallas, TX

BenBella Books, Inc.
10440 N. Central Expressway, Suite 800
Dallas, TX 75231
www.benbellabooks.com
Send feedback to feedback@benbellabooks.com

BenBella is a federally registered trademark.

Printed in the United States of America
10 9 8 7 6 5 4 3 2 1

Library of Congress Cataloging-in-Publication Data
Names: Turow-Paul, Eve, 1987- author.
Title: Hungry : avocado toast, instagram influencers, and the modern search
  for connection and meaning / Eve Turow-Paul.
Description: Dallas: BenBella Books, 2020. | Includes bibliographical
  references and index.
Identifiers: LCCN 2019056912 | ISBN 9781948836975 (hardback) | ISBN
  9781950665167 (ebook)
Subjects: LCSH: Food—Social aspects. | Social media—Social aspects. |
  Twenty-first century—Forecasting.
Classification: LCC GT2850 .T87 2020 | DDC 394.1/2—dc23
LC record available at https://lccn.loc.gov/2019056912

Editing by Leah Wilson
Copyediting by Karen Wise
Proofreading by Michael Fedison
  and Karen O'Brien
Text design Publishers' Design
  and Production Services, Inc.
Printed by Lake Book Manufacturing

Indexing by WordCo Indexing Services
Text composition by PerfecType,
  Nashville, TN
Cover design by Matt Chase
Cover photo © Shutterstock/ Elena Shashkina
  (avocado) and M Kunz (toast)

Distributed to the trade by Two Rivers Distribution, an Ingram brand
www.tworiversdistribution.com

Special discounts for bulk sales are available.
Please contact bulkorders@benbellabooks.com.

For Jason and Liv, who fill my life with comfort, love, and meaning.

contents

It is then fair to characterize the whole organism by saying simply that it is hungry, for consciousness is almost completely preempted by hunger. All capacities are put into the service of hunger-satisfaction, and the organization of these capacities is almost entirely determined by the one purpose of satisfying hunger.

—Abraham Maslow, *Motivation and Personality*

introduction

Flecks of sand sat between my sandaled toes and the warmth of the descending sun kissed my shoulders as I leaned forward and scoured the menu.

My husband, Jason, and I had traveled to the resort town of Playa del Carmen, Mexico, for a brief respite from New York's lugubrious winters. I intended to take advantage of our short stay culinarily, and had made a mental list of all the regional flavors I wanted to indulge in, from piquant tacos al pastor to bright ceviches.

On this, our second night, we had walked across town to a highly recommended seafood restaurant. Soon, we placed an order for a towering seafood tostada and tangy, lime-soaked aguachiles. Our waiter nodded in approval of our selections.

"And to drink?" he asked, motioning for us to look at the back of the menu where I anticipated finding a handful of standard beer and fruit-forward cocktails to choose from. But as I flipped the page, I was stunned to see a list of nearly seventy beer options, with Mexican states like Jalisco, Quintana Roo, and Baja California Sur noted alongside each item.

"What do you like?" the waiter questioned. "IPAs? Saisons? Pilsners?"

"These are all made in Mexico?" I asked him, bewildered. The waiter nodded. Historically, the category of Mexican beers has fit into a rather narrow box: golden, low-alcohol lagers made by industrial breweries that pair well with a slice of lime and a day of continuous drinking by the pool. But here in front of me was an extensive list of breweries and beer styles that directly challenged this tenet. Suddenly I was overwhelmed. The craft beer revolution, it seemed, had arrived in Mexico.

Back in the United States, the small-batch, artisan brewing craze had already hit a high. In the decade between 2008 and 2018, the number of US craft breweries tripled to an astounding 6,500. New boutique brewhouses have been reimagining what beer can be. They toss in unique ingredients like habanero chiles, mangos, and coffee, utilize obscure hop varietals, and even toy with new production methods like aging brews in whiskey barrels. With these innovations, the beer drinking experience has become more sophisticated, playful, and regional.

I later learned that Mexico has been experiencing its own craft beer movement, though on a smaller scale. In 2008 there were only twenty craft breweries across the entire country. By 2018, some eight hundred Mexican craft breweries were fermenting their unconventional creations. All thirty-one Mexican states now have a state brewery.

"We are growing at an amazing rate," Ariette Armella of Acermex, Mexico's Craft Brewers Association, told me, citing their astounding rise and continued year-on-year development. Though still just about 0.2 percent of all beer brewed in Mexico, the craft beer scene is catching on, she said, especially among those ages twenty-five to forty.

While I have always thought of Mexico as a flavor haven—home of complex moles, acidic escabeches, and fiery salsas that illuminate each and every taste bud—the idea of Mexico as a craft beer destination had never crossed my mind. Yet, I shouldn't have been so surprised that the beverage trend had been fermenting south of the US border. This rapid and radical shift is emblematic of the larger changes that have taken place across the food industry over the last decade, by and large fueled by those under the age of forty. This era has given rise to the colloquial term "foodie," a title proudly adopted by roughly half of all Millennials (those born between 1980 and 1996) and members of Generation Z (those born between 1996 and 2010) worldwide.[1] Together, these generations make up just over half of the global population, which means that *at least* one quarter of all people in the world consider themselves a part of the modern foodophile community.

Gourmet food experiences used to be a hobby for older, upper-class bon vivants, not recent college graduates with four roommates and a bikeshare membership. But here we are, in a world where twenty- and thirtysomethings fawn over uni, chamomile Saison beers, and Chemex pour-over coffee, and treat reservations at Copenhagen's Noma, New York City's Momofuku Ko, Bangkok's Gaggan, and Lima's Central with the same excitement as tickets to Broadway's *Hamilton*.

"Food has become a bit like pop music," Indian food blogger Amit Patnaik told me over Skype in 2017 of his own observations in Mumbai. "Food has become a hobby for young people. They say, 'Let's go out and have a meal.' In India," where, he said, the culture has historically revolved around home cooking, "this is new, seen only the last five years."

An obsession with all things food has taken hold in nearly every nook and cranny of the globe. In India, people chew on fusion dishes like chutney grilled cheese and offer culinary critiques that emulate the judges they watch each week on *MasterChef*. In Nairobi, Kenya, folks can bite into grass-fed beef hamburgers topped with chili mango sauce and grab tacos from street-side food trucks. "Young people are definitely crowding new bars and bistros," Della Mbaya, a Nairobi-based lifestyle journalist, confirmed for me. In Hong Kong, veganism is the latest fashion statement, and restaurants boast locally brewed kombucha. Craft beer festivals are hosted in Ho Chi Minh City, São Paulo, Cape Town, and yes, Mexico City, among other places. I've heard stories of young Berliners leaving desk jobs to become butchers, Londoners waiting in hours-long lines for Filipino fried chicken, and Buenos Aires residents hopping from speakeasy to speakeasy.

I have witnessed firsthand the virality of foodie culture. During a 2017 trip through Southeast Asia, on the Bangkok Skytrain, I stood across from a twentysomething Thai woman wearing a T-shirt that read: "Fuck love, I have food." And in Myanmar—where the Internet only recently arrived and most of the country remains campestral copper dirt roads and vast rice fields—a barista at a small café in Yangon presented Jason and me with a coffee flavor wheel to help us choose the beans for a custom pour-over coffee. What flavors, she inquired, would we like our coffee to exhibit? Hints of raisin? Rum? Chocolate? I ended up ordering locally bottled cold brew with the tasting notes of "cherry cola" and "lemon citrus" printed on the glass. Myanmar is the poorest nation in Southeast Asia.[2] Still, they have cold brew.

This youth-based gastronomic fever has spread to all aspects of lifestyle culture. You can find Beyoncé donning a "KALE" emblazoned sweatshirt in a music video and Katy Perry singing in food metaphors ("I'm a five-star Michelin/A Kobe flown in/You want what I'm cooking, boy"). In the US, new parents are popularizing food-centric baby names like Kale, Saffron, and Maple.[3] In Japan, the bestselling shōnen manga series Shokugeki no Soma focuses on a boy who wants to become a chef. In Korea, livestreams of people eating have become one of the most popular forms of online content. Food ingredients are spilling over in beauty products and textiles. Sitcoms and films glorify the lives of chefs and farmers. Hotels are touting on-premise farms and organic ingredients, and find that even their mini bar menus play an increasingly important role in traveler decision-making.*

The gaming industry, too, has embraced the global food mania. In 2018, Nintendo released *Sushi Striker: The Way of Sushido*, in which players help the main character "end the Empire's tyrannical monopoly of the world's sushi supply" by devouring conveyor-belt sushi and matching plates and sushi types.

Part of what's so revolutionary about today's food trends are the particular kinds of food and food experiences raking in the most bites, slurps, snaps, and shares. New concerns and interests are influencing people's food choices. All around the globe, there is a call for products with greater transparency, made with local ingredients, by brands with a clear value system. These tenets—of openness, connectedness, and purpose—are rattling the food industry as newbie upstarts, able to address these modern criteria, begin to steal shelf space and dollars away from veteran brands.

In the food and beverage arena, there is a popular rebuffing of genetically modified ingredients, gluten, and any flavor or coloring agent deemed "unnatural." People want simple and clean products with easy-to-understand ingredients and access to behind-the-scenes information about sourcing and processing. Products that invoke a sense of intimacy by focusing on "artisanal," "heritage," and "local" ingredients are resonating. In restaurants, diners welcome shared tables and plates, open kitchens, and direct chef-to-patron interaction. Finally, there's robust enthusiasm for prosocial brands that put their dollars to wide

---

* Food is not just influencing where we stay, but often where we travel to. More than two-thirds of US Millennials will recommend a destination entirely based on cuisine, according to a survey commissioned by food company Harry & David and reported in "Intrepid Adventure Travel Index 2018."

use. Fervent demands for eco-friendly, responsibly sourced, and fair-trade food items continue to grow louder.

All of these trends run counter to decades of food and beverage marketing that, by and large, focused on flavor and cost-savings above all else. For the past few generations, shoppers have celebrated the reliability and consistency of industrialized food. Now, restaurateurs, consumer packaged goods companies, grocers, and farmers are all tossing their former rule books out the window as they try to meet these new, game-changing expectations.

Some members of the food and beverage industry aren't managing these changes well. Since 2009, the top twenty-five American food and beverage companies have lost more than $18 billion in market share, unable to appropriately respond to customer wants, according to analysis by Credit Suisse.[4] Many veteran companies continue to experience a precipitous loss of market share to new, smaller startups that embody the candid, humanistic, and socially responsible values today's shoppers crave. Once-favored sit-down restaurant chains like TGI Friday's, Ruby Tuesday, and Applebee's are all facing sales slumps, while upstarts like Blaze Pizza and Honeygrow—which emphasize handcrafted, gluten-free, and vegan options—reel in visitors. In China, new chain restaurants like Grandma's Home and Xibei Youmian Cun—which highlight shared plates and organic items such as "self-made fresh tofu"—are nabbing fast-food frequenters from staples like McDonald's and KFC.[5]

Farmers are also impacted by changes in supply chain demands; they're facing decisions like whether to forgo GMOs, raise their hens cage free, or supplement their waning dairy milk sales by sowing flax or brewing beer. "Meet Your New Boss: Moms, bloggers and foodies these Millennials are driving the new food and ag economy," read the cover of a 2016 edition of *Successful Farming* magazine. Many are flummoxed by the market shifts and point fingers at "hipsters" as villainous instigators of upheaval.

Novel Millennial and Generation Z standards aren't just impacting our food; they're shaking up nearly every lifestyle industry, including travel, hospitality, auto, beauty, fitness, and fashion. Just as "free from" proliferates on food labels, fashion and cosmetic brands now promote products sans parabens, BPA, and other controversial ingredients. By 2020, market researchers expect the organic cosmetic market to be valued at $66.1 billion.[6] Meanwhile, interest in shared products and experiences is pushing the automobile, fitness, and hospitality industries to rethink their business models and product offerings: Legacy hotel chains are struggling to attract young people who prefer Airbnb, couch surfing, and glamping, while big box gyms have watched their numbers fall as memberships at boutique gyms rose by 121 percent between 2013 and 2017.[7] Unique, handmade home goods, personal care items, and accessories are all the rage. And just as shoppers want their food dollars to go toward social and environmental causes, fashion houses are now dancing around clientele who want "upcycled," wasteless retail options and brands that "give back" to charitable causes. Today's teens, twenty-, and thirtysomethings are less likely to affiliate with political parties or religious faiths. Instead, they're increasingly interested in unorthodox concepts like astrology and in expressing their value systems through product choices. A yearning for meaning and self-reflection is also supporting the rise of a potent global wellness industry.

Still, the greatest changes are occurring across the food system, from farm to fork, where those under forty are spending a record amount of their discretionary time and income. Globally, Millennials purchase organic goods more often than members of any other generation, driving double-digit yearly growth in the organic food industry. This is especially true of young parents, who are now the biggest group of organic buyers in America and across Europe.* Similarly, twenty- and thirtysomethings spend the most on specialty foods, infusing couture coffee shops, bone broth pop-ups, and small-batch brands with ample cash.[8] (In fact, according to a 2017 survey, almost half of US Millennials have spent more money on coffee than they've invested in retirement savings.[9]) Millennials around the world—from Spain to India to the United States—are also spending the most on meals out.[10] In Asia Pacific, one in three eighteen- to twenty-nine-year-olds eats at a fine dining establishment at

---

* The Organic Trade Association reports in "Millennials and Organic: A Winning Combination" that the shopping habits of Millennial parents have spurred the more than 200 percent rise in US organic produce sales between 2005 and 2015. Among US parents, more than half (52 percent) of organic buyers are Millennials. And according to a 2017 Mintel survey of ten thousand individuals, this behavior pattern holds true in France, Germany, Poland, Spain, and Italy as well.

least once a month, which is more often than those thirty years old and above, according to Mastercard.[11] Meanwhile, Visa confirms that Millennials in Singapore, Hong Kong, and China allocate 18 percent of their personal budgets to dining and eating out, more than any other expenditure.[12] Millennial spending power is vast, and some view their tastes and preferences as a tsunami, smashing down and creating chaos. In 2017, then CEO of Buffalo Wild Wings Sally Smith directly blamed foodie Millennials for her company's downturn in a letter to shareholders.[13]

Generation Z has similarly picked up the epicurean torch. "Generation Z spends more of their entertainment budget on eating out at their age than any past consumers," Steve Gundrum, Chairman and Chief Creative Officer at food and beverage development firm Mattson, told me. On average, he noted, Gen Zers spend 20 percent more than Millennials did at that age. According to financial services company Piper Jaffray, teens are now, for the first time, spending more on food than on clothing.[14] And in a somewhat bizarre statistic, Chicago's restaurant research firm Technomic notes that the second biggest age group visiting high-end fine-dining restaurants, behind Millennials, are young tween and teen Gen Zers.* Dining hall offerings are now an influential criterion for college-bound Gen Zers,† and Food Studies programs are popping up at universities across all continents.

It's easy to make fun of this youthful food obsession, and many do so with great zeal.‡ Many characterize these younger generations as

---

* According to the 2018 Technomic Future of FSR Consumer Trend Report, 41 percent of Generation Zers who dine at a high-end restaurant attend the meal with their "partners," 34 percent are with family, 26 percent with friends, and 15 percent dine alone.

† For some college students, the craving for high-end and sustainable coffee has become so essential that they're complaining to their universities. According to a September 6, 2017, story by Quint Forgey and Patrick McGroarty in the *Wall Street Journal*, titled "College Activists March on the Cafeteria: What Do We Want? Hydroponic Cilantro!", Virginia Tech's head of dining services flew to Nicaragua to handpick the free-trade, organic coffee beans now used at the school in an effort to assuage the coffee-coveting student body.

‡ Foodie-mocking memes abound. "Care to see pictures of every meal I've ordered in a restaurant in the past 45 years?" one *Bizarro* cartoon reads, with the caption "Future Millennial Grandparents."

entitled, lazy, and naive for spending their limited discretionary funds on evanescent goods. "I have seen young people order smashed avocado with crumbled feta on five-grain toasted bread at $22 a pop and more," social commentator Bernard Salt writes in the October 15–16, 2016, edition of *The Australian*, taking aim at what he sees as youthful fiscal irresponsibility. "Twenty-two dollars several times a week could go towards a deposit on a house," he admonishes. While I'm not sure savings from avocado toast alone could put more young people into home ownership, Salt has a point: Australians now spend more on restaurants and takeaway meals than they do on electricity, gas, or even secondary education, all while lamenting being unable to afford the overpriced real estate market, among other financial woes.[15]

A global youth food craze makes very little rational sense when juxtaposed with this same cohort's economic reality. In 2008, at the precipice of a global recession, most Millennials were just edging into adulthood, either in college or recently graduated. I, myself a Millennial, graduated college in 2009 and very clearly remember one of the commencement speakers saying something to the tune of: "You've paid into society and done everything we've asked of you. Society is not about to pay you back." That year, the usual financial institutions were not on campus to recruit potential employees. Instead, we walked across the stage, took our degrees in hand, and moved back in with our parents— packing $1.5 trillion of student loan debt into our luggage.[16]

The Great Recession kept career-ready Millennials on the lower rungs of professional development. Unemployment of American college graduates nearly doubled between 2007 and 2010.* The rest of the world didn't fare much better. Youth unemployment in Europe rose above 17 percent in 2012, double the unemployment rate for the general population. Greece and Spain fared the worst, with over half the young labor force out of work.

For many, unemployment has been paired with years of stagnant wages and rising living costs. Average Millennial salaries often pale in

---

* The year 2012 marked the lowest rate of youth employment in the US since the government started keeping records in 1948.

comparison to what generations prior were making at the same age.* Concurrently, living expenses, like the cost of housing, continue to rise, pushing youth away from the home-buying market and into their child-hood bedrooms.† For the first time in the modern era, US adults ages eighteen to thirty-four are more likely to live with a parent than with a romantic partner, a trend that echoes worldwide.[17] As of 2015, roughly half of Japanese Millennials lived with their parents.[18] Meanwhile, those who rent face astounding prices and competition. Renters in Sydney and Melbourne routinely spend over 30 percent of their income on housing, a stat mirrored in London, Hong Kong, New York, and San Francisco, among other large cities.

"My friends and I know our salaries will never be enough to buy a house or be very wealthy," my friend Hyunjee Cho, then thirty-four, told me from her home in Seoul, South Korea, where the global recession and controversial labor policies have been negatively impacting youth employment rates and wages.[19] While her parents' generation saved up, Hyunjee says that the mindset of the young has shifted to *Why even try?*

In the US, many twenty- and thirtysomethings are also choking down the brutal reality of student loan debt. Three-quarters of American Millennials are in debt, and nearly two-thirds say they don't know when, if ever, they will pay off what they owe.[20] The Consumer Financial Protection Bureau reports that one in four student loan recipients is either in delinquency or default on their student loans.[21] The World Economic Forum cites similar debt woes for Millennials in the United Kingdom and Japan, caused by education and housing costs.[22]

With these hardships, more and more young people—even those living independently—are turning to their wealthier Baby Boomer parents for help. Somewhere between 40 and 50 percent of American

---

* In 2016, median earnings for college grads stood at $24.99 per hour, about 1.5 per-
cent less than in 2000, according to the Economic Policy Institute. The Federal
Reserve notes that US Millennials are less well off than members of earlier generations when they were at the same life stage, noting this generation's "lower earnings,
fewer assets and less wealth," as written in "Are Millennials Different?" published in
Finance and Economics Discussion, November 2018.

† US Census data shows that only 39 percent of Millennials owned homes in 2015,
compared to 47.5 percent for that same age group in 2007.

Millennials rely on financial assistance from their parents to cover the costs of rent, groceries, and health insurance, a relationship that often continues after Millennials themselves become parents.[*, 23]

Though financial challenges have kept many Millennials from buying homes and cars, getting married, or having children, many still seem to find it worthwhile to invest their recession-dented incomes in an ephemeral commodity: food.[24]

Between 2010 and 2014, the years hardest hit by the recession, there was a 10 percent increase in US Millennial food spending.[25] Millennials are more likely than members of other generations to consider food items splurge-worthy; only half of American Millennials think it's important to make their food purchases fit into their budgets, compared to 61 percent of non-Millennials, according to a survey from Mintel.[†] Another study notes that US Millennials are more willing to overspend on restaurants than on any other shopping category, including technology.[26] Again, these behaviors are evident internationally, where people attend supper clubs that they travel to in ride shares while wearing secondhand clothes.

Back in Mexico, craft beers are three times as expensive as their industrial beer counterparts, Ariette Armella told me. Why, I asked her, are young people choosing to spend their limited income on this costly experience?

"Our income right now, it doesn't get us as far as past generations," Armella, herself a Millennial, said, referring to the incomes of Mexico's burgeoning population of middle- to upper-class Millennials. "Buying a

---

* "House prices are so inflated, particularly in London, that the Bank of Mum and Dad now helps fund 26 [percent] of all property transactions in the UK, providing deposits for more than 298,000 mortgages in 2016," reports Sophie Smith for the *Telegraph*. "That means the Bank of Mum and Dad has become the equivalent of the ninth-biggest mortgage lender in the UK."

† While over a third of Americans say they can't afford to fund a retirement plan because they don't have enough money, and a shocking 60 percent of adults don't have enough money in savings to cover a $1,000 emergency expense, Americans spend an average of $18,000 a year on "nonessentials," the most frequent of which includes restaurant meals, drinks, and delivery food, according to a survey by One-Poll and insurance company Ladder, reports Maurie Backman for *USA Today*.

house is off the table for many. I think our generation is tilting to luxuries they can afford. Maybe I need to share my apartment, but I get to go out and have these beers that I completely love."

Affordable indulgence is one possible explanation for these incongruous trends. But is it really that simple? And why is artisanal food the luxury of choice, rather than concert tickets, new clothes, or a nice car?

In 2010, I moved to New York City for graduate school and found myself scraping by on a student budget, yet investing what little extra income I had on underground dinners and Sottocenere truffle cheese at Whole Foods. At the time, I was fresh off a brief stint at a Washington, DC, economics think tank, where, as a part of their communications team, I had worked to tease out the difference between unemployment and underemployment. With consistent exposure to the latest economic numbers, I became keenly aware that in terms of income, my generation would be behind Generation X (those born between 1960 and 1980) for at least a decade, if not our entire lifetimes. Yet, just a few months later, I was living in one of the most expensive cities in the country, spending well over a thousand dollars a month to rent 250 square feet, and choosing to forgo taxis, new clothes, and movies (not to mention contributing to my savings account) in order to enjoy great meals out. What was motivating me to make that trade-off?

With our financial realities, Millennials should not be waiting in lines around the block for raw cookie dough or leaving lucrative jobs to become pastry chefs, yet that is exactly what so many of us are doing today. Why, at this moment in time, has food culture become a fetish of the young, the up-and-coming? *Is* it irresponsible for a generation facing horrendous debt and financial insecurity to be spending our time and money on artisan ice cream, single-origin chocolate, and home sous vide machines? What is it that we are so hungry for?

Eventually, I decided to look into the "why" behind my own behavior and that of the people around me. And what I began to learn was so complex and enthralling, I haven't stopped studying it since.

Though it's easy to label today's twenty- and thirtysomethings as careless, misguided kids, our seemingly incongruous behaviors are not a reflection of arrogance or extravagance, but rather the direct result of the unique environment we were raised in: the Digital Age.

In my own research, I began to see link after link between the anomalous and nascent digital world that defines Millennial and Gen Z youth, and the often-mocked lifestyle trends shaking up global industries. I began to see interest in things like adult coloring books, the Paleo diet, and learning to bake sourdough bread not as hobbies, but as coping mechanisms for this extraordinary, bizarre, and unprecedented digital world we live in.

While a love of food makes the Millennial and Z generations unique, it's the relationship to technology that truly sets these generations apart from all others. Millennials were the first guinea pigs for lives tethered to digital screens. We recall the days of landlines, floppy disks, and fears of Y2K, but our fingers now use phone keyboards with second-nature agility. Meanwhile, Gen Zers don't know a world without social media, email, and texting. They're the first generation born directly into the Digital Age. They speak a digitally influenced language that sometimes even leaves Millennials flummoxed.

Given the staggering impact of these technologies on our lives, it's important to pause and ask: How is this unique backdrop driving our current obsessions?

In the blink of an evolutionary eye, our worlds have been irreparably altered. In 1991, the world welcomed the World Wide Web. In less than thirty years, we've catapulted from dial-up and Ask Jeeves to Snapchat and geo-tagging. Since the release of the iPhone just over a decade ago, in 2007, the social impacts of technology have become even more widespread. Technologies unknown just a decade or two ago are now treated as essential appendages. Nearly three-fourths of Millennials and half of Baby Boomers now believe that they "can't survive" without their smartphones—a device that literally didn't exist until just over a decade ago.[27] People sleep with their phones, take their phones with them to the bathroom, and even check their phones while having sex.[28] Among the world's three billion smartphone users, the average person unlocks their phone eighty times a day, which comes out to six or seven times every hour.[29] What else do you do that often besides breathe and blink?

Yet, as the environment around us has shifted, we, as *Homo sapiens*, haven't changed all that much, which is why, to assess the impact of this remarkable climate, I've found it useful to place this era in the wider context of human history. For about forty thousand years, humans lived as foragers.[30] The past two hundred years drove us away from the fields and down to our desks, yet evolutionarily speaking, we remain our hunter-gatherer selves; some evolutionary psychologists say we still carry around "stone-age" brains.[31] Our eyes, noses, and ears are attuned to the outdoors. Our bodies are best fed by a wide variety of foods collected based on season and location. We cannot concentrate on many things at once, having evolved to maintain focus on the dangers or opportunities in our surroundings and to block out the rest. We are tribal by nature, convivial and comfortable in groups, and we find purpose in manual competence, completing tasks that we can see and hold in our own two hands.

Today, our Paleolithic selves live in an antiseptic, hyper-scheduled Twitterverse. Instead of convening, we iMessage. Instead of crafting, cultivating, or building something, we export a Keynote presentation. Instead of finishing our work with a sense of accomplishment, we wade endlessly through a persistent bombardment of emails, Slack posts, and text messages. And this dissemblance appears to be taking a toll.

Sure, Millennials and Gen Zers are foodies; we're also the loneliest and most anxious, stressed out, and depressed generations on record. Though the years since Y2K are often talked about as the most "connected" period of all time, numerous studies from around the globe show that people of all ages feel far more isolated. Numbers of close confidants have plummeted worldwide, and people are spending less and less time in person with friends.[32] Concurrently, stress is mounting. According to an online survey of over two thousand people ages eighteen to thirty-three by the American Psychological Association, 52 percent of US Millennials have lain awake at night due to stress.[33] In the UK, the British charity YouthNet reports a third of young women and one in ten young men suffer from panic attacks.[34] There has also been a stark rise in depression. Major depressive episodes, reports of self-harm, and attempted suicide are becoming alarmingly common among adolescents.[35]

Many analysts point to common culprits such as helicopter parenting, tough economic realities, and political unease as the foundation of these debilitating mental states, but others see a different catalyst for angst: the Internet. The cycle of 24/7 news puts us into an anxious tizzy. Social media makes us jealous and insecure. Email makes our existence seem nugatory.

It should come as no surprise that the first Digital Age generations spend their time and money in novel ways. The human experience has drastically changed, and with it, so have our demands and desires. So, the questions we should be asking are: What needs—what hungers— are we trying to satisfy today? And how is food culture—among other things—helping us fulfill these basic needs?

In *Hungry*, we will explore the ways in which today's top lifestyle trends—with a core focus in food—are tools for well-being. In each chapter, we will focus on unique trends—from an interest in delivery services to the popularity of unicorn cakes to the DIY movement—and assess why these trends have come into being. We will dig into our core human needs and discuss the ways in which the Digital Age is challenging or aiding the satisfaction of these needs. Along the way, we will not just learn about the movements upending the lifestyle industries, but gain insight into the physiological and psychological impacts of our new technologies and our inherent well-being needs.

In the late 1940s, famed psychologist Abraham Maslow became the first academic to theorize what each of us needs to lead a fulfilling life. He hypothesized that all humans share five core types of needs: *physiological*, which includes the basics of survival like water, air, food, sex, and sleep; *safety*, meaning a sense of security, societal order, law, and stability; *love and belonging*, which Maslow defined as "hunger for affectionate relations with people" and a place within a group; *esteem*, described as achievement, mastery, and independence that leads to self-respect and respect from others; and finally, *self-actualization*, realizing one's potential by seeking out personal growth and peak experiences. Maslow became a seminal figure in the creation of humanistic psychology, and his Hierarchy of Needs remains a touchstone concept for many business, healthcare, education, and psychology practices.

In recent years, other, similar philosophies around human well-being have been developed. In 2000, University of Rochester social science professors Richard M. Ryan and Edward L. Deci introduced what they call Self-Determination Theory (SDT), which states that all human beings possess an inherent desire to feel autonomous, competent, and connected to one another, and says that the fulfillment of these needs is essential to personal growth and well-being. Put another way, human beings must feel empowered, emotionally bonded to others, and capable of achieving our goals in order to feel well. Since its introduction, SDT has become one of the most widely researched and applied theories in the field of psychology.

You may notice that Deci and Ryan's theory aligns rather nicely with Maslow's. I can't say that any one scientist has figured it all out, but I am struck by the confluence of themes—those of control, belonging, and purpose—in these two theories. As such, I've used these themes as the structural foundation for this book.

This book will evaluate the human experience in today's world, and the ways in which food culture and other disruptive lifestyle trends act as an antidote to the stress, loneliness, and anxiety generated by the Digital Age, to create a sense of safety, love, and purpose in our lives by tapping into our core, innate needs as human beings.

In the first section, "Control," we'll explore the impact of 24/7 news, readily accessible information, the rise of Internet addiction, and our growing desire to find something within our direct control. We'll touch on transparency trends and dig into the psychological underpinnings of the anti-GMO movement, interest in delivery services, and subscriptions, as well as restrictive diets, such as vegan, Paleo, and gluten-free.

In the second section, "Belonging," we'll investigate the effects of social media on human bonding. We'll look at the uptick in online bullying, performance via online avatars, and the waning frequency of eye-to-eye contact. In direct antithesis, we'll cover the renewed interest in dining out, the success of tribal fitness practices and communal events, and our desire to get to know creators, as seen in the potent power of social media influencers.

Finally, in "Purpose," we'll examine the repercussions of time spent in the digital space on our sense of meaning and personal value. We'll look at the popular online trends around sensory experiences and reconnecting to our bodies, such as the DIY movement and ASMR videos. We'll also discuss the growing interest in unplugging, shutting down our phones, and getting back outside into nature to cook, garden, and sometimes, just breathe.

In writing this book, I traveled the world to witness firsthand the cultural trends driven by modern consumer behaviors and to speak with experts who could help me make sense of all I was observing. I spoke with evolutionary biologists and psychologists, neurobiologists, sociologists, anthropologists, and those who study robotics. I spoke with happiness experts and teen addiction experts, along with young farmers, social media influencers, and food entrepreneurs.

I also ran my own study with trend research firm Datassential. Together, we surveyed 1,100 individuals across the United States on food-related behaviors, attachment to technology, interest in social media influencers, life satisfaction, and more. Throughout the book, I will reference our findings and this project as the Hungry Study. (And if you want *all* the data, you can find the full Hungry Study online at TheHungryBook.com.)

I should also note that while this book will mainly focus on Millennial and Generation Z data, the behaviors it describes are not limited to those born during the last few decades. The themes I've uncovered during my research have less to do with age and everything to do with the modern world we're living in. Plenty of Gen Xers and Boomers live similarly to tech-savvy Millennials. They, too, are often online, keep their phones bedside at night, know that Kim Kardashian is married to Kanye West, and can easily identify a stellar rendition of a poke bowl.

Most studies categorize demographically rather than psychographically, which is why in this book I rely mostly on data around Millennials and Generation Z, where we see these novel behaviors concentrated. But worry not, you digitally astute Gen Xers and Boomers: I see you. I recognize that the year you were born does not dictate your habits or desires. The best indication of someone's wants and needs in this Digital Age is how they spend their days. Therefore, when I am speaking about those of *any* age whose lives are steeped in this quick-paced, screen-based world, I will refer to them as the Digital Generation.

By the same token, there are plenty of Millennials and Gen Zers who simply don't fall into the category of digitally savvy—who don't have a Facebook page, have no idea what Snapchat Lenses are, and honestly do not care one bit about Monsanto, gluten, or CBD. It's important for us not to forget these folks, nor assume that all Millennials and Gen Zers fulfill their needs via the same mechanisms.

It's for this reason, in my evaluation of the Hungry Study data, that I do not rely simply on demographic divides but also on psychographic subgroups, such as the Tech-Tethered Cohort—those who express anxiety when away from their devices—and Pro-Social Dieters—who attach a strong value system to their ways of eating.

Here, I hope to reveal not just what the trends are but *why* they are the trends, all while digging into human truths, avenues to well-being, and the realities of our digital world. People today aren't just hungry for avocado toast and "likes"; we're hungry for meaning and a life worth living. By exploring our motivations and these transformative trends, we can, perhaps, all walk away with a new understanding of today's Digital Generation, and a greater sense of how to fulfill our deepest needs and find happiness in today's tech-obsessed world.

PART I

control

Future shock . . . [is] the shattering stress and disorientation that we induce in individuals by subjecting them to too much change in too short a time . . . [It is] a product of the greatly accelerated rate of change in society . . .

Now imagine . . . an entire society, an entire generation . . . suddenly transported into this new world. The result is mass disorientation, future shock on a grand scale. This is the prospect that man now faces. Change is avalanching upon our heads and most people are grotesquely unprepared to cope with it.

Alvin Toffler, *Future Shock*, 1970[1]

CHAPTER ONE

transparency
& anxiety

We hopped in our DiDi ride share and ventured across the city. The sky was a persistent pale gray—as though someone had lassoed all the blue and hit "delete"—a constant reminder of Beijing's suffocating pollution. The car dropped my translator, Ellen,* and me on a bustling street, in front of a building just as silver as the air above. There, we saw the logo we were looking for: a small cartoon face of a hippopotamus.

We had arrived at the flagship location of Hema Xiansheng, e-commerce giant Alibaba's new-age grocery store. In English, the name (盒马鲜生) roughly translates to "packaged freshness," but when mispronounced in Mandarin with the final tone going up instead of down, it has a different translation: "Mr. Hippo." The punny mascot sets the tone for a grocery experience that feels more like a trip to an amusement park than down the frozen food aisle.

The store entrance was flanked by miniature blue shopping carts for children; above, dreamy, iridescent images of clamshells, starfish, and other aquatic creatures silently floated on a panoramic bright blue screen running along the ceiling's edge, a cue that Ellen and I were walking directly into Hema's famed seafood section. Inside, open tubs of abalone, oysters, and mantis shrimp greeted us. "Please use a net for

---

* Name has been changed.

the aquarium," a sign read in both Mandarin and English. A young woman dressed in a white fedora and Gucci T-shirt stood across the tank from Ellen and me. She used one hand to hold her phone to her ear and the other to scoop up the shrimp she desired using a bright orange net.

The adjacent tank housed an undulating carpet of gray turbo flatfish. Above, a sign told us they were "fresh" from Huludao, Liaoning, a seaside city northeast of Beijing. "High in polyglycoprotein content, delicious," the sign read.

Across the aisle, there were stacked tanks filled with giant lobsters, geoduck, and crabs. Each aquarium sported a small white card that provided the name and price of the swimming invertebrates, along with a pattern that looked like a miniature black and white magic eye puzzle. This was the unique product QR code. Ellen reached into her purse for her phone and opened the Hema app so she could test the feature we had trekked all this way to see. She bent down, eye to eye with a tank of bubble-blowing crabs, held out her phone, and snapped the matrix barcode on display.

"Let's see," she said, looking down at her screen.

In seconds, a page loaded with a crisp picture of a bright red crab against a pure white background. With Ellen's quick translation, I learned that we were standing in front of Canadian Fresh Treasure Crab. Customer reviews commented on the product. "So good," one person wrote, "except that I didn't buy enough, haha." As Ellen continued to scroll, we reached a step-by-step recipe for Scallion Treasure Crab. With all the details available to us, the crustaceans pinching and puttering in the tank came to life in a whole new way. I could imagine their path from Canada all the way to the store in Beijing, and picture myself cracking into a stir-fried claw.

Impressed, we decided to try another product. We walked a few steps to our left, into the produce section and its mountains of colorful fruits and vegetables, and stopped in front of a package of white mushrooms that pillowed out like pom-poms. Ellen reopened the Hema app and scanned the correlating QR code. A picture appeared of the farm where the fungi grew and we learned that the agribusiness sources its energy from solar panels.

"That's pretty cool," I remarked, of both the app and the eco-friendly shrooms. Ellen seemed equally impressed.

We continued to meander, pausing every few feet to try out our new superpower. Eventually, we landed in the butcher section. I picked up a package of bone-in meat wrapped in a gold and white label and whipped out my own phone, also loaded with the Hema app. I was holding Zhili Organic Black Pig Bone, sourced from pigs raised on a pure-grain diet. I scrolled down to learn more about the thick trotter slices.

The pigs were raised in Baoding City in Hebei Province, ninety-three miles southwest of Beijing. "Rest assured," the text declared, set atop an image of an ivory foot bone with striations of bright red flesh attached to it that looked a whole lot like the product I held in my hand.

As I continued to scroll, I saw a picture of a tiny black pig mid-dive between a metal slide and a pool of wavy gray water. Fellow pigs paddled in front of him. "Diving pigs," the image was labeled. From afar, the scene could easily have been mistaken for a picture of kids at summer camp frolicking in a lake. Below that, three additional photos captured the pigs at ages zero to three months, four to five months, and six to ten months, each captioned with information on what they ate and the activities they were exposed to at each life stage. (Camp Zhili Organic Black Pig activities include diving and swimming in the summer and running in the winter.)

Below the images of the merry piglets were product attributes, including "high-protein fascia," and then a brand introduction with a brief history of the pork processing company, including their address. Next, images appeared that most Western meat eaters try to avoid. Under a red-and-black section title that assured "strictly controlled" "scientific management," I saw pictures of swine carcasses hanging in a row, snouts toward the ground, with men in deep-blue jumpsuits inspecting the blush-toned skins. Another photograph showed the workers alone, dressed in hooded, all-white medical garb, with their mouths and noses covered by light blue masks. At the bottom of the lengthy parallax scroll were images of the company's three "comprehensive" organic certification forms, including nutrition tests from both Beijing and Hebei Province. "Good water, good Earth, good pork," it concluded.[1] It felt as though I had every possible detail about this product right there at my fingertips.

Hema's parent company, Alibaba, has found immense success with the grocery chain. They have opened over 160 Hema stores in twenty-one Chinese cities since their 2015 launch and have plans to open about two thousand additional branches in the next few years.[2] Many shoppers find the innovative consumer experience enthralling. But their success raises the question: Why do we want to know all this stuff?

Hema's app requires endless updating from stocked brands as well as the company's staff . . . all to tell me that my mushrooms were grown using solar power, that my crab is best prepared with scallions, and that the pig feet I'm about to simmer into a stew come from animals who once paddled in pools? Why is this transparency-centric shopping experience revolutionizing the Chinese grocery market?

Our Basic Safety Needs

Every day, we look for people, institutions, theories, or products that we can trust. This search is a small part of a much larger, perpetual human desire: for safety.

All of us—no matter our race, socioeconomic status, or religion—share a deep desire for the things vital to our survival, such as reliable shelter, food, sleep, and sex, and our bodies are hardwired to reward us for securing these essentials. Yet we yearn not just for the physical fundamentals of safety, but also for a *sense* of safety.

Over the last many decades, researchers across many scientific disciplines, from psychology to sociology, have determined that we feel safe when we feel that we're in control. Dozens of studies illustrate that those with a greater *internal locus of control*—a belief that success or failure, security or danger, lies within our own hands—report higher rates of well-being.[3] This makes rational sense: We feel less anxious if we're confident in our own abilities to protect ourselves, and that our fates are not simply at the mercy of others, or luck. But how do we secure this sense of autonomy?

One way we can gain a sense of control is through knowledge. In 2009, Ethan Bromberg-Martin, senior scientist in the Department of Neuroscience at Washington University School of Medicine in St. Louis, found that the very same neural systems that urge us to find food also encourage us to seek out information.[4] Every time we learn something new, our bodies ping us with the feel-good hormone dopamine.[5] Our brains reward us for acquiring new insights.

"We actually *do* have a hunger for knowledge," Bromberg-Martin said with enthusiasm over the phone. This hunger, he noted, is part of our evolutionary fitness; people who know what's up are, hypothetically, in less danger. Consider the evolutionary advantage knowledge can bring: areas with a sick tribe to avoid, a coming storm, where the bison like to roam, or what plants are poisonous. Any form of information places us in a greater position to avoid threats, or secure those survival basics like food and water. And so, we became *informavores*: animals that seek and digest information.[6]

Our search for safety and desire for details is particularly salient in the context of food. Nature, as any botanist will tell you, is mother to many lethal concoctions: water hemlock, nightshade berries, and white snakeroot all hold deadly toxins, as just a few examples. What we eat can kill us. And as such, we have a natural skittishness around food, and exhibit many subtle, adaptive behaviors that help us better avoid these baleful bites.

For example, it's common for children to become picky eaters once they learn to walk. One can easily imagine the dangers avoided by becoming a youthful culinary skeptic. Just think of what could happen to a toddler, waddling about on the plains or along a city street, if they eagerly picked up anything in sight and stuck it in their mouth.

In a similar fashion, multiple studies show that children are more likely to eat foods that they have repeatedly observed a trusted friend or adult eating.[7] Once children see that a food is safe, they are more willing to consume it.

These ancient instincts show up in adult consumer preferences as well. As one example, people seem to prefer products with clear origins, which some have hypothesized is because knowing where a food comes from or how it was processed provides a sense of safety.[8] Recent studies show that people consider a product to be of higher quality when its origin is known,[9] and these sourcing details can even make an eating experience more satisfying.[10]

"If there's a good story about what you're eating, [for example] that the animal has had a good life or that the wild garlic (ramson) has been picked in a certain forest," the meal will be more satisfying, an eighteen-year-old female focus group participant commented in one study, noting the impact of knowing a food's "story." "Don't know if it can override the actual taste experience. But it can help," she added.[11]

This is one reason why a technology like Hema's app can be a potent attraction for shoppers. What Hema is offering is not just groceries, but endless knowledge about each item: where it's sourced, by whom, at what time. These insights feed an innate craving lying within each of us to understand what it is that we are putting inside our bodies. The more information, the better. Would I enjoy the Zhili pig trotters more knowing they come from happy, swimming pigs? Science says yes.

Additional studies have found that regional products are more successful when their characteristics match consumer expectations of that location.[12] This means that an extra-virgin olive oil from Greece will be more trusted than an extra-virgin olive oil from Thailand. This is our evolutionary poison detector on display, looking for signs of deception within our food sources.

Modern food trends and consumer demands reflect this desire to know our food. In one survey, more than half of 1,300 respondents from across North America, Europe, and Asia-Pacific said that they were willing to pay 10 percent more for a food or drink product if it contained known, trusted ingredients, and that recognition of ingredients was one of the biggest reported drivers of product choice.[13] The 2017 James Beard Foundation Consumer Research Project came up with similar data: Of one thousand individuals surveyed, over three-quarters said they "want to know where their food comes from" and the "environmental impact" of those foods.[14]

It makes sense that people prefer some knowledge of what it is that they're consuming, even if that intel is limited to a product's country of origin or that taking a bite of it didn't kill their friend.

The trouble is, we know less about our food today than perhaps ever before.

All We Don't Know

In recent years, our desire for food knowledge has run into a unique hurdle: Human beings have never been more detached from our food sources than we are today.

Up until the last century or two, by and large, we knew the people who grew our food, who cared for the soil, who raised our livestock. Historically, most people harvested and butchered their own food or purchased goods from reliable sources. We didn't look for a certificate of proof to corroborate any claims, because we didn't have to; if we didn't know the farmer personally, we at least trusted the person we purchased the item from—a well-known vendor was there to vouch for the quality and safety of their wares.

While spices and other exotic delicacies like grains, nuts, oils, fruit, and wine have long been traded via road systems and sailing routes dating back to the Roman Empire, large-scale trade was impossible until the advent of refrigeration, which didn't arise until the nineteenth century. The first commercial refrigeration ship set sail for England in the late 1800s, departing New Zealand's shores with approximately five thousand mutton and lamb carcasses aboard.

After home refrigeration became widespread in the 1940s, the shelf-stable and frozen processed food industries blossomed, and advertising agencies began to sell the concepts of convenience and sanitary factory-made foods. Since that time, our grocery aisles have become exponentially more global. Modern preservation and transportation technologies have turned ingredients into assets to pick, package, and ship anywhere around the world.

"The origins of the food, in our ancestral environment, were very local. We knew the origin of our foods, for sure, because you got it yourself," prolific evolutionary culture psychologist Paul Rozin pointed out to me over the phone from his home in Pennsylvania. "We don't know where our food comes from anymore. It doesn't come from one place, but many places all over the world. Where does an Oreo cookie come from? My gosh, I don't know," he said with a chuckle.

The globalization of our food system has accelerated in recent decades, a trend exemplified by the US produce market. In 2000, just 12 percent of fresh and processed vegetables consumed in the US were imported. By 2016, the import share increased to over 30 percent for fresh vegetables and 22 percent for processed vegetables.[15] As of 2018, the majority of fresh fruit and nearly a third of fresh vegetables purchased by Americans came from other countries.[16] Other categories of food are even more heavily reliant on international commerce; 80 percent of fish consumed in the United States is caught in waters outside our borders.[17]

The same trends are reflected in China. Just a few decades ago, towns relied on their own harvests to make it through the year. Now, even in remote outskirts, locals can get fresh crabs—perhaps those Canadian Fresh Treasure Crabs—delivered within a day via drone, as I learned on a media trip to the Beijing headquarters of Jingdong, the second biggest e-commerce company in China.

Meanwhile, economic waves of the last century have pushed people from the fields toward factories and desks. Over the last two hundred years, the number of agriculture jobs has plummeted, due in part to automation, globalized commerce, and, most recently, climate instability and diminishing crop returns. With this shift, our collective knowledge of food production has dwindled to a pitiful state of ignorance. While the vast majority of Americans say that how a food is grown or raised influences their purchases, the same number admit they know nothing or very little about farming.[18] Most people today don't even know a farmer.

Just how removed from our food system have most of us become? Let's take a quick quiz. Think of a run-of-the-mill cheeseburger. Can you identify whether the meat patty, cheese, lettuce, tomato, pickle, onion, and bun each come from a plant or an animal? If so, which plants and animals?

In 2010, Alexander Hess, an agricultural teacher at Davis High School in Davis, California, and Cary Trexler, an associate professor of agricultural education at UC Davis, set out to explore elementary students' grasp of the agricultural system.[19] They interviewed eighteen ten- and eleven-year-olds, recruited from the Boys and Girls Club of Long Beach, California, and asked them to identify the seven components of a cheeseburger, state if each component originated from a plant or an animal, and describe the agricultural crop that produced the components.

Hess and Trexler found that only four students out of the eighteen knew that pickles are cucumbers. One student, Lynn, claimed confidently that pickles come from lions and tigers. Nine students stated that hamburger buns are made from animals and another four students said they just didn't know if a bun was made from plants or animals.

The researchers also asked the students how food gets to their plates. Over half of the students appeared to have partially accurate understandings of the food system. They documented one conversation with a child named Denise:

INTERVIEWER (I): Why do we have farms?
DENISE (D): So we so we can have lots of food and stuff to drink.
  I: Lots of food and stuff to drink. And what do we get to drink that's from the farm?
  D: What do we get? We get milk.
  I: What kind of food do we get from the farm?
  D: We get meat and chicken wings and pig feet.
  I: Where do you think they grow tomatoes?
  D: In the backyard.
  I: So you think Jack in the Box got their tomato from someone's backyard?
  D: No.
  I: Where do you think they got it?
  D: The store.
  I: From the store, OK. Where do you think the store got it?
  D: I'm not sure.

Now, before you shake your head and lament, "Kids these days," you should know that adults don't fare much better. In the 1990s, the US Department of Agriculture interviewed over two thousand Americans to get a sense of our agricultural literacy. They found that one in eight respondents didn't know that hamburgers come from cows.[20] And before you say, "Oh, those ignorant Americans," a 2015 survey of British youth found that one in five respondents did not know that bacon comes from pigs, while one in twenty survey takers believed that cheese comes from humans. Sixty percent didn't know that lettuce grows in the ground, and nearly four out of five respondents didn't know that broccoli is a plant.[21] These findings are shocking until you consider how little time—if any—most people today spend on a farm. After all, one-third of the youth surveyed had never heard a cow or sheep noise in real life.

I asked Hess if he had been surprised by Lynn's fantastical theory on the origins of pickles. "While her answers were wildly far from the desired understanding, or general expectation, this young lady was making meaning of the world with what she had been exposed to," Hess wrote me. "The creativity and purposeful desire to make connections was wonderful; she just didn't have a basic understanding to draw from."

The students interviewed, he notes, "knew" that lettuce and pickles were plants. But, he said, "Seeing a pickle on a hamburger, iceberg lettuce in a salad, or a bowl with salsa is still disconnected from growing, processing, and experiencing edible plants."

Because of this knowledge gap, the vast majority of today's eaters are unable to accurately judge origin stories or even product safety for themselves. Instead, they have handed off this responsibility to government regulation agencies and large food companies. No longer able to rely on our direct, *internal* judgments about our food, we have, in recent years, shifted to reliance on *external* sources.

An *external locus of control* is a person, concept, or institution outside the self that helps us feel protected—be it government, God, or Grandma Nan's undeniably accurate premonitions. In *Motivation and Personality*, Maslow argues that we all want a sense of "security; stability; dependency; protection; freedom from fear, from anxiety and chaos; need for structure, order, law, limits; strength in the protector; and so on."[22] Often, societal structures like regulations and religion become external resources to fulfill these emotional needs. "The peaceful, smoothly running, 'good' society ordinarily makes its members feel safe enough from wild animals, extremes of temperature, criminals, assault and murder, tyranny, etc.," writes Maslow. Whether it's a social code of conduct or a belief that a higher power is offering us protection, these external forms of control are essential "adaptive tools" that can quell fears of things outside our purview. When these emotional needs go unfulfilled, Maslow notes, our well-being is compromised by worry, stress, and anxiety.

In our modern industrialized food system, where the eater has largely been removed from the growing and sourcing process, the very practical responsibility of keeping the eater safe now falls on food companies and all others who have a hand in the supply chain. When it comes to what we eat, the pressure is on our external forms of control to make us feel secure and protected.

The problem is, sometimes others fail to uphold the same safety standards that we, as individuals, would enforce ourselves.

Food Fraud

Since the turn of the twenty-first century, Chinese citizens have become accustomed to the idea that they can't trust their food. In the early 1980s, China underwent an unexpected shift toward capitalism. After the death of Mao Zedong in 1978, Deng Xiaoping became leader of the People's Republic of China and, in a momentous policy change, began to encourage private business enterprises. Slowly, autonomy seeped into China's Communist culture. Citizens were allowed to take on second jobs; they no longer needed approval from their "work units" to get married or divorced, or travel outside the country.

Soon, money, esteem, and success began to dominate Chinese culture. The average Chinese income catapulted from $200 in 1978 to $6,000 in 2014—a staggering 3,000 percent rise in less than four decades. It was during this time that the Chinese attitude toward personal success also underwent an abrupt one-eighty. The bourgeoisie were no longer vilified but revered. Suddenly, it was anyone's race to the top. And with this race came a lot of cutting corners.

In his book aptly titled *The Age of Ambition*, American journalist Evan Osnos, who lived in China from 2005 to 2013, documents the rapid development of a capitalistic culture. By 2007, the top 10 percent of city-based Chinese were earning 9.2 times as much as the bottom 10 percent, Osnos writes. "The more that people became aware of the widening gap, the more desperate they became" to not be left behind.

The wealthier and growing urban populations had new food desires: more meat and bigger portions. Inexperienced and pressured farmers began to rely heavily on pesticides and hormones to boost production speeds and lower costs. These tactics spurred noxious results that continue to plague the modern Chinese food system: contaminated water, soil, and air. Issues like irresponsible livestock management conjure headlines that haunt many.

For example, in March 2013, sixteen thousand dead pigs were discovered floating down the Huangpu River, a Yangtze River tributary that provides drinking water to Shanghai. There were more pigs than fish in the river, a forty-eight-year-old local fisherwoman wryly told a reporter for *The Guardian*,[23] as a dead piglet, partially submerged in the polluted black and green bayou, bobbed like a buoy near her feet. Early tests of the river hogs confirmed they died of contagious porcine circovirus, but Shanghai's municipal water department maintained its conviction that the water met national standards for safe drinking water.

Stories of fraudulent food have become disturbingly commonplace as competitive suppliers routinely adulterate food items along the supply chain to augment output. Watermelons exploded after being treated with growth accelerator.[24] Rancid mushrooms were bleached to look fresh.[25] A recent discovery revealed that forty-year-old frozen meat, smuggled in through Vietnam, had infiltrated the poultry and beef markets.[26] With each interview in China, I learned about a new food to fear: fake alcohol, adulterated honey, plastic rice and eggs, cardboard cabbages.*

I am an adventurous global eater. I have devoured tarantulas in Cambodia, squirming raw octopus in Korea, and charred pig intestines in Argentina. But I made an exception in China, where I purchased Australian muesli for breakfast instead of venturing out onto the streets for steamed buns or noodle soup. I didn't feel sure of anything I ate, except for my time in Hema. The food paranoia had its grip on me.

There were no reported deaths from the porcine circovirus incident, but the same cannot be said for all of China's food scandals. Years

---

* Want a few more? In 2016, a man purchased ninety-two pounds of pork to make sausage. He seasoned it and left it to marinate overnight in a bucket. On a mid-evening trip to the kitchen for a glass of water, he noticed that the bucket was glowing. Upon further inspection, he realized the pork itself was emitting the blue rays of light. Later, officials would suggest it was the result of pigs fed high levels of phosphorus. Delish. This story was reported on by Sophie Williams for *Daily Mail* in 2016: "Chinese Man Finds Meat He Bought from a Market GLOWING Blue in the Dark."

prior, in 2008, an infant formula product was spiked with melamine, a chemical compound most often used to make flame-retardant plastic. It was added to boost the protein levels of otherwise watery milk. When the milk producer, Sanlu, discovered the doctored product, they didn't report it to authorities. Instead, they bribed local officials to censor media from reporting on it. The product was fed to nearly three hundred thousand babies. Six children died. Chinese authorities jailed nineteen people and executed others in the scandal.

The event was a tipping point for fearful citizens who had long suspected the dangers lurking in their food. Wealthy mothers started to fly to Hong Kong, where international imports are far easier to come by, to purchase baby formula. This gambit became so popular that the government had to implement a limit on the quantity of formula allowed back on each trip.

Multiple public surveys have shown that nearly three-quarters of the Chinese population, about one billion people, are concerned with food safety and the impact of that food on their own health.[27]

"I don't trust any of the food I eat," Nanjing resident Mr. Fung commented to a researcher, "but I just eat it and hope for the best. I worry for my children, but it's what there is here in this country."[28]

Resentment among frightened eaters rose again when media revealed that the government was maintaining its own private organic farms for officials and all-star athletes.[*, 29] After the story broke, all other news about the government-only organic farms was banned from publication.[30]

With food scares seeping into headlines, and good reason to suspect inside cover-ups, wariness has become a mainstay of the Chinese consumer psyche.[†]

---

* At one such farm, "a sign inside the gate identified the property as the Beijing Customs Administration Vegetable Base and Country Club," reported Barbara Demick for the *Los Angeles Times* in 2011. "The placard was removed after a Chinese reporter sneaked inside and published a story about the farm producing organic food so clean the cucumbers could be eaten directly from the vine."

† "There are rumors that we have much higher cancer rates than other countries," one contact in Shanghai told me, citing the excessively heavy-handed use of pesticides.

While China is certainly the apex of food fraud, food scandals are not limited to China's borders. In the 1980s, mad cow disease took the lives of 166 Brits. Before that, wheat treated with mercury-based fungicide was imported to Iraq from Mexico, which led to over 450 deaths and permanent brain damage for many more. And then there are the less fatal but still icky stories, like how pink slime—a meat by-product added to processed beef to lower its overall fat content—was (is?) used in everything from McDonald's burgers to lunch-line sloppy joes, without eaters' knowledge. Yet, globally, today's true food danger lies not with fraudulent items, but popular snacks, meals, and other processed goods—yet one more consequence of a depersonalized food system.

Over the past three decades, the percentage of people worldwide considered overweight or obese has increased 28 percent in adults and a staggering 47 percent in children, a contemporary crisis spurred, many believe, by modern diets chock-full of foods with ingredients that come from all over the world, processed through complex supply chains and food engineering, and sold in mass quantities across global markets.[31] Researchers point to increasingly Westernized diets, including multinational food and beverage company products like soda, packaged snacks, and fast food, as the main culprit. An estimated one-third of the global population is overweight or obese and therefore at greater risk of developing cardiovascular disease, type 2 diabetes, asthma, hypertension, and other weight-related illnesses. One in every five children on the planet is either obese or overweight. *One in five.*[,][32] There is even an obesity epidemic in sub-Saharan Africa and in the favelas of Brazil. In Nigeria, Africa's most populous nation, hypertension, also known as high blood pressure, now ails nearly a quarter of the population. Ghana's obesity

---

"But we can't be sure," she said with a shrug, "as the government won't release the data."

* This shift in global health has been rapid. Until 1980, fewer than one in ten people were obese across the Organisation for Economic Co-operation and Development (OECD)'s thirty-six member countries. Now, one in five adults across the OECD countries are obese—more than one in three adults in Mexico, New Zealand, Hungary, and the United States, and more than one in four in Australia, Canada, Chile, South Africa, and the United Kingdom, the OECD reports in their 2017 Obesity Update.

rates have surged more than 650 percent since 1980.[33] For the first time in the modern era, life expectancy is decreasing in America.[34] One in four Americans dies from heart disease, and treatment for this avoidable ailment accounts for one of every six dollars spent on healthcare in the US, adding up to nearly $1 billion a day.[35] Alongside obesity, the global prevalence of type 2 diabetes nearly doubled between 1980 and 2016, rising from 4.7 percent to 8.5 percent in the adult population.[36] In the US, the number of diabetics multiplied nearly twentyfold, from 1.6 million in 1958 to 30.3 million in 2015.[37] Stories of developing countries and once-healthy nations such as Japan and Greece battling heart disease, type 2 diabetes, and obesity very clearly trail the introduction of cheap processed foods.

This health epidemic has spurred a growing distrust of government and business. Some global citizens are asking: If these products are so bad for our health, why are they on the market? Who are the people selling and approving these products?

Everyday consumers, writes food columnist Tamar Haspel for the *Washington Post*, are focused "on a sense that they've been misled by the people and companies selling them food." Many feel that corporations' intentions are not just to sell products but also to hide the truth about them. Many people believe that certain food items never would have gained traction if companies had been transparent about the health impacts, marketing schemes, and addictive qualities—if these products, say, carried the same warnings now required (in many countries) on cigarettes, or were labeled with more practical serving sizes.[38]

Suspicion and mistrust of big food companies have seeped into nearly every nation. Only 44 percent of global consumers now say they trust industrially prepared foods.[39] Eighty-one percent of US and UK Millennials believe that Big Food pursues policies that do not have consumers' best interests in mind,[40] and nearly half of all American Millennials say they don't trust large food manufacturers.[41]

This lack of trust also negatively impacts the public's perception regarding the safety of the wider food system, including aspects overseen by government agencies. In 2016, a proprietary survey of over eight hundred US consumers by Bernstein Research found that 55 percent of consumers—across generations—agreed that they are becoming more distrustful of the food system, up from 48 percent in 2013.[42] In our

Hungry Study, 70 percent of participants said that they worry about the safety of their food and another 66 percent shared the same concerns about water.

"Sometimes I worry that I'll mutate because of the strange things in food," an American high school senior confessed to me, conveying the angst many harbor about the health and safety of the foods they consume.

In reaction, customers worldwide are increasingly expressing a fervent desire to know more about what they're putting in and on their bodies—be it skincare items, kitchen cleaners, a new pair of jeans, or Sunday brunch. Ultimately, people want to know where items are made, how they're made, what's in them, and where those ingredients come from.[43] And they want companies to offer up this information. In short, people want greater "transparency," a term that has become a marketing buzzword over the last decade. In many ways, these trends are illuminating a human need that is currently going unmet—the need to feel safe, to feel knowledgeable about the things we're consuming and placing on our bodies.

Products increasingly tout labels like "clean" and "simple." Nielsen calls this a "mainstream movement," citing that 93 percent of US households have now purchased a "clean"-labeled product at grocery stores—be it food, vitamins, or personal care items.[44] People are gravitating toward products with ingredients they understand. Often, this means shunning ingredients that are less familiar, like artificial colors, flavors, and fragrances.[45]

Globally, people are avoiding brands that refuse to comply with these transparency demands. A survey by Label Insight and the Food Marketing Institute found that three-quarters of shoppers say they would switch to a brand that provides more in-depth product information.[46] Meanwhile, 70 percent of survey takers queried by the Atlanta-based brand communications firm Response Media said their purchases are "always or often influenced by transparency content."[*, 47] When the 2017 James Beard Foundation Consumer Research Project looked

---

[*] Respondents named things like ingredient sourcing, production and manufacturing processing, shipping and handling, and sustainability information as influential in their purchase.

into this topic, a whopping 90 percent of respondents said they want to "understand the ingredients in their foods" and "see truthful nutritional information."[48] (Interesting that "truthful" was included in the survey language, suggesting that not all nutritional information provided is forthright.)

Over the last few years, the way to market a product has shifted from *entertain and delight* to *inform*. Data from a survey conducted by website host WordPress revealed that 81 percent of people prefer to be informed by a company's content, such as advertisements, websites, videos, articles, and pictures, while only 19 percent said they want to be entertained.[49]

Many food marketers attempt to fill our knowledge gap through storytelling, much like Hema's expository app. Brands—in food, fashion, and beauty, in particular—have come to focus on company founders, sourcing methods, or sustainability initiatives, in the hopes of making shoppers feel connected and at ease.

Still, this solution of transparent marketing doesn't always work. Here's why: In order for labeling to make you feel safe, you have to trust that the information that's being provided is accurate. And increasingly, trust is the one ingredient that's hard to come by.

Today, it's not just food companies and government institutions that are facing a crisis of trust; studies around the world are reporting a general drop in faith in others. Ready for a jarring statistic? Only 19 percent of Millennials believe you can trust most people.[50] In a 2014 social survey, Pew found that less than one in five American Millennials (then ages eighteen to thirty-three) have confidence in the honesty of others, while two in five Boomers said that, yes, "most people can be trusted."

These findings were no fluke.* Over a third of surveyed Millennials from around the world told Global Shapers, a subset of the World

---

* In 2016, Snapchat and Luntz Global joined forces to survey one thousand Americans ages eighteen to twenty-six and ask what professions they respect most. Given a list of sixteen options, respondents overwhelmingly expressed respect for nurses, doctors, and teachers, while only 6 percent chose "business leaders," 4 percent chose "elected officials," and a bleak 2 percent expressed respect for "bankers." Sixty-six percent of respondents agreed that corporate America "embodies everything that is wrong with America."

Economic Forum, that they do not trust federal and local government, news media, religious leaders, armed forces, or multinational corporations to be "honest and fair," with the highest concentration of skeptics located in China and Latin America.[51]

Throwing more weight behind this burgeoning worldwide trend, the 2017 Edelman Trust Barometer Report showed the largest-ever year-over-year drop in trust across government, business, media, and even NGOs. "The implications of the global trust crisis are deep and wide-ranging," Richard Edelman, president and CEO, is quoted as saying. "It began with the Great Recession of 2008, but like the second and third waves of a tsunami, globalization and technological change have further weakened people's trust in global institutions."[52] The report cites economic and societal fears, such as corruption, immigration, and the pace of innovation, as catalysts for the plummeting sense of trust in business and government.

The instability caused by unreliable external *and* internal forms of control is creating a worldwide bellyache of anxiety—the worry and stress Maslow warned of. In the food and agriculture arenas, this deep-seated fear and mistrust is driving one of the most controversial food trends of the last decade: the non-GMO movement.

Who's Afraid of GMOs?

"Why are Millennials willing to eat at Chipotle—whose food has killed people—but won't eat GMOs, which haven't killed anyone?" an audience member asked me one afternoon in a windowless Houston hotel conference room. There I was, the lone urbanite twentysomething standing in front of about two hundred middle-aged commodity soybean farmers, gathered together in the heart of Texas. They were waiting for an answer.

Over the past decade, you've likely noticed a growing number of little green-and-blue non-GMO (genetically modified organism) labels on the food packages that line your grocery store shelves and even on your farmers' market signs. The rise of the non-GMO movement has been rapid, with new non-GMO product launches ratcheting up at warp speed.

Standing before these farmers, I was tempted to start my reply with the fact that, no, the Tex-Mex fast-food chain's scandals of *E.coli*, salmonella, and norovirus poisoning didn't actually kill anyone (though the fifty-some infected diners certainly spent some immensely unpleasant days curled up in bathrooms). But I knew that wasn't the response my audience was interested in. Many of the farmers who sat in front of me were part of a long line of corn and soybean farmers, who for generations have relied on GM (genetically modified) seeds. They just wanted to know why they were making less money and getting less market return for their GM crops than in years past.

The term *non-GMO* was barely a part of the public vernacular until 2012, yet half of all global citizens now say that purchasing non-GMO goods is a priority for them, especially Europeans and Latin Americans.[53] The demand is so strong that food purveyors have started to stick the non-GMO label on fruits and vegetables where no genetically modified version exists.*

Many members of the general public consider GM products to be "generally unsafe," and those ages eighteen to twenty-nine are most likely to believe that GMO foods are worse for our health than non-GMO foods.[54] But are they?†

---

* There are a limited number of genetically modified products available in the marketplace. In the US, 90 percent of the 170 million soy and corn acres are dedicated to growing GM varietals developed to resist pests, to enhance specific features (like high oleic acid oils), or to be tolerant to common herbicides. These two grains make up the majority of GM ingredients found in the American food system, though we also grow GM sugar beets, cotton, canola, alfalfa, potatoes, and virus-resistant papaya and squash. As of 2017 there's also a GM apple on the market, which doesn't brown. In India, farmers make use of a modified eggplant breed, and Nigeria just approved a GM cowpea. Research is being conducted on a number of additional grains, fruits, and vegetables, but they have yet to be approved for market. All this to say: If you see "non-GMO" on a product like oats, salt, or kale (all of which I have personally witnessed), a company is misleading you to think that a GM version of that product exists . . . when, at least for now, it doesn't.

† Genetic engineering can alter an apple so that it doesn't brown, create glow-in-the-dark fish, or allow yeast to create insulin. Some of the most common edible GMO seeds are edited to be resistant to particular herbicides and insecticides. Decades ago, Monsanto altered commodity crop corn and soybeans to be insecticide (Bt toxin)

Most doctors and scientists agree that genetically modified foods are a net benefit and perfectly safe for consumption. A 2016 letter from 107 Nobel laureates to Greenpeace notes: "There has never been a single confirmed case of a negative health outcome for humans or animals from [GMO] consumption." In fact, they note, GMO products "have been shown repeatedly to be less damaging to the environment, and a boon to global biodiversity."[55] The World Health Organization, the American Medical Association, the European Commission, the Royal Society, and the American Association for the Advancement of Sciences have all released statements affirming GM foods' safety for humans. There are some two thousand scientific studies that have found no ill effects on humans or animals from consuming GMOs.

Still, nearly all of the latest diets, such as Paleo and Whole30, scorn GMOs. A recent national survey in China found that over 45 percent of Chinese consumers oppose putting GM foods on their plates.[56]

Often, farmers, scientists, and pro-GMO advocates say that non-GMO eaters are denying science. But the reality is, most people don't know enough of the science to deny it.

Here's a fun fact to tell at dinner parties: Over one-third of Americans don't know that non-genetically modified foods have genes. In 2017, Michigan State University sent out their annual Food Literacy and Engagement Poll to more than a thousand US residents and asked people whether it was true or false that "genetically modified foods have genes and non-genetically modified foods do not." Thirty-seven percent of respondents answered "true."[57] (All food has genes.)

This all leaves us with the question: How have people come to so vehemently fear something when they don't even know what it is?

As we reviewed earlier, insights and learning are a conduit to a sense of personal control and empowerment, and it's for this reason that *not* knowing can put us on edge. The things we don't understand often cause

---

and herbicide (Roundup Ready) resistant. Initially, these products reduced farmers' pesticide use, but their consistent application has led to resilient superweeds and pests, essentially expediting Darwinian evolution. Now, many farmers are applying *more* pesticides in order to combat these antagonists. This trend is detrimental not just for human health, but planetary health, as soils become damaged and polluted. Here, however, the issue is not genetic modification itself, but its implementation.

us great angst, a characteristic easily observed in food culture. In fact, one convincing argument as to why the non-GMO movement exists is that people are rejecting this new technology explicitly *because* they don't understand it. The concept of genetically modified anything is foreign and confusing. *Why should I put that in my body?* some ask themselves. Especially when many don't trust the companies and institutions creating and evaluating the GM products.

In 2016, two university researchers, Nan Yu and Qian Xu, decided to look into the Chinese public sentiment around genetically modified organisms by analyzing two thousand social media posts related to the topic.[58] While the vast majority of posts spoke negatively of GM foods, nearly half didn't provide any specific reasons why the posts' authors felt GMOs are hazardous, nor did they cite any particular risks of consuming modified foods. In fact, Xu later told me, she suspects that most of the people who post about GMOs don't know what a genetically modified organism is. But that wasn't the part of the study that interested her.

"We actually discovered that GM is not just a topic about food," Xu said. She and her co-researcher found that the conversation around GM was often "about defending accessibility to the information about GM foods."

As the two summarize in their publication: "Most posts viewed the government, lawmakers, and scientists as those responsible for guaranteeing the safety of genetically modified foods." The "cyberactivism," as Yu and Xu call it, of citizen pushback against GMOs "goes beyond the scope of public health and extends to discussions about human rights, the government's ability to supervise the market, and even national security."

Here, Xu and Yu hit on an important insight: Genetic modification of foods, for many, is less about personal health than it is about the right to know. "The public may have distrusted GM foods only because they felt their individual rights were not respected," Professors Yu and Xu's paper states. "Many of the posts about human rights expressed concerns that the government and media had hidden the truth about the safety of GM foods."

"Some mobile social media users worried that the GM food industry was controlled by interest groups such as the government, big business, and scientists . . . This perceived inequity of power and broader concerns about 'the right to know' led to the negative perception of GM foods," they summarize.

By and large, the non-GMO pushback in the US reflects the same cynical "right to know" mentality. The main argument that many Western anti-GMO activists rely on is this: Scientific analyses say GMOs are safe, but Big Industry controls access to GMO seeds and therefore also controls which research projects get taken on, so how can we trust any of the existing science?

This contention has merit. At one point, Monsanto owned 90 percent of the American GMO market.[59] The large agrochemical company, now owned by Bayer, has long dominated the GMO development scene and, with that power, has been able to approve or quash nearly all research related to the safety of GMOs.

To make matters worse, when the public first began to push for companies to label GMOs, Monsanto and big food companies, through the Grocery Manufacturers Association, pushed back. They said mandatory labeling could imply that food products containing GMOs are somehow inferior to conventional or organic counterparts. (As a compromise, all parties eventually agreed to add a QR code to packages—immediately cueing the public to claim obfuscation. While QR codes are everywhere in China, they are seldom utilized in the Western market, and bar the more than 20 percent[60] of low-income US citizens without smartphones from exercising their right to know what's in their food.)

What these companies clearly didn't realize at the time was that their pushback against transparent, accessible labeling was going to make the public's desire to know only that much stronger.

"It's like Trump and his tax returns," I told the crowd in Texas. Perhaps not the ideal audience for the comparison, but they understood my point. "If someone doesn't want to reveal something, we immediately assume there's something worth hiding." Though their product hasn't changed, I explained, consumer sentiment had, buoyed by a food-fueled public health crisis and other economic and political undercurrents.

Many feel that there's a theft taking place: the theft of agency over their own food, their own safety.

Now, as much of the world eyes politicians, the news media, and businesses with deep misgivings, folks are left in a bizarre limbo: If we cannot rely on these cultural expert systems, where does that leave us? Company-controlled barriers to information, and lack of personal knowledge of GM science, appear to be the chief catalysts for GM distrust. Many are clamoring to regain the personal power we abdicated. And many are going online to do so.

The Desire to Know

In 2009, the Internet and social media came barreling into Chinese culture. Suddenly, Chinese citizens were offered a portal to more information than they'd ever had access to before.

User-generated information became an attractive addition to the usual state-controlled media landscape.[61] Handed a microphone for the first time in modern Chinese history, citizens began to talk. A lot. Just as Yu and Xu observed in their own study, social media platforms very quickly became a place for uncovering suspected corruption, most often related to politicians, but nearly just as frequently about food.

Social media platforms WeChat and Sina Weibo anchor the country's Internet use. WeChat dominates the market, with 963 million active users who can send a friend money, make a doctor's appointment, place an order for dinner, and debate genetically modified organisms all within a single interface. (Many stores no longer accept cash. "WeChat?" people inquire instead, pointing to a QR code to scan as payment.) In a distant second, Weibo, a Twitter-like messaging platform, enchants over 360 million active users,[62] just a hair more than its Western counterpart. Weibo is known for its virality, spreading messages to millions within minutes. In less than a decade, both have become foundations of Chinese communication.

"Chinese people are not stupid. They know that a lot of information is censored," Ashley Galina Dudarenok, a Millennial with long blond hair and a model-like figure, told me over video call from her Shanghai apartment. Russian-born Dudarenok moved to Chongqing, China, at the age of seventeen to earn a language and business degree, convinced that China's economy would become a global powerhouse. After graduation, she founded Alarice International, a Hong Kong–based digital marketing agency. Initially, Dudarenok helped international companies break into the Chinese market, but as the strength of social media platforms intensified, she pivoted and now focuses entirely on social media, helping Western clients with WeChat and Weibo marketing initiatives. Today, her self-published book *Unlocking the World's Largest E-Market: A Guide to Selling on Chinese Social Media* is a bestseller on Amazon. I caught her on a busy weeknight evening, after a trip to the gym.

The introduction of social media platforms, Dudarenok explained, "was the first time in [Chinese citizens'] lives when they could go online and anonymously share information and discuss things." In a country where Facebook, Google, and Twitter are all banned, WeChat and Weibo, among other early social media sites, suddenly opened people's doors to the outside world, and also to one another.

The platforms connected a nation spread across 3.7 million square miles, and created channels of communication that had never before existed. "The whole huge country was connected," Dudarenok recalls of the 2009 Weibo launch. "Whatever happened in Ürümqi or Guangzhou was known within Beijing," she told me. And the information was not being passed "through fake media, but through social sharing. That was powerful. People felt empowered, interested, and extremely excited about that change. Literally within a year, the whole of China was on social media."

Alongside cat videos, reports of illness and fraud are rampant on social media. A 2015 study found that 15 percent of all rumors on WeChat are related to food and health, specifically food safety and disease; food is the second most common conversation topic, behind politics.[63] Often, stories that reveal the nefarious state of the nation's food system go viral.

In February 2017, a ten-second video made its way through the arteries of WeChat that showed what appeared to be a home cook discovering a long, thin piece of plastic in a bag of seaweed. A day after the video was uploaded, the recording leapt over to Weibo, where it was reposted and shared with over two million viewers. Weeks later, the wholesale price of seaweed was down by 50 percent in Jinjian, China's biggest seaweed processing hub.

Inspired by the original post, others filmed themselves struggling to tear strands of seaweed. One of these individuals was a forty-year-old woman with the last name of Zeng, who was arrested by the Jinjiang Public Security Bureau for allegedly damaging the reputation of the aquatic commodity. In her video, Zeng uses a clip to fasten one end of the seaweed as she pulls on the other. "It's made of plastic," she says to the camera. "These ruthless businesses. This is going to kill people when they eat it." Zeng uploaded the clip to a group board on WeChat. It was shared so widely that a seaweed company claims her testimony cost them over a half million dollars, 4.68 million yuan, in sales.

"I got on a call with several of the seaweed businessmen," Echo Huang, a Hong Kong–based journalist, recalled of her time covering the seaweed scandal, "and they were so upset and didn't know what to do. Of course, they were telling me that they had never sold any fake products. But," she confessed to me, "even at that moment, I was still questioning them: Are you sure it's not real? Are you sure you didn't miss a step, maybe along the supply chain?" Huang's skepticism reflected the common public sentiment.

"Whenever these food rumors break out, people from the government come out to say, 'This is a rumor. How could you guys trust this?'" Huang explained. But the government rebuttals only affirm cynics' suspicions. "When officials come out to say, 'This as a rumor,' the overriding public response is: 'Well, then we can regard this as real.'"

"I think there's a complete lack of trust in the system," she concluded.

All around the world, people are hungry for more information. With less and less trust in our external loci of control, people are looking for answers themselves. In an era of mistrust, industry- and government-skeptical eaters are clamoring online to discover the "truth."

In China, that personal power is arriving in the form of social media posts. There, citizens are empowering each other by putting others in the know. Outside of China, warnings and information arrive not only via social media, but also in the form of influencer blog posts, television talking head analyses, and tell-all books. But our independent search for clarity may be backfiring.

While we have access to more information than ever before, our evolutionary desire for safety through knowledge is, in this Digital Age, put into overdrive—placing much of the global population in a persistent state of alarm.

The Sky Is Falling

"I'm anxious to turn my phone on in the morning because I'm worried, like, what now? What's the latest worst thing that's happened?" British expat Alex Tew told me over the phone from his San Francisco apartment. It's a relatable concern, and one that has fueled Tew's personal financial success. He is the co-founder of the meditation app Calm. Named Apple's favorite app of 2017, Calm has amassed over thirty million downloads since its release in 2012.

"Like, this morning I was on Facebook and saw that one of my friends marked himself safe in the attack in Stockholm and I was like, 'For fuck's sake, what is it now?'" On a beautiful April afternoon in 2017, a hijacker drove a truck at high speed down Drottninggatan, one of Stockholm's main shopping streets, killing five in the rampage. The environment we're in today, Tew said, makes it so that "you're not only worried about your own life, but you're worried about what's happening ten thousand miles away."

We are living in a new era of information, where tales of wars, disease, and natural disasters arrive on our screens continuously throughout the day, from a tsunami over in the Philippines to a terror attack down in Miami. At no other time in human history have we had this much knowledge about goings-on around the world.

The human mind did not evolve for an environment with round-the-clock news. The worries of our ancestors were constrained by location and population, as well as more limited means of communication. The *Homo sapiens* brain developed to take in intimate details of a select few tribe members, along with a select few dangers, like local predators, weather patterns, or poison fruits. Today, our communities know no limits, linked by broadband and 4G networks.

Access to these stories generates palpable anxiety—about our food, about nuclear war, about terror attacks—because we are not just evolutionarily driven to acquire information, but particularly adept at seeking out and remembering warnings of danger. It's self-protective to pay attention to bad news.

"Since news of death or other disaster may presage the nearby existence of a predator or of raiding parties from neighbouring tribes, or of disease, it must have been adaptive for bad news to increase anxiety and promote activities to ward off occurrence," the late evolutionary psychiatrist John Scott Price hypothesized in 2012.[64]

And in fact, humans have a unique ability to "rapidly process things with a bad outcome," whether we've experienced the calamitous event ourselves or simply learned about it on the radio, according to Jon Kaas, a Vanderbilt University biology professor who specializes in mammalian brain evolution. But this talent is causing some serious problems for us in this Digital Age.

As Kaas explained to me, the inundation of bad news beamed onto our many devices keeps us in a fixed state of anxiety, alert to "dangers" that in all likelihood pose no threat to us. "Every day, if you watch the news, somebody's killed, and there are many ways that they're killed," he said, as his eightysomething-year-old voice wavered, "and you have the impression that the world is very dangerous." News stories on topics like robberies, shootings, and poisonous processed foods affect the emotional system "so that you're more attuned" and "more ready to protect yourself or to escape," Kaas said. "In earlier times, we would never really know about most of this stuff."

"Bad news, of deaths and other disasters . . . has been available to our ancestors over the last few million years since language evolved," evolutionary psychiatrist Price echoes in his writing, but "since these ancestors lived in groups of about 150 individuals, the amount of bad news they could generate was limited, even if we add in bad news from neighbouring groups. Now, we have available the bad news of many billions of people."[65]

Many of the devices and platforms that we've integrated into our lives over the past decade exploit our tendency to scour our environments for more information and warning signs. As a result, we've become afraid of things that pose no direct danger. Clickbait leaves us in a tizzy, sticking in our minds no matter how irrelevant. Rather than giving us survival advantage, each scroll or swipe in our hunt for the latest pieces of newsworthy information just elevates our stress hormones unnecessarily. The cacophony of social media fuels a sense that the world is spinning out of control—a sense of chaos that may also factor into our global crisis of trust.*

Yet we keep scrolling, swiping, and clicking. Aristotle began *Metaphysics* with the observation that "all men by nature desire to know," and now, with nearly all information just a click away, many minds are swirling with the endless race to know more.

This information-seeking symptom of the modern era is evident in a 2016 addition to the *Oxford English Dictionary*. That year, the word *infomania* was added, defined as "the compulsive desire to check or accumulate news and information."

Washington University neuroscientist Dr. Bromberg-Martin compares our desire for information to our desire for sugar: Just as our evolutionary infatuation with sugar has been exploited by food companies, so has our innate desire to know been exploited by newsfeeds and social media.

Because of our innate drive to protect ourselves through knowledge of potential threats, we click on negative information more often than happy stories. This inclination becomes additionally problematic when paired with Twitter, Google, Facebook, and YouTube's algorithms, which make the most-clicked-on headlines more readily available to users.

"When you open up the blue Facebook icon, you're activating the [artificial intelligence], which tries to figure out the perfect thing it can show you that'll engage you," former Google ethicist and co-founder of

---

* "The human mind tends to estimate the probability of an event from the ease with which it can recall examples, and scenes of carnage are more likely to be beamed into our homes and burned into our memories than footage of people dying of old age," writes cognitive psychologist Steven Pinker in his book *The Better Angels of Our Nature: Why Violence Has Declined*. As more and more stories of terrible things are beamed into the devices we interact with throughout the day, many of us are set in a persistent state of worry. For example, you're more likely to be killed crossing the street than flying in an airplane, but it doesn't feel that way. Pedestrian deaths are so common that news organizations don't report them with the same urgency as a plane plummeting into the ocean; the plane accident is newsworthy because it's rare. But the human mind does a terrible job at evaluating which threat is more significant. This is why, Jon Kaas says, more people are afraid of flying in airplanes than crossing the street.

the Center for Humane Technology Tristan Harris explained to journalist Ezra Klein on *The Ezra Klein Show*.[66] Harris is a steadfast critic of today's big tech companies, like Facebook, Apple, and his previous place of work, Google. The AI "doesn't have any intelligence, except figuring out what gets the most clicks. The outrage stuff gets the most clicks, so it puts that at the top." These algorithms, Harris argues, make it so that we're all outraged, all the time.

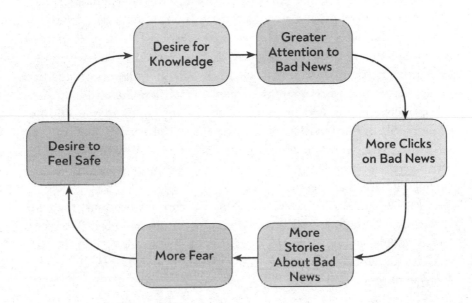

Harris explains to Klein: "People in tech will say, 'You told me, when I asked you what you wanted, that you wanted to go to the gym. That's what you said. But then I handed you a box of doughnuts and you went for the doughnuts, so that must be what you really wanted.' The Facebook folks, that's literally what they think. We offer people this other stuff, but then they always go for the outrage, or the auto-playing video, and that must be people's most true preference."[67] The algorithm responds not to happiness, but to engagement—comments and clicks.*

---

* To make matters worse, these companies make money based on clicks, so they're essentially incentivized to keep us outraged and clicking. Happy stories simply don't inspire the same platform engagement.

And so, each of us is likely to see newsfeeds packed with headlines that spark outrage (and therefore more engagement). Soon, each of us is suffering under the weight of cortisol-sparking information.

In the Hungry Study, we found an interesting correlation between people's attachment to their devices and their rates of anxiety. "How often," we asked in a series of questions, "would you say you worry about your own safety or the safety of loved ones?" "How often do you worry about climate change, terrorism, healthcare, hate crimes, and debt?" "How often do you get anxious when you read, watch, or listen to the news?" We had over 1,100 responses from Americans across genders, ethnicities, regions, and age groups. And while different demographics exhibited varying worry and anxiety trends (for example, women worry more than men, and Millennials and Gen Zers show more anxious tendencies than Baby Boomers), there was only one cohort within our study that on every one of these worry and anxiety questions was, with statistical significance, more likely to worry than the average respondent: those who spend the most time online and engaging with their phones.

In this era of 24/7 news, social media, and notifications, many of us are beginning to feel that we're drowning in things to fear. We often have trouble seeing the good news, the uplifting tales, the progress, amidst the weeds of worry writhing through our day-to-day content consumption.

To make matters even worse, sometimes we're fretting over issues that simply don't exist.

The Anxiety Economy

Gaining reliable, trustworthy knowledge is far more difficult than it seems. Assessing food safety based on blog posts, Weibo videos, and influencer recommendations is, at times, misdirecting public attention and exacerbating unnecessary fears.

It turns out that the Chinese plastic seaweed rumor really was just that—a rumor. A total of eighteen people were arrested in connection with the fake news story.[68] After inspecting seaweed products from over fifty-five different companies, the government said they found no evidence of counterfeit or adulterated products. What they did find were dozens of copycat fake seaweed videos littering the Internet.

"I didn't think about whether it was true or not," Zeng, who uploaded the original "fake" seaweed video, told the Chinese publication *The Paper.*[69] "There's too much fake stuff nowadays—I don't feel safe."

What's not clear from Zeng's interview is whether or not she believed at the time that the seaweed truly was counterfeit; what is clear is her distrust of the Chinese food system and, in turn, her lack of faith that the Chinese government is working to keep people like her secure from harm. Either way, the clarification that the seaweed story was a fabrication didn't seem to alleviate consumers' concerns.

When the seaweed company put out a release that the scandal was hogwash, one Weibo user commented, "I don't care if this is real and I won't buy your food products anyways . . . I have to be careful, after all." The doubt became indelible.

"There's nothing to lose by believing it," Yun Wuxin, a Chinese food industry observer, is quoted saying in an article by Echo Huang (published on *Quartz* under the section header "Trust No One"). "There's no simple way to tell if the news or the [food] companies' announcements are true."[70]

In this era of little food knowledge, erosion of expert systems, and ample access to information, many are steeped in an interminable state of anxiety. The stories pouring into our newsfeeds are sometimes important, at times pure falsities, and often irrelevant. But how can you tell which stories are which? Which opinion should you listen to?* What if you follow the wrong advice? Individuals, equipped with little expertise to help them, are attempting to parse an overwhelming amount of content. Most of us click on it all, exposing ourselves to a mass propagation

---

* For example, a search as simple as *Are muffins healthy?* will dole out arguments every which way: No, gluten is toxic and will kill you. Yes, follow your inclinations and enjoy. No, the muffin was likely made with wheat milled months ago and has retained no nutritional value. Yes, especially if it's from a local baker who your money will support. Maybe—why don't you meditate on it?

of opinions, comments, and reports, absorbing stories by experts, bloggers, and conspiracy theorists alike—a recipe for infinite anxiety.*

Food-specific fear-mongering flows onto newsfeeds, social media
pages, and forums all around the world. Eating soy will lead to a "tes-
tosterone imbalance, infertility, low sperm count, and increased risk of
cancers," one popular blogger writes.[71] The Internet is rife with worry
that ingesting GMOs can lead to food allergies or resistance to antibiotics. Others warn that gluten causes depression or promise that putting
butter in your morning coffee is the key to avoiding dementia.

"From reading the inextricable mesh of advice, warnings, scare stories, irreproducible results, quack theories and serious science, advertising and PR that is the daily ration of anyone reading the news with
a food and nutrition biased eye, one would be led to believe that there
actually are other options besides not eating," writes famed French social
scientist Claude Fischler in an article titled "The Nutritional Cacophony
May Be Detrimental to Your Health," published in the academic journal *Progress in Nutrition*. He then notes as an aside, "People who do not
eat die, too, but usually quite a bit faster" (a riff on a famous quote from
the Czech physician Petr Skrabanek, who once wrote: "People who eat
die").[72]

Some are so overwhelmed and frightened by what may lurk
within their food that they're facing a new disease, orthorexia, known
as the fear of food. Most often, orthorexia (sometimes referred to as
"orthorexia nervosa") refers to an extreme preoccupation with the production method, origin, health, purity, and ingredients of food.[73]

Of course, we're not just in a state of paranoia about food; we're
anxious about everything, in part because what's "real" has never
been more difficult to pin down. Worries about legitimate dangers are
lumped together with far-fetched scandals. Vaccines are imagined to be
as threatening as the climate crisis, immigrants as villainous as heart

---

* Amidst the cacophony, some are turning to new "expert" systems. Yet these new
  beacons of direction are often those who seem approachable, rather than those who
  are accredited. Friendly, sympathetic bloggers with little nutrition or health backgrounds are instructing readers on what to eat and how to exercise. Authoritative-
  sounding talking heads parrot conspiracy theories and bunk science. Meanwhile,
  legitimate experts find it difficult to break through the surrounding noise.

disease—because, as we've seen, the human mind is particularly good at absorbing warnings and particularly bad at evaluating what is and isn't a true threat. This, paired with the unending inundation of bad news stories, has become a recipe for debilitating anxieties.

My friends talk openly about their dosages of Lexapro and Zoloft. People twirl fidget spinners below their desks, flicking the whirling star of plastic meant to soothe frayed nerves. The phase "I can't even" has taken hold, used to indicate a situation or conversation that is beyond one's perceived abilities to tackle. People have even turned anxiety into a descriptor, calling people "anxy."

"Anxiety is starting to seem like a sociological condition," observes *New York Times* reporter Alex Williams in an article titled "Prozac Nation Is Now the United States of Xanax."[74] This angst, Williams writes, is now "a shared cultural experience that feeds on alarmist CNN graphics and metastasizes through social media."

In the last few years, anxiety rates have risen sharply for all generations, yet the greatest leap is concentrated among the world's youth. Starting in 2009, anxiety overtook depression as the top concern among college students, and the number of students experiencing anxiety has steadily increased since then.[75] In its annual survey of students, the American College Health Association found a significant increase—from 50 percent in 2011 to 62 percent in 2016—in undergraduates reporting to have experienced "overwhelming anxiety" in the previous year.

Signs of the anxiety epidemic are all around us. More and more people are avoiding crowded concerts and busy airports and skipping trips abroad because of the fear that they'll be unsafe.[76] Some view the future through such a fatalistic lens that they're forgoing parenthood, citing things like "global instability" as influencing their decision not to bring new life into this world.*,[77]

---

* For the first time in thirty years, the birth rate in the US is decreasing. While economists originally blamed the 2008 recession for this dip, the number of babies born each year has not rebounded in line with the stock market. A recent survey, conducted by Morning Consult for the *New York Times*, of nearly two thousand men and women who say they had or expected to have fewer children than they considered ideal found that 37 percent of respondents listed "worried about global instability"

Frayed nerves are also fueling a bustling self-care industry that some call the "Anxiety Economy." There are now more than a thousand meditation apps, some of which have been downloaded by as many as ten million people—or, as with Alex Tew's Calm, thirty million.[78] Tew says Calm's guided meditations, nature soundtracks, and bedtime stories, designed to help people sleep or simply pause, serve as a "pressure release," an antidote to our modern disaster narrative. In 2017, the wellness industry raked in $3.7 trillion, with a growth rate faster than the global economy.[79] Its burgeoning trends include meditation classes, floating tanks, infrared saunas, CBD supplements, ayahuasca "trips," destruction therapy,* and slow entertainment.† People are jumping on any bandwagon that promises tranquility, quiet, or some form of "toxin" banishment.

---

as a factor in their decision. Thirty-three percent directly named the climate crisis as their impetus to put family on hold.

Multiple news reports document the climate-based angst that twenty- and thirtysomethings are feeling while considering parenthood. As just a few examples, see "No Children Because of Climate Change? Some People Are Considering It" by Maggie Astor for the *New York Times*, "Should We Be Having Kids in the Age of Climate Change?" by Jennifer Ludden for National Public Radio's *All Things Considered*, and "How Do You Decide to Have a Baby When Climate Change Is Remaking Life on Earth?" by Madeline Ostrander for the *Nation*.

* "Destruction therapy" is pitched as a way to release budding aggression. Be it at Ikari Area in Hong Kong or Rage Room in the US, entrepreneurs are handing angsty customers bats, metal pipes, and axes and encouraging them to start swinging.

† People are finding moments of Zen through "slow entertainment," which includes television and radio shows designed to soothe viewers. Netflix's *Terrace House* is a sloth-paced Japanese reality show with episodes "calm as Quaker meetings," writes Troy Patterson for the *New Yorker*. Stressed-out viewers can also quiet the mind with four-hour episodes of *National Knitting Evening*, six hours of chopping and burning of wood on *National Firewood Night*, or a seven-hour train ride from Bergen to Oslo, all hosted by the Norwegian Broadcasting Company. (In 2012, the Norwegian Broadcasting Company mounted a camera to a cruise boat that sailed down the coastline from Bergen to Kirkenes. They aired the entire journey—all 134 hours of it. At one point in the broadcast nearly half of Norway's population was watching, according to media reports.) Folks are tuning in to, effectively, tune out.

But here's the kicker: We're most afraid in an era when we should be least afraid.

Climate breakdown aside (which, granted, is legitimate and should deeply alarm you. Sorry.), multiple historians argue that we're living in the most peaceful era of our species' existence.* Rates of hunger and violent crime are at their lowest points ever; we're developing vaccines and therapies that save people from flesh-eating diseases like Ebola; there are even lots of promising solutions to the climate crisis waiting to be put into use (if only public sentiment were stronger and corporate greed weaker).

Yet, while we may *be* safer than ever, life *feels* inordinately more dangerous, with worries of things like government corruption, debilitating debt, and identity theft frequently impinging upon our waking hours. Beyond downloading a meditation app or stocking up on adult mandala coloring books, what else are we to do to soothe our unease?

At the very least, many feel, *in a world that feels increasingly out of control, I should be able to control what I put into my body. I should know what I'm eating.* Food is one of the only areas of respite, where people are able to demand greater information and control.

While the twentieth century drew us farther and farther away from the origins of our food, new technologies and localized food systems have the opportunity to bring us closer. And unlike nearly all other modern woes, like fears of terror attacks or superstorms, the food system is an issue that can be broken down into understandable, sometimes even tangible, parts. Today, people are looking to food companies to provide the sense of control we crave, by clamoring for greater access to information.

The push for transparency is a call for agency—for personal power and autonomy. And, perhaps unsurprisingly, no country is seeing as much food industry investment in retail transparency innovations as China.

---

* The decades since the end of World War II have been "the most peaceful era in human history—and by a wide margin," argues historian Yuval Noah Harari in his book *Sapiens: A Brief History of Humankind*. "In the year following the 9/11 attacks, despite all the talk of terrorism and war, the average person was more likely to kill himself than to be killed by a terrorist, a soldier, or a drug dealer," he notes.

Digging for Answers

On a pasture in Cha'an, located in the eastern landlocked Chinese province of Anhui, more than a hundred thousand chickens scuttle about, wearing high-tech black anklets that track their every step. The clip-on monitors have been with them since birth and provide their eventual buyer with every possible detail about their four to six months of life.[80] These cluckers are a part of the GoGo Chicken project.

Spearheaded by the Hong Kong insurance company ZhongAn, GoGo Chicken employs a mix of state-of-the-art sensors and tracking systems to farm verifiably "free range" chicken. Whether a chicken qualifies as "free range" depends on how much space it is allotted, and an auto-tracker of a chicken's steps is a reliable measure of that feathered friend's lifestyle. While this may seem over the top, Chinese customers are finding comfort in the added assurance.

"[Transparency] is something that consumers want, and we can't ignore it anymore," an industry expert who works in the Chinese market and asked to remain anonymous told me. Years prior, "companies could have changed the way they tracked and traced manufacturing, but there was no incentive. Consumers weren't pushing before. Social media wasn't around. It wasn't a PR disaster, and retailers were previously OK with a few issues. When companies say, 'We cannot or don't know where our products are coming from,' it's because they don't want to know, not that they can't." Now, with calls for greater transparency at a fever pitch, a number of companies are utilizing the messy Chinese food system to test out groundbreaking food tracking systems and sensors.

ZhongAn documents the chickens' age, location, and steps, the surrounding air quality, daily drinking water quality, when the chicks are quarantined, and when they're killed—all on a digital register, using blockchain technology. A blockchain is a decentralized ledger shared on a peer-to-peer network—a supposedly inalterable master list of interactions—and can be used to do everything from track the journey of diamonds to authenticate the voting process. Blockchain implementation is gaining interest throughout the Western world, too, as IBM, Walmart, Tesco, and other high-powered companies experiment with the new tracking system. Don't be surprised if in a few short years, you are able to scan your produce to see exactly where and when it was picked, what chemicals were applied, how far it traveled, and perhaps the carbon footprint it racked up along its journey to you, all inputs monitored and housed on a blockchain. At ZhongAn, inputs to their blockchain are made both manually by farmers and automatically through the smart sensor bracelets attached to each chicken's ankle.

ZhongAn also provides an extra touch of personalization to the novel chicken-buying experience: People can choose a baby chick and watch it grow via online video streams. Through this program, they're allowing folks to essentially adopt a chicken, enabling them to become virtual, voyeuristic farmers. And when that butchered chicken is delivered, the company employs facial recognition technology (yes, to recognize the face of the chicken) to confirm that a customer is receiving the same chicken they'd selected weeks or months ago. In doing so, ZhongAn is using technology to close the knowledge gap between farmer and eater.

Many companies—in both China and the West—are also testing sensors that give customers the power to check for any unscrupulous contaminants or even nutrient loss caused by extensive storage time or damaging travel conditions. It's easy to imagine that a few years down the line, the discerning public will no longer accept *any* label as sufficient, and instead will pull out their toxin spectrometer to scan produce for signs of glyphosate residue or to check nutrient density.

People are no longer just asking for a great story; they want tracking systems for behind-the-scenes access and certification. Blockchain and sensors, many believe, further reduce the possibility of fraud.

Still, blockchain and sensor technologies are in their infancy and, in the meantime, customers are eager to become omnipotent rulers of their diets. And so, companies like Hema are incorporating other methods of control and transparency, such as their extensive brand stories accessed by QR code, and the opportunity to literally catch your own dinner. Meanwhile, smaller startups are looking to a more basic tactic to engender trust: rethink the supply chain.

During my time in Shanghai, I visited a location of Hunter Gatherer, a chain of fast-casual restaurants and retail stores boasting local and "chemical-free" produce. There, I found myself transported to a haven of superfoods and clean eating. I arrived at lunchtime, and nearly every seat was filled with twenty- and thirtysomethings, most of whom seemed to be on breaks from office jobs. Patrons were devouring items like the Koreatown LA rice bowl, topped with pepper-crusted roast beef, kimchi, bulgogi sauce, and a tangy avocado slaw, or the Mala Spice bowl, with chicken thigh, bacon-braised cabbage, and a cucumber relish. As people waited in line to place an order, they passed a market-like produce section offering "chemical-free" fruits and vegetables. Near the cashier, a refrigerator housed local beverage options, like Beijing's Papp's Tea kombucha and Jova honey vanilla nut milk. I ordered an iced coffee that arrived in a glass branded with the phrase: "Celebrate real food."

"We talk about the food being transparent and real," explained Anmao Sun, the young owner of Hunter Gatherer, who returned to his birth country after graduating from Tufts University in 2012 with the hope of shaking up the food industry. "Our company is largely based on the fact that we actually have our own farms that we operate. We found that in the beginning, when you are trying to establish a brand that people will trust, you obviously need credibility, and to do that, you need to control the supply chain." With four locations spread across Shanghai, Hunter Gatherer relies on two company-owned 165-acre farms for the bulk of their ingredients. "We are a seed-to-table ecosystem that serves and celebrates real food," the Hunter Gatherer website proclaims, and offers brief details on the proprietary farms and farming techniques.

Hunter Gatherer's job, as Sun explains it, is to convince people to trust them, and then work to maintain that trust. To open doors, Hunter Gatherer regularly hosts farm dinners for key opinion leaders (referred to as KOLs), who then post their stories to social media for followers to view. The influencers' visits serve as brand validation. And the push seems to be working, evidenced by Hunter Gatherer's rapidly growing business.

Hunter Gatherer works in partnership with a sister company called Yimishiji, an online farmers' market that focuses even more intensely on sourcing. The two companies share an investor, Shinho, as well as office space in Shanghai, as they work together to build a reliable ecosystem of trustworthy food.

"We are really trying to disrupt the transparency of the supply chain for China," Matilda Ho, the thirtysomething founder of Yimishiji explained to me. On Yimishiji's website, shoppers can place their weekly grocery orders and look through offerings sourced from local farms. Ho has settled on a balance, as she puts it, between art and science to keep her business reliable and functioning. It's not enough, she said, to label things as "organic."

"A lot of Chinese consumers don't trust organic labels," she told me. Players "without integrity" destroyed what reliability the organic label used to carry, she said, citing stories of fraudulent organic-labeled goods that hit the market years prior. "So, no matter how hard you try to say that your food is safe and clean, it's still very difficult for the buyer. How can they trust whatever you say?"

As one part of their trust-building, Yimishiji offers frequent farm visits for customers, and one morning, I was lucky enough to attend one of these excursions. Two Yimishiji employees picked me up from my Shanghai Airbnb and drove me an hour outside the city to BIO-Farm, one of Yimishiji's largest suppliers. There, we walked among hoop houses where rows of deep verdant zucchini tendrils with canary-yellow flowers cascaded down like a curtain. Suspended pumpkin vines swept the length of another greenhouse; the bright orange gourds appeared to float in the air, and below, in the soil, rows of stout salad greens punctuated the cornucopia. As we walked, our host, farmer Xiao Lu, talked about BIOFarm's dedication to rotational crops and biodiversity, and their efforts to educate Chinese farmers and the public about sustainable farming practices through classes, farm tours, farm produce box subscriptions, and farmer training programs. On our visit, the Yimishiji staffers, my translator, and I spent time gamboling in the fields, gawking at purple artichoke flowers, and snorting at pet pigs. But these bucolic farm visits alone are not enough to convince patrons that their food is safe, Ho said.

Yimishiji also focuses on testing and certification. Ho has implemented strict standards for vendor acceptance on the Yimishiji marketplace. "Everything is zero tolerance towards pesticides, chemicals, antibiotics, and hormones," she explained. Samples from each of Yimishiji's participating and pending partner farms are sent to a lab, where they're screened for two hundred types of pesticides to ensure they meet the company's standards. The results of this screening can be found on the Yimishiji website under each purveyor's profile. Then, to confirm that there is no funny business, they again sample items from each vendor every quarter and make personal visits. Sometimes, she said, you'll see a nonapproved bag of fertilizer tucked in the corner of a greenhouse and you'll know that someone is cutting corners. She's convinced that every measure to ensure honest and chemical-free food is needed in the Chinese market.

Ho attests that each day more and more Chinese consumers are learning how to take control of their food. Currently, she says, Yimishiji's core shoppers are Millennial parents concerned for their children's safety, as well as those who have been diagnosed with cancer or diabetes and have been instructed by doctors to eat organic foods. Those folks simply have the greatest motivation to seek out safe food. But, as "chemical free" becomes an accessible and more affordable option, she anticipates that their consumer base will grow. And this seems to be a realistic forecast.

While still a niche market, the concept of local and "chemical-free" foods is gaining traction across China. Prior to my visit to Yimishiji, I toured a weekly farmers' market pop-up in Beijing with coordinator and local agriculture expert Tianle Chang. "When we started," Chang told me, "it was mostly Westerners coming. Now, it's mostly locals." With growing demand, Chang explained, farmers are able to sell more and therefore lower their prices. More and more locals are simply finding it worthwhile to buy produce from farmers they can actually shake hands with. It puts customers at ease to look into the eyes of the person they're buying from. On our visit to the Sanlitun market in the heart of Beijing, surrounded by restaurants that offered paninis, Chemex coffee, and, yes, avocado toast, I saw mostly locals wandering between the tables of locally grown produce.

Still, the Yimishiji staffers told me that they are surprised that there aren't more customers clamoring for farm visits or rushing local farmers' markets. While many of their customers make the trip out to the farm, and, in fact, far more Chinese Millennials are making the effort to visit livestock or seafood farms than their over-fifty-five counterparts, the number of farm-curious shoppers is still less than some in the industry would anticipate.[81] Instead, many shoppers seem to be satisfied with the information they find online and testaments from trusted KOLs.

Yimishiji's core Shanghainese shopper "works a lot," I heard from a member of their marketing team. Though most of the farms are just a short ride away, time for day trips is limited. Many of their customers, this team member explained, rely on Yimishiji for not just safe food, but also the speedy delivery that's become a necessity for today's oversched-uled professionals. This is a part of Hema's allure, as well. All Hema locations guarantee thirty-minute delivery within a three-kilometer radius of any particular store. While food safety is a must, urbanites are also limited by other practical constraints. After all, in our always-on era, who has time to stroll through a strawberry field?

CHAPTER TWO

delivery &
distraction

Tickets are printing faster than the prep cooks can keep up with. At ten individual stations, workers hover over their tables of pre-sliced and sorted ingredients, awaiting the incoming orders. With tickets in hand, they're off, tossing ingredients into bowls, layering them across sandwich breads, or blending them into smoothies. Usually, a cold dish takes no more than ninety seconds to prepare before it's pushed across the table to the sorting area, where another employee organizes and stacks items in to go bags branded with the Sweetheart Kitchen logo. With a pulse-like rhythm, motorbike drivers arrive and depart from the kitchen, tucked in the hipster Prenzlauer Berg neighborhood of northeastern Berlin, to deliver grub to the outer arteries of the city.

Orders from sixteen different DoorDash menus, each branded with a different restaurant name, all collide here in the hub of Sweetheart Kitchen, a restaurant company that focuses entirely on delivered meals. Each evening, the screech of the printer and the sea of white tickets it churns out represent the collective forfeiture of grocery shopping, dinner prep, and cleanup among the city's exhausted yet starved workforce.

Meanwhile, five thousand miles across the ocean in Houston, Texas, Rachel unpacks a black-and-white cardboard box that arrived at her doorstep. Inside are a month's worth of prepped and frozen meals created by the startup Daily Harvest. Each morning, after an early workout, Rachel reaches into the freezer to select a smoothie cup, chock-full of pre-cut and frozen mostly organic produce, seeds, and grains. She lifts the black plastic lid from the white paper cup, dumps the frozen ingredients (today, perhaps, it will be a carrot and chia mix, with sweet potatoes and walnuts) into the blender, adds her liquid of choice for the day (almond milk, for example, or coconut water), and hits the "on" button. Soon, she'll have her breakfast. During her workday, she'll reach back into the freezer for a Daily Harvest harvest bowl and zap her way to lunch.

Roughly a dozen hours later, Kainaz starts her day in New Delhi, India, by awaiting her morning delivery from FoodCloud, a delivery network of home-cooked meals. For the past three years, she has relied on FoodCloud for her breakfast and lunch thalis—"a couple of Indian dishes with a roti and rice or salad." Most often she orders Mughlai dishes like tikka and biryani (meat and rice) from Ruchhi's Homemade; occasionally she opts for more global flavors—be it nachos or Bengali mangsho jhol with aloo (curried lamb with potatoes)—from Ranu's Ranna. Each morning, Kainaz choses from the menus posted online by the independent cooks and submits her order through the FoodCloud system; her selected cooks then prepare the thalis in their own home kitchens and the orders are picked up by motorbike drivers and delivered to Kainaz's home.

Over the last decade, the mealtime experience has undergone a radical shift. Eaters are now able to get food-on-demand from a record number of sources.

Around the world, food delivery services are reeling in customers with astounding success. In India alone, there are now over four hundred food delivery apps.[1] In Latin America, a startup called iFood completes about 1.7 million deliveries a month in Mexico and Brazil. Meanwhile, in Europe, the London-based Just Eat has delivered over three hundred million meals across the western continent, as well as overseas in Australia, New Zealand, and Mexico. These services are so highly valued by patrons that many plan their budgets around their weekly, if not daily, delivery habits. Australians, Deloitte consultancy found, are cutting back on basic household expenses rather than giving up "little luxuries" like restaurant delivery, for which they gladly shell out about $2.6 billion each year through companies like Menulog, Uber Eats, Deliveroo, and Foodora.[2]

Others who want a low-effort meal but appreciate the process of cooking are turning to another innovation: the meal kit. In kitchens around the globe, from Australia to Belgium to South Africa, people open packages of prepped ingredients and follow a recipe card—like an IKEA manual for dinner—to assemble the many parts. Those in India can choose from among a number of meal kit delivery options such as iChef, Let's Chef, SnapCurry, and Burgundy Box, with each brand targeting a different diner: those who like Western food, those who want to try new global flavors, those who want all organic. The popularity of these kits has risen with astronomical speed. Blue Apron, one of America's first successful meal kit concepts, saw its net revenue grow 338 percent between 2014 and 2015 and another 133 percent between 2015 and 2016; at one point, the company was valued at over $2 billion.[3]

And then there are those who opt to skip "meals" altogether, and instead graze or snack throughout the day. You can walk into any market and see the evidence of the snack boom along the aisles: Shelves are stuffed with granola bars, miniature yogurt cups, and a vast array of dry meat snacks like jerky and biltong. Where Frito-Lay, Utz, and Rold Gold once reigned, innumerable specialty brands now urge you to pick up a colorful bag of kale chips, quinoa puffs, or gourmet air-popped Amish popcorn. An astounding 94 percent of Americans now snack at least once per day, a far higher percentage than in decades past.[4] For many, this rise in snacking isn't in addition to meals; nearly half of those who've boosted their snack intake say they've also slashed the number of full meals eaten in a day.[5] This insight was reflected within our own study group. Forty-four percent of our Hungry Study participants said they eat a snack on the go at least once a week, and 41 percent reported that they eat a meal while working and/or at their work desk at least once a week. Nearly a quarter of our respondents said they replace a full meal with a snack at least four times a week. Who needs a salad when you can have a yogurt cup, chickpea chips, and a Clif bar?

Many loudly lament this delivery, meal kit, and snacking revolution. Numerous individuals and organizations claim that Millennials simply have no cooking skills. Or that we're impatient. Many blame laziness for these trends. In 2016, *New York Times* food writer Kim Severson set off a firestorm of tweets and articles when she suggested that Millennials don't eat cereal because we can't be bothered to clean up after ourselves. She supported this assertion with this finding from research agency Mintel: "Almost 40 percent of the Millennials . . . said cereal was an inconvenient breakfast choice because they had to clean up after eating it."[6] Cue the groans. Soon the clickbait story was everywhere: "The baffling reason many Millennials don't eat cereal," a *Washington Post* headline read; "Millennials Think Eating Cereal Is Way Too Difficult," from *Fortune*; "Millennials Literally Too Lazy to Eat Cereal," by *New York Magazine*'s "The Cut"; and "Millennials don't like cereal because they hate doing dishes," from *Vice*.[7]

One journalist, Luke Darby, on behalf of *GQ* magazine, reached out to Mintel to get the background on the hysteria-inducing statistic.

"I don't think it's that Millennials are lazy," Amanda Topper, senior food analyst at Mintel, clarified for Darby, pushing back against the narrative spreading across the Internet.[8] Instead, she says, she interprets the data as a comment on time management: "Consumers are increasingly pressed for time, so for breakfast specifically we're not necessarily sitting down at the breakfast table each day, so when it comes to finding products that are going to satisfy those needs, we need convenient, portable food." She references the success of McDonald's all-day breakfast menu and the explosive sales of on-the-go meals.

"It all ties back to being too busy to have a sit-down breakfast at home, and that's impacting product development across the board." A close look at these delivery, convenience, and snacking developments reveals a consumer group not defined by laziness, but by stress and overwhelm.

Over the last few years, the number of people who report experiencing a time crunch has skyrocketed. The terms *time famine, time crunch*, and *time poverty* have become popularized in reference to the growing sentiment that there are simply not enough hours in the day to do everything we'd like to accomplish. Nearly a third of parents today claim to always feel rushed, while more than a third of Millennials say they do not sleep at least eight hours a night because they do not have enough time; they simply have too many things to do.[9] This time crunch is markedly evident, of course, in the way people are eating—or not eating.

Full meal replacement products are another food sector that has grown rapidly over the last decade. At the checkout counter of my local convenience store, brick-like rows of meal replacement bars have taken over the prime shelving real estate once held by goodies like Twizzlers and Sour Patch Kids. Over in the beverage aisle, liquid meal replacement options boasting high protein or caffeine contents are slotted alongside sodas and kombucha. Often, the taste of these meal replacements leaves something to be desired, but who cares? They're efficient.

This time crunch has also spurred the rise in delivery. Who has time to go shopping? It's not just restaurant-prepared meals that are being delivered these days; everything from cat food to diapers are being packed in boxes and bags and transported directly to people's homes and workplaces.

"I get about fifteen boxes a week," confessed Maggie, a Millennial mom of two living in the suburbs of Chicago, as we spoke over video chat. "That's a little embarrassing," she said with a faint eye roll. I asked Maggie, then at home with her three-week-old daughter, what, exactly, she has shipped to her front door.

"Everything. Literally everything," she replied, and began listing the items: groceries, personal care products, cloth diapers, chef-prepared meals, feed for their chickens, dog food. "I don't go shopping," she told me, then wondered out loud how people in generations past ever possibly had the time to go out and run all those errands. How, she pondered, did people manage before delivery?

Similarly, Daily Harvest devotee Rachel isn't sure how she'd make it through each day without the convenience of her delivered frozen meals. With two kids, a career in real estate, and a husband who spends at least twelve hours a day at a demanding job in medicine, she finds there's little to no time to cook. Sometimes, she admits, even the few seconds it takes to blend her breakfast or microwave her lunch bowl is a stretch. Often, she eats Daily Harvest for breakfast and lunch, then she and her husband order in a delivered meal for dinner.

But this is not to say that her blended, microwaved, and delivered eating routine is what she prefers. "I actually love to cook. I cook whenever I can," she tells me, and says that sometimes just going to the grocery store and looking through produce "is a pleasure," a "pause in the day." The problem is, she rarely has time to indulge in such an experience.

Similarly, Kainaz's fondness for FoodCloud is not just about the fabulous dal. Ironically, Kainaz works as a chef at both her own restaurant and a nearby café, but with the demands of her career, she is unable to find time to prepare proper meals for herself. So, as she cooks and sends out orders for delivery across Delhi, she awaits her own twice-daily thalis crafted in kitchens just a few miles away.

Many in the food industry read reports about the rise of delivery and snacking and draw the most straightforward conclusion possible: Young people really love snacks and delivery. But it isn't so simple.

We asked our Hungry Study participants to rank their *preferred* meal experiences, assuming that time is not an issue, and a resounding 81 percent put "Home-cooked meal, eaten at home" at the number one or two position for most preferred way to eat, followed by "Leftovers eaten at home" and "Going out to eat at a restaurant" in third. Only 9 percent of participants said they favor eating at their desks, and a scant 7 percent prefer to snack on the go.

It's hard to argue that a yogurt cup and breakfast bar are as satisfying as a warm omelet with hash browns, or that eating dinner out of a plastic container is more pleasant than a meal on a ceramic plate. The *why* behind convenience trends is not wants. It's needs.

Young people love food. Multiple surveys, including the Hungry Study, show that well over half of US Millennials identify as "foodies" and list going out to eat as one of their favorite things to do—more than attending concerts and playing video games. In fact, one survey found that over half of Millennials say they enjoy eating as much as sex, and over a third would choose fine dining *over* sex.[10] Yet, the same demographic reports eating an increasing number of on-the-go meals over the past half decade.[11] The question then becomes: What is causing this modern time crunch?

Workin' 9 to 5?

Does your employer expect you to be accessible after you leave the office? If yes, until what time? If you're like many modern office workers, the lines between when you start and stop work have become blurred by the ability to answer emails and text messages from home.

"Employees are more and more connected during hours outside of the office," Myriam El Khomri, France's minister of labor, said in 2016. "The boundary between professional and personal life has become tenuous."[12] The comments came as a justification for a new French labor initiative known as the "right to disconnect," which went into effect on January 1, 2017. The policy requires offices with more than fifty employees to incorporate rules that ban work-related emails on days off or after work hours. Sounds pretty lovely, right?

Just as technology is disrupting the way we eat and the way we shop, it is impacting our relationships to the workplace, too. For tens of thousands of years, humans "worked" as foragers. About two hundred years ago, after another ten thousand years as farmers and herders, we left the great outdoors for desks and factory lines. And then, decades later, we plunged into the era of cell phones, email, and text messaging. And we haven't stopped clicking, scrolling, and swiping since.

Smartphones have penetrated the world market faster than any other modern technology. In 2011, only one-third of US adults owned a smartphone. Less than a decade later, 95 percent of Americans own a cell phone of some kind.[13] There is greater access to smartphones than toilets on this planet. Two-thirds of all people on Earth now own a handheld gadget that buzzes and dings and acts as a portal to the entire globe. This Digital Age shift has, with unprecedented velocity, transformed the way we engage with one another, how we shop, how we consume the news, how we assess our own self-worth—and, yes, how we spend our waking and working hours.

In France, the minister of labor is paying attention to the impact of this societal shift specifically on the workplace experience, but many employees in other countries are subject to antiquated work policies yet to be updated for our digital work environments. Best practices in this era of round-the-clock connection are not yet defined; office etiquette has yet to be rebooted. As a result, many employees face the burden of untenable workplace expectations.

In early 2019, Buzzfeed News reporter Anne Helen Petersen penned an article that quickly went viral: "How Millennials Became the Burnout Generation." In it, she writes: "I'm burned out. Why am I burned out? Because I've internalized the idea that I should be working all the time."[14] Just a few months after the article's release, the World Health Organization reclassified "burnout" as a "syndrome" caused by "chronic workplace stress." The "occupational phenomenon" the WHO outlines is characterized by "feelings of energy depletion or exhaustion; increased mental distance from one's job, or feelings of negativism or cynicism related to one's job; and reduced professional efficacy."[15]

The topic of workplace-based burnout has been percolating in the media for years. "Feeling Burned Out at Work? Join the Club," read a 2017 *Wall Street Journal* headline. "The problem appears to be worsening, resulting in steep turnover and health costs," the article subhead summarized.[16] Gallup polls from 2018 show that more than 40 percent of workers in the US are so stressed they feel "burned out," and global workplace wellness programs are reporting more stress- and anxiety-related calls to phone-counseling lines.*, [17]

Globally, people are clocking in more working hours while technically off the clock.† In 2015, a poll of one thousand American working professionals found that 65 percent of those surveyed expected to be available outside of work both by email and by phone.[18] Another work-time analysis of executives, managers, and professionals found that 60 percent of those who carry smartphones for work are connected to their jobs 13.5 or more hours a day on weekdays, and about five hours on weekends, which adds up to about seventy-two hours each week.[19] The days of landlines, fax machines, and snail mail seem quaint in comparison to today's always-on-call professional environment.

The latest food trends reflect our society of time-crunched workers. "Wherever you see major office centers, that's where you see the most lunchtime orders," Matt Maloney, co-founder and CEO of America's restaurant delivery sector leader Grubhub, confirmed for me over the

---

* Seventy percent of the calls in 2017 placed to phone counseling lines at Workplace Options, an employee well-being company, were stress and anxiety related, up from 50 percent of calls just three years earlier, as reported by Rachel Feintzeig for the *Wall Street Journal* in the article "Feeling Burned Out at Work?"

† Gallup reports that the number of working hours for US full-time employees has held fairly steady over the past fourteen years, at around forty-seven hours a week, but likely doesn't account for time working at home or on the go. "The '40-Hour' Workweek Is Actually Longer—by Seven Hours," Gallup's headline reads.

phone. In Shanghai, I saw a horde of office workers swarming a food delivery kiosk around noontime. Some meal-delivery companies, in fact, deliver exclusively to offices.

Office workers also support sales of fast food. Contrary to the common belief that the majority of American fast-food consumers are low income, a 2018 CDC study reports the exact opposite: It is in fact *affluent* Americans, those raking in six-figure salaries, who are the most likely to eat fast food—specifically, affluent folks ages twenty to thirty-nine, the same age bracket that represents the largest portion of our labor force.[*][20]

Ultimately, many people are forfeiting a mealtime pause to continue plugging away, eating a snack or delivered meal that sits next to their keyboard. Some are nibbling on jerky while on a conference call, chugging a Soylent on the morning commute, or slowly working their way through a bag of peanut butter pretzels throughout the day. A study of American workers discovered that about half of employees feel that they cannot get up for a break at all, and just under half regularly eat lunch at their desks.[21] A quick search of the hashtag #SadDeskLunch produces images of reheated takeout, gray sandwiches, and limp salads propped up against keyboards or computer monitors, a symptom of people who feel obligated to keep their rumps glued to their office chairs even through the traditional noontime break.

These modern pressures are even convincing many workers to leave vacation days unused. One survey by Project: Time Off (run by the US Travel Association) found that more than half of American workers left vacation time unused in 2015 because they couldn't find the time to take it "due to a heavy workload."[22] American employees, who typically get a mere ten days of paid vacation to begin with (compared to most other developed nations, which offer around a month paid vacation annually[23]), are forfeiting that break, saying, *Nah, I'll skip the beach*.

"It is commonly assumed that economic trends are driving the decline" of vacations or an increase in the actual amount of work, notes a press release from the project. Instead, they found, "America's time off

---

* According to the CDC report "Fast Food Consumption Among Adults" by Cheryl D. Fryar, one-third of respondents who earn below the federal poverty line eat fast food daily. Meanwhile, over 40 percent of those earning 350 percent or more above the poverty line (about $112,950 a year per family) are daily fast-food diners.

habits closely track technology innovation and adoption trends, suggesting that connectivity has intensified Americans' attachment to work and reduced their ability to break free of the office." Added up, Americans are forgoing 658 million vacation days annually because they feel they just can't get away.

"There's no more vacation," Rachel, the Daily Harvest customer, told me. "If you're on vacation, you're on your email. There's never a true break." What's the point of flying to an exotic location if you're just going to be working the entire time?

Information Overload

While it's tempting to point the time-crunch finger entirely at employer policies, the reality is that each of us bears some responsibility for this new on-call environment. There is little data to show that we're actually given or completing more work during these extra on-call hours. Instead, there's plenty of evidence that we're simply taking longer to accomplish the same number of tasks we've always had. Why would that be?

In 2016, University of California–Irvine Department of Informatics professor Gloria Mark looked into how email use impacts rates of productivity and stress.[24] Along with her research team, she assembled a group of forty volunteers, all of whom worked in the research division of a large corporation, and gathered data on the employees' computer activity, perceived productivity, and time spent on email over the course of nearly two weeks. The researchers also monitored whether the workers primarily checked email after a self-interruption or relied instead on notifications to indicate that there was a new message awaiting in their inboxes. Finally, the researchers also measured the volunteers' stress levels via digital heart rate monitors, which were worn during all waking hours for the duration of the study.

In the end, the research findings were clear-cut: "When an individual spends more time on email during the workday, it is significantly related to lower assessed productivity and higher stress," their final study states. In fact, the same was found for spending time texting and on phone calls.

Why would time emailing equate to lower productivity and more stress? Shouldn't it be the opposite, since more time on email means more messages answered and more tasks completed? One factor is information overload.

Email was initially thought to be a time saver—no postage stamps, no trips to the post office, no waiting for the fax signal. But a number of new studies point to what many of us know from personal experience: We spend far more time corresponding now than ever before.

By opening our inboxes or checking our phone messages, we subject ourselves to a flood of information. In Mark's study, those who spent more time on email, phone calls, and texting—likely those sorting through a greater amount of content overall—experienced higher levels of stress.

In this digital era, messages rush forth like water from a broken faucet. It takes far less time to type an email than to pen a letter and it's free to send, disincentivizing us to be economical with our time or words. (Would you have sent the last twenty emails in your outbox if you'd had to handwrite them, add postage, and drop them in the mailbox?) But it's not just email that's occupying our time—it's reviews, tweets, gifs, videos, and more.

"Today we are confronted with an unprecedented amount of information, and each of us generates more information than ever before in human history," writes neuroscientist Daniel Levitin in his book *The Organized Mind: Thinking Straight in the Age of Information Overload*:

> Information scientists have quantified this. In 2011, Americans took in five times as much information every day as they did in 1986—the equivalent of 175 newspapers. During our leisure time, not counting work, each of us processes 34 gigabytes or 100,000 words every day. The world's 21,274 television stations produce 85,000 hours of original programming every day as we watch an average of 5 hours of television each day, the equivalent of 20 gigabytes of audio-video images. That's not counting YouTube, which uploads 6,000 hours of video every hour. And computer gaming? It consumes more bytes than all other media put together, including DVDs, TV, books, magazines, and the Internet.

Yet we are evolutionarily unequipped to parse through this onslaught of content. "Our brains evolved in a much simpler world with far less information coming at us," Levitin writes. "In a real biological sense, we have more things to keep track of than our brains were designed to handle." In other words, we literally do not have the capacity to sort through all the information being tossed our way—it is untenable for the human mind to manage.* This incongruence, between our new Digital Age tools and the capabilities of the human mind, inevitably creates a sense of overwhelm. In fact, there's a term specific to this condition: *technostress*.

Clinical psychologist Craig Brod introduced the term, which he defined as a "modern disease of adaption caused by an inability to cope with the new computer technologies in a healthy manner," in the 1980s. Later, other academics further defined the term as stress due to information and communication overload.[25]

The modern downpour of content, alone, can elevate our stress levels. "So many of us find life increasingly chaotic as opposed to even twenty years ago," Levitin told me over the phone from California, having just returned from a trip to India to visit the Dalai Lama. There's only so many things we can do at once, only so much information we can attempt to tackle.

This general sense of chaos has contributed to another successful retail market—that of limited choice. Many brands are restricting options, freeing up cognitive space that would otherwise be occupied by price comparisons, brand reviews, or the plagues of paradox of choice.†

---

* It's because of this overload, Levitin surmises, that our society is leaning toward visual communications. Our brains, he writes, "have trouble separating the trivial from the important, and all this information processing makes us tired." So, we look for shortcuts, like emojis, infographics, and listicles. Another mental shortcut is to choose only a few resources—whether news stations, religious leaders, or bloggers—to listen to.

† Contrary to what one might think, having a lot of choices doesn't make us feel powerful; it stresses us out. This is called the *paradox of choice*, a term coined by psychologist Barry Schwartz. Studies show that we feel better about our decisions when choosing from among a few things, rather than lots. For example, 401(k) participation rates fall as the number of fund options increase. People are more likely

For example, in the US, Quip sells one kind of toothbrush. Casper sells three variations of a mattress. Brooklinen sells four (similar) types of sheets. And that's it!

Limiting choice is also a commanding theme in grocery. German supermarket chain Aldi is one of the largest retail groups in the world, with ten thousand locations in twenty countries. Their stores stock between 1,300 and 1,600 items, a sliver of the 120,000 one can find in a Walmart Supercenter.[26] Trader Joe's employs a similar model, offering a small handful of items, each highly differentiated from one another. (For example, there aren't multiple brands of garlic hummus. Instead, there's one garlic hummus, and the other hummus options are wildly different flavors: chocolate, buffalo-style, and spicy avocado.) Online packaged goods site Public Goods offers just one of everything: one kind of ketchup, one toothbrush, one type of hand soap. Why waste time and space offering a gazillion variations of tissues or pasta when you can simply trust a brand to test and create the optimal product for you.

"The next big breakthrough in design and technology will be the creation of products, services, and experiences that eliminate the needless choices from our lives and make ones on our behalf, freeing us up for the ones we really care about," Aaron Shapiro, CEO of global digital marketing agency Huge, prognosticated back in 2015.[27] And that's exactly the mindset Brandless has taken on. Limited-option businesses are a salve for a demographic steeped in information overload.

Services like subscription boxes—another modish business model—provide the same cognitive stress relief. They remove the fear of missing out on a "best" face cream or salsa by letting you sample a new variety each month. Why look through product reviews when you can hand

---

to buy items in the grocery store if there are six varieties than if there are twenty-four. Many think choice is a liberator, but with too much of it, we can become paralyzed. For more on these experiments, see "When Choice Is Demotivating: Can One Desire Too Much of a Good Thing?" by Sheena Sethi-Iyengar and Mark Lepper published in the *Journal of Personality and Social Psychology* and "How Much Choice Is Too Much? Contributions to 401(k) Retirement Plans" by Sheena Sethi-Iyengar, Gur Huberman, and Wei Jiang, in the book *Pension Design and Structure: New Lessons from Behavioral Finance*.

that time-consuming evaluation off to a company you trust to provide you a set of quality options?

Other subscriptions services simply automate common errands, freeing up both the time you'd spend at the store and the mental space commonly dedicated to remembering to restock your must-have items, be it new underwear each season, or prescription medications once a month. Now, you can even sign up for a toilet paper subscription, offered by companies like Smartass in New Zealand and Who Gives a Crap in the US.

Delivery-maven Maggie finds herself relying on subscriptions for a number of everyday items. She used to order organic meal kits but has since given that up—though, when we talked, she was considering restarting her Sun Basket subscription. Her cloth diaper delivery is on a weekly pickup/drop-off schedule. A subscription company called Fresh Little Love even delivers a new assortment of clothing for her children every three months. "Every box includes 5–8 items that are nontoxic, eco-conscious, and totally cute," their website explains. Maggie's subscription-reliant routine is becoming the norm. Overall, between 2014 and 2017, the American subscription market increased by an astounding 831 percent.

For those cognitively exhausted by the roil of emails and texts—which Dr. Mark's study shows is likely anyone who answers emails or texts or phone calls at work—the economy of limited options, subscriptions, and delivery is there to help them make it through.

Distraction

Yet it's not just the quantity of information that's an issue—it's also the unpredictability of it, the unending bombardment and interruption.

The human mind doesn't do so well with distraction. It takes us more than nine minutes—in fact, some studies claim it's over twenty minutes—to refocus after being interrupted in the midst of completing a task.[28] But when we hear or see one of those ever-present buzzes, dings, or alerts, it causes exactly that—a distraction. *Stop what you're doing*, it says, *and pay attention over here instead!*

This incessant interruption is another factor in our modern inability to complete work in a timely manner (or our "reduced professional efficacy," as the World Health Organization put it). In Dr. Mark's email use experiment, more time on email meant more opportunities to be distracted, and more opportunities for distraction meant it took her subjects more time to complete their work.

You know what this feels like: You're in the zone working on a project when you receive an email or a text. It's a breaking news story or a notification about a super sale at your favorite retail store. You click on the link to see more and become enthralled. Perhaps you message a friend to let them know, as well. Minutes later, you close the computer window or set down your phone and turn back to your work. What was it that you were doing again?

Refocusing is just part of the issue. Switching from one task to another creates what business professor Sophie Leroy calls "attention residue."[29] In 2009, Leroy found that those who move from one task to another leave a portion of their attention on the original task. This mental juggling depletes our mental resources. In other words, if you're interrupting yourself throughout the day to check your email or texts, you're inevitably making yourself less productive by drawing mental energy away from your main task and distributing bits and pieces of that energy to all those other interactions.

No matter how confident you are in your multitasking skills, numerous studies highlight the human brain's blatant failure at managing multiple to-dos at once. Some studies suggest that multitasking can even negatively alter the physical makeup of our brains. Researchers have found that those who multitask exhibit lower gray-matter volume in the brain's anterior cingulate cortex, a region that regulates emotion processing and decision-making.[30] (This is the same part of the brain that's been shown to become strengthened by meditation, perhaps the exact opposite activity to multitasking.[31])

Yet, most of us feel an immediate desire to respond or follow up on messages. Common Sense Media, a media watchdog group in San Francisco, found that 72 percent of teens and 48 percent of their parents feel the need to immediately respond to texts, social media messages, and other notifications.

Some of us have even convinced ourselves that our texts and emails are so urgent that we sacrifice our own safety to reply. One study estimates that the desire to immediately respond is partly responsible for the sixfold jump in hospital emergency room visits for phone-related injuries between 2005 and 2010.[*, 32] Researchers also credit this connection compulsion for the rise in distracted driving accidents. In 2014, more than one in four motor vehicle accidents involved cell-phone use.[33]

But is our immediate response really necessary? Harvard Business School professor Leslie Perlow found that the professionals she surveyed spent twenty to twenty-five hours a week outside the office checking emails, often under self-imposed pressure to answer messages within an hour of their inbox arrival. "There is no impetus to question whether the work actually requires 24/7 responsiveness; on the contrary, people work harder and longer, without stopping to explore how they could work better," she assesses.[34]

While we tell ourselves that people on the other end *need* a response, the reality is that we're reacting to an ancient mental cue: Do it now or you may forget later. (Our ancestors didn't have Siri reminders or Post-its. We do.) Once we're aware of a task, our innate cognitive processes conjure a feeling that we need to act promptly.

Simply *knowing* we have a message waiting for us can negatively affect both our problem-solving skills and IQ.[35] Just like switching tasks, awareness of an awaiting task lures a portion of our focus and attention away from the immediate goal before us. This means that a notification telling us that we have new email, or an unread text, can cause us to work more slowly and poorly.[36] Studies show that our anxiety levels spike when we're aware of an incoming call or text yet unable to respond.[37] (Think: Your phone buzzes in your pocket as you sit at dinner. You don't want to be rude, so you don't answer. But your mind begins to tune out the table conversation anyhow and instead fixates on the vibration. *Who is calling?*)

---

* Some descriptions of these phone-related injuries include: "28 year old male walked into pole talking on phone and lacerated brow" and "14 year old male walking down road talking on cell phone, fell 6–8 ft. off bridge into ditch with rocks and water, landed on chest/shoulder, chest wall contusion," as documented in "Pedestrian Injuries Due to Mobile Phone Use in Public Places" in *Accident Analysis & Prevention*.

One night I was prepping dinner while my husband, who had recently returned from work, sat in the kitchen to keep me company. As I was telling him a story about my day, I looked up to see him staring down at his phone. I knew that there was hardly any chance he was listening to me, a suspicion that was confirmed when he didn't look up after I stopped speaking—and even started typing.

"What are you doing?" I asked.

"Responding to an email," he replied. "It will only take a second."

"Does it have to be responded to right now?" I questioned. He paused, cradled the phone in his hand, and looked at me.

"No," he replied, "you're right." He put the phone down and we continued our conversation.

A buzz on Jason's phone had alerted him to an incoming email and, without making a conscious decision, he opened his inbox. Then, a mental cue made him feel that the message he received *had* to be responded to right that instant. This pull was so strong that it caused his mind to shift focus entirely, giving the email message (a task) precedence over the real-life engagement (a nontask). But this is an antiquated response that, in our modern environments, isn't usually warranted.

The only way around these distractions is to eliminate the interruptions: silence all alerts or put our phones away. Otherwise, it's a catch-22: If we see the message and don't respond right away, our productivity is compromised. If we see the message and pause what we're doing to respond, our productivity is compromised. Our only hope is to avoid knowing about the message in the first place.

"I feel distracted all day," mom-of-two and delivery devotee Maggie told me over video chat.

"Why?" I prodded.

"My phone," she said with a sigh. I asked Maggie what notifications show up on her phone. As her newborn lay on her chest grunting and sighing, Maggie listed them off: CNN, HuffPost, fantasy football, Amazon Prime Now, her smart doorbell, an app she uses for lists and reminders, Grubhub, shared iPhoto streams with her family (she's alerted whenever anyone adds a photo), Calendar, group texts, Facebook, and then there's her Chicago Chicken Enthusiasts group, for which she is sent an email any time someone posts or responds to a post. Just listening to her list made me anxious.

When her notifications pop up, she says: "I start thinking about all the things I have to do." Often, a notification will cause her to stop whatever task she was working on to place an order on Amazon or check the weather or set herself another reminder.

Perhaps, I floated, she might have more time in her day if she didn't keep her phone close by? She took a moment to let the idea sink in. Her eyes wandered up, as though someone from above would provide the answer. She said she wasn't sure. And I think that's how most people would answer. But when you consider the number of times each of us checks our phones per day, the number of times a notification jerks us away from a task at hand, interrupts our concentration, and then pleads with us to continue engaging, it's hard to believe that phones *aren't* stealing minutes and hours of productivity from our days.

The 2017 Stress in America survey by the American Psychological Association found that employed Americans who are "constant checkers"—those who say they constantly check their email, texts, and social media accounts on a typical day, workday *or* weekend—report the highest overall stress levels.[38] According to the APA's findings, 44 percent of working adults in America qualify as "constant checkers."

With all we now know, it makes logical sense that "constant checkers" would be more stressed than others; these folks likely feel that they have less time, and less cognitive energy, to complete their daily tasks, and reduced productivity translates into greater levels of stress, as it takes us more time to complete our to-do items.[39]

Teens are also feeling the impacts of their distracted, on-call existence. In fact, technology use correlates with some of the highest rates of stress on record, which is especially evidenced among young people.*

---

* In the US, over half of Millennials say stress has kept them awake at night, and more than nine in ten Gen Zers say they've experienced at least one physical or emotional symptom because of stress, such as feeling depressed, sad, or lacking interest, motivation, or energy, findings that have been replicated by a number of institutions. Stress causes the persistent elevation of adrenaline and cortisol, which are known to be detrimental over the long term and cause ailments like anxiety, depression, digestive problems, heart disease, difficulty sleeping, and even debilitations of memory

In the UK, a study conducted by the University of Cambridge found that 38 percent of ten- to eighteen-year-olds feel overwhelmed by technology, an even higher percentage than the 34 percent of twenty-five- to thirty-four-year-olds who said they felt the same way.[40] One teen told me she daydreams of chucking her phone out the window, just to avoid the persistent barrage of incoming messages.

These online obligations, along with our compromised productivity rates, are contributing to a worldwide scarcity of shut-eye. The US Centers for Disease Control and Prevention has declared insufficient sleep a "public health problem," noting that more than one-third of American adults are not getting enough sleep on a regular basis.[41] Citizens in the United Kingdom are clocking in an average of only six hours and forty-nine minutes of daily rest. In 1942, just under 8 percent of the UK population slept six hours or less; now, it's 50 percent. Meanwhile, folkloric tales of excessive workdays in Japan are cited for the insufficient average night's sleep, which has shrunk to just six hours and twenty-two minutes.[42] (These conditions have popularized the terms *karōshi*, meaning "death from overworking," and *inemuri*, which means "to fall asleep in public.")

The ties between technology and sleep deprivation are undeniable. At the same time that the number of smartphone users doubled, the number of sleep-deprived teens jumped 58 percent.[43] In 2015, 40 percent of adolescents slept less than seven hours a night. Compared to 2009, that's a 17 percent increase in sleep deprived teens.[44] In the Hungry Study, one-quarter of our Gen Z respondents said they lose sleep almost every single night because they are spending time online. Beyond our inability to break away and put our phones down, numerous studies highlight the detriment of bright screen light stimulation, as well as the general stress associated with being within arm's reach of our communication portals as causes of this sleep loss. A meta-analysis that examined screen use among more than 125,000 kids, curated by researchers at King's College, London, found that simply having a media device *in the room* can impact a child's ability to get a rejuvenating night's snooze.[45]

---

and concentration—all increasingly common ailments in the Digital Age. These statistics are documented by the American Psychological Association in the reports "Stress in America™ Generation Z" and "Stress in America 2017: Technology and Social Media."

Social media and our devotion to our screens are, without question, provoking this shut-eye scarcity.

Perhaps our inability to catch enough z's is the catalyst behind yet another prevailing food trend of the last few years: cold brew coffee. In Japan, cold brew cans drop down from street-side vending machines. In Korea, cold brew, Americanos, hazelnut ice coffee, and iced macchiato packets could be mistaken for convenience store wallpaper, arranged floor to ceiling like a patchwork quilt. Nitro brew taps (cold brew infused with nitrogen) line coffeehouse bars around the globe, be it Santiago, Chile; Cape Town, South Africa; or Brooklyn, New York. In 2017, the global ready-to-drink coffee category ballooned to about $19.05 billion, with much of that growth driven by cold brew.[46]

The latest trend is coffee infused with "functional" ingredients like cannabidiol (better known as CBD) and ashwagandha, which promise to deliver a sense of calm. If you believe the marketing, these products will give you an energy boost while reducing your stress and anxiety— the ideal creation for this sleep-deprived, stressed-out cohort. And people seem to think these concoctions are worth their investment. According to one survey, the average US Millennial spends more than $2,000 a year on coffee—a shocking statistic when you consider the trillion dollars of student loan debt this generation is staring down.[47]

It's hardly a wonder that those of us living in this new on-call, technostressed reality are finding and investing in time-saving and energy-boosting solutions, whether in the form of delivery, snacks, or coffee. While we think of our always-on habits as productivity boosters, the reality is that "checking in" checks us out of the work that we need to get done; ultimately, we may be wasting chunks of time we could be spending, say, enjoying an afternoon tea while seated at a café.

One has to wonder: Why don't we just take a cue from the French and put down our phones?

Some say we just don't have the willpower. But that's not the whole story.

Nomophobia

Do you feel anxious when your phone's battery bar turns red, or when you realize you've accidentally left your phone at home? If you do, then you're not alone. In fact, you're part of the majority. About two-thirds of mobile users report distress when separated from their phones, a proportion that only grows when you look at younger users.[48] And these numbers are consistent around the world.[49]

This phone-specific anxiety actually has its own term, *nomophobia*, defined as the fear of not having or not being able to use your cell phone. "In 2015, there were 280 million smartphone addicts. If they banded together to form the 'United States of Nomophobia,' it would be the fourth most populous country in the world, after China, India, and the United States," observes Adam Alter in his book *Irresistible: The Rise of Addictive Technology and the Business of Keeping Us Hooked.*

In the Hungry Study, we asked participants a series of questions to assess their level of attachment to technology, inspired by validated nomophobia assessments.[50] We asked survey takers how much they agree or disagree with the following statements:

- I find myself wasting time on my phone but find it hard to break away.
- When I have a moment alone, I find myself reaching for my phone.
- When I wake in the morning, one of the first things I do is reach for my phone.
- My grades or work suffer because of the amount of time I spend online.
- I would rather spend time at home online than go out with others.
- I get nervous when my phone runs out of battery.
- I feel uncomfortable if I am unable to find a data signal or cannot connect to Wi-Fi.
- I find myself looking at my phone when I don't know what else to do.
- I feel a persistent desire to check my phone.
- I feel anxious when I do not have my smartphone with me.
- I feel uncomfortable when I cannot stay up-to-date with social media/online networks.
- I feel anxious when I can't check my email messages.

In order to qualify for our Tech-Tethered Cohort, respondents had to "agree" or "slightly agree" with five or more of these statements. Fifty-six percent, or 628 of our 1,106 respondents, made the cut.

In the blink of a historical eye, digital devices have gone from nonexistent to what many consider to be vital appendages. One comprehensive survey found that about half of respondents ages sixteen to thirty would rather give up their sense of smell than be separated from their devices.[51] People are so nomophobic that they keep their phones next to their beds, take their phones into the bathroom with them, and bring them to religious services; they even look at their phones while having sex.[52] Three-fourths of US Millennial smartphone users say that they "can't survive" without their phones—and half of Baby Boomers say the same.[53]

How have we become so dependent on a type of device that didn't exist just over a decade ago? Why can't we just put our phones down?

On a spring afternoon, I dialed up Dr. Larry Rosen at his oceanside home in San Diego. I needed his help, I told him, to understand what exactly is happening in our brains that keeps us checking our phones and email, even when it is counterproductive.

Rosen's work focuses on the psychological and physiological impacts of technology. He is professor emeritus and past chair of the psychology department at California State University and coauthor of the book *The Distracted Mind: Ancient Brains in a High-Tech World*. Of late, he's been interested in monitoring people's relationships with their phones, specifically the frequency of and motivations behind our phone interactions: How often are we checking our phones—and why?

Half the time we check our phones because we receive a notification, "but half the time there's no good reason," he told me with exasperation. "There's no visible reason, or auditory reason, or vibration reason. There's nothing—you just do it. Those are the times that I'm most concerned with."

Rosen started by walking me through the physiology of our phone-checking behavior. Each of us has adrenal glands that leak cortisol, the stress hormone. We need this little drip, drip, drip of cortisol to keep us awake throughout the day. But our adrenal glands also secrete things like adrenaline. "As those chemicals leak into your brain and body, you start feeling the physiological signs of anxiety: sweaty palms, you feel a little light-headed maybe, your heart feels funny, butterflies." When those chemicals build up, he says, studies show that people are more likely to pick up their phones.

Many phone interactions produce feel-good hormones in our brains, in much the same way that common drugs do. Remember, we have a natural hunger for information, and when we unlock our phones or open our email and happen to gather a juicy tidbit of useful information or see that we received a "like," our bodies release a bit of the feel-good hormones dopamine and serotonin. "People are carrying around a portable dopamine pump," says David Greenfield, assistant clinical professor of psychiatry at the University of Connecticut School of Medicine and founder of the Center for Internet and Technology Addiction.[54]

Of course, we don't get a hit of dopamine every time we interact with our phones. This concept is called "intermittent variable reward" and was coined many years ago by American psychologist B. F. Skinner, who found that if he administered the same reward (sugar) to a rat every time the rat pushed a lever, then the rat would, ultimately, only push the lever when hungry. However, if he varied the reward, sometimes providing the sugar and sometimes not, the rat would push the lever all the time. This is exactly how our phones operate. Sometimes there are no messages, or we read an upsetting article or see a photo of a friend's party that we weren't invited to. Other times, we read a compelling article or see that a post earned a record number of retweets. And this unpredictability of our Internet interactions, it turns out, makes them that much more addictive.

The concept is akin to gambling. In fact, many have begun to refer to smartphones as slot machines. Just as a slot machine keeps gamblers pulling the lever with the temptation of rewards, so do emails and notifications. Each check-in has the potential to deliver a hit of dopamine to the brain, and that potential leads to a persistent craving for one more possible hit, one more heart, one more piece of news to chew on. With this in mind, it makes sense that we find ourselves always connected, even when the incessant use of these devices may compromise our well-being. It's the allure of knowing—and the fear of not knowing—that keeps us checking in.

This urgent need to check in is driven by FOMO, or the fear of missing out. FOMO is the fear, worry, or anxiety of being out of touch with, or missing out on, events, experiences, or conversations.[55] Nearly a quarter of global Internet users say that fear of missing out is the main motivation for their online connection.[56] In order to stay on top of our digital communications, 78 percent of teens and 69 percent of teen parents check their devices at least hourly, according to Common Sense Media. This modern dilemma arouses insecurities and has been found, time and again, to be associated with smartphone as well as social media addiction.[57] FOMO is, in part, what makes putting our phones down so difficult.*

Nearly half of the digitally connected global population is thought to suffer from some form of Internet-related addiction, be it to email, gaming, Snapchat streaks, or porn.[58] More than one-third of eighteen- to twenty-nine-year-olds are online almost constantly.[59] A 2018 survey of over 1,500 US respondents found that 55 percent of Gen Z claim they can't go more than five hours without Internet access before becoming uncomfortable. Twenty-seven percent can't go for more than an hour.[60] Children and adults alike are claiming that they simply cannot live without their Internet-connected devices by their sides at all times.[61]

In 2016, Dr. Rosen asked his students—a mix of older and younger Millennials—to install an app on their smartphones that would monitor how many times they unlocked their phones each day and how many minutes they kept the phone unlocked. At the end of the semester, the results showed that the students checked their phones on average fifty-six times a day, which, he notes, "is about every fifteen minutes or so of waking time." Each time they unlocked their phones, they would spend an average of four minutes on the phone, which adds up to nearly four hours a day. (Shockingly, this rate is lower than the US average.[62] In 2017, Deloitte's Global Mobile Consumer Survey revealed that those ages eighteen to twenty-four check their phones a record-setting eighty-six times per day, on average. This is up from eighty-two times a day in 2016. The average number of check-ins for all age groups in 2017 was forty-seven times per day, a number that also continues to rise.[63])

---

* Young kids are most prone to FOMO, as well as to general technology addiction. The part of our brains that manages distraction and temptation is called the prefrontal cortex. This area of the brain isn't fully developed until our twenties. Furthermore, children have a hyperactive risk-reward system that allows them to both learn and become addicted—to anything—much faster than adults.

Rosen assumed that once he alerted his students to the number of waking breaths spent staring at a phone screen and the drawbacks of distraction, they would change their habits. But that's not what happened.

Rosen always asks his students: "Did you look at these data?" Usually half to two-thirds of the students say, "Yes, I looked at the data."

"Were you surprised?"

"Yes, I was surprised," half of them say. "Yeah, it was more than what I expected."

"Did you do anything?"—meaning, did you change your smartphone behaviors?

"No." Only 30 percent of the students say they did anything based on what they saw. They agreed that they could be spending their time differently, but weren't able to break the habit.

To state the obvious, hours spent on our phones are not just moments not spent doing other things. "If you're talking about someone with a spouse and kids, what's being sacrificed is time spent in connection with the spouse and kids," Rosen reasons. "If you're talking about somebody in school, what's being sacrificed is productivity or more importantly sleep, because everything now takes longer."

"You can't donate that much time [to one device] and not have an impact on your relationships, your productivity, your brain. You just can't," he emphasized.

But instead of putting down our phones to regain our daily time lost to them, we're finding other ways to cope with our new time-crunched existence—like convenience foods, delivered meals, snacking, and other tools for time optimization.

We've created a world in which the hours in each day feel shorter and, in so doing, we're encouraged to optimize every minute and every bite. What product or service will save you time? And when you do have time available, what's the best possible way to spend that time? Sometimes, all people want is a product or service that will make them feel like their lives have a bit more order.

CHAPTER THREE

diets & order

When I first saw her, all I could think is that she must have been very cold. Asha was waiting for me at the entrance of my neighborhood Whole Foods Market. Rainbow boxes of La Croix sparkling water were stacked from the floor up to her belly button, which peeked out between the top of her black yoga pants and the bottom of her black mesh halter bra. It was summer, but inside the heavily air-conditioned grocery store, I could see the hair follicles on her arms puckering up like chicken skin. Asha's blond bob cradled a round face that she had patted with foundation and subtly tinted with makeup.

"So, what are we making today?" I asked her.

"I'd like to do what's kind of a basic lunch bowl for me," she said as we walked through the automatic doors and into the produce section. An opera singer turned food entrepreneur, Asha ran, at the time, a vegan, gluten-free, refined sugar–free baking kit company from her home in Vermont. She was in New York to visit a friend, and I jumped at the opportunity to meet up and learn more about Asha's eating habits, something she's eager to discuss with others.

"On any given day I have at least three people texting me, like, 'What should I do about this?' Or like, 'I'm trying to eat less sugar. What do I do?' And so, you know, I'm actually right now starting a little project," she explained, where she'll post videos online that answer her followers' food-related questions. Asha has no formal nutrition education but, she tells me, she reads nutrition textbooks for fun. On this particular afternoon, I was the single student receiving Asha's lessons.

I asked about her daily food routine. For breakfast, she said, "I usually have a smoothie or oatmeal. Sometimes I have [vegan and gluten-free] banana bread with almond butter and berries on top. But 99 percent of the time it's a smoothie." Most often, she blends frozen cauliflower or zucchini with blueberries and mixes in some seeds, almond butter, or tiger nut flour (a gluten-free, grain-free, nut-free, Paleo-friendly flour made from the tubers that cling to the roots of an ancient weed species) to round it out. For lunch, she almost always makes what she calls a "grain bowl," though no grains ever make an appearance. In winter, she uses quinoa or buckwheat as the base. In summer, she rips up fistfuls of curly kale to layer at the bottom, a tactic she would employ later that day while building our lunch bowls.

As we walked among the vibrant palette of summer produce on display—school bus–yellow summer squash, royal purple and white graffiti eggplants, and crimson heirloom tomatoes—Asha added a bunch of broccoli, a couple of tawny sweet potatoes, and ruby grape tomatoes to her basket.

Asha is about four and a half years into her life as a mostly gluten-free vegan, and it's a commitment she takes seriously. As we strolled, she told me about her honeymoon in Bali ("vegan paradise"), from which she had recently returned with her new husband, Andy. How, I asked, is she able to maintain her stringent diet while traveling?

"Well," she said with a smile, "I *have* traveled with my Vitamix." Yet, for her most recent trip she left her blender at home. Instead, she relied on a bag full of other items like vegan protein powder and a "toolkit" of adaptogens and spices. Without these supplements, "I knew I was going to be subsisting on rice and fruit," she told me of her time in Indonesia, "and I didn't want that. It's very important to me to make sure that I'm getting a balanced diet."

To many, this way of eating sounds foreign and perhaps a bit extreme. But to Asha, her choices are perfectly normal. "If there's anything I've learned from Vermont, it's that I am a lot less extreme than all of my neighbors," she said with a laugh, and told me of one friend who knits and sews her own clothes, even hand-dyes some of the raw materials with colors derived from fruits and vegetables grown in her own garden.

Asha downplays the uniqueness of her own habits: "I want to be pure. I want to be clean with my lifestyle." At the end of the day, she summarizes, "My obsession is optimal function."

In today's food culture, Asha isn't an anomaly. She may be on the more radical end of the restrictive spectrum, but being a vegan and going gluten-free are no longer rarities. In fact, in some demographics, it's quickly becoming the norm.

Rates of veganism are on a steep climb, especially in the UK, where the vegan population rose by 600 percent between 2016 and 2018.[1] In the US, the *Economist* correspondent John Parker declared 2019 "the year of the vegan," citing sales of vegan foods in America, which, in 2018, rose ten times faster than food sales as a whole.[2] While only a small minority of global citizens identify as full-fledged vegans (6 percent of Americans identify as vegans as of 2017, up from 1 percent in 2014; 7 percent of the population in the UK are reportedly vegans[3]), a whole lot of folks are taking on new eating habits that prioritize plants over animal products. (In fact, a 2019 survey by Whole Foods and You-Gov found that nearly two-thirds of US Millennials are trying to incorporate plant-based proteins into their diet.[4])

Globally, the concept of plant-based eating is taking hold with such fervor that it is infiltrating the most mainstream food scene of all: fast-food chains. In 2017, the McVegan burger became a permanent menu item at McDonald's across Finland and Sweden. In the US, fast-food empire White Castle integrated the Impossible Burger (made mainly from soy protein concentrate and coconut oil) into their menu, and Burger King followed suit with a test run of the Impossible Whopper. In Hong Kong, you can now find the Impossible Burger on over 150 restaurant menus.[5] Meanwhile, KFC launched their Beyond Fried Chicken with Beyond Meat chicken product (made from soy protein isolate, pea protein isolate, and amaranth) in the test market of Atlanta, Georgia, and sold out the first day.[6] These menu offerings appeal to both vegans and nonvegans alike as plant-based, "clean" eating habits take hold around the world.

The groundswell toward plant-based alternatives has also made itself blatantly apparent in the milk industry, where dairy farmers are now struggling to maintain footing. "In the last 10 years, the Australian almond industry has grown from 10,000 tonnes to 78,000 tonnes in 2013, as Paleo and vegan consumers alike shun dairy and soy in favor of nut and seed milks," Mintel's Senior Trends and Innovation Consultant Jane Barnett told *Australian Food News.* "Almond milk has experienced growth of 93 percent and oat milk has risen 38 percent. New milks including quinoa, coconut, and blends of different nuts and seeds are also increasing in popularity." Similar trend lines around the globe are causing concern among dairy farmers. In the US, sales of nondairy milk grew by 61 percent between 2012 and 2017, while dairy milk sales dipped by 15 percent.[7] Currently, dairy farmers are selling their milk at a loss, and stories are surfacing of farmers looking to alternative crafts—like brewing beer—to make ends meet.[8]

Of course, these new ways of eating reach far beyond almond milk. Just about everyone, it seems, is limiting something within their diets these days, be it animal products, gluten, sugar, soy, dairy, or GM ingredients. Often, I hear people lament the difficulties of going out to eat with friends, or the hurdles of hosting a dinner party, as we attempt to navigate each person's food restrictions.

All kinds of dietary restrictions are taking center stage as more and more individuals test their bodies for "reactions" to a variety of common ingredients. For example, an approach once prescribed only by doctors to identify food sensitivities, the elimination diet, has entered mainstream diet culture. Self-experimenters remove nuts, corn, soy, dairy, citrus fruits, nightshade vegetables, wheat, gluten, pork, eggs, seafood, sugar, alcohol, and caffeine from their diets for approximately three weeks. After that initial "detox" phase, elimination dieters reintroduce items one by one to observe whether their bodies have a "reaction" to any one of them. Some use the eating practice to identify food allergies, while others use it as an exercise in mindfulness or holistic living.

One of the most popular diets of the last couple years is Whole30, in which adherents banish alcohol, grains, added sugar, legumes, dairy, carrageenan, MSG, sulfites, baked goods, GMOs, and junk food for thirty days in an effort to "reset" the body.* After that, everything is fair game (though it is recommended to add items back into your diet one by

---

* There are some exceptions to these rules. Ghee is allowed, along with green beans, sugar snap peas, snow peas, vinegar, coconut aminos, and salt.

one, much like the elimination diet, in order to identify any "food sensitivities"). New Year's Day is a common time to start the Whole30 diet, with many folks using the regimen as a "cleanse." While the name of the diet itself nods to a mere thirty days of dedication, the diet's founder, Melissa Hartwig, maintains a Whole30-like diet all the time, keeping grains, dairy, beans, and caffeine out of her diet. (She admits to the occasional consumption of sugar and alcohol.)

Today, when it comes to our dietary choices, everything is on the table—or rather, off the table. Whether it's gluten or animal products or anything a caveman wouldn't have eaten, more and more foods and food categories are considered off limits. The question is: Why are so many people restricting their diets?

After nearly a decade spent speaking with people around the world, many of whom follow restrictive diets—be it veganism, Paleo, keto (short for "ketogenic," a high-fat, low-carb diet), or Whole30—I developed a theory that many find jarring: We are a generation of disordered eaters.

One afternoon in New York City, I put forth this theory to therapist, podcaster, and influencer Megan Bruneau. "Oh my god, it is so true," she said.

Deepak Chopra has called Bruneau "the Millennials' therapist." She specializes in anxiety, depression, and eating disorders, and as a Millennial with her own history of disordered eating, I thought she'd be an excellent resource to discuss whether or not my hunch—that the Digital Generation as a whole exhibits a high frequency of eating disorder–like behaviors—holds water.

Restrictive diets, Bruneau said, can be used as a socially accepted cover for calorie avoidance. "If you are vegan or gluten-free, you can very easily say no to a lot of things and restrict yourself from certain things that you wouldn't have otherwise," Bruneau explained as she bit into a slice of (cow's milk, glutenous) cheese pizza. She gave me an example of a friend who said she couldn't eat a sundae with ice cream and hot fudge because of her veganism. Then, Bruneau followed up by offering the friend a vegan sundae made with coconut ice cream. That was a no-go as well, a hint to Bruneau that the issue was, in fact, not the animal products but the calories. Phrases like, "I am vegan, I can't have that" or "Oh no, I'm gluten-free" are sometimes used as an excuse to avoid consuming high-calorie foods, she said. The other hint of disordered motives for following a restrictive diet can become evident when someone's inhibitions are lowered, Bruneau told me, providing examples, again of experiences she has had with friends. "They're like, 'I'm gluten-free. I'm vegan.' And then they get drunk and they're not, all of a sudden; they're eating pizza and a hamburger and you're like, 'What? Okay.'"

I asked Bruneau to walk me through the emotional drivers known to spur most eating disorders. Social pressures and genetics play a large role, she said, but underlying it all is a sense of chaos and lack of control. "Feeling powerless, feeling uncertain, feeling anxious, scared, ashamed, guilty. There are all sorts of things that come up with feeling out of control," she said. "Managing difficult emotions," she clarifies, "is a huge piece of eating disorders."

Bruneau then explained that just as "likes" and information give us a hit of those feel-good hormones dopamine and serotonin, so do disordered eating behaviors. Let's say Doug is feeling anxious. Lunchtime comes around and he is faced with the decision of what to eat. His co-workers are all going to the new fried chicken spot down the street. Doug tells them he'll join them next time and instead heads to the grocery store to get a salad (dressing on the side). Ultimately, he feels very satisfied with his ability to say no to the fried chicken and yes to a nutritious, low-calorie salad. This kind of experience, said Bruneau, can give someone the feeling of *Okay, I am able to manage this*. While everything else in your life may seem like too much to handle, at the very least, you can control your meal, and that feeling of control triggers a release of dopamine. "The behaviors themselves have these sorts of addictive qualities to them," she says. "It can be like a drug." Ultimately, the act of restricting—or bingeing and purging—can become, as Bruneau described it, an addictive "coping mechanism."

"Not all diets cause eating disorders," Bruneau summarized, "but every eating disorder starts with a diet."

———————

On a cool early spring afternoon in New York, I met up with food writer Gena Hamshaw at a coffee shop in Manhattan. A freshly inked shoulder tattoo of a stinging nettle peeked out from beneath the wide neckline of her milk-white sweater. Her straight brown hair dangled down to her defined collarbone. With a soy latte in hand, she curled up on a bench and turned her back to the cold winds streaming in from the waving café door.

Hamshaw is a prolific vegan recipe writer and mealtime influencer in her mid-thirties. Beyond her successful blog, *The Full Helping*, she has penned three cookbooks: *Choosing Raw: Making Raw Foods Part of the Way You Eat*, *Food52 Vegan: 60 Vegetable-Driven Recipes for Any Kitchen*, and *Power Plates: 100 Nutritionally Balanced One-Dish Vegan Meals*. Her eating habits have been documented and lauded by *Washingtonian* and *SELF* magazines.[9]

Viewed by many as a trusted authority on what to eat and how to cook, Hamshaw has a long history of disordered eating. During her adolescence, when her mother had breast cancer, she told me, her matter-of-fact facial expression unwavering, "I didn't even cry. I wouldn't let myself feel the panic." Instead, she told me, "I internalized a lot of that and became very controlling about my food. It felt like the one thing in my life that I could pour all of my energy into, and I would have complete control and it would never fail me. There was such a clear linear relationship: restrict calories and lose weight. That was one thing I could count on."

Hamshaw's lifelong struggles with disordered eating are no secret to her fans. She has woven her experience directly into her brand and curates a series of guest posts on her blog under the headline "Green Recovery," where she seeks "to explore the link between plant-based diets and recovery from disordered eating." As a certified nutritionist, Hamshaw also works as a dietitian and often writes about the complexities of maintaining a "selective" diet while in recovery from disordered eating. But little online reveals just how deeply anxiety and trauma have influenced Hamshaw's relationship with food.

Minutes after meeting me for the first time, Hamshaw promptly dove into the nettled nest of her past, telling me stories of her challenging childhood: an unpredictable and often absent father, deep attachment to her mother, and intense fear of change. She described her younger self as "a serious, thoughtful, worried kid."

"I was always sick to my stomach," she recalled, and told me of "psychosomatically mediated" childhood digestive afflictions.

"I somaticized my anxiety from a young age," Hamshaw self-diagnosed, and explained how her unease quickly came to fuel a rejection of food. At eight years old she saw *Bambi* and, in a disavowal of the hunting-related death of Bambi's mother, gave up red meat. In her middle school years, the restrictions piled, mostly focused on quantity. At one point, she lost twenty pounds and had to complete a weight-restore under the guidance of a doctor. Her battles with food continued through college and were exacerbated at moments of stress, as when her mother was diagnosed with cancer and then again in her twenties after a painful breakup. "My eating disorder was the one domain in my life where I called all the shots. It was my little secret, and no one else got to interfere. As crazy as it sounds, it was a form of self-expression," she explained.

Eventually, Hamshaw decided that not thinking about food, or making food less important in her life, was not a rational solution for her. Instead, she thought that perhaps she could "transmute" her preoccupation with food "into something good." She was already avoiding chicken, fish, and red meat. A gastrointestinal "mind-body" doctor had suggested that she cut out dairy ("He might have been trying to offer me something that would make me feel empowered and give me the expectation of feeling better," she now admits), and she had never liked eggs. So, she began to flip through vegan cookbooks. Eventually, she landed on the raw diet, and the promises of the regimen sang to her.

The raw food literature gave her the impression that "if I eat all the right things, I won't get cancer, I won't age, I won't get sick, I'll sleep." She did not recognize the warning signs of a new form of her eating disorder, she tells me, because her rigidity around food was no longer about a weight-loss goal but about "healthy eating." She soon fell down the "raw food rabbit hole," which spurred the launch of her successful blog and well-reviewed cookbook. But at a certain point she noticed that her social circle had become small. She was spending more and more time at home. "It's funny how I've been saying no to things because there are no raw vegan options," she remembers musing. Yet again, she had to press reset.

Today, Hamshaw considers herself ten years "recovered." She maintains a vegan diet and claims that she no longer feels guilt for eating a few processed foods here and there, or items with preservatives. She says that she is back to baking—and eating—cake (provided it's made with no eggs or butter).

But that is not to say she no longer feels the pull of strict behaviors. When it comes to her diet, she later wrote me, "Restriction no longer feels like an option, and without it, I sometimes feel powerless and unmoored." She has begun to observe her "impulse to exert control" presenting itself in other habits: rigidity about scheduling and making plans, "compulsive phone checking or ruminating on a fear or a worry."

"This is something I wasn't prepared for at the start of recovery: the fact that the impulse to control can get rerouted to other places," she commented. "Nothing about the way I eat makes me feel sheltered or distinctive anymore. I really miss it. And in the moments where I really miss it, I think a lot of what I'm missing is the sense of freedom, the sense of autonomy and control."

Restriction as Order

Refusing a particular ingredient is not always a covert attempt to restrict calories, but a craving to be the conductor of one's own life, a concept illustrated in Gena Hamshaw's turn to excessive scheduling. Losing weight is not the goal—gaining a sense of authority is

This idea of using a diet as a lever of control surfaced during my time with Asha as well. While she was away on her Bali honeymoon, I followed the journey online via Instagram. One afternoon I came across a post of hers. The photo captured a dark wood staircase decorated with golden flowers that spelled out the words, "Peace is in every step you take." Alongside the image, Asha provided an update to her six hundred or so followers:

Andy and I are spending today on a #juicecleanse . . . Meditation this afternoon at the ashram in town (our first), followed by a trip to the pool and the movies. Contrary to what you may have heard about juice cleanses (lay low!), I like to fill my day chock-full with restorative, comforting, feel-good activities, which helps distract me from the compulsive desire to eat . . . Drinking lots of water, lots of herbal tea as well. Will break the fast with some rich nut-based chocolate milk tonight. Tomor-row, back to the gorgeous culinary fuel that is everywhere here. Any juice cleanse questions? Ask away. #reset #restoration #recovery #juicecleanse

Later, Asha explained to me that after consuming "all this gluten" and drinking cocktails at her wedding, her body was "crabby" at her. "Usually I do a three-day cleanse," she told me of her typical liquid diet reset routine. Her cleanse in Bali was only one day, she said, downplay-ing the intensity of her honeymoon detox. Here, I was able to see how one could use a diet to fix past wrongs, or undo self-assessed mistakes or blunders. Didn't follow through on your diet ideals perfectly? No wor-ries, you can always "cleanse." It's this kind of reset that seems to appeal to many.

Correlations between vegetarianism/veganism and disordered eat-ing have been found repeatedly across the psychology and nutrition fields, as have correlations between eating disorders and a sense of lack-ing control.[10] A secondary analysis from the broad 2012 US National Health Interview Survey reveals that over half of those who report using vegetarian or vegan diets for health reasons say that these diets provide "a sense of control" over their health and help them "feel better emo-tionally."[11] (Notably, fewer participants said that the diets "make it easier to cope with health problems," despite having answered "yes" to using vegetarianism or veganism specifically for health reasons.[12])

"I've seen people told by their psychiatrist that they should try a gluten-free diet," said Dr. Peter Green, founder and director of the Celiac Disease Center at Columbia University, over the phone. Green has been in the field of celiac and general gastrointestinal research for longer than I have been alive. He explained the difficulty of addressing this kind of chosen restriction with patients who come in to be tested upon the advice of a life coach or therapist. Sometimes Green must tell them that, according to the laboratory results, they do not show a physi-cal reaction to gluten—a finding that is often met with anger or frustra-tion. "But I feel better when I don't eat gluten," the patient will tell him. "Well," he has to reply, "that's all right, but it's not because you have a physical sensitivity or intolerance to gluten."

Gluten is a protein found in certain grains, like wheat, rye, and barley. People who have celiac disease, an autoimmune gastrointestinal disorder, cannot consume gluten because their small intestine will become inflamed and prevent nutrient absorption. Celiac is diagnosed through a genetic test, and patients are treated through adherence to a gluten-free diet. According to the latest statistics, approximately 1 percent of the globe's Western population has celiac.

Nonceliac gluten sensitivity (NCGS) is a term used to categorize those without celiac disease who nonetheless report gastrointestinal discomfort caused by gluten. There is no proven way to diagnose NCGS; it relies on self-reporting of symptoms and symptom relief. And in recent years, Green said, he's seen a steep rise in people who "self-identify as gluten-sensitive." As he put it, "Celiac doctors around the world started lamenting, 'Why are all these people saying that they're gluten sensitive?'"

Between 2009 and 2014, the number of nonceliac Americans following a gluten-free diet tripled, and gluten-free became the diet most frequently searched online across most of the United States.[13]

Though only 1 percent of Americans are estimated to have celiac disease and only 0.1 percent more are affected by wheat allergies, research firm Packaged Facts estimates that US sales of gluten-free foods and drinks are projected to exceed $2 billion by 2019. And like most food trends, Millennials and Gen Zers are at the forefront of the gluten purge. According to a Nielsen survey, 37 percent of Generation Z respondents and 31 percent of Millennials are "very willing" to pay a premium for gluten-free products, while only 22 percent of Baby Boomers say the same.

This new demand for gluten-free foods has been the catalyst for an entirely new section in many grocery stores. While the overall packaged foods category grew just over 4 percent in 2016, the gluten-free category leapt 12.6 percent.[14] The global gluten-free retail market is expected to nearly triple in size between 2011 and the end of 2020.[15] From bean-based pastas to almond-flour cookies, gluten-free packaged goods are replacing wheat-laden shelf items.

Perhaps nothing indicates the impact of this gluten-phobia more than pasta sales in Italy, which fell by 2 percent between 2011 and 2015.

By 2016, one in three Italians said they had eaten gluten-free pasta.[16] Folks around the world now shop for spiralizers, a device that turns zucchinis and sweet potatoes into spaghetti-like ribbons, a veg-tastic way to avoid gluten.

While Dr. Green appreciates the new public attention paid to gluten—and the truly painful disease of celiac—he remains vehemently skeptical of the general movement toward a gluten-shunning diet.

To begin with, he said, "If you take people who self-identify as being gluten sensitive and do a double-blind placebo diet study, only 30 percent of those people will perceive that they're getting gluten in their placebo-controlled state," citing work he had recently completed. In fact, similar findings were uncovered by the person who first created the term NCGS, a gentleman by the name of Peter Gibson.

In 2011, Gibson, a professor of gastroenterology at Monash University and director of the GI Unit at the Alfred Hospital in Melbourne, Australia, published a study that found that gluten can cause gastrointestinal distress in patients without celiac disease. Soon, folks around the globe began to declare themselves gluten-sensitive. But, a couple of years later, he revisited his findings. As reported by *RealClearScience*, Gibson expressed misgivings that his original study did not provide any clues as to what caused his subjects' discomfort from gluten.[17] So, in 2013, with the help of additional researchers, he completed a new study.[18]

Thirty-seven nonceliac subjects, each with self-reported gluten sensitivity as well as irritable bowel syndrome (a functional bowel disorder often abbreviated to IBS, also currently without clear structural or biochemical explanation), participated in a double-blind study in which subjects were randomly assigned to one of three groups. All participants began the experiment by adhering to a low-FODMAP diet* for two weeks. Then, they were given one of three diets—high gluten, low

---

* Though the cause of IBS is unclear, patients diagnosed with IBS often see their symptoms dissipate with a low-FODMAP diet, which means a diet low in fermentable oligosaccharides, disaccharides, monosaccharides, and polyols—ingredients that draw water to the intestinal tract. Folks on the low-FODMAP diet are instructed to avoid fructose; lactose; fructans, such as wheat, onions, and garlic; galactans, which are legumes; polyols, which include sugar alcohols; and fruits that have pits or seeds, such as apples, avocados, cherries, figs, peaches, and plums.

gluten, or a placebo diet with whey protein isolate—for one week. No one knew which diet they were adhering to. (A second experiment was also run to ensure the suitability of the whey protein as a placebo.)

Ultimately, Gibson and his team found that all subjects reported worsened GI symptoms during the low-FODMAP round, no matter which regimen they were on. Those on the high-gluten, low-gluten, and whey protein diets all reported an increase of pain, bloating, nausea, and gas over the baseline low-FODMAP diet. Moreover, bloating and tiredness "significantly worsened" for those in the low-gluten group, far more so than in the high-gluten scenario. In the end, the researchers concluded that the reports of gluten sensitivity could be categorized as a "nocebo" effect ("a strong anticipatory symptomatic response"), where people's expectations of feeling cruddy caused them to, well, feel cruddy.

It is findings like this that seem to drive Dr. Green up the wall. During our conversation, he listed caveat after caveat that all point to the nonexistence of "gluten sensitivity." People who claim gluten sensitivity are overwhelmingly white and high-income earners.[19] In addition, he told me, recent work has shown that those who self-identify as gluten intolerant are generally more likely than those with celiac to believe that vaccines are "unsafe," more likely to avoid genetically modified foods, more likely to prefer organic foods, and more likely to be skeptical of expert systems like the Food and Drug Administration, university researchers, and gastroenterology/nutrition professional societies. While this study was rather small—only 217 gluten-sensitive participants and one thousand celiac patients provided their responses—it points to an interesting connection between anxiety, lack of trust, and a desire for control.

Sure enough, we found similar trends in our own survey. In fact, in the Hungry Study, we found that individuals who voluntarily restrict items in their diets—be it gluten or GMOs—report lower rates of trust and greater worries than the general public. They are more likely to say they worry about the safety of their food and water, are less likely to trust food companies, and are generally more likely to worry about everyday economic and political issues like debt, healthcare, terrorism, climate breakdown, and hate crimes.

Just as mistrust is driving much of the non-GMO movement, it seems that similar anxieties are propelling the success of many restrictive diets. Suspicion and conspiracy theories regarding vaccines swirl around Paleo diet websites.[20] Pew Research has found that both vegetarians and vegans are more likely than omnivores to be concerned about avoiding genetically modified foods.[21]

It's possible that anxiety, not physical sensitivities, is driving people toward a gluten-free diet. It may not be the removal of gluten that's the cure-all, but an increased sense of control. For those who are anxious about the state of the world and untrusting of their external loci of control—like government and Big Food—the attempt to create a sense of safety through rules (in this case, food rules) can be comforting.

"People can change what they eat as a control mechanism," Dr. Green hypothesized. In the end, "people are looking for ways to be happier."

Restrictive dieting has found a profoundly enthusiastic audience in Silicon Valley, where anxiety, stress, "time crunch," and burnout run high. There, so-called "tech bros" have adopted concepts like "biohacking" and "body optimization," which treat the body as an object to be molded into perfection. They take on intermittent fasting, keto, or the Bulletproof diet; put themselves in cryotherapy chambers, saltwater float tanks, or infrared saunas; and note their progress (or lack thereof) in the form of productivity, weight, and muscle tone. Through fitness trackers and "macro" trackers, they measure every input and output with the goal of achieving peak physical and mental performance.

"With 'biohacking,' the effects are ephemeral and the health claims are dubious. But what these crude approaches *do* offer is a sense of control in the moment—a way to tell yourself that you're willing some change into being," writes *Boston* magazine senior editor Thomas Stackpole in a *New York Times* op-ed. He's a self-described biohacker who has dabbled in the keto diet, raw foods, intermittent fasting, and other modish self-molding fads. "In an era when so many of us feel the world spiraling out of control, maybe it's just the promise of being able to control something—to will a change, any change, into being—that's the draw."[*, 22]

---

* It's worth noting that doomsday preppers appear to also be fans of biohacking, which points to a potential correlation between anxiety (*the world is ending*) and a desire for control (*I can be the strongest, smartest version of me*). In *The Cut*'s "The Rise

The other allure of many of these diets relates back to the paradox of choice. By adhering to any eating regimen, you are automatically reducing the number of options in your life. Often, people on restrictive diets will take on a routine and eat similar meals each day, to easily satisfy the rules. Choosing a restaurant or looking at a menu suddenly becomes less overwhelming when only one or two options fit your diet plans. It is possible that those overburdened by other cognitive loads—be it from 24/7 news, email, or other stressors—find solace in the removal of choice.

In my travels around the world, the conversations often circle back to a mounting anxiety that goes somewhat like this: *I have no idea if I'll ever be able to buy a house, or a car, or pay off my debts. I don't know if my city will be under water in fifty years, or if there will be a global water war. I don't know if I've been hacked or had passwords stolen, or even how to safeguard myself against these things. I don't spend enough time with friends or family because I'm always working. But there's one area of my life that I feel like I should, without question, have authority: I should have full control over what I put into my body.*

I would like to clarify something very important: I am not, nor is Dr. Green, asserting that every person who adheres to a restrictive diet has an eating disorder. But it's worthwhile to recognize that much of the restrictive habits frothing to the forefront of modern eating embody a hunger for a sense of structure and autonomy amid the chaos. Unlike the climate or the economy, food provides a tangible means to make an impact, and some find that exerting control over this one area can provide a sense of calm.

The Illusion of Control

"We may generalize and say that the average child and, less obviously, the average adult in our society generally prefers a safe, orderly, predictable, lawful, organized world, which we can count on and in which unexpected, unmanageable, chaotic, or other dangerous things do

---

of the Silicon Valley Diet Hacks" by Allison Davis, Soylent co-creator Rob Reinhart says doomsday preppers are one of the company's biggest demographics.

not happen," writes Abraham Maslow in *Motivation and Personality*.
Hundreds—if not thousands—of studies showcase the human desire
for order, stability, and dependability, all assets that ward off stress, fear,
and anxiety.

Of course, nearly nothing in life is truly controllable, so we human
beings have found creative ways to soothe ourselves even when life is not
predictable or orderly (aka reality).

"The tendency," Maslow writes, "to have some religion or world-
philosophy that organizes the universe and the men in it into some sort
of satisfactorily coherent, meaningful whole is also in part motivated by
safety-seeking." Decades before any definitive research had been completed to support Maslow's assertions, the psychiatrist shone a light
on one of *Homo sapiens*' least recognized yet, perhaps, most influential tendencies: We create philosophies of order. We write rules, put up
guardrails, categorize, and theorize our way to making the unreason-
able sound reasoned, the unjustifiable seem justified, and the irrational
appear rational.

This process of creating order out of chaos has been illustrated
repeatedly in lab settings, and some studies show that this tendency
to impart rules becomes even more common as individuals experience
greater and greater anxiety about the world around them.

In 2008, Jennifer Whitson, assistant professor of management and
organizations at UCLA, and Adam Galinsky, professor of business at
Columbia University, tested "whether lacking control increases illusory
pattern perception." The authors were not examining just our desire for
control, but how that desire for control may intensify with a growing
sense that we are no longer omnipotent rulers of our lives. Lack of control, they hypothesized, may lead people to see order where there is
none, a perception "designed to restore feelings of control."

For the study, Whitson and Galinsky conducted six different experiments where participants' feelings of control were manipulated through
various modes of priming. In the end, they found their hypothesis to be
correct: "Participants who lacked control were more likely to perceive
a variety of illusory patterns," they write. These kinds of "illusory patterns" included "seeing images in noise, forming illusory correlations
in stock market information, perceiving conspiracies, and developing
superstitions."

In one of the six experiments, Whitson and Galinsky asked participants to recall in detail a situation in which they either did or did not have complete control over an event's outcome. Then, participants were presented with scenarios in which one event was preceded by a separate, unrelated event. For example, one scenario involved a person knocking on wood before an important meeting and then getting their pitch approved. Participants were then asked whether they thought the first event (knocking on wood) was related to the later outcome (getting a work concept accepted) and how important it would be to them to perform that same superstitious behavior in the future. Those who had been primed to recall an experience in which they lacked control perceived a greater connection between the two unrelated events than did those who recalled a time when they were in control.

In another study, participants who had been asked to think of a time when they felt powerless were more likely to see images in visual static than those who had been primed by being asked to think of a moment of great personal control. "The need to be and feel in control is so strong," the researchers write, "that individuals will produce a pattern from noise to return the world to a predictable state."[23]

Though perceiving order or structure does not actually provide greater control, the idea that the world has an order to it minimizes the sense of randomness that we find so deeply unnerving. "When people are gripped in the emotional vise of uncertainty . . . they will engage in mental gymnastics to imbue the world with order," the same researchers note in a later study.[24]

In a set of follow-up experiments, Whitson and Galinsky, along with Duke University professor of psychology and neuroscience Aaron Kay, found that a sense of unease also encourages belief in conspiracy theories (for example, believing a co-worker sabotaged your promotion opportunity) as well as "paranormal beliefs" like astrology.* Similarly, additional studies find that when we have a lower sense of personal control, we tend to have greater faith in external loci, like government

---

* This theory about control and belief in horoscopes has been repeated by additional researchers. (Wang, Cynthia S., Jennifer A. Whitson, and Tanya Menon. "Culture, Control, and Illusory Pattern Perception." *Social Psychological and Personality Science* 3, no. 5 (September 2012): 630–38. https://doi.org/10.1177/1948550611433056.)

bodies or an all-powerful higher being.[25] For example, "economic bad times," like the Great Depression, "increase the rate of conversions to authoritarian churches, while economic good times increase the rate of conversions to nonauthoritarian churches," Stephen Sales, then a professor at Carnegie Mellon University, found back in the 1970s. During the Great Depression, one of the greatest times of economic instability in the modern era, churches that celebrate an almighty God—such as Catholicism, Mormonism, Baptist Christianity, and Seventh-Day Adventism—added converts. Meanwhile, less dogmatic denominations, like Presbyterianism and Episcopalianism, lost members.[26] (In subsequent studies, Sales found that turbulent times also correlate with an interest in "attack dogs" like Doberman pinschers or German shepherds, and a love for powerful protagonists like Superman, Dick Tracy, and the Lone Ranger.[27]) When life hands us lemons, we look to a strong protector who promises us a glass of sweet lemonade.

Religion has traditionally played a strong role in the human experience, and often provides the human psyche with a reliable external form of control. People may rationalize horrible events, gain confidence in positive future outcomes, or derive a sense of purpose all from a belief in a higher being (or beings). Some evolutionary theorists hypothesize that this is why human beings created the concept of religion in the first place, and for this reason its role can be vital to emotional well-being.[28] But, just as faith in government bodies is at basement lows, faith in another common comfort, God, is also capturing fewer and fewer believers.

Church attendance has plummeted. Nearly one-third of American Millennials are not affiliated with any religion, the highest levels of religious disaffiliation recorded for any generation in the last quarter century.*,[29] "In fact, in 46 countries around the world, adults under age 40 are less likely to say religion is 'very important' in their lives than are older adults," notes Pew Research Center.[30]

Religion and law have traditionally offered us the sense of predictability and order we need for well-being. In today's world of skepticism

---

* The percent of people between the ages of eighteen and twenty-nine who "never doubt existence of God" fell from 81 percent in 2007 to 67 percent in 2012, according to Pew Research Center's "American Values Survey Question Database."

and fear, these expert systems and spiritual guidance frameworks are on shaky ground. Youth around the world are growing distrustful of police and politicians. They see big business and policy makers ignore their calls for movement on climate, gender equality, and labor issues. And exposure to scandals within the Catholic Church is driving disillusionment with once-revered religious leaders. Still, our need for a lawful, organized world remains unaltered.

In an era when faith in our usual outside protectors is shattering, we must ask: Where are people finding their sense of safety? Who and what are the external sources of order and calm in the Digital Age?

Though traditional religious beliefs are on the decline, interest in "spirituality" is on the rise. More than half of young adults in the US now believe astrology is a science, and the psychic services industry (which includes practices like palmistry, cartomancy, mediumship, aura reading, and astrology) grew 2 percent between 2013 and 2018; it is now worth $2.2 billion annually, according to industry analysis firm IBIS World.[31] Reflecting this boom, fashion-focused website The Cut saw clicks on their horoscopes rise 150 percent from 2016 to 2017, the horoscope website AstroStyle experienced a doubling of web traffic in 2017, and the newly launched app Co-Star—which "uses NASA data, coupled with the methods of professional astrologers, to algorithmically generate insights about your personality and your future"—was so overwhelmed by new users it crashed three times in its first week after release, according to an article from MarketWatch.[32]

Some in the astrology industry credit Donald Trump's election as the catalyst for astrology's trending success in the US. Aliza Kelly, the astrologer-in-residence at Sanctuary, an app that provides monthly astrological consultations and daily horoscopes, told the New York Times that she believes Hillary Clinton's unforeseen defeat spurred an interest in astrology "in order to create some sense of structure and hope and stability in [people's] lives."

Crystals are also trending. In 2015, Kuwaiti royalty Sheikha Fatima Al-Sabah and her mother, Sheikha Intisar Al-Sabah, launched the beauty brand Prismologie, which incorporates powdered gemstones in their Meridian balms "to enhance the flow of positive energy in the body." Earth-made minerals are also being used in water, including London-based brand Blue Moon Dream Water, which is "charged" with lapis lazuli. Glacce sells water bottles with a large crystal at the base for the hefty price of $80 (crystal-enveloped steel straws sold separately). Beauty leader Bite released a line of astrology-themed lipsticks ("for earthy Virgo, Bite mixes up a shade inspired by the fruit of the vine"[33]).

Of course, others are looking not to the stars but to the devices in their pockets. Increasingly, teens are drawn to the curated and predictable form of life offered online. Kevin Ashworth, the clinical director at the NW Anxiety Institute in Portland, Oregon, warns parents of the "illusion of control and certainty" offered by the Internet. Teens, he says, are prone to pick up their phones "if they feel like they know everything that will happen, if they know everyone who will be there, if they can see who's checked in online."[34] Often, the online world feels more predictable and manageable than reality. Kids find comfort in the ability to think through their responses before texting, posting, or emailing, a power unavailable in a free-flowing in-person conversation.[35] These certainties can be a soothing antidote to life's messy and sometimes awkward interactions.

Several studies extrapolate upon this finding. One of them, based in Taiwan, found that the more people feel a loss of personal control, the more they rely on their phones to provide a sense of internal autonomy. "Individuals with an external locus of control," those who tend to believe that their lives are highly influenced or controlled by fate, luck, and/or other people, "are more likely to use their smartphones compulsively," the study concludes. In these instances, people are using their phones—whether commenting on a social media post or checking for likes, or even the simple act of unlocking the phone—to make them feel more in control. This experience is something cookbook author and blogger Gena Hamshaw can relate to. She has observed that without her extreme food restrictions, she finds herself compulsively checking her phone as a self-soothing mechanism.

Back in the 1980s, German sociologist Ulrich Beck, author of *Risk Society: Toward a New Modernity*, posited that our sense of control is under greater threat today than ever before. Prior to the industrialized world, Beck argues, all disasters, hazards, and dangers were deemed as acts of God, fitting squarely into the religious paradigms proven by research to soothe us. Today, advancements in technology and culture tell us that if only we understood all elements, we could control the system. But, as Beck flatly stated in an interview with the *Guardian* in 2006, "We are living in a world that is beyond controllability."[36]

In the Digital Age, many people are simply looking to new avenues for a feeling of control. People are identifying new external forces that provide a sense of order—even when that structure may all be an illusion.

Common Illusions

You may think you do not fall into the category of illusory control-seekers, but I can almost guarantee that you do. I know that I do. The product details I felt complete faith in at Hema are not foolproof. The information was provided by the individual brands. Who's to say the images, facts, and stories were true? I too had bought into the illusion of control. Access to information at Hema made me feel safe. But did that information actually make me any safer? Not one bit.

In chapter one we reviewed how the call for GMO labeling is a call for transparency. But what happens once you get the label to tell you something is GMO or non-GMO? What changes? I assumed that the answer to this question was simple: People who want to avoid GMOs are better equipped to avoid them. But it turns out the reality is far more complex.

Years ago, researchers in Italy took on this question as they tried to discern the public attitude toward genetic modification and labeling.[37] A group of folks at the University of Milano-Bicocca, led by sociology professor Andrea Cerroni, administered a survey to about five hundred residents of the Lombardy region of Italy on the potential benefits and risks of biotechnologies, and the role of labeling biotechnologies.

Considering the overwhelming skepticism around GMOs, the researchers were a bit taken aback when 61 percent of survey takers said that they would not mind the introduction of GMOs into the market as long as they were labeled as such. Even more stunning, perhaps, was the 60 percent who said, sure, I'd buy those labeled GMOs.

The label, they found, is perceived as a valid reassurance of the product's safety. "But," they write, "it should be noted, the labeling 'contains GMO' does not provide any specific information on the dangers of the product, because it is absolutely generic." Instead, the label serves a psychological function: It creates the illusion of control. This illusion, Cerroni asserts, is enough to reduce one's sense of risk.

With a keen eye, you can spot similar illusions of control everywhere in the food, beauty, fashion, and personal goods industries. In fact, labels that provide the illusion of control are some of the most in-demand keywords of modern sales.

Let's look for a moment at the term "natural." The global natural beauty industry is forecasted to double in size between 2016 and 2024.[38] Makeup mega-house Sephora now has a "Naturals" landing page.[39] Nordstrom launched a natural-only beauty section in its stores, and bargain-hunting spenders can find an expansion of natural beauty options at Target. Meanwhile, in the food industry, "foods with all natural ingredients . . . are each considered very important to 43 percent of global respondents," according to a 2015 worldwide Nielsen survey.[40] Sales of US products with "natural" claims grew 7.5 percent from 2015 to 2016.[41]

Cultural psychologist Paul Rozin has explored the concept of "natural" over his long career, and has found that it is associated with feelings of health and considered "more moral, more aesthetic, or simply 'right.'"[42] But what is "natural"?

The term "natural" may be one of the greatest cons of the last decade, bringing in enormous sales while promising nothing in return. "Natural" has no regulation. The US government has long dodged the philosophical question and has refused to define the term, much less regulate its use. Still, consumers find comfort in the label and have globally boosted sales of "natural" items in food, personal care, home care, and fashion over the last decade.

"Artisanal" is another claim that means little by definition but a lot when it comes to sales and marketing power. In 2015, the journal *Appetite* published a study by two business school students, Nathalie Abouab and Pierrick Gomez, that looked at our affinity for items referred to as "artisanal" and "handmade."[43] They presented 130 of their business school classmates with one of three descriptions for the process of making grapefruit juice and asked them to rate the "naturalness" of the final product. Participants read about either an entirely by-hand production, a machine-automated production, or a vague baseline description saying the fruit was harvested, sorted, and pressed within twenty-four hours. In all three conditions, the juice came entirely from grapefruits—no additives, no preservatives, nothing extracted. But study participants did not view the three grapefruit juices as equals.

Instead of accurately reporting the juices as identical in "naturalness," the hand-harvested and manually pressed juice was deemed to be "more natural" than the juice harvested and pressed by machine. Why? The authors conclude that terms that hint at human contact fulfill our ancient evolutionary desires for familiar and safe foods. The more human contact imagined, they found, the more natural and higher-quality a product was considered to be. (This finding is in line with others, like the fact that we consider foods made by loved ones to be extra tasty.[44])

Our innate reaction to these cues of human involvement and care let us better understand why marketing Dunkin' Donuts bagels as "artisanal" may sway hungry visitors, or why beauty brands are making waves by introducing "ancient recipes" produced in "small batch" installments. But, of course, the sense of safety these claims provide is all a farce, an illusion by our own making.

Still, we gravitate toward these claims. Even myself. Knowing all this, I still find myself scouring the shampoo aisle for items that include things like avocado oil, jojoba oil, and green tea, assuming that these "natural" ingredients are safer for me than the alternatives, which I often can't pronounce.* Each of us, every day, selects items that give us a sense of security. Some of us just go further down that road than others.

---

* In 2009, the academic journal *Psychological Science* published a study titled "If It's Difficult to Pronounce, It Must Be Risky: Fluency, Familiarity, and Risk Perception" by psychologists Hyunjin Song and Norbert Schwarz from the University of Michigan, in which the researchers reported that people perceive hard-to-pronounce (imaginary) food additives as more dangerous. For example, which word sounds better to you: magnalroxate or hnegripitrom? If you're like most, you'll choose magnalroxate. It's less of a tongue-twister and, therefore, according to the study's findings, perceived as less threatening. No surprise, then, that global shoppers gravitate toward words like "coffee essence" instead of pyrazines or 5-P-coumaroylquinic acid (both of which are found in coffee).

The Elixir Aisle

"Here I am with my little deities," Asha said as she leaned over a chopping block of diced vegetables, with jars of tahini, sauerkraut, and powdered nutritional yeast crowding the board.

Earlier in the day, Asha had introduced me to more of her talismans, walking me through her methods, doses, and timing of use for peak impact. After leaving the produce section back at Whole Foods, Asha and I had cruised past the seafood and poultry area and straight to the supplements aisle.

There, Asha paused in front of a box of mushroom tea. "Adaptogens are my life, they are everything," she gushed. Sales of adaptogens—such as ginseng, moringa, maca, and ashwagandha—and other herbal dietary supplements are on the rise in the US; the category exceeded sales of $8 billion in 2017, up 8.5 percent from 2016.[45] The term *adaptogen* refers to any substance that theoretically "adapts" to your body's needs. Though the science on adaptogens is as murky as a mud mask, many claim that these medicinal plants can influence adrenal glands to reduce stress and balance hormones. (None of these items or claims are reviewed by the Food and Drug Administration.)

"I don't drink coffee," Asha told me. As an alternative, she dabbled with raw maca, a powdered form of a radish-like Peruvian root. "The first time I took maca, I got kind of rage-y. I read that it would pep me up." Later, she read that gelatinized maca does not have the same effect but has still decided to avoid maca for now.

Instead, "Ashwagandha is my go-to. They say that it's cortisol-lowering, which is a quality of a lot of adaptogens," she explained. "It's best if you take a little bit every day so that it's integrated into your system, like a vitamin, I guess. It makes me feel mellow and hyper-focused"—similar, she noted, to how she feels when taking cannabidiol, also known as CBD, a nonpsychoactive chemical compound found in hemp. According to *Hemp Business Journal*, CBD sales are expected to surpass $645 million by 2022, a giant leap from 2016's $129 million.[46]

You may have noticed—and even contributed to—this spike yourself. Lately, the acronym CBD has popped up on coffee shop chalkboards, chocolate bar wrappers, and even body lotions and lip balms. Pitched as an elixir that will relieve you of dry skin, puffiness, and acne, as well as banish your anxiety, stress, and insomnia, "CBD" is now searched for on Google even more than "gluten-free." While studies validate the efficacy of CBD in treating some forms of epilepsy and schizophrenia, as well as its ability to relieve joint pain, the indications most often advertised to the general public—like relief from anxiety and stress—have yet to be verified in any scientific setting.[47] Still, that has not stopped the trend from stoking interest and a growing number of devotees.

Asha said she takes CBD only "situationally," like when her family came for a visit and she felt the need to calm her nerves. Other items she keeps in her "toolkit" include an Ayurvedic gooseberry herb called amla powder, moringa, reishi mushrooms, spirulina blue-green algae, a derivative of vitamin E called tocotrienols, turmeric, carob, cocoa powder, and Ceylon cinnamon.

"Everybody's talking about L-theanine," she said, "but I haven't tried it yet. The thing is, I feel like there are only so many things I can do."

The world of supplements that Asha eagerly participates in has gone from stigmatized hippie-dippie hooey-dooey to celebrity panacea. Actress Gwyneth Paltrow brought many of these supplements into common nomenclature through her website Goop, which sells items like Brain Dust, "an adaptogenic blend of enlightening superherbs and supermushrooms that help combat the effects of stress to align you with the cosmic flow for great achievement."[48] Goop notifies readers that Gwyneth drinks a smoothie with Brain Dust every morning. A 1.5-ounce jar costs $38—or $2.71 per teaspoon—and is packed with many of the items Asha showed me. The ingredients sound like they should be sold by a staff member in the Herbology Department at Hogwarts instead of a Hollywood sweetheart: maca root and ashwagandha root, as well as lion's mane mushroom extract and astragalus root extract.

A tea shop I passed in New York offers lattes with these additives. For $8, you can get a Vanilla Zen matcha latte, with MCT oil (oil with medium-chain triglycerides, a favorite of those on the ketogenic, Paleo, and Bulletproof diets), vanilla, ashwagandha, cinnamon, and maple, or the Moonberry Magic, with elderberry elixir, blue-green algae, and maple. If you'd like, CBD, MCT, and collagen are available as additions to any of the café drinks for a few extra bucks.

Some supplement devotees use adaptogens for a full-body boost, while others utilize them primarily for mental acuity. Nootropics, a subset of adaptogens centered entirely on the mind, emphasize focus, clarity, and energy. Overall, nootropics peddle the promise of cognitive perfection. For example, nootropics company HVMN sells one supplement for memory, mood, and long-term cognitive resilience; another for alertness, focus, and relaxation; and a third for healthy sleep.

In an era of high stress and tumultuous nights, nootropics are finding an audience hungry for reassurances and the promise of a cognitive boost. L-theanine, mentioned by Asha, is one of the most popular nootropics; it appears in two of HVMN's nostrums. Many mind-body doctors recommend L-theanine as an alternative to psychopharmacological anxiety treatments like Zoloft or Lexapro. Meanwhile, an extract of the root of the rhodiola plant is marketed as a way to combat stress, anxiety, and depression, as well as cancer and aging. Participation in the world of supplements is all about finding the ingredients that will make you the most productive, well rested, and virtuous version of you. And often, those devoted to these supplements have full faith that the regimen they have identified is, in fact, bestowing them with a longer, healthier, more mentally acute life.

Another common supplement craze is probiotics that feed the bacteria in our gut, aka our microbiome. Most probiotics claim to improve digestive health; others say they support immune health or even alleviate depressive symptoms. Entrepreneurs are now integrating probiotics into everything from kombucha to body soap. But while mesmerizing studies have been conducted on the connection between the microbiome and obesity, arthritis, and even autism, the findings are still preliminary. Dr. Bruce German, a nationally recognized microbiome researcher at UC Davis, calls current microbiome knowledge "draconian."

"We don't know much about what we're doing. The microbiome is really important for a variety of things. We just don't know how to manage it yet," he told me. Even simple product claims of boosting "good bacteria" are a stretch based on the existing science; researchers are not quite sure yet which bacteria are "good" and which are "bad," or which are good for some people and bad for others. For now, perhaps the idea that you are doing something positive for yourself is the real placebo-like benefit of most probiotics, and of supplements as well.

"All my anxieties are related to longevity and cancer," Asha admitted, a fear that seems well aligned with the promises peddled by the nootropics market. She believes that every bite of her selected foods, every supplement swallowed, is putting her on a trajectory toward a longer, healthier life. And with this belief comes some self-admonishment for not adhering to these rules earlier. "Do I wish that I'd had my health awakening earlier in life?" Asha mused later that afternoon as she prepared our "grain" bowls. "Yeah, I honestly think my skin would be better. I think that my digestive system would be better."

The problem, of course, is that the idea that we can have full autonomy over our own fates is a fallacy. Who knows if Asha's skin would be clearer, her stomach less fussy, had she been popping supplements since her teen years? Still, that kind of physical omnipotence is something all people yearn for.

Asha revealed that a recent exam found a cell abnormality on her cervix, a sign of potential cancer.

"Of course," she remarked with an eye roll, cancer is "the one thing I can't eat my way out of." Although "maybe," she thought aloud, "if I'd started my health kick earlier, I wouldn't have an abnormal Pap right now."

During my time with Asha, I could not help but think of her supplements as, indeed, deities. Her devotion to her own practice of eating felt religious and, in some ways, I became envious of the sense of assurance she created for herself. I could see how, for someone who openly battles anxiety, relying on a toolkit of ingredients could offer a sense of stability. Her interaction with these items felt similar to the Peruvians who believe that affixing a small bull to the top of your roof will bring a fertile harvest, or to those who swear that burying a Saint Joseph figure in your yard will help you sell property or that a large cup of Indian sweet curd slurped down before an exam will help boost your performance. These belief systems act as emotional support beams along the path of life, saying, "You can do it."

In this age of anxiety, where we are working longer but not better, learning more but becoming more fearful, and losing faith in the safety nets we've long trusted to have our best interests in mind, each of us is working to create a sense of safety in our own ways. Be it through restricting our diets, looking to the stars, formulating a supplement regimen, or signing up for a subscription box, each of us is striving to create order, predictability, and autonomy in a chaotic world.

Yet feeling safe and in control is just the beginning of well-being. After we create a sense of security for ourselves, the next element of well-being is awaiting those ready to take steps toward deeper connection.

PART II

belonging

Whatever the technological advances of modern society—and they're nearly miraculous—the individualized lifestyles that those technologies spawn seem to be deeply brutalizing to the human spirit.

—Sebastian Junger, *Tribe: On Homecoming and Belonging*

CHAPTER FOUR

influencers & loneliness

As the sun went down, my friend Hyunjee and I boarded the Seoul-bound bus, took out our phones, and loaded that night's livestream of Ddungnyeo (a name that roughly translates as "Fat Girl"), who over the next hour would cook and devour a quantity of food one might serve a dinner party of eight. The video feed showed Ddungnyeo in her home studio sitting behind a phalanx of ingredients propped up so high that they took up the entire bottom half of the frame. As Ddungnyeo ate, comments flowed onto the right-hand side of the livestream where viewers expressed their pleasure, asked questions about the food, and said hello. Some asked Ddungnyeo to eat specific things, and seeing the requests on her own monitor, the host nearly always obliged.

Min Boram created the avatar of Ddungnyeo in the summer of 2015. Every evening, the Incheon native livestreams herself eating dinner. This is her full-time job. And every night, hundreds of people tune in to watch her live, in action.

Earlier that day, Hyunjee and I had traveled to Suwon, a suburb about ninety minutes outside Seoul, to visit with Min. We arrived as she and her husband were prepping a wide array of ingredients for that night's broadcast. Min's hair was pulled back into a bun, secured with a bedazzled headband that framed her rotund face, amply patted over with white powder. Her gangly husband wore Harry Potter–like circular glasses. They were both dressed in simple black T-shirts.

Min ushered us into her living room, where she had laid out sweet treats for Hyunjee and me. A framed silver plaque from YouTube commemorating Ddungnyeo's passage of one hundred thousand subscribers sat under the television. Beside it was a print of the Ddungnyeo bitmoji giving a double thumbs-up.

The duo introduced Hyunjee and me to their newly adopted kitten and showed us their broadcast studio in a converted second bedroom. There, two wide computer monitors sat on a broad white desk with three light boxes propped up behind it. A flexible microphone arm covered with a professional pop filter was clamped to the side of the desk, and a complex side panel of audio/visual buttons and plugs sat on the desk's lower edge.

That night, Min was preparing a menu of Korean barbecue. The intricate meal required multiple packages of peppers, mushrooms, herbs, meat, and seafood to be sliced. Hyunjee and I joined Min and her spouse in their modern open kitchen as they finished their preparations. While her husband handled the beef, Min pulled an octopus from a small Styrofoam box—a gift sent by one of her viewers. It wriggled in her hands as its tentacles twitched. "It's moving!" she squealed. She dropped the creature into the metal kitchen sink and raised her hands in horror. Her husband stood by and laughed. He instructed her to drop the octopus into a nearby pot of boiling water.

As the broadcast hour neared, a smorgasbord of ingredients was arranged in the studio, propped up on a jerry-rigged pedestal made from shoeboxes and rolls of toilet paper. Asparagus, whole garlic cloves, and thick trumpet mushroom slices filled a foot-wide plate like a shield. Thinly cut bright-red ribeye beef was piled high. Verdant herbs and long green chiles were stacked in a wicker basket. Next to it was a plate of cooked and sliced tentacles from the creature alive just minutes prior. A portable grill was plugged in and arranged directly below the camera. Min poured a healthy cup of spicy ssamjang dipping sauce into a Mickey Mouse–shaped white ramekin. Arrangement was key—everything had to fit in the frame, and all items had to be easily visible, a task that, on a night like this, felt like playing a game of Tetris. Moments before the meal was set to begin, Hyunjee and I waved goodbye and left them to concentrate on their broadcast.

Usually, Ddungnyeo is a one-woman show, but on that barbecue-themed night, she called on her spouse to be a co-star. She needed the extra pair of hands for on-screen grilling, as well as an extra stomach to digest the mounds of food they'd prepared. Throughout the broadcast, her husband added piece after peice of bulgogi to the grill. The microphone captured the bubble and hiss of beef searing, which brought viewers further into the pair's home.

As Hyunjee and I watched the performance on our phones on the bus ride home, we saw that Min's viewers were clearly thrilled by her spouse's presence. Hyunjee translated from Korean as comments scrolled down the side of the screen. Voyeurs urged them to feed one another. Min's husband rolled a cut of browned bulgogi ribeye into a traditional palm-shaped perilla leaf and placed it gently into the mouth of his longtime partner. She devoured the roll in one large bite. Hyunjee and I watched in awe as the mounds of food were swiftly ingested.

In less than sixty minutes of chewing, it was all gone. The pair wiped their mouths and cleared away the plates, then Min reappeared by herself holding a super-size container of instant ramen. *More?* I thought with disbelief. She snagged a bunch of crimped noodles with her chopsticks, held them high, and brought them toward the camera for viewers to take in. Her eyes went wide in anticipation and then, in a flash, they disappeared into her mouth. The microphone captured the slurping whoosh of the noodles slithering against her lips. "Mmm," she groaned. Between subsequent bites, she talked to her viewers and laughed as she read their comments. She appeared as amused by her viewers as they were by her. With yet another meal consumed, she said goodbye and transitioned into the two-hour chatting segment of her evening, called Ddungseobang Real Sound.

Well over 250 people watched the night's stream in real time, but a few days later the number of viewers had soared to well over thirty thousand, about average for Ddungnyeo's daily videos. Some of her greatest hits have lured in as many as 1.4 million pairs of eyes.

Mukbang is a combination of the Korean words for eating (*muk-ja*) and broadcasting (*bang-song*). Mukbang videos bring in millions of viewers, sometimes hundreds of thousands at a time, who watch individuals eat. These performers are called broadcast jockeys, or BJs for short. Most mukbang streams showcase a BJ consuming large amounts of food, be it a pile of fast-food hamburgers stacked in a tower or a vat of deep red tteokbokki, where oblong white rice cakes bob among a hot pepper and anchovy stew. But the quantity of food is not the only draw. ("I am not really a heavy eater among mukbang BJs," Min told me. "Some people can finish ten packages of instant noodles, but I can only eat five.")

Viewers home in on the BJ's enthusiasm for eating, their consumption tactics, and their personalities. Many BJs, like Min, use microphones that sit just below their mouths, which allows their mastication to be picked up with such clarity that viewers can virtually feel their own molars cracking through the shell of an orange crab leg or sinking into squares of fleshy meat.

Some mukbang BJs also film beauty tutorials, livestream their car rides, and develop recipe videos. Min livestreams her vacations, shopping trips, and other escapades that she thinks her viewers will enjoy. But traditional eating videos remain her true bread and butter.

The trend of Korean mukbang became widely popular around 2012. According to the Korea Press Foundation's "2016 Youth Media Usage Survey," over a quarter of South Korean teenagers have watched a mukbang broadcast.[*,1]

Many mukbang BJs make a good living from their routine performances. On the South Korean social media site AfreecaTV, viewers can buy virtual "star balloons" for about ten US cents to send to the BJs. With thousands, sometimes millions, of viewers, these gratuities can add up to something significant. Many fans also send real-life treats in the mail, like Ddungnyeo's gifted octopus. One of the most notorious mukbang performers, a mysteriously fit Millennial who goes by the name Banzz, has over three million YouTube subscribers, and rumor has it that his annual income exceeds $8 million, in large part due to

---

* The public obsession with mukbang has encouraged more traditional media mavens to get in on the game. South Korea's television networks are now crammed with food-centric programming, such as *Tasty Guys*, which showcases celebrities eating; *Please Take Care of My Refrigerator*, where Korean chefs compete to create impromptu dishes that feature ingredients found inside a guest star's personal refrigerator; and the talk show *Wednesday Food Talk*.

his sponsored product posts, which have their own category on his You-Tube channel.

Since 2016, the mukbang trend has proliferated outside of Korea, quickly becoming a global phenomenon. About 20 percent of Banzz's viewership streams in from abroad.[2] Stateside, one of the most successful mukbang BJs is Gen Xer Bethany Gaskin, who goes by the nickname Bloveslife. An African American mother of two living in the American Midwest, Bloveslife's 1.3 million YouTube subscribers support her branded apparel and product lines. Up in Canada, Veronica Wang, who also has over a million YouTube subscribers, shovels bathtub quantities of ramen into her tiny frame. With a simple search, you'll find people of all different backgrounds doing mukbang: families, straight and gay couples, devoted vegans, junk food enthusiasts, and black, white, Asian, and biracial individuals all chowing down for anyone to watch.

"Do your parents understand what you do?" I asked Min as we sat on the floor around her coffee table before her nightly broadcast, sipping iced coffee and nibbling on sticky pastel sweets. Hyunjee translated Min's responses.

Min tilted her bobblehead face to the side and shrugged. "They vaguely know what I am doing," she said, noting that the "elderly" are less acquainted with mukbang. "My parents learned that I am famous two years ago. My mom noticed that many people recognize me and ask me to take photos with them."

Min's street recognition goes to show just how deeply mukbang culture has infiltrated the Korean media scene, and yet, many still observe the trend with confoundment: Why are droves of people watching strangers eat?

Some attribute the wild popularity to a growing diet culture and call mukbang "surrogate satisfaction."[3] This theory has merit, says Min, who believes that, at first, her audience clicked on her stream to gawk at her ability to eat ten pounds of sushi and fried chicken in one sitting. But over time, she says, as people got to know her, her viewership changed. Now, a regular cohort of two hundred people participate in the nightly chats that take place after the mukbang performance.

What, I asked, do people talk about for those two hours?

Lots of things, she told me. They share their life hardships, like experiencing depression. Some ask Min about her marriage. A bit like a radio show, this segment allows people to call in on the phone, and conversation progresses via online chats as well.

I asked Min when she thinks she will stop broadcasting, and she looked at me wide-eyed. This is "endless," she replied. "At first, we weren't so attached to one another, as we didn't know much about each other," she said of her viewers, "but now we have more shared memories." She has talked with one fan through her pregnancy into early motherhood. "We try to support each other, cheer each other up, and share good news as well."

Some of her viewers, she reflects, now consider the Ddungseobang Real Sound community a "family."

Honbap Living

Having a community, a sense of belonging, is a core part of well-being. Maslow calls these "the love and affection and belongingness needs." Without these needs fulfilled, "he"—Maslow writes in terms of "man"—will "hunger for affectionate relations with people in general, namely, for a place in his group or family, and he will strive with great intensity to achieve this goal. He will want to attain such a place more than anything else in the world." Maslow cites the "deep importance of the neighborhood, of one's territory, of one's clan, of one's own 'kind,' one's class, one's gang, one's familiar working colleagues."[4]

Our thirst for fellowship has core evolutionary roots. In our hunter-gatherer days, those who belonged to a tribe were more likely to survive and procreate; those who lived as a part of a group had a support system for assistance and defense. As such, we evolved to crave these social protections, and belonging became inextricably linked with our well-being.

Belonging to a group provides each of us with three vital requirements: a sense of self, a sense of worth, and a sense of connectedness. Our tribes help us define who we are. Very often, our group affiliations dictate core parts of our personal identities, be it how we talk, dress, and eat or what we believe in. Belonging is also essential for the development of our self-esteem. By bonding with others, we gain confidence in our own value as individuals. And finally, belonging to a group opens doors to positive, reliable, and loving social bonds, sometimes referred to as "relatedness" or "connectedness." These needs are so essential to our well-being that for nearly all of human history, people thought of themselves not as isolated individuals, but as part of tribes, clans, dynasties, kingdoms, and nations.

South Korean culture has long maintained a strong Confucian emphasis on community and family units. One's place in the Korean societal hierarchy is generally determined by where one comes from and who one associates with.

"Our culture is collectivistic," Dr. Andrew Eungi Kim told me of his fellow South Koreans as we sat in his office, located down a stark corridor of the International Studies Building at the Korea University campus in Seoul where he teaches courses on contemporary Korean society. "We are always trying to have relationships. Whereas in the West, it's okay to be by yourself . . . here, if you're going home right after work instead of going out with a group of friends, it's like saying you don't have any friends to hang out with," he said, leaning back in his office chair.

Yet in the last decade, South Koreans are spending more time alone than ever before. The number of one-person households, a concept once unheard of in South Korea, now hovers just above 30 percent and is expected to continue rising. In fact, as of 2015, single-person households are the most common type of living arrangement in South Korea.[5] Lured by job opportunities, young people who used to live at home until they wed are now venturing out on their own and settling into the solo lifestyle. Meanwhile, the elderly find themselves abandoned by kin once expected to be end-of-life caretakers.

Compounding the trend is a growing indifference toward marriage. Divorce is losing its stigma, and more and more women are shunning the long-held cultural expectations of females as homemakers. "This generation is called 'Sampo Generation (삼포세대)' in Korean. Sampo means that young people these days give up on three things: relationships, marriage, and birth," South Korean journalist Sohn JiAe explained to me. South Korea's birth rate hit a record low of 0.95 in 2018, well below the rate of 2.1 needed to sustain a population. In Seoul, the birth rate is even lower, sitting at 0.84.[6]

Eating as a group has long been considered a core tradition of affiliation and affection in Korean culture. Eating alone, be it at home or in a restaurant, says Dr. Kim, has always been culturally taboo, a sentiment I'd heard from others as well.

"I saw a Korean movie years ago where, in one scene, a guy goes out to a barbecue restaurant and eats by himself. There's this very forlorn scene of him cutting the meat by himself," American journalist and Seoul resident Steven Borowiec told me. The scene was clearly meant to illustrate the character's mental instability, he analyzed.

Now, with more and more people living alone, people previously accustomed to large communal meals are dining by themselves, a concept once unthinkable to many Koreans.

A few years ago, Borowiec began to hear rumblings about *honbap*, a portmanteau of the Korean words for "alone" and "rice." There was a new type of restaurant popping up around Seoul, one that served only single diners. He pitched a honbap story to his editor at *Korea Exposé*, an English-language South Korean news and culture magazine, and with editorial approval, Borowiec boarded the subway and rolled just west of Seoul to a barbecue restaurant in Bucheon called Dokgojin to investigate the solo-eating trend.

Unlike nearly all other Korean barbecue restaurants, where groups gather around a large, circular, communal table that features a center grill, Dokgojin is designed for people eating by themselves. Inside, the restaurant looks more like a computer lab than a restaurant, with partitioned wooden cubicles fanning either side of an aisle. Each compartment has a small desk-like table with a personal grill, television, and condiments, along with a poster of instructions and, of course, the Wi-Fi password. "The only sounds were the sizzle of fatty meat, and the K-pop blaring from outdoor speakers," Borowiec writes of his experience dining there.[7] "I realized what was missing: human voices." Barbecue establishments are usually a stage for boisterous exchanges; this one was hushed with the tones of whispers and searing beef.

While in Seoul, I wanted to experience honbap for myself, so I dropped by another solo eating establishment, called Ichi-men, located in the University district of Seoul. There, ramen-loving diners are partitioned off from one another—as well as from the restaurant staff. Upon entering the restaurant, patrons place food orders at a vending machine that prints out a paper ticket. Once you are seated in a cubicle, a pair of anonymous hands appear from beneath a curtain to take the ticket.

Minutes later, the curtain rolls up, just high enough to get food passed through, and diners eat their meals, essentially, in secrecy. Ichi-men originated in Japan, where mindfulness informed the restaurant's design. The privacy was supposed to force diners into a sort of meal meditation. But once adopted in South Korea, the setting transformed from facilitating a Zen experience to a cover for taboo solo dining.[8] After all, as Dr. Kim noted, stigma remains for those seen eating out alone.

For this reason, many prefer to honbap at home, spurring the explosion of Korean delivery services over the last decade. Now, seven in ten Koreans have used a food delivery app, and other subscription services are likewise multiplying.[9] At home, people can eat in peace, without the judgmental gaze of others. And they can turn on their favorite shows to watch as they eat.

After Borowiec's visit to Dokgojin, he began to see the signs of solo culture simmering everywhere, including television, where shows like *I Live Alone*—which documents celebrities who, you guessed it, live alone—were becoming increasingly popular. He noted that more solo activity terms have begun to enter common nomenclature, like *honsul*, drinking alone; *honhaeng*, traveling alone; and *honyoung*, going to the movies alone (a demand so significant that movie theaters have added "single seats" separated from the rest of the row by a foot-wide insert).[10] All around Korea, people are learning to adjust to a life lived without companions.

Belonging Well-Being

The trend away from communal living and tribal associations is not unique to Korea. In general, we are living in a world where people spend more time alone. Just as in South Korea, single-family households around the globe are splintering into single-person units. In 1950, only 6 percent of American households were single-person; now that figure is over 30 percent.[11] In Japan, solo dwellers are expected to account for 40 percent of households by 2040.[12] Researchers estimate that China could have upwards of 132 million single-person homes by 2050.[13]

It's not just living situations that have changed, but the role (or lack thereof) of our wider communities. "We have been pulled apart from one another and our communities over the last third of a century," writes political scientist Robert Putnam in his 2001 book, *Bowling Alone: The Collapse and Revival of American Community*. Suburban sprawl and divorce, he notes, are trends loosening long-held social ties, along with dips in political involvement, civic engagement, volunteer work, ties to religious groups, and attendance at workplace events.[14]

These societal shifts have taken a toll on our community connections. Between 1985 and 2004, the number of Americans who said there was no one who they could discuss important matters with nearly tripled, according to nationally representative data.[15] A quarter of 2004 respondents said that they have no one to confide in. The data also revealed that the modal number of close confidants dropped from three to one, a data point that highlights our increasing isolation.

Community ties have further weakened since the introduction of the Internet and social media. Between 2005 and 2015, there was a "very large decline" in "belonging well-being" among twentysomethings, according to a 2018 analysis by an independent UK think tank called the Intergenerational Foundation, which assessed statistics gleaned from three points in time—1995, 2005, and 2015.[16] Through an examination of twenty-four indicators, the nonprofit found a 32 percent drop in belonging well-being between 2005 and 2015. The index focused exclusively on the responses of those ages twenty to twenty-nine at the times of the surveys.

Young people in 2015 reported having fewer close friends than twentysomethings of past decades. The Intergenerational Foundation attributed this dip in belonging well-being to "falls in volunteering, interest in politics, and observing a religion," as well as moving away from home. "It could also have something to do with technology," the report states, citing the impact of social media as a potential cause for the significant drops in closeness between 2005 and 2015.

Our use of technological devices is clearly eating up hours once spent face-to-face with others. In 2013, Scott Wallsten, president and senior fellow at the Technology Policy Institute, analyzed data from the 2003 to 2011 editions of the American Time Use Survey and found that "leisure time online . . . crowds out other activity" such as socializing offline, spending time at parties, and attending cultural events. According to Wallsten, each minute of online leisure is correlated with

less time working, sleeping, traveling, doing educational activities, playing sports, helping other people, eating, drinking, and participating in
religious activities.[17] These patterns continued into 2018; time spent
hosting or attending social events fell by 30 percent between 2011 and
2018. Time engaged in religious and educational activities continued to
drop as well. Meanwhile, computer use for leisure trended upward.[18] In
essence, if you're online, you're less likely to be spending time with others IRL,* as the kids say.†

Less time spent with others in person is having very trackable
results, particularly among youth: Teens today are less likely than youth
of generations past to be sexually active, smoke, drink, or participate in
physical fights.[19] While some celebrate these statistics as positive mile-
stones, others read between the lines with concern, noting that perhaps these data are indicative not of responsible adolescents but rather
of lonely adolescents.

Even when we are with other people in person, many of us are
absent. Sometimes when we are with others, our attention is elsewhere,
lost in an abyss of apps, messaging, and newsfeeds. This is called phubbing ("phone snubbing"), and it is the act of looking at your phone
instead of paying attention to those who are with you in person.

Phubbing is an all-too-common social faux pas of the Digital Age.
In the Hungry Study, 54 percent of all respondents (and 70 percent
of Generation Z respondents) admitted that they occasionally, often,
or always ignore others around them because they are looking at their
phone, tablet, or computer.

Common Sense Media, a nonprofit that provides research on children and technology use, notes that 77 percent of parents feel as though
they often can't commandeer their children's attention away from their
devices.[20] Yet the phubbing frustration goes both ways. While completing research for her 2013 book, *The Big Disconnect: Protecting Childhood
and Family Relationships in the Digital Age*, author and psychologist Catherine Steiner-Adair reports that many of her one thousand interview

---

* In real life.

† The 2017 Stress in America report by the American Psychological Association found
  that people who constantly check their phones are less likely to meet with family and
  friends in person.

subjects, ages four to eighteen, complained of feeling ignored, angry, or lonely while vying for their screen-addicted parents' attention.[21]

In our current solo living, phubbing/phubbed world, people report having fewer and fewer close friendships. An analysis of 65,045 social relationships across Kenya, Ghana, and India found that the number of reported friendships has decreased by approximately 2.4 since the introduction of the Internet.[22] The plague of friendlessness is most rampant among youth. In one European multigenerational survey, the number of close friends among twentysomethings fell by over 6.5 percent between 2005 and 2015.[23] In a 2019 survey by YouGov, over one-fifth of the American Millennials polled said they have *zero* friends.[24] In addition, 27 percent said they have "no close friends" and 30 percent said they have "no best friends." (In comparison, just 16 percent of Gen Xers and 9 percent of Baby Boomers said they have no friends.)

Though we have the opportunity to have more "friends" than ever before, we're living in an era of overwhelming isolation and loneliness.

Loneliness Epidemic

Today, a record number of people all around the world report feeling lonely. US rates of loneliness have doubled since the 1980s.[25] In 2018, Cigna, a global health services company, and Ipsos, a global market research firm, found that 46 percent of some twenty thousand American respondents said they sometimes or always feel lonely, and only around half said they have meaningful in-person social interactions daily. Two in five said that they sometimes or always lack companionship and/or that they are no longer close to anyone.[26] Meanwhile, 60 percent of the 3,100 respondents in a national Australian survey reported that they "often felt lonely."[27] And, in January 2018, Britain became the first European country to name a "Minister of Loneliness," after studies laid bare the crushing isolation among its citizens. Subsequently, residents in Switzerland, Sweden, and Germany have pondered if they should have a minister of loneliness as well.[28]

Traditionally, loneliness most commonly plagues the elderly, but modern loneliness data challenges this long-held truism. In 2019, You-Gov found that 30 percent of Millennials say they always or often feel lonely, twice the rate for Baby Boomers surveyed.[29] Similar findings were reflected in Cigna's loneliness index. There, Generation Z (a demographic not assessed by YouGov) showed the highest rates of loneliness.

Loneliness is not simply an emotional ill, but a physical one as well. The need for community runs so deep that without it, our health is proven to suffer. "We are biologically, cognitively, physically, and spiritually wired to love, to be loved, and to belong," relationship guru Brene Brown has said. "When those needs are not met, we don't function as we were meant to. We break. We fall apart. We numb. We ache. We hurt others. We get sick."[30] Today, some claim that we are facing a loneliness epidemic more dangerous than the soaring rates of obesity or diabetes.[31]

"Over thousands of years, the value of social connection has become baked into our nervous system such that the absence of such a protective force creates a stress state in the body," former US Surgeon General Vivek Murthy warns in the *Harvard Business Review* while walking the reader through the impact of losing these essential affiliations. "Loneliness causes stress, and long-term or chronic stress leads to more frequent elevations of a key stress hormone, cortisol. It is also linked to higher levels of inflammation in the body . . . This in turn damages blood vessels and other tissues, increasing the risk of heart disease, diabetes, joint disease, depression, obesity, and premature death. Chronic stress can also hijack your brain's prefrontal cortex, which governs decision-making, planning, emotional regulation, analysis, and abstract thinking."

On the flip side, filling our lives with strong community connections and close relationships buoys our well-being. Love and connection are like human vitamins. Endorphins, released when we look at or touch a trusted person, trigger a cascade of killer T cells, which give our bodies an immunity boost.

People with more deep, loving relationships in their lives are less prone to heart disease and more resistant to illnesses like the common cold, and statistically live longer.[32] In fact, an academic analysis of a hundred years' worth of research, covering more than three hundred thousand participants across all ages, reveals that those with a solid social network live longer lives.

A sense of belonging and connection is core to our well-being. And so, in this era of solo living, phubbing, and friendlessness, many are searching for other ways to feel like they belong.

I'll Follow You

"The act of creating daily interactions with other people such as family members and friends is a primitive act for human survival and life," two researchers from Seoul Women's University outline in an academic article published by the *Korean Journal of Broadcasting and Telecommunication Studies.*[33] Yet, they note, "when that ritual is suppressed or unsatisfactory," mukbang can fill the void, becoming a "surrogate fulfillment" of our primitive needs. They call the phenomenon "a kind of 'healing therapy' that fulfills hunger and emotional hunger" at the same time.

A study by the Korea Health Promotion Institute found that 38 percent of thirtysomethings say the reason they watch mukbang is because they simply have no one else to eat with.[34]

"I give viewers the sensation of eating with a friend," mukbang BJ Banzz has said, explaining the popularity of his mukbang channel.[35]

Min relayed a similar sentiment: "Many people live alone and they feel lonely when they have a meal by themselves, so they need a pal," she told me as we sat around her coffee table. "They turn on mukbang and feel they are having a meal together."

Most of Min's fans are Millennials who live by themselves, she tells me. Other BJs report similar viewership demographics. Some say that their viewers prop up phones on their dining tables and stream mukbang while eating dinner so that they can feel like they are eating with someone else. Some BJs provide the night's menu in advance so that fans can order or prepare the same thing.

With belonging needs unmet, many hang out online in search of camaraderie. And mukbang is unique in its ability to conjure a sense of intimacy.

"They like to see me eat, but we also have lots of conversations," BJ Lee Chang-hyun, who boasts nearly two million subscribers on his YouTube channel, told BBC News of his followers.[36] "We talk about everything. I even give them counseling about problems they might have, so we have a real relationship."[37]

Unlike many media formats, mukbang platforms allow for immediate feedback and audience interaction. Viewers directly barter with BJs and ask them to perform certain tasks, like eating spicy food, or an extra hamburger, in exchange for star balloons. The ability to directly speak with the entertainer facilitates a sense of intimacy.

Often, BJs will respond to star balloons with a sign of thanks. Researchers Soo-Kwang Oh at William Paterson University and Hyun-Ju Choi at Johns Hopkins University observed twenty BJs and found that 80 percent of them "engaged in some behavioural action expressing gratitude" in response to receiving a star balloon. "Most of these cases involved the BJ stopping the live show to scroll up the chat window to identify and read the donor's username. When reading the names, female BJs used the term 'oppa', which means 'older brother' and have [sic] affectionate connotations. Other BJs bowed to the camera or showed a subtle dance move, which garnered satisfaction from viewers."[38]

The relationships between BJs and their viewers do not adhere to the typical performer/viewer roles. For example, viewers may provide feedback to the BJ on their performance, or offer tips on how to operate equipment. "Slide the controls to the bottom for better sound," one spectator notes as a BJ struggles to improve audio quality. "Tell us . . . what the chicken tastes like—don't just eat it," another person critiques.

Communities develop around the BJs, and often, fans bond and converse with each other. *Do you remember that amazing junk food from the '80s?* a BJ may ask, after which chatroom participants will chime in and create a dialogue not just with the BJ but also among themselves. Sometimes, viewers even develop inside jokes that the BJ is unaware of. Oh and Choi cite one example of this in their paper: "When a 'mukbang' BJ adjusted the camera, one viewer noticed a funny calendar on the wall. While the BJ did not notice, viewers were joking among themselves: 'Did you see the calendar picture? . . . How cheesy!' Those who did not miss the moment were laughing and recognized each other, saying, 'You have good eyes! That made my day.'" The virtual community ends up expanding far beyond the broadcast jockey, and envelops all those logged on at the same time.

Ultimately, many viewers develop a sense of kinship with one another and the BJs they follow. "I feel a sense of belonging to this virtual community," one interviewee in another study says of her mukbang community, noting: "I consider it a cure for loneliness."[39]

This same search for connectedness plays out on Western social media sites like Snapchat and Instagram with popular "influencers." Today, people yearn for "celebrities" who they can relate to and potentially even interact with. We've transitioned from a culture obsessed with rock stars and movie stars to a culture enthralled by influencers and KOLs (Key Opinion Leaders). Some of the most popular and powerful influencers entertain through the mundane: They lip-synch, play video games, review toys, eat food, and apply makeup. It's all about authenticity and accessibility—people who you can imagine hanging out with.

"Many people see me as a friend they can chill with for 15 minutes a day," Swedish gamer Felix Kjellberg, aka PewDiePie, told the *Guardian*. "The loneliness in front of the computer screens brings us together."[40]

In today's world of always-on social media, people are able to conjure a potent sense of intimacy with perfect strangers. Content isn't limited to an influencer's specialty, be it healthy recipes or meditation tactics. Many post about everything and anything: Influencers livestream their commutes, exercise regimens, and Minecraft adventures, and sometimes just talk to the camera about whatever is on their minds. Content churns out with such regularity that many feel like they're in conversation with a friend.

"If you go through [influencer] Deliciously Ella's Instagram timeline, you won't only see a plate with granola and organic vegetables and almond butter and banana bread," University of Sheffield Information School Data Science PhD candidate Alexandra Boutopoulou told me. "You're going to see Deliciously Ella's engagement announcement; you're going to see her wedding on a beautiful island; you're going to see her husband; you're going to see her dog; you're going to see her house, her bedroom, and her yoga routine that she practices every day in her bedroom." As one of her 1.6 million followers, it would be easy to assume you know everything about her.

Wellness blogger Ella Mills, better known as Deliciously Ella, entered the social media universe in 2012 at age twenty-one and quickly became a British household name. While she positions herself mainly as a health food guru, her social media presence extends far beyond cookbook promotions.

I'd reached out to Boutopoulou to better understand influencer culture. At the time of our conversation, Boutopoulou had just finished collecting three thousand Deliciously Ella social media images, which she planned to spend the next year analyzing to assess the social impacts of wellness bloggers and why people follow them.

Upon Boutopoulou's recommendation, I opened Instagram to see for myself what she was talking about. That day on Instagram Stories I learned that, at 10:01 a.m. GMT, Ella drank a green smoothie made of frozen bananas, spinach, juiced cucumber, hemp seeds, chia seeds, dates, almond milk, and almond butter (an ingredient list detailed enough that, if I wanted to, I could have emulated her meal). A few hours later, she munched on a Deliciously Ella–branded nut butter energy ball, and an hour or so after that, she posted a recipe for marinated mushroom and aubergine noodles with miso, spring onions, toasted cashews, and fresh chiles. "Who wants the recipe for this beauty?" she asked her followers. Just two hours after posting, the image had more than eight thousand likes and well over two hundred comments, such as, "That looks beyond tasty. Please set a place for me I'm coming over. 😋 🍵 🍴," "omg this sounds DIVINE," and "Ah yes it looks so good 😍 🙌."

Earlier in the week, Ella took to Instagram to show her fans an enormous, organically homegrown butternut squash gifted to her by the CEO of a food supplement company. "Any suggestions or recipe ideas for this giant beauty, please let me know," she asked of her followers.

Just like the relationship cultivated between mukbang BJs and their fans, wellness bloggers like Deliciously Ella can create a sense of closeness by sharing daily diary-like updates and posting user-engagement questions. Every few days, Deliciously Ella will put a question to her audience, asking if they liked something, what suggestions they have, or whether a recipe was difficult to make. This type of interaction gives you "this feeling that you actually talk to this person," said Boutopoulou, and Deliciously Ella's fans respond in kind.

Her followers often write "positive messages, acting as though she is their friend," Boutopoulou explained to me. They tell Ella that their children love her recipes or that they'll be dropping by Ella's London café. "That doesn't mean that Deliciously Ella is going to be at the deli waiting for this person, but this person acts as if she would have been there."

In all likelihood, Boutopoulou hypothesized, people respond as though Ella is their friend because, in a way, they believe she actually is.

"Social media creates this proximity; you're now part of [an influencer's] everyday life . . . People might feel, I suppose, this kind of closeness."

Many become emotionally attached to those they follow. "If I were lucky enough to meet one of my favorite celebrities/influencers, and he/she asked me to do something illegal as a favor, I would probably do it," agreed just under half of the Hungry Study respondents who follow celebrities online. Even more agreed that when something bad happens to their favorite celebrity or influencer, they feel like it happened to them as well.

Our influencer culture seems, more than anything else, like a symptom of a society yearning for connectedness. And in the place of real friendships, or dinner partners, we learn all we can about strangers, and imagine ourselves as a part of their lives, be it a mukbang BJ, gamer, or wellness guru. Today's icons are not idols, they're confidants. The role of influencers is not to impress with talent, but to attract with approachability and realness to, ultimately, make us feel less alone.

Amidst a loneliness epidemic, perhaps watching others eat, talking to a group of like-minded strangers, or learning all you can about an influencer quells a deep hunger within us. We require connectedness for our physical and emotional well-being, but while our traditional routes to these supportive communities are evaporating, our desire for camaraderie has not. And so here we are, "sharing" meals online instead of around the dinner table.

Social eating serves many roles: It makes us feel bonded to others, and it makes us feel better about ourselves when we share a meal.[41] Watching someone eat seems to be a coping mechanism for the loss of an activity that, while seemingly mundane, aids human happiness. With fewer opportunities for eating together, in person, we're turning to digital supplements.

But influencer and BJ culture cannot fulfill all our belonging needs. While we can feel some intimacy through these interactions, it's much harder to feel validated by these relationships. We may not feel alone, but we still want to feel "liked."

CHAPTER FIVE

"likes" &
self-esteem

The posting rules:

Step 1: Before putting any picture of friends on social media, share a selection of photos with your "Group Chat," a single text message thread with many participants, so that each person can vote for which image they like best and nix any they vehemently disapprove of.

Step 2: With one winner in place, edit the file with color filters, text additions, or body enhancement apps like Facetune to erase freckles, define jawlines, or zap inches off someone's waist. Create a few different versions of the image and then resubmit the options to the Group Chat for review.

Step 3: After all opinions are in, discuss how to caption the photograph. (This debate can become a lengthy one.)

I heard variations of these rules repeatedly while interviewing people in their teens, twenties, and even thirties about how they choose what, and what not, to post online. One interviewee from a Tier 3 city in China revealed that one of her childhood friends stopped talking to her after she posted a nonapproved photo of the two of them on WeChat. Those under forty know better than anyone just how much an image can matter.

In 2018, I traveled back to my former high school, New Trier Township, in the northern suburbs of Chicago, keen to observe how smartphones and social media have transformed the adolescent experience. New Trier is notorious for its stress-inducing academic rigors as well as its mostly upper-middle-class suburban student body (picture *Mean Girls* or *The Breakfast Club*). I was ready to compare today's environment to the one I experienced in the pre-Facebook, pre-emoji days of the early 2000s. I found a few students willing to let me shadow them and was immediately flung back into the catacombs of high school life.

I spent a spring Friday with Lizzy,* one of the "cool kids," who was going through the steps of college applications while managing her day-to-day schoolwork and social pressures. On that day, she wore a torn jean jacket snugly layered over a black-and-white striped hoodie. Her auburn hair was tied at the nape of her neck, revealing ear piercings that trailed up her lobes like icicles.

After a morning of Algebra 2, Chinese, and two periods of Chemistry, Lizzy brought me to Physical Education (more commonly known as "gym class"), during which the teachers decided to host a "meditation" period. The sixty or so students were told to remove their shoes and sit anywhere they pleased in a large basement room where the floor was covered in cushioned wrestling mats. I followed Lizzy to the edge of the room, where we huddled side by side, our backs against a large brick wall. Then, the teachers turned out the lights and left the students to their own whims.

Within moments, Lizzy took out her iPhone and opened Instagram. I peered over her shoulder as she rapidly scrolled through her photo feed and double-tapped images with the pad of her thumb. She was moving so fast that my brain didn't have time to process each post.

"Are you actually looking at them?" I asked, in part wondering if I was just a slowpoke.

"Some of them," she replied. I asked why she bothered "liking" the images if she didn't actually see them.

Lizzy then, with gracious patience, explained the politics of Instagram to me, in a way that, at the age of thirty, made me feel like a geezer. For celebrity posts and even ads, she "likes" them if (in the

---

* Name has been changed.

nanosecond she spends looking at the content) they appeal to her in some way. She "likes" images of those she knows personally because, she reasons, they'll be more likely to "like" her posts back. It is an exchange made in goodwill: You help me, I'll help you. But, she warned me, you never "like" someone's older post; it indicates that you've been sleuthing around on that person's page. And *that* could suggest that you have a crush. Major no-no.

Before leaving the app, Lizzy also checked the "likes" on her own posts. Images that underperformed were removed, while those that raked in a solid number of Internet approvals remained a part of her Instagram collage. The process reminded me of a magazine editor or marketing director choosing the content that would most appeal to buyers, and is a tactic practiced with regularity by Instagram users.* Lizzy's editing process had a clear goal: maintain an amply "liked" online persona. Only the socially approved posts would stay. The rest would be deleted, forever erased from her public digital memory.

I began to see that, unlike my often torturous years of adolescence spent learning and guessing what others would think was cool or interesting or nerdy, Lizzy and her peers no longer have to wonder what others think of their outfits or weekend activities or vacation destinations— they have the data to tell them what people think. Lizzy's methodical "liking" of others' photos and assessments of her own "like" data is not just a fun pastime, but a self-esteem and social acceptance tactic. Un-"liked" photos are plucked out of profiles like an unruly eyebrow hair. By following these rules, Lizzy and her peers can each become someone they *know* will be accepted and envied. The agony of wondering *Do they like me?* is gone. You can just look at the comments feed.

Her work complete, Lizzy closed Instagram. Next on the agenda: Snapchat.

---

* In 2017, LendEDU, a financial marketplace geared toward students, sponsored a survey of nearly ten thousand Millennials who were asked if they know someone who deletes Facebook or Instagram posts if they don't get enough likes. In their summary report, "Millennials Say Instagram Is Most Narcissistic Social App," LendEDU reveals that a shocking 78 percent said they themselves or someone they know practice this profile editing regimen.

Self-Esteem

"All people in our society (with a few pathological exceptions) have a need or desire for a stable, firmly based, (usually) high evaluation of themselves, for self-respect, or self-esteem, and for the esteem of others," writes Abraham Maslow in *A Theory of Human Motivation*. All people want to feel good about themselves.

Traditionally, self-esteem and a sense of worth would be based on one's group and one's role in a community. We develop high self-esteem when others view us as having desirable group member qualities—as being competent, skilled, reliable, or friendly. Traditionally, these sentiments would be expressed through some form of affirmation: a high five, a kiss, a nod, an invitation to a dinner party. Each of these social interactions boosts our confidence that, yes, we really are rather awesome.

Most of the confidence-building cues we, as a species, have always relied on require one vital element: that we spend time in person with others as a part of a community. And in recent years, this simple act has been disrupted.

Several studies now claim that most Millennials and Gen Zers communicate digitally more than they do in person.[1] A 2015 survey published by Common Sense Media found that American teenagers ages thirteen to eighteen average six and a half hours of screen time per day, and a report from Pew that same year found that nearly a quarter of teens ages thirteen to seventeen report being online "almost constantly."[2, 3]

Some estimate that, based on today's rates of social media use, the average person will spend five and a half years of their lives on social media.[4] Others say it is more likely to take up a full one-seventh of the average American existence, which comes out to roughly *eleven* years.[*, 5]

---

* Data from GlobalWebIndex, gleaned from interviews with over four hundred thousand Internet users around the world, shows that the average Gen Zer spends just over three hours a day on social media. According to GlobalWebIndex's 2018 "Flagship Report on the Latest Trends in Social Media," the most social media–obsessed teens and twentysomethings reside in the Philippines, where average daily use is above four hours, yet those in Brazil, Indonesia, Argentina, Thailand, Mexico, the United Arab Emirates, Malaysia, South Africa, and Saudi Arabia are not far behind—a sign that this youthful attachment to social media is not defined by

While most teens still see their friends outside of school during the week, Pew Research finds that just a quarter of American teens spend time with friends outside of school daily. Instead, a greater number text their friends.

Online platforms have become mediators of communication. After-school hangouts are intercalated by a screen. Video game battles are no longer played in your neighbor's dingy basement; instead, they're played alone, from your bedroom with the door shut to the outside world. Instead of staying behind at the library to study alongside friends, kids are heading home and opening Houseparty, where they livestream themselves completing their homework, as the rest of their video chat group does the same.

Today, with less and less time spent with others, pats on the back are traded in for 🙌, vocal agreement for 🎉 , and signs of a valuable opinion for 👍 Like .

What happens when our self-worth is drawn less and less from in-person relationships and increasingly through digitized emojis, gifs, upvotes, and memes?

Social Validations

A few hours after gym class, I joined Lizzy and several of her friends in the cafeteria for lunch. I asked what they do during their free time.

Weekends, the girls said, are often spent at parties. As a post-drinking salve, groups usually end up at some kind of fast-food estab-lishment. This surprised me, as I hadn't pegged them as a fast-food crowd: The girls adhere on and off to a vegan diet, and Lizzy had spent the weekend making raw Paleo energy balls. Cost, they admitted, is a factor, along with indulgence. Fast food, they explained, is associated with being hungover or still intoxicated, states that many high school-ers consider admirable, in a novel or rebellious way. (This association also suggests, of course, that one would not go to these establishments

---

borders or culture. Based on these numbers, the average Internet user worldwide will spend ten years of their lives online.

sober.) One girl explained: People "want to fulfill the expectation of the night and take a funny Snap of, like, me spilling fries all over the place."

The *image* of the experience, they said, was a core part of why they ventured out to Steak 'n Shake or McDonald's at two in the morning. How else would everyone know what kind of a raucous, drunken night they'd had? I imagined the girls feeling tired and craving bed yet motivated enough by the promise of social bragging to pose for photos while nibbling half-heartedly on burgers.

And during the day? "Driving around is a big thing. We Juul in the car. We go to the beach." On a recent weekend, Lizzy told me that she and her friends went to a local café to pick up food and then "had a beach picnic because, obviously, that's a good photo op."

I asked for clarification: You did that because of the photo opportunity? Lizzy nodded. "Yeah, people will say, 'Let's go here, I think it's going to be a great photo op.'"

All young adults have a need to belong to a social group, to feel popular and accepted by their peers, but with fewer hours spent in the presence of others, and fewer group affiliations, many are looking to "hearts," "thumbs-up," and Snapchat streaks as evidence of social acceptance. As such, several studies have confirmed that online approvals can have a direct impact on how young people weigh their own self-worth or personal achievements.[6] For example, young people love to cook, but a survey by Scripps Media found that 40 percent of young Millennials say they don't feel great about a dish they've made unless they receive compliments from others online.

These nods of social approval act like a pat-on-the-back affirmation.[7] A digital tip of the hat can trigger the release of a feel-good shot of dopamine (just like receiving a new tidbit of information). Our desire for connection, approval, and belonging turns social media sites into validation dosing machines.

In order to boost personal happiness and self-esteem, many feel the desire to gain the greatest amount of social envy and applause possible online, and find themselves persistently searching for photo opportunities that can drive the online validations they crave. Many choose how to spend their time, what to buy, and even what to say based on what they think will earn them the most social media praise. Nearly half of Gen Z girls and a third of Gen Z boys surveyed by consumer research firm Open Mind Strategy say they are more apt to do things because "it will give them something good to post." Likewise, Lizzy and her friends' decisions to go to the beach or out for fast food is not motivated by what they feel will be enjoyable, but what will earn them the most social media attention.

Food Porn

"We like going downtown to eat," one of Lizzy's friends told me. She recommended that I check out the restaurant Velvet Taco for their "Instagrammable tacos." She didn't mention how the food tasted.

According to youth research agency YPulse, nearly two-thirds of American thirteen- to thirty-two-year-olds have posted an image of food online, and China-based global brand agency Labbrand claims that 60 percent of all Chinese mobile users "consistently" take pictures of their food.[8] The practice of sharing images of our meals has become so commonplace that most of us participate without pausing to ask: *Why are we doing this? Why do we want others to see pictures of our meals?*

Often, if we're being honest with ourselves, it's all about the "likes."

"They line up for hours to get things like ice cream or French bread," Shanghai-based chef and food blogger Jenny Gao tells me of Shanghai's young foodophiles. But the "foodies" she observes queueing up prioritize something other than eating the desired delicacies: Instead of immediately chowing down, the scenesters pull out their phones. "They [stand in line] so they can take a million photos and share it on social media," she said.

Today, with a persistent mind to "likes," the pictorial value of a food is often prioritized over flavor. College food media company Spoon University found that over half of surveyed Gen Zers would pay an extra 10 percent for an "epic burger" that they can Instagram rather than two "non-photo-worthy burgers." Similarly, according to research conducted on behalf of the Food Network, more than a third of younger American Millennials believe that sometimes the photo of a dish they've cooked is more important than the dish itself.

With an emphasis no longer on flavor but on ocular opulence, many of today's most disruptive food trends are the direct result of an image-obsessed culture. This fixation has generated food trends that, I believe, without social media simply wouldn't exist. Think: poke bowls, rainbow bagels, sushi burritos, galaxy donuts, and mermaid toast—all foods that are pictorially provocative but gustatorily unremarkable. In 2018, the food item with the greatest spike in Google searches was "unicorn cake," a simply flavored, Care Bear–multicolored confection. These rainbow-tastic foods don't taste better than their less colorful cousins; they just look great on camera.

Several "stunt food" dishes around the world are now optimized not for flavor but for visual shock. In Budapest, the doughnut shop Mr. Funk serves "Freak Shakes"—milkshakes topped with things like a hat of multiple donuts, a drizzle of chocolate syrup, and splash of confetti sprinkles. Each shake looks like a hallucinogenic concoction from the fantastical mind of Willy Wonka. Meanwhile, at New York City's M. Wells Steakhouse, French Canadian chef Hugue Dufour put a "bone-in burger" on his menu, where a giant shank protrudes from an otherwise common-looking beef burger. The bone has no culinary purpose; it just looks cool. In fact, the restaurant has admitted that the bones come from a variety of animals—they use whatever bones they can secure. The chef has said that he is entertained by watching people attempt to eat the unwieldy burger, which quickly rose to fame on social media after its release. Similarly, in Sydney, Australia, Aqua S layers vibrantly colored soft-serve ice cream—like magenta pomegranate, glacier blue sea salt, and verdant pandan—with toasted marshmallows and caramel popcorn, and places the whimsical sugar-bomb atop a throne of cotton candy. Online, it looks as though the twisted icy treat is emerging from an ethereal sugar cloud. Though befuddling to eat, the accoutrements transform a simple ice cream cone into something "Insta-worthy," and with that, the ice cream parlor has earned a flock of fanatics. The point is not piquancy (or practicality), but optical enticement.

Over-the-top visuals have also dribbled off the plate and into the dining room, where patrons eat in spaces framed by bold chevron-patterned tiles, metallic fixtures, cursive neon lights, and dangling plants that have been chosen by designers specifically for their social media pizzazz. For example, in 2017, the year of "Millennial Pink," several New York City cafés opened that, in person, look like a flamingo's 1983 prom party, but when captured online create rosy, vibrant images that jump out from a crowded scroll.

In Bangkok, decor is the main draw for café visitors—forget the food. "People are concerned about the backgrounds. Each café has decor just for Instagram. That's what people are thinking about," Pieng-or Fai, a food blogger from Bangkok, told me. She says that young people are "café hopping," bouncing from one coffee shop to the next to accumulate social points as they document each visit for their followers. "The cafés are now competing with their interior design," she relayed. These establishments understand the visual motivations, and they happily feed into this novel social need.

Similar desires for visual interest over experience are transforming the travel industry. A UK survey of one thousand Millennials found that "how Instagrammable the holiday would be" was overwhelmingly the most important factor to them when choosing a vacation destination.[9] Similarly, social media is driving Chinese youth to prioritize food and travel experiences. "You don't want to be the only one who's never traveled and never had any cool experience on your WeChat moment feed," Chinese food tour founder Hu Ruixi wrote me.

The Instagrammability of travel moments is so prized that there are several new vacation photo management businesses. The Flytographer app connects travelers with professional photographers and has partnered with Fairmont Hotels & Resorts to offer the service at thirty-five of its properties. Meanwhile, a Swiss hotel chain, Ibis, offers guests a $90-and-up service called "Relax We Post," where someone will take photos and post them to Instagram on a traveler's behalf. The package lets "vacationers take a break from social media, while still maintaining a jealousy-inducing presence online," reports *Quartz*.[10]

Another symptom of this photo fetish is the growing prominence of pop-up "museums" where there's nothing to learn beyond how to find the right camera angle. These spaces, now found all over the world, offer visitors the opportunity to create images that will conjure online approval and awe. Whether you're at the Museum of Ice Cream, 29Rooms, Rosé Mansion, or Museum of Candy, the only activity within these "galleries" is selfie-taking.

The need-to-be-seen is even impacting the housing market as young first-time buyers schedule photo shoots to highlight their big purchase. They then post these pictures online; spouses carry one another over the threshold, snuggle on the stoop under a "sold" placard, or cradle keys in the palms of their joined hands. Personal achievements alchemize from intimate experiences to public announcements.

Finally, and most critically, some are even putting their lives at risk in the name of an Insta-worthy photo. More than 250 people have died over the last few years from selfie-related accidents, mainly in India, the US, Russia, and Pakistan. Signs warn Tokyo train commuters that use of selfie sticks is not permitted on the platform.

Ultimately, social media, once considered an avenue for personal expression, has transformed into a canvas for personality contests—a game, if you will, of who can post the most jealousy-invoking, humorous, desirable content (while avoiding embarrassing pitfalls).[11]

Social media offers the ability to project a false reality. That idyllic-looking vacation may have been crippled by flight delays, a twisted ankle, or food poisoning, and the house purchase may have put you into immense debt, but viewers online will never know. One of the trendiest Instagram travel locations of 2019 was a blindingly blue Siberian "lake" that was actually a toxic dump.* The ombre Starbucks frozen drink tastes unremarkable and may give you a stomachache, but it shimmers with color on others' screens.

Often, stunt foodies don't even eat the items they've purchased. In fact, a study by Sainsbury's supermarkets found that Instagram may be contributing to food waste in Britain. "Desire to explore the latest foodie trends is contributing to food waste with 86 percent of us [admitting] to buying ingredients for one specific recipe, knowing we will struggle to use it again," they cite. The study ties this habit directly to creating

---

* "We ask that in the pursuit of the selfie, not to fall into the ash dump!" the Siberian Generating Company warned in response to Instagrammers posing along the shore of the waste pool while in bathing suits or wedding dresses or while standing in yoga poses. Some photo seekers ignored the warnings and waded into the calcium salt waters, all for the 'gram, according to reporting by Salvador Hernandez for *BuzzFeed News* in "Instagrammers Are Swarming This Turquoise Lake. It's Actually A Toxic Dump."

foods to "look great on our Instagram feed."[12] New York City ice cream Instagrammer Eric Mersmann admits that three-quarters of his photographed icy treats end up in the trash. "Once it gets too melty for a good shot, it goes out," he tells his friend and journalist Amanda Mull.[13]

Some are beginning to rebel against—and sound the alarm on— the false realities conjured online. A young Australian model named Essena O'Neill garnered a half million followers on Instagram by posting images of herself lazing on a beach, sipping cocktails poolside, and hiking in the Australian foliage. Each image highlighted her abnormally narrow, long midriff and dainty limbs. But a few years into her reign as an Instagram influencer, O'Neill boldly changed her account name to "Social Media Is Not Real Life," deleted most of her photos, and re-captioned those that remained. One image of the starlet on the beach was re-captioned: "NOT REAL LIFE—took over 100 in similar poses trying to make my stomach look good. Would have hardly eaten that day. Would have yelled at my sister to keep taking them until I was somewhat proud of this. Yep so totally #goals."

What O'Neill had been doing on her page isn't very different from what most social media users do every day: posting idealized images of her life online. In an effort to be liked, we are editing out our least-liked attributes and overselling our accomplishments.

The Envy Machine

The fallacies of online personas are becoming a common topic of conversation, as various influencers and celebrities draw back the social media curtain to highlight rampant digital distortions of reality—be it waist size or store-bought cake posing as homemade. But knowing about the prevalence of online fallacies does not stop us from comparing ourselves to these concocted versions of reality.

Repeatedly, studies show that the more time we spend on social media, the more likely we are to feel dissatisfied with our lives, depressed, and isolated.[14] Use of social media sites correlates with elevated levels of envy and lower rates of life satisfaction.[15]

These platforms can cause users to fall into something called an "envy spiral." It's all too easy to become envious of other people's vacations, weddings, or families, even when we know that what others choose to post is a selective slice of their lives. *Everyone else seems to be happy, accomplished, and living exciting lives*, people think. *Why am I such a failure?* For example, the Hungry Study participants most tethered to their devices were likelier than the general population to say that their friends are more interesting and more successful than they themselves are.

Soon, envy translates into self-doubt. Persistent exposure to a flawless gallery of social media imagery can make many feel inferior. "I feel like I look at other people's lives [on social media] and think, 'Why can't my life be like their life?'" a Millennial who lives in Brooklyn remarked to me. She has to remind herself, she said, that though others may have more followers, comments, and views, they are no better than her. This quicksand of self-doubt is so intense that she had the word "enough" tattooed on her wrist.*

In 2018, a comprehensive study titled "Perfectionism Is Increasing Over Time: A Meta-Analysis of Birth Cohort Differences from 1989 to 2016" found that perfectionism among college students is on the rise. "This finding suggests that recent generations of college students are demanding higher expectations of themselves and attaching more importance to perfection than previous generations," the researchers Thomas Curran, a lecturer in the Department for Health at the University of Bath, and Andrew Hill, an associate professor of sports psychology at York St. John University, note in their paper. Curran and Hill examined twenty-seven years' worth of responses to the Multidimensional Perfection Scale, from more than forty-one thousand college students in the United States, Canada, and Britain, and found an increase in perfectionism across all genders in all three countries.

As more and more young people absorb a curated social media mirage, many are doubting their own lives and placing unrealistic

---

* Relatedly, in the Hungry Study, we found a direct relationship between those who are most attached to their devices and sentiments of self-doubt. Those who qualified as a part of the Tech-Tethered Cohort were more likely than the general population to agree with the statements *I worry about what other people think of me*; *When at work or school, I worry others will think I don't know what I'm doing*; and *I feel dissatisfied with myself much of the time.*

pressure on themselves to live up to the deceptive representations they see online. "The unrealistic expectations set by social media may leave young people with feelings of self-consciousness, low self-esteem, and the pursuit of perfectionism, which can manifest as anxiety disorders," Curran and Hill posit.

Reports of body dysmorphia and eating disorders have risen significantly among adolescent girls since the dawn of social media.[16] Unrealistic body types, highlighted and created through photo-editing apps and illusory poses, may be behind the uptick. Globally, young people are also likelier than ever before to feel the need to diet and undergo plastic surgery.[17]

"Young people appear to have internalized irrational social ideals of the perfectible self that, while unrealistic, are to them eminently desirable and obtainable," Curran and Hill write, highlighting the disconnect between curated posts and reality. With the cultural bar set higher than ever before, aiming for perfection is the only way one can feel secure. "Broadly speaking, then," they hypothesize, "increasing levels of perfectionism might be considered symptomatic of the way in which young people are coping—to feel safe, connected, and of worth."

Socially prescribed perfectionism, note Curran and Hill, is closely related to depression and anxiety.[18] These new social pressures and perceived expectations are likely "important in terms of explaining recent increases in mental health difficulties among young people," including the rising prevalence of depression, anxiety, and even suicidal ideation.

Today, global communities are reporting alarming spikes among teenagers of major depressive episodes, self-harm, and death by suicide.* [19] "In just the five years between 2010 and 2015, the number of US teens who felt useless and joyless—classic symptoms of depression—surged 33 percent in large national surveys," notes prolific researcher and a professor of psychology at San Diego State University, Jean M. Twenge.[20] Between 2010 and 2016, the number of American adolescents

---

* Globally, the total estimated number of people living with depression increased by 18.4 percent between 2005 and 2015, outpacing the general population growth. In "More than a Mental Health Problem," the Centers for Disease Control and Prevention (CDC) notes that of all recent suicides in the United States, over half of the victims had no known mental health condition.

who experienced at least one major depressive episode leapt by 60 percent, according to a nationwide survey conducted by the US Department of Health and Human Services.*

Globally, suicide is now the second leading cause of death among fifteen- to twenty-nine-year-olds, and seems to affect people of all socio-economic statuses, races, and ethnicities.† The CDC reports that while suicide rates among those ten to nineteen years of age dipped by 15 percent between 1999 and 2007, they increased by a horrifying 56 percent by 2016.[21] Between 2010 and 2015 alone, "the number of thirteen- to eighteen-year-olds who committed suicide jumped 31 percent," notes Twenge in her review, and the CDC website states that occurrence of teen suicide in the United State overall has tripled since the 1940s.‡

While there is no single catalyst of the youth mental health crisis, our digital connections have been identified as a key culprit.§ At the

---

* According to Health and Human Services' "United States Adolescent Mental Health Facts," 13 percent of surveyed adolescents, ages twelve to seventeen, reported that they had at least one major depressive episode during the twelve months before the 2016 survey, up from only 8.7 percent in 2005, a nearly 50 percent increase over just eleven years. Similar findings are reflected in the article "National Trends in the Prevalence and Treatment of Depression in Adolescents and Young Adults," by Ramin Mojtabai et al, published in the journal *Pediatrics*.

† In line with these findings, the number of hospital admissions for suicidal teenagers more than doubled over a study period of 2008 to 2015, according to "Trends in Suicidality and Serious Self-Harm for Children 5-17 Years at 32 U.S. Children's Hospitals, 2008–2015" by Gregory Plemmons, presented at the 2017 Pediatric Academic Societies Meeting in San Francisco. Nearly half of these hospital admissions were for children between the ages of five and twelve. To add to these shocking statistics, the CDC found in a 2017 study that over 17 percent of high school students—more than one in six—had seriously considered killing themselves in the year prior.

‡ The suicide rate for females ages ten to fourteen tripled from 0.5 per 100,000 in 1999 to 1.5 per 100,000 in 2014, and continued to notch up to 1.7 in 2016, as documented in the National Center for Health Statistics Data Brief "Increase in Suicide in the United States, 1999–2014" by Sally Curtin, Margaret Warner, and Holly Hedegaard.

§ Of course, the Internet is not the only cause of this mental health crisis. Issues like debt, personal relationships, and bullying are also cited as causes for these emotional debilitations.

same time that we entered the Digital Age and handed our time and attention over to folks like Steve Jobs and Mark Zuckerberg, just one decade after Google search altered the way the world accesses information, three years after Facebook—the "connector"—debuted, and the very same year the iPhone allowed each of us to unlock a virtual world, the rates of teenage depression, anxiety, and suicidal ideation began to tick up, rising bit by bit every year since.

In 2016, clinician and professor Brian Primack, along with his colleagues at the University of Pittsburgh's School of Medicine, undertook a comprehensive survey of nearly two thousand adults to assess social media use and depression. "We thought we would see sort of, what I would describe as a U-shaped curve," Primack explained to me. The researchers expected people with the lowest amount of social media use to "be more depressed, more anxious," because these folks would, hypothetically, be missing out on the benefits of connecting with hundreds of "friends" online. Average social media users, they anticipated, would exhibit the greatest benefit from social media, and extreme social media users—those who use the platforms for nearly all their waking hours—would show higher rates of anxiety and depression. But it turns out that they were wrong across the board.

"What we found was basically a straight line that goes up. Meaning that every level of social media use was associated with an increase in depression.[22] We found the same thing for anxiety," Primack told me.[23]

No One Knows Me

"How many people do you talk to on a regular basis every day?" I asked a group of tenth, eleventh, and twelfth graders one afternoon in the New Trier library. A mix of boys and girls were huddled around a table in the back corner of the expansive, quiet room.

Between their group chats on iMessage and Snapchat, and comments and "likes" on other sites, most agreed that they interact with over two dozen people every day.

"How many people do you feel, like, really know you?" I followed up.

"That's a hard question," one student replied.

"No one knows me," said another, shrugging and smirking.

"My mom?" offered a boy across the table from me.

"Do you feel like you have anyone who you can go to who knows the core of you, who is not going to judge you?" I asked.

"Less than 10 percent of my friends," a girl beside me said matter-of-factly.

"I probably have five people like that. Most people would not say that the overwhelming majority of their friends are like that," another offered.

According to a McCann survey, 56 percent of eighteen- to thirty-year-olds, globally, claim that if they didn't have their mobile device or mobile service even for a short while, their personal connection with others would suffer. But I'd begun to wonder: What kind of human connections are forged online? With all the correlative data between social media and envy, jealousy, and depression, I'd begun to seriously question the value of digital friendship. With curated posts and strategic profile editing, how much can you *really* know about someone based on their virtual feeds and profiles?

The next day, I tried out the same question—"How many people *really* know you?"—on a different group of students, this time eleventh-grade girls more interested in talking about Mary Berry than Velvet Taco. During lunch, a group of about ten sat in a wide circle in the second-floor rotunda. I plopped myself down on the beige laminate floors, unchanged since my time meandering those halls.

"Could it be your family?" one girl asked in response to my inquiry. I said it could.

"A couple. A handful," she replied.

"That actually, like, *know me* know me? Like, two," said another.

Earlier that week, Lizzy had told me about the importance of keeping up with messages on Snapchat. "I religiously streak with my closest friends," Lizzy said, referring to a long ongoing Snapchat message exchange. (Snapchat keeps track of how many days you and a contact have sent each other direct messages; if you continue messaging back and forth for several consecutive days, the app will notify you that you're on a "streak" and eventually reward you with an emoji.) When I asked why, she said that it "shows you're close with that person." Shows to whom was not clear to me.

Many, like Lizzy, say that online interactions serve as an extension of real-life relationships. Well over half of global social media users say they go on social sites to keep up with friends.[24] Similarly, a study by the Girl Scout Research Institute found that more than half of girls ages fourteen to seventeen say that social networks help them feel closer and more connected to their real-life friends.[25] But a curious insight is revealed once you dig a bit deeper into these assertions.

While in the rotunda, a girl beside me paused a moment and looked at me quizzically. "The funny thing is," she said, "the people that, like, know me really well, I don't Snapchat or I talk to on a very infrequent basis."

"No, I've noticed that too," another excitedly averred, nodding with agreement.

I heard a very similar sentiment in the other group.

The people who truly "know you," a boy beside me in the library reasoned, "don't talk to you on social media. Those people, they know you, they know you as a person. They know what you're all about and they know, like, your flaws and everything. So they can actually differentiate between a perception of you and who you actually are." In essence, he was saying, there is no point in talking to them through social media because they'll see through the façade.

Nearly all the students I spoke with said that only a select few of their friends really know them. *What about all those other "friends"?* I wondered. *Who are they and what kind of friendship is that?* I started to realize that this generation has two categories of friends: real friends, and those you Streak with.

"The key mechanisms for building relationships and their stability over time is the endorphin system in the brain," famed evolutionary anthropologist Robin Dunbar explained to me from his home office near Liverpool, England, as he fiddled with his graying whiskers. Intimate interactions like eye contact and touch trigger the release of endorphins, neurochemicals that help us feel closer to others. This, he says, "in turn, seems to elevate your sense of well-being and contentedness."

"Certainly," Dunbar continued, "our data shows that the more friends you have, the more often you see them, basically, the happier you are, the more contented you are with your life."

And do social media or text-based relationships facilitate that same bonding, I asked? "No" was the short answer. While "likes" provide a feel-good hit of dopamine, dopamine is different from endorphins. Dopamine provides a brief neurochemical reward, while endorphins help create lasting bonds—and provide those physical, immune-boosting health benefits correlated with deep relationships.

"There is no point in having five hundred 'friends,'" Dunbar told me, using air quotes, "if you actually don't know any of them. It's all about this more intimate, inner layer of friendships."*

Dr. Primack echoed Dr. Dunbar: "We found that when you ask questions like, 'Do you feel like people have your back?'" even those with seven hundred friends claimed that only a few of those connections were folks they could rely on.[26] Maintaining a well-"liked" social media profile, these researchers agreed, does not indicate anything about one's deep friendships—the people they would "consider going to for advice or sympathy in times of great emotional or other distress."[27] And it's those relationships, the experts maintained, that really matter.

---

* In fact, Dunbar explained to me, it's not even possible for us to have five hundred meaningful friendships. While each social media site preaches the benefits and allure of hundreds, if not thousands of friends and connections, it turns out that human beings have a very limited capacity for human connection, and the closest relationships we have require a great deal of time and energy to maintain—far more than an emoji or a Snap.

According to Dunbar, *Homo sapiens* evolved in communities no larger than 150 people. Thus, our species evolved to firmly grasp—at most—the ins and outs of 150 individuals living in one location. Still, the human mind is not adept at holding 150 simultaneous deep relationships, so, according to Dunbar, we prioritize some relationships over others. Many of us have about two dozen family members and besties who will help us with things like home projects or childcare. Then, we have a few dozen additional good friends and, perhaps, another hundred run-of-the-mill friends. Beyond these relationships, argues Dunbar, we can maintain up to five hundred "acquaintances" and manage to recognize up to 1,500 people, a number that, again, makes sense considering our evolutionary roots: In all likelihood, a hunter-gatherer would encounter no more than a thousand individuals in an entire lifetime. But under no circumstance, argues Dunbar, can anyone develop, maintain, and enjoy deep friendships with hundreds.

While one can perceive social support through social media friends, multiple studies show that those who look to online contacts for support in times of need are likelier to experience depressive feelings.[28] In fact, turning to social media for support may exacerbate loneliness, as the support received by an online acquaintance will never provide the same physical or emotional benefits as the support from a close, trusted confidant.*

Online relationships, by and large, are not an adequate replacement for our in-person connections. In the Hungry Study, those who rely on social media "friends" to fulfill their relationship needs are more likely to believe that no one in their lives really knows them well and are more likely to say they wish they had a stronger community.† Other studies confirm that those with the most social media connections are more likely to feel socially isolated.[29] Meanwhile, those who use social media as a tool to coordinate *offline* meetups are *least* likely to feel socially isolated.[30]

Findings like this make Primack wonder "whether that special sauce that we truly need as human beings is part of the [social media] package. Maybe [an] emoji smile sort of fulfills a little bit of that Paleolithic need for a smile. But on the other hand, maybe it's a pale comparison. Maybe it's an Apple Jack to an apple." In other words, in most of these online associations, the essential parts of friendship are missing.[31]

Primack says that the difference between real friendship and online friendship is the same as the one between downhill skiing and taking out your Wii Fit for a simulated skiing experience. Maybe the Wii Fit is a good idea if visiting a ski slope is absolutely not an option and you really want to ski, but it is not a substitute for the real experience. In the same vein, if someone is isolated or challenged by in-person social interactions, online relationships will fill an important void; for lonely or socially insecure adolescents and children, online interactions provide a

---

* Research psychologist Dr. Larry Rosen has found that virtual empathy and support does exist, but, he notes, "it's only one-fifth or one-sixth as good as empathy in the real world."

† In the Hungry Study, those with the most social media "friends" were most likely to agree with the statements *If I wanted to go on a day trip, I would have a hard time finding someone to go with me* and *If a family crisis arose, it would be difficult to find someone who could give me good advice about how to handle it.*

space to practice social engagement, self-disclosure, and identity explo-ration.[32] But by and large, the social benefits of online relationships end there; they are still no replacement for in-person *can you come over right now, I'm in crisis* friendships.

Similarly, mukbang can be a welcome stand-in for those who have no one else to eat with. But social bonds formed through YouTube and AfreecaTV will never rival the strength of the ones sown between those who meet in real life for a shared meal. And for people who are lonely, collecting "likes" may be a temporary boost, but it's no replacement for a friend who brings over chicken soup when you are sick.

Each group of students I spoke to willingly admitted the vapidity of their online exchanges. When it comes to the students' close friends, they take the time to make plans with them or, at the very least, call them on the phone. They put in effort, and take the time to see them in person. Meanwhile, their time "liking" images and gathering these dopamine-inducing online approvals, I saw, has very little to do with forming deep, meaningful relationships.

People often talk of this generation as kids who "share" too much of themselves online. But perhaps "connection" and "sharing" are mis-nomers when it comes to social media. The more time I spent thinking about online social approvals, the lengths to which people go to gar-ner those social points, and the emotional impact of seeing manicured image after manicured image, the more I observed just how difficult these young kids have it—how nearly impossible it is for them to meet their self-esteem needs.

The marketing of social media sites makes us think that by shar-ing an image of our bubble tea, lakeside picnic, or cookie dough, we are opening ourselves up to more friendships than ever before. But by focusing our attention on screen-based interactions, we're prioritizing acquaintance over close friends, the ones who will have your back when you're in need, come water your plants when you're out of town, or listen as you grieve. In many cases, people are sifting through a bag of Apple Jacks hunting for a bite of fresh, nutritious fruit.

Further, we need to feel liked, appreciated, of value. Each of us wants to be accepted by those around us. But how do we really achieve that sense of belonging in a world where most of our "friends" don't know who we are?

CHAPTER SIX

diets & identity

H i," I said to the restaurant host who waved me in from the rainy New York City night. "I'm here for the vegan speed dating event." She smiled and directed me to the back staircase of Urban Vegan Kitchen.

As I reached the stairs, I heard a ruckus of voices. Twenty-seven people had signed up for the event hosted by Find Veg Love, a vegan dating company, in hopes of meeting a like-minded opposite-sex partner. I headed down to the basement dining room, where white twinkle lights dangled from the ceiling. Graffiti covered one wall, while the other showcased framed photos of pop stars. The room was no more than 250 square feet, and two-tops were arranged along the walls. I quickly saw that people had sectioned themselves off into groups, finding safe, same-gendered faces to mingle with before the one-on-one sessions were to begin. A plate of seasoned seitan buffalo wings made its way around the room.

The crowd reflected the diversity of New York City. I briefly joined a table and met a twentysomething Latina nurse who told me she was there to find a long-term serious relationship with someone who shares her "ethics" and "lifestyle." Next to her, a jazz voice graduate student from the suburbs of Osaka, Japan, talked about the unspoken understanding that accompanies relationships with fellow vegans. Next to her, a woman originally from Serbia was keen to find her match.

I moved across the room to speak with three men huddled in the center of the floor, all of whom, I learned, were proud vegans. "Would you date a vegetarian?" I inquired. Elijah, a middle school math teacher with wet curls flopping across his forehead, visibly cringed. The others—Naveet, a banker in a well-ironed blue button-down, and Andrew, who sported a jet-black manicured beard—laughed at the idea. "I'll let you answer that one," Elijah responded, motioning toward his two new friends.

"No" was the final answer from Naveet. Andrew said it was a possibility—if it was a vegetarian who shared his ethical beliefs. That kind of vegetarian, he argued, could be swayed to become a vegan.

Soon, attendees were instructed to find a table. Each couple would have five minutes to chat before the ladies moved on to the next date. With everyone in their seats, the timer began, and a hushed room soon sang with conversation.

Vegans Karine Charbonneau and Andy Brighten launched Find Veg Love in February 2017. Years before, after a move to the Bay Area, Charbonneau, an experienced event planner, saw business potential in the niche arena of vegan events. She began organizing vegan Iron Chef competitions, plant-based fitness retreats, and vegan weddings. Quickly, she became known as *the* vegan event planner.

Soon, she noted a common complaint from many of her friends and clients: I can't find a vegan partner. Inspired, she and Brighten hosted her first vegan speed dating event, and two people who met there were married a few years later.

Now several years into the business, Charbonneau and Brighten are no longer together and Charbonneau heads up the company on her own. She sees endless potential and is expanding the business— eventually she wants to offer a wide array of vegan- and vegetarian-friendly services. "We're going to be working with a vegan dating coach, a vegan astrologist, a vegan beauty expert," she tells me of her big-picture plans.

Meeting someone who shares one's vegan values "can be a very powerful experience for people," Brighten had explained to me months earlier during our first conversation, when he was still working alongside Charbonneau. The vegan lifestyle, he noted, "can bring you together in a shared identity in a stronger way than just something that is a mere preference." Here, he made the point that many interpret veganism not as a diet, but a way of being. As such, what could be more important than meeting a partner with the same ethos?

Where Are "My People"?

Each of us has the desire to belong to a group. Being a group member provides not just an immediate source of support and self-esteem, but a form of personal identity.

Group identification "provides us with a sense of who we are that prescribes what we should think, feel, and do," writes social psychologist Dr. Michael Hobb in a paper titled "Uncertainty-Identity Theory," published in the Elsevier book series Advances in Experimental Social Psychology.[1] Many times, communities offer a shared system of "beliefs and values that explain and justify the world, our place within it, our relationship with others, and our own and others' actions." Associating with a particular group—be it *Mean Girls'* Plastics ("On Wednesdays, we wear pink") or Seventh-Day Adventism—provides us with guidelines on what to believe, what to wear, what to eat, even how to speak.

Group identity produces a feeling of rootedness and a strong sense of self, all the while reducing the number of decisions one has to make about what to believe and how to act. Depending on which identities you subscribe to, you may cheer for a specific team, vote for a particular politician, believe or disbelieve the science around climate breakdown, or opt for black instead of pink nail polish. You can think of your identities as the filters you choose on your newsfeeds. This form of belonging informs nearly every aspect of the way we live.

So, what happens to us when these traditional filters fall by the wayside?

Over time, global culture has become less group-anchored and more competitive, capitalistic, and meritocratic. We're obsessed with rankings, SAT scores, "likes," job titles, and income over group achievements. This shift strips us of common group identity markers. Traditionally, our personal identities were largely informed by our hometown, religion, and politics; today, we're identified by the corner office and our online profiles. We are moving away from home for school or job opportunities, and our other traditional group-identity systems, like religion and political affiliations, are falling out of favor.

These trends are particularly stark among Millennials. In its 2015 Religious Landscape Study, Pew Research Center found that nearly 23 percent of US adults do not affiliate with any religion, up from about 16 percent in 2007. That number is even higher among Millennials, where 34 percent claim no religious affiliation.[2] Some youth express hostility toward traditional forms of religion; in 2016, only 55 percent of American Millennials agreed that churches have a positive impact on the nation, a number that just five years earlier was at 73 percent.[3]

Further, Millennials are famous for being politically independent and refusing to adhere to party lines—crushing another traditional form of collectivism.[4] Pew Research claims that half of US Millennials now describe themselves as political independents, which means that at least an eighth of the US electorate is not strongly tied to any political party.[5]

Sociologists like Hobb argue that people without identity parameters can feel uneasy, forced to consistently ask oneself: Who am I, what do I believe, what should I wear, what should I eat, who should I vote for? Further, the loss of these foundational group identities leaves us without a clear group who, simply put, gets you.

As such, individuals who shun the group labels of the past are engineering new ways to express their identities and find like-minded individuals.

Food Identities

Food has long played a crucial role in identity. Food invokes history, ethnicity, tradition, and income.[6] Each of us takes on food identities of some kind—maybe we're a "meat and potatoes" or a "dressing on the side" type of person—but historically, other cultural, social, and geographic forces, such as religion, class, and region, have most impacted what we do and do not eat.

Religions often delineate particular diets. Under kashrut, Jewish dietary law, Jews are prohibited from eating pork and shellfish, among other restrictions; religious Muslims adhere to halal jurisprudence; Jains avoid meat and eggs, as well as tubers; Mormons denounce the consumption of caffeine and alcohol. Historically, class has also influenced what foods end up on the table. Medieval peasants ate gruel as the nobility chowed down on an array of game, fruits, vegetables, and cheese, all devoured with wine or beer. And up until recent decades, all diets were curated by season and locale. Depending on the time of year and region, only a select few fruits, vegetables, grains, and legumes were available.

Only in the last century have these class, religious, and regional food identities become less potent. Our globalized and subsidized food system has erased many geographic and monetary boundaries. Starting with refrigeration in the mid-twentieth century, a family in New York could sit down and unwrap the very same TV dinner as a group of friends in Utah—and they could eat that meal no matter the season. As people immigrated and assimilated, their diets also adapted, and cost-friendly processed foods meant people at nearly all income brackets could enjoy a pan-fried Wonder-Bread-and-American-cheese sandwich. (Where cost barriers remain, our globalized food system has homogenized the diets of the poor. Those at low income brackets in Brazilian favelas eat many of the same processed foods as those living in subsidized New York City Housing Authority buildings.)

As such, in the 1960s, young Baby Boomers turned to fashion and music as personality markers; food was no longer the main way to express your beliefs, your heritage. Yet in the last decade, this trend has shifted once more. Food has again become a key form of identity, especially for Millennials and Gen Zers.

Young people today are increasingly likely to say that what foods they buy and eat are reflections of their personal identities. More than two-thirds of American Millennials agree that the foods they buy "say a lot about the kind of person I am," a Kantar Future Company survey found. Sixty-six percent say that what they eat and cook are significant factors in their identities.[7] In parallel but unrelated studies, nearly 60 percent of Millennials in a Scripps Media survey and 80 percent of Hungry Study respondents agree that food is an important part of their identity.

The connection between food and identity is so strong that two-thirds of the Scripps Media respondents believe that you can tell a lot about a person by what they bring to a potluck. When attending a party, the dish you bring is more important than what you wear, the vast majority agree—a stat that underlines the transition from fashion as identity marker to food.

One of the most pervasive modern food identities, one that has infiltrated global nomenclature, is the term *foodie*. According to Mintel,

62 percent of American Millennials consider themselves to be foodies and think of a sophisticated palate, cooking skills, and culinary knowledge as desirable traits.[8] The foodie identity is inspiring revolutions in food culture around the globe, as people embrace new ingredients, bold flavors, innovative dining experiences, and a passion for home cooking. In Bangkok, twentysomethings can stop in Tep Bar for cocktails made with housemade syrups and seasonal fruits, go around the corner to Teens of Thailand for a true speakeasy experience, and then down the road to Pijiu for global craft beers. In Buenos Aires, twenty- and thirty-somethings file into underground restaurants known as *puertas cerradas* for secret pop-up dinners hosted by Instagram stars and notable chefs. Across the ocean in Cape Town, foodies order matcha lattes and stop by the farmers' market for a fresh loaf of sourdough bread and a selection of artisanal cheeses.

Foodie-ism often cuts across geographic, economic, religious, and racial boundaries as a sign of education and worldliness. In China, Angela Xu of Labbrand, a global brand consultancy headquartered in Shanghai, writes that foodie culture has become an exclusive club. "There are multiple closed WeChat groups on which foodies of different levels share their recommendations and creations," she reports. "By mastering foodie culture and becoming a recognized expert, young Chinese can reach a level of projected sophistication that is usually reserved for the super smart, super beautiful, or super affluent."[9]

Parents even attempt to instill foodie-ism in their children, as they feed their Generation Alpha offspring (those born after 2010) bold flavors like kimchi, harissa, and nori and then gloat about their children's consumption of these exotic foods to anyone who will listen. Farming and cooking camps are simmering with success, and kid couture kitchen sets are the new "it" playtime item; some are outfitted with stainless steel play pots, espresso machines, and farmhouse sinks. Meanwhile, media companies celebrate and amplify kids' food knowledge with shows like *Chopped Junior*, *MasterChef Junior*, and *Kids Baking Championship*.

"It's a good time for foodie kids," Jill Colella, editor-in-chief and founder of two kids' food magazines, *Ingredient* and *Butternut*, tells *Ad Age*. "It's what Mandarin Chinese lessons were 10 years ago . . . Food literacy is a competitive advantage in our world."[10]

Foodie interest in high-end, small-batch, and unique foods is supporting the growth of the specialty food market. Those between the ages of twenty-five and forty-four are the most common purchasers of specialty food in the US, followed closely by even younger customers, ages eighteen to twenty-four, notes the Specialty Food Association.[11] This remains true no matter one's income, according to Boston Consulting Group.[12] Food is no longer viewed as sustenance, but social currency.

Many young consumers are turning away from mass-produced products and are instead looking for brands that reflect their personal values. Often, these items are created and sold locally. To support this interest, farmers' markets are expanding around the world, and locally produced goods fill grocery store shelves. Single-origin coffee, regional honey, and small-batch kombucha are just a few examples of in-demand items.

Over the last few decades, across Asia and Africa, access to Western food became a symbol of affluence. Now, many nations are turning away from the West's influence and focusing again on local talents, ingredients, and methods. While a nice dinner out used to mean a trip to a five-star Western hotel restaurant, today people are looking to younger, local chefs who utilize techniques and ingredients from the region.

"We make our own mustards, sausages, and work with local cheesemakers," Millennial hospitality marketing expert Kunal Chandra told me as he sat out on his apartment porch in the town of Noida, just outside New Delhi. At the time, he was working for a hip restaurant company with brands throughout India. "No more importing," he proclaimed of his restaurant group's sourcing methods. Instead, they source their brie and camembert from a local cheesemonger. For chocolate, the restaurant group works with Indian bean-to-bar producers. For a risotto dish, they use local short-grain rice instead of shipping in Arborio from Italy. It's time, Chandra told me, that people start celebrating the talent and resources available in India.

There is a "heightened demand for different foods" in Nairobi, Kenya, I was told by Della Mbaya, a member of the Nairobi media, "as well as a changed perspective on why we eat what we eat, and where we eat."

The biggest food trend at the moment, Mbaya said, "is multi-ethnic, derived from our own traditional food—maize and beans, chapati,

Ugali—all flipped into something new for a fresh and more experimental audience," much like the trend Chandra told of in India. Mbaya told me about "homegrown products made by young Kenyans—from chilli sauce, to marinades, to chilli flakes, to pestos and other condiments. That's where the excitement is."

Shoppers all around the world are more likely to pay a premium for local goods, and data from McCann shows that about 70 percent of global respondents say they would "rather buy local brands than global brands."[13] Why? Each purchase feeds a sense of connection with a local community or land. A 2014 Packaged Facts National Consumer Survey found that 53 percent of US adult respondents specially seek out locally grown or locally produced foods, citing freshness, a desire to support local businesses, and taste as the primary motivations.[14]

Food allows eaters to show their pride in and connection to their heritage. All around the world, indigenous cuisine is gaining praise, and global tastes are being replicated with local ingredients, creatively adapted by local talent. For many, choosing a product from their hometown fills them with pride—and a sense of connection to the place and the people who are there.

A devotion to local goods is not just a celebration of heritage, but also—and equally relevant—a rebellion against a globally homogenized food culture. Reliance on local talent and ingredients can reduce a country's economic reliance on large powerhouse nations. In Accra, Ghana, the Republic Bar and Grill serves cocktails infused with local herbs and alcohols like akpeteshie, hibiscus flower, and ginger. Their menu is described as "Nouveau-Ghanaian" and lists items like vanilla ice cream blended with fruit from the native baobab tree. "The traditional marketplace is heavily reliant on the importation of commodities—products and even services," co-owner Raja Owusu-Ansah tells *Food Tank*. "We're at a point where everything is imported, literally. The toothpick is imported, so a shift in paradigm will go very well for the economy at large. There is really no need to be importing almost everything from elsewhere, primarily because you possess the capacity to produce it," he reasons. "That's the ethos and philosophy behind our food and drink."[15]

This renewed focus on local crops and artisans is stoking a wider appreciation for *topophilia*, meaning "love of place." While our mid-twentieth-century food system thrived on mass accessibility, today's chefs are turning inward in search of inspiration. Many of the most highly acclaimed international restaurants of the last ten years have been the work of chefs who display a painstaking devotion to their homelands. At Noma, in Copenhagen, chef René Redzepi garnered worldwide acclaim for his reinvention of Nordic cuisine. Each plate celebrates the rare plant varietals of the Nordic landscape. The boyish Dane first made a name for himself in the restaurant scene by shocking diners with dishes featuring edible moss, insects, and tubers, presented in a fashion that often looks more like a small-scale nature model than a meal. When Noma moved, briefly, to Mexico, Redzepi's restaurant's dishes were as different as the new setting: Plates were filled with ingredients collected from the tropical surroundings, like melon clams, avocados, and ant eggs.

Similarly, the menu at Lima's award-winning restaurant Central encapsulates the various altitudes and ecosystems of Peru. Young Peruvian chef Virgilio Martínez Véliz builds his plates with novel grains, algae, and fruits discovered on foraging trips around his home nation. Each dish celebrates the diversity of flora and fauna blanketing the country. You could not re-create Véliz's or Redzepi's dishes anywhere else. These aren't accessible recipes, and that's a large part of the attraction.

Today, topophilia is influencing not only elite restaurant menus but coffee shop bean listings, chocolatier signs, and craft beer lists. An obsession with terroir is spreading beyond the world of wine. Now, customers can learn how the topography, climate, and soil conditions create the honey notes in their coffee, the sweetness in their bean-to-bar chocolate, or the force of the hops in their small-batch IPA.

Yet some of today's most recognizable and influential food identities embody far more particular dogmas and value systems than simple geographic affiliation or appreciation for high-end ingredients. While some eaters may casually identify themselves as "foodies" or "locavores," others are more specific about their devotions to particular ways of eating and what those regimens mean to them.

Diet Tribes

"How do you know if someone's a vegan?" a common joke goes. "Don't worry, they'll tell you."

Today, people confidently identify themselves explicitly by what they don't eat. It's not uncommon to come across a profile that reads something like, "I'm Bob, a Paleo musician from Boulder," or "I'm Suzanne, a gluten-free mama from Boise." The diet detail is included because, for many, their way of eating indicates much more than what is in their refrigerator; it's a sign of what they believe in, what they care about, and who they want to be affiliated with.

Many modern diet identities "very much parallel how people construct a racial identity and other identity domains such as religion or political orientation," Daniel Rosenfeld, then a psychology undergraduate student at Cornell University, explained to me. A vegan himself, Rosenfeld said that the experience of "going vegan" changed "how I thought about myself, how people viewed me, and my interactions." The label of veganism began to define him in a way that he had thought only race or religion had the power to.

Just like the more traditional identity markers, he noted, vegans and vegetarians share particular behaviors that many use to label themselves, and through this signify group membership. "When I meet another vegan, there's this connection—we share this social experience," Rosenfeld reflected, and this familiarity "fosters a sense of belongingness."

Rosenfeld studied veg*n (a shorthand term used when referring to both vegans and vegetarians) identities during his undergraduate years working at Cornell's Purpose and Identity Processes Laboratory, where he quickly uncovered the complexities of these new personal labels. Essentially, not all veg*ns fit the same mold.

First, he found, not all people who do not eat meat identify as vegetarian. Second, not all vegetarians entirely abstain from eating meat.[16] Confused yet?

"Eating a vegetarian diet and having a salient vegetarian identity are distinct constructs," document Rosenfeld and his advisor, Dr. Anthony Burrow, in a 2017 paper published by *Appetite*. By analyzing the thoughts, feelings, and behaviors of vegetarians, Rosenfeld and Burrow were able to decipher that the label of being a vegetarian is something separate from the actual adherence to a vegetarian diet. Vegetarianism, for some, is simply a set of practical food restrictions. These vegetarians would likely never think of attending a Find Veg Love event. For others, vegetarianism serves as a way of understanding oneself, sort of a life philosophy.[17] These folks are far more likely to seek out like-minded vegetarian partners and friends.

So, what does it mean to "be a vegetarian" or "be a vegan"? In the Western world, veg*nism is often associated with being "crunchy" or a "hippie." People often assume that all veg*ns have an activist bent, that they care deeply about animals and, perhaps, the environment.[18] Others associate it with healthism and a concern for personal nutrition. What Rosenfeld and Burrow uncovered is that while some veg*ns welcome these associations, others prefer to avoid them. So, just because someone avoids animal products doesn't mean they'll label themselves a veg*n. Likewise, someone who occasionally eats meat may call themselves a vegetarian because they want to associate with others who fit the vegetarian stereotype.

The values and behaviors associated with veg*n identities shift depending on where you live. In Hong Kong, there is a strong association among veganism, celebrity, and sustainability fads. Along the dense, stacked city streets, competing restaurant signs brag about the recent introduction of the meat-free Impossible Burger and Beyond Burger onto their menus. Chic plant-based restaurants are sprinkled throughout the city, and during my visit there, it seemed as though every stoplight had a Tesla silently hovering in neutral. While standing in line at a couture coffee shop, I picked up a copy of the wellness magazine *Liv*. The cover promoted an "indispensable guide to plant based Hong Kong life." Another magazine behind it offered a guide on "Green Weddings: How to turn your celebration into a planet-friendly affair."

While in Hong Kong, I met up with David Yeung, a vegan entrepreneur who jump-started the Green Monday movement, which encourages companies and schools to establish one meatless day a week. He is also the founder of Green Common, a chain of vegan supermarkets and restaurants in Hong Kong. He understands that not every person is motivated by the usual vegan arguments of animal rights, but believes that a global diet with fewer demands on our environment is necessary to combat climate breakdown. So, Yeung has set out to make veganism cool.

"In terms of penetrating the mainstream, [veganism] has to make people feel like a part of . . . a cool community," Yeung, a Gen Xer, explained as we sat in a Green Common dining room. In his work,

Yeung has codified a new form of vegan cool by bringing in celebrity brand ambassadors, and the Green Common establishments are blatant Instagram-fodder. Quotes decorate the mellow pink and green walls (the one behind us displayed a decal that read "Be kind to every kind"). Statistics on calories, saturated fats, water use, and carbon footprints adorn the aisles and menus and congratulate visitors on their devotion to healthier, more environmentally friendly choices.

Meanwhile, up in mainland China, vegetarianism carries an entirely different association. Though the eating rules are identical, mainland China's version of vegetarianism is inextricably linked to Buddhism. Though China is technically a secular country, vegetarian restaurants sometimes serve as a gathering place for people in search of moral and ethical guidance.[19] "Buddhist notions of karmic merit, compassion, and the protection of life permeated the pamphlets, seminars and informal discussions held at Buddhist vegetarian restaurants, despite restrictions on religious proselytising," observed social anthropologist Jakob A. Klein during his visit to vegetarian establishments in the Yunnan Province capital city of Kunming, in southwest China.[20] Zhai jie, a traditional Chinese purity meditation, talks of the vegetarian diet as a conduit to an environmentally friendly, compassionate, and frugal existence. Thus, by saying you are a vegetarian, you are also indicating that you adhere to Buddhist-like beliefs.

———————

No matter what connections a culture may have with the terms *vegan* and *vegetarian*, those who outwardly identify themselves by these diets are associating themselves with a wider group of people. They are placing themselves in a community with a shared system of beliefs and values that influence behavior and, in a way, finding a substitute for the group associations, once more commonly provided by religion or tribes or political affiliations, that are essential to our well-being. By developing a strong connection to one's way of eating, people are taking on a set of rules that helps them identify what to believe and how to behave. It also makes it easier to find others with belief systems that match your own.

In the Hungry Study, we found that those whose diets are motivated by belief systems tend to feel a camaraderie with others who follow their way of eating. We call this group of eaters Pro-Social Dieters, since they take on certain diets because of animal rights, environmental concerns, or another ardent ethos. Rosenfeld uncovered a similar finding in his own research among vegans. When people embody a strong vegan identity, they hold on to it and embody it with fervor, he told me. This affiliation makes vegans more prone to crave connection with other vegans and, as Rosenfeld found in a small online survey, exhibit positive feelings toward those who share their diet—their "ingroup," to use the psychology term.

The inverse also holds true: Those who hold strong diet identities are more judgmental of those who eat differently—their "outgroup."[21] In our study, 50 percent of Pro-Social Dieters said that they are bothered when people eat foods that go against their way of eating.* Likewise, Rosenfeld found that those with a strong vegan identity evaluate non vegans more negatively.

This negative bias, at times, spurs controversy among diet groups. Some people argue that their diet is "right" and other diets are "wrong." Within the veg*n communities, a battle between animal rights and animal welfare takes center stage.

"You can't really be motivated by animal rights and still be vegetarian, unless you're not aware of the fact that animals are used for eggs and dairy," one vegan explained to me with more than a tinge of condescension. While vegetarians believe in animal welfare—that people should minimize animal suffering and be mindful of their experiences—vegans are proponents of animal rights, believing that animals have the autonomous right to life and that people should not use animals as commodities. This is why vegans disapprove of animal testing for beauty products as well as the consumption of eggs and dairy.

Find Veg Love's founders are all too aware of the tension between vegetarians and vegans. Some vegan speed daters have requested vegan-only events, a move that Charbonneau and Brighten had initially resisted. "As a business, we serve anyone who's vegan or vegetarian equally," the duo was careful to clarify to me when we first spoke. "We

---

* Nearly three-quarters of Hungry Study Pro-Social Dieters also agreed that they feel bad about themselves when they stray from their chosen diet, a sign that their way of eating is a value system standard they attempt to uphold for themselves.

don't prioritize one or the other or anything like that, so everything that we do is open to both." It felt like they were walking the PR tightrope, afraid of being accused of vegetarian bigotry.

These ingroup/outgroup mentalities are commonly observed among people of a particular heritage, race, or religion, but such ardent ingroup/ outgroup behavior among dieters is something rather new.

"Is it possible," I asked Rosenfeld, "that we're seeing these passionate diet identities gain in popularity because religious identities are falling out of favor?"

The benefit of belonging to a group, Rosenfeld explained, is that it promotes one's self-esteem by providing a sense of relatedness of identity and security. "So, yes," he replied. "When people would, say, become less religious, they would be inclined to compensate in another identity domain and make that one more central to who they are." As our traditional ways of communing and self-identifying are disrupted, we're forced to look elsewhere. And today, people are looking to food.

After all, it's not just vegans and vegetarians who are forming their personal identities around their diets. Another identity gaining followers is the Paleo diet. Paleo centers around the concept of eating only those foods that were available to humans during the Paleolithic era, which began about 2.6 million years ago and thus predates agriculture and all forms of food processing. Also called the "caveman diet," the doctrine excludes modern dietary additions such as dairy products, grains, sugar, legumes, processed oils, salt, alcohol, and coffee. According to the founder of the Paleo concept, Loren Cordain, just over half of one's daily calories should come from seafood and lean meats, with the remaining calories derived from fruits, vegetables, nuts, and seeds.

Since its debut in 2002, the Paleo diet has transformed the consumer packaged goods marketplace. Although the term *Paleo* is still found on less than 1 percent of US menus, its prevalence on menus grew by 77 percent between 2014 and 2018, according to research from Datassential, and strategy firm IRI Worldwide estimates that the Paleo market will reach $4 billion by 2020.[22] The fad has spurred an interest in meat snacks—like jerky and biltong—as well as bone broth, a product that saw its US sales triple to $19.7 million between 2016 and 2017.

Soon after its introduction, the Paleo credo gained popularity among Silicon Valley residents, who buoyed sales and deluged social media with posts about the doctrine. The obsession falls squarely within the big tech interest in biohacking, and the diet quickly became affiliated with sister fads like intermittent fasting, Bulletproof coffee, Cross-Fit weight training, and nootropic supplements, which transformed the diet from weight-loss tactic to lifestyle.

Like veganism, the Paleo diet has clear-cut principles and rituals. "There's a sort of evolutionary philosophy which underpins [the Paleo diet]," doctoral student Tim Squirrell mused over the phone from his home in Edinburgh, Scotland, citing the diet's anthropological rationalizations.

At the time of our conversation, Squirrell had spent over two and a half years studying the social dynamics of online fitness and nutrition communities, with a particular interest in the Paleo community, and had decided to make it the central theme of his PhD at the School of Social and Political Sciences at the University of Edinburgh. His research has focused on analyzing conversations held on the user forum Reddit.

Soon after his research began, Squirrell observed a stark difference in online behaviors among diet groups. While some people, such as those on the keto diet, seemed to be drawn to their diet as a swift weight-loss tactic, Squirrell noted that the conversations taking place on Paleo community boards had a more ideological bent. He found people talking about diet as a lifestyle and a belief system. He also noticed a proselytization element, in which people tried to bring others aboard, as well as frequent conversation of things being "sinful" and "indulgent" or "clean" and "pure." These same words, he noted, "wouldn't seem out of place in a religious service or sermon." With this religion-like ideology in place, the emphasis on weight loss, he said, is almost entirely "stripped away."

He also began to observe "intra-community conflicts" between types of Paleo dieters, just like the ones Rosenfeld and the Find Veg Love founders saw between vegetarians and vegans. Squirrell saw bickering and tension building among members who advocate different interpretations of the same Paleo dogma.

"Like Catholics and Protestants?" I asked him.

"Exactly!" Squirrell replied with enthusiasm.

Paleo food blogger Michelle Tam has seen the same friction among her Nom Nom Paleo followers. "My basic tenets revolve around eating great, healthy fats, more vegetables, and well-raised protein," but, she noted, she does not follow these rules hard and fast, and she has noticed that some of her fans have an issue with her flexible interpretation of the rules.

"Nuance is something that people have issues with, and context. The recipes that I put up on my blog are Paleo and Whole30 friendly, but on Instagram, I might visit a gluten-free bakery and post a picture of a gluten-free cupcake." Posts like these, she told me, cause some of her fans to cry foul, noting the Paleo taboo of eating anything made with dairy products or added sugar. "They're okay with a Paleo pancake" made with coconut or almond flour, "but freak when there's a potato in something," Tam said.

Daniel Rosenfeld says reactions like this are the result of "identity threat." Again, one of the core reasons we associate with group identities is to help fortify our own personal identities, so when a member of our group does something that we don't agree with, it can feel like an attack on that personal identity; when an ingroup member violates a norm—like no dairy—it can threaten the overall group dynamic, a pattern Squirrell continues to watch unfold on Reddit, while Tam sees it in her Instagram comments section.

Divisions within the Paleo community continue to proliferate in part, said Squirrell, because of the wellness leaders who found new sects, if you will, of the Paleo ideology. For some, social media influencers are not just virtual friends or examples of perfection—sometimes, they take on the role of spiritual and moral leaders as well.

Wellness Gurus

"The most important part" of what these wellness influencers do, researcher Alexandra Boutopoulou told me as she leaned forward at her desk in her home office in the UK, is that they "talk a lot about a promise of a good life, of a healthy life, which means essentially a longer life." Although, she admits, most personalities do not explicitly promise a longer life, "they talk a lot about being healthy, and being healthy means not being sick, and not being sick suggests that you don't die." Here, Boutopoulou introduced an element of influencer culture that I had not yet considered. Beyond a stand-in for our friendship needs, perhaps many of these color-filtered talking heads are also modern stand-ins for the social roles once filled by shamans, priests, and rabbis, guiding people on how to live their best lives. At times, the draw of these wellness personalities stretches beyond community and into the realm of doctrine leaders.

"I'm not sure if you know this," Boutopoulou said, but Deliciously Ella's blog, like the blogs of "loads of other wellness bloggers," began with a story of illness. In 2011, Mills was diagnosed with a rare medical condition called postural orthostatic tachycardia syndrome, an ailment that kept her in and out of the hospital for months while she battled digestive and cardiac issues.

With little success managing her symptoms through Western medicine, Mills began to experiment with her food and lifestyle choices. When she began her journey into medicinal treatments, she had no cooking skills and no knowledge of plant-based eating, and was feeling deflated and hopeless, she notes on her website. But she channeled what little energy she had into creative kitchen choices. This was the start of her career as a food blogger. She documented her struggles, successes, and failures on DeliciouslyElla.com, which eventually earned her over 130 million site visits. Plant-based living, writes Mills, "gave me my life and health back." And, she notes, it can do the same for you.

There's a common allegorical trope known as the "monomyth" or "hero's journey," in which a character experiences personal transformation by overcoming an internal or external obstacle. These tales of crisis, victory, and transformation are a recurring archetype found throughout folklore and modern fairy tales. Think: Katniss Everdeen, Lisbeth Salander, Luke Skywalker, and Simba. Or Moses, Christ, and Siddhartha. In each allegory, an individual faces a physical or emotional challenge and emerges from their journey a changed person, ready to share their learnings—be it the power of the Force or how to reach Nirvana—with the greater world.

Many wellness bloggers promote personal stories that fit the monomyth archetype. Wellness guru and Oprah favorite Kris Carr is the author of the award-winning Crazy Sexy Cancer book series and uses her story of overcoming cancer—allegedly via the adoption of a plant-based diet—to promote anyone's ability to take charge of their "health and happiness by adopting a plant-passionate diet," along with other lifestyle changes.[23]

Meanwhile, Whole30 founder Melissa Hartwig, arguably the most influential wellness blogger of the 2010s, openly discusses her past battles with drug use and positions clean eating as her avenue to a healthier life. "I smoked weed all the time, I did a lot of acid, I dabbled in coke, but the thing I really liked was ecstasy, especially in combination with other things," Hartwig recounts in an interview with the addiction and recovery publication *The Fix*.[24] "I particularly found X and heroin to be brutally effective at completely wiping out every thought of my real life—which is what messed me up the most, of course." Now, she says, "My addiction and recovery experience play a huge role in how I support people who are doing the Whole30." One recurring Whole30 tagline is: "Quitting heroin is hard. Beating cancer is hard. Drinking your coffee black. Is. Not. Hard."[25] The Whole30 website has an entire article series called "Coming Clean" that focuses on overcoming addiction and eating disorders, and how to change your habits. Each of these wellness promoters, said Boutopoulou, talks about how others can borrow elements from their own experience "in order to create different lives, or in order to make their lives better and change their lifestyles."

Hartwig, Squirrell observed, "literally calls herself a headmistress," and with her "tough love doctrine," speaks to her followers "like a wayward flock, like a preacher would."

Michelle Tam's Nom Nom Paleo founder story reflects this hero archetype as well. After moving to the suburbs with her family, Tam vowed to lose her "muffin top" and borrowed from the tried-and-true diet methods of counting calories and exercising. But after a year or so, her results were not satisfactory. Meanwhile, her husband, Henry Fong, discovered the intense cross-training program P90X and "the whole primal movement." He came home and told her, "There's this way of eating that sounds kind of crazy: It's kind of the opposite of what we're doing." At first, she thought he was nuts. But "he got a six-pack right away, which was super annoying," she recalled.

On the Paleo diet, Tam felt like they had discovered a hidden health secret. "I felt like I was in the Matrix," she reminisced with excitement. "I was like, 'Why don't people talk about this?'" Tam and Fong decided to start a Tumblr page to document their Paleo diet and workout successes.

Fong styled the site with a red, white, and black bitmoji that slightly resembles Tam; the icon's tongue sticks out irreverently and the ovular face is framed by two long black pigtails. At first, the couple didn't expect anyone to read the blog; a few years later, the site was doing so well that Tam was able to quit her decade-and-a-half-long career as a nighttime hospital pharmacist (or "zombie drug dealer," as she put it) to focus entirely on the Nom Nom Paleo brand.

Now, the spunky fortysomething has two *New York Times*–bestselling cookbooks under her belt, an award-winning cooking app, and over three million website page views a month. In January 2018, her brand took over hot bars at Whole Foods Markets around the US, where shoppers could grab "Nom Nom Paleo To Go" dishes, each selected from her cookbook. Around the rest of the store, bright yellow "Nom Nom Paleo Pick" signs were attached to Tam's favorite Paleo-friendly products, like sugar-free dry-rubbed bacon and coconut aminos. With these labeled guides, followers could shop the Paleo lifestyle with ease.

Individuals who speak about personal transformation are becoming "figureheads" of new Paleo sects, Squirrell said. Each successful wellness personality "seems to fit this sort of mold: They use scientific language, but not too much; make it accessible to the layperson—interpret the scriptures, I suppose—and overall, be a charismatic figure, but one who is approachable." And each creates their own, slightly unique dogma for their followers to sign on to. Whole30 is an offshoot of the Paleo diet. Other Paleo variations allow dairy, while some, like Tam's, preach the importance of intermittent fasting (which, she told me, is shown to reduce one's risk of breast cancer). Some emphasize the importance of physical activity in the lifestyle and encourage followers to sign up for a membership at CrossFit or join an Ironman race. Meanwhile, traditionalists stick to the original Loren Cordain dogma, unwilling to accept any variation. Still others travel whole-hog down the keto rabbit hole and give up all Paleo association along the way, like a Unitarian Universalist becoming an Evangelical Christian.

Diet communities fulfill group identity needs and direct people on what to eat, how to behave, and often what to think. In this way, many of today's most popular diets fulfill our desires to belong and identify with a group.

"Is Paleo a religion?" I asked Tam.

She paused and with her inimitable humor replied, "Well, I'm an atheist. But yes, it is a religion."

––––––––––––

We are tribal beings who increasingly find ourselves without a tribe. With fewer pillars of identity to attach ourselves to, but the same core need for community identity, we are finding our sense of self through what we do—and do not—eat. Whether we label ourselves as pescatarians, or take pride in local cuisine, or learn all we can about Chemex coffee, more and more people are expressing their values and beliefs through food choices. And importantly, we are using those interests to connect with others, be it through speed dating or simply joining a Reddit board of sourdough bread bakers.

Still, calling oneself a "foodie" or an intermittent faster is often not enough to fulfill all our belonging needs. We need something tangible, something real. Just as an emoji is no substitute for seeing a loved one's smile, a Reddit board exchanging Paleo diet tips is not able to make us feel sufficiently connected to others. While we may feel understood, and proud of our contributions, we are beings who evolved to spend time together in person. Our needs extend beyond self-esteem and personal identity.

And so, many people are putting down their phones to pick up a fork, a rope, or a yoga mat, and are heading out into the world to interact with people, eye to eye, bar seat next to bar seat, Warrior I alongside Warrior I.

CHAPTER SEVEN

shared experiences & relatedness

S hreya Soni hid out of sight in a darkened corner of the restaurant, peering out at the table of twenty-eight guests. In the weeks prior, each invitee had received an email from a mysterious person named "Stevie" informing them that they had been chosen to attend the Delhi Secret Supper Club. Now, here they were, a group of complete strangers who had all RSVPed yes to a dinner despite not knowing who had invited them, sitting down for a meal together in South New Delhi at a pan-Asian restaurant called Shiro.

The restaurant was palatial, with ceilings well above thirty feet high. Red up-lighting illuminated the dimly lit room, and imposing statues of the Buddhist goddess Tara—tall enough for her crown to nearly touch the wood latticed ceiling—overlooked the dining tables. Small sculpted faces of Gautama Buddha, with long earlobes and curly hair, flanked the walls.

The grandiose environment only added to the thrill. As the group of twenty-, thirty-, and fortysomething guests arrived, Soni, then in her mid-twenties, watched her social experiment unfold. She had researched each person, their interests and dislikes, what they did for a living, and where they had studied. If they seemed interesting, their names and contact information were added to a spreadsheet and, eventually, a select few were invited to the launch event.

To Soni's amazement and delight, the dinner lasted four hours. Just as she had anticipated, breaking bread with others became a social lubricant. Entrepreneurs, designers, artists, chefs, activists, CEOs, and homemakers—strangers all—shared in conversation. The usual bondage of social cliques unraveled before her eyes. She knew she had a repeat concept on her hands, and guests were soon clamoring for a follow-up meal.

Shortly, the number of events, and the invite list, snowballed. Initial attendees recommended others who would like to attend. The mystery of the dinner's founder didn't matter. In fact, it added to the allure. Who had deemed them worthy of such an exclusive invitation? Those who participated were flattered that this well-connected individual thought of *them*. And those who hadn't received invites asked their friends to go to bat for them, and explain why they would be a good addition to the supper experience.

"South Delhi thrives on exclusivity," Soni explained of her decision to host the events in secrecy in Delhi's thriving urban area. The concept originated around 2013 when she returned to Delhi after completing her studies in London and felt that "weekend after weekend" was spent "having the same set of conversations with the same set of people." In London, the concept of a dinner club was already well established. There, at least eighty versions had taken root that offered meals in basements, on the London Tube, or in people's homes, all with different themes. But the idea had yet to arrive in India. With Delhi Secret Supper Club, all that changed.

Today, Delhi Secret Supper Club has transformed into DSSC, an events website and company with an "exclusive member base," though DSSC still runs invitation-only dinners as well. Soni revealed her identity four years into running the company.

With DSSC, Soni feels that she is helping people close their computers, turn off their phones, and get out into the world to meet people and simply enjoy the moment. "We're so deeply engrained in the digital world, a lot of people want to break away, and they want on-ground, real-time, real-life experiences," she told me, citing this craving for real-world connection as the reason for her success.

IRL Needs

French sociologist Émile Durkheim believed that sharing experiences with others is an essential part of human life. In 1912, Durkheim broke with the conventions of his time by arguing that any form of shared social practice—not *just* religion—can serve as a societal glue, and create an energy, an electric charge, that bonds us to one another.* Durkheim created a term for this sense of camaraderie, calling it "collective effervescence." Perhaps you have felt this kind of sensation at sports events, political rallies, or even during color war at summer camp—a shared energy connecting you to those around you. This physical and emotional response to a shared experience, Durkheim believed, is necessary for any functioning society, and serves as the foundation of belonging.

What Durkheim couldn't have known at the time is that this sense of "bonding" was not caused by an electric charge, but the release of neurochemicals such as endorphins—the same neurochemical produced with eye-to-eye contact that Dr. Dunbar spoke of.[1] Activities like eating, laughing, singing, and dancing with others fill us with these feel-good chemicals. Seeing someone else smile can trigger a genuine sense of joy, relaxation, and contentment, and the hormones released during these real-life interactions facilitate a sense of trust that helps us bond to one another.[2]

Humans have evolved over millions of years in a world that relies on in-person social interactions. We are hardwired to read and respond to others' bodies. We notice one another's posture, tone of voice, facial expressions, physical tics, and scent. Creasing around the eyes, the movement of eyebrows, and the length of sustained eye contact can communicate a world's worth of encouragement, shame, or seduction. A light touch of someone's hand can be playful, flirtatious, powerful, or soothing.† We learn how to be empathetic and develop intrapersonal

---

* "What essential difference is there between an assembly of Christians celebrating the principal dates of the life of Christ or of Jews remembering the exodus from Egypt . . . and a reunion of citizens commemorating the promulgation of a new moral or legal system or some great event in the national life?" asks Durkheim in *The Elementary Forms of Religious Life*.

† In fact, our perception of touch is so nuanced that, in one study, two strangers, separated by a barrier but able to touch each other's forearms, were able to accurately interpret expressions of anger, fear, disgust, love, gratitude, and sympathy at above-chance levels, simply through touch. For more, see "Touch Communicates Distinct Emotions" by Matthew J. Hertenstein et al, published in the academic journal *Emotion* in 2006.

emotional skills by spending time with others.* Shared in-person experiences color our lives, bringing in a soundtrack and a rhythm for us to feel and see and hear. And no technology will ever be able to stand in for these elements of in-person interaction—a truth that many of us seem to recognize implicitly.

While much breath—and many pages of this book—have been spent discussing the youth attachment to technology, the true secret of the Digital Age generation is that, although they're sometimes held back by anxieties, they prefer in-person experiences over online. In a survey conducted by the Girl Scout Research Institute, 92 percent of their young female respondents noted that they would rather spend an hour socializing with their friends in person than socializing through their favorite social networking site.[3] Similarly, generational researcher Noreena Hertz writes that 80 percent of her surveyed Millennial subjects "prefer spending time with their friends in person rather than on the phone or online."[4]

As screen-based interactions take up more and more of our time, there is a counter-movement underway. Though most cultural shifts are pushing people toward more isolated days, a boomerang industry is simultaneously ratcheting up that creates spaces and opportunities for people to put their phones away and make eye contact—both with friends and strangers.

---

* Cues like voice, touch, and eye contact are learned. Some scientists are finding that without constant exposure to tone of voice, touch, and eye contact, children are not developing the ability to pick up on key social cues needed for empathy and judgment. The prefrontal cortex, a part of our brain that is critical for interpreting human emotion, doesn't fully develop until a person's mid-twenties and can, some studies are showing, be thrown off course by constant distraction and less in-person contact. Preliminary research suggests that children who communicate mainly through devices are growing inept at interpreting nonverbal cues. For more, see: "Face Time vs. Screen Time: The Technological Impact on Communication" by Chandra Johnson in *Deseret News*, and "Five Days at Outdoor Education Camp without Screens Improves Preteen Skills with Nonverbal Emotion Cues" by Yalda T. Uhls et al, published in the academic journal *Computers in Human Behavior* in October 2014.

The Experience Economy

"I would rather live a life filled with great experiences than a life filled with beautiful possessions," agree 73 percent of eighteen- to thirty-five-year-olds around the world, according to a survey by creative agency McCann.[5] In response to a culture focused on the individual, young people are increasingly opting to spend their limited cash not on houses and cars, but on shared, in person experiences like festivals, overseas travel, Jeffersonian dinners, and community-centric gyms. Events company Eventbrite found that 78 percent of American Millennials now choose to spend money on experiences over material items, and 55 percent of those surveyed by the company say they are spending more on events and live experiences now than ever before.[6] This particular Millennial and Gen Z spending habit has become so influential that it has garnered its own title: the experience economy.

While we can conjure a sense of connectedness over social media and boost our self-esteem with posts, no virtual exchange will ever adequately fulfill our needs for connectedness. For that, we must spend time engaging with others face-to-face, and the experience economy reflects a growing desire for in-person, intimate interactions.

Concepts like DSSC are proliferating around the globe. At these dinner clubs, conversations are nearly always table-wide, not cordoned between those who already know one another. "Family-style," tapas, or meze plates are passed around and, often, the chef will engage with guests, and sometimes dine alongside them. At Buenos Aires' puertas cerradas, chefs often invite diners into their homes.

"People want to have a special moment and have a direct interaction with the chef," says Magdalena Bermúdez about the popularity of these private eateries.[7] Bermúdez is co-founder of Cookapp, an app that allows users to cull through the hundreds of puertas cerradas currently in the market to find an underground dinner of their choosing.

This public craving for greater intimacy has also influenced restaurant design. Sometimes it feels like every "hip" restaurant now utilizes community tables, shared plates, and open kitchens in their design schemes. Kappo dining, a concept that originated in Japan, in which the chef stands behind a counter and serves a small group of customers, has become popularized around the world. Many modern restaurants have knocked down walls and opened their kitchens to the dining rooms, which allows patrons to watch as their meals are charred, basted, and tossed together.

Some new establishments take personalization and intimacy to the extreme. As one example, an itsy-bitsy speakeasy opened in New York in 2017 called The Threesome Tollbooth that fits (you guessed it!) only three people: one bartender and two patrons. There, a ninety-minute custom-cocktail tasting session will run you about $100 per person.

This same demand is transforming the travel industry. Millennials are a wanderlust generation, with many dedicating their time, attention, and money on exploring the globe.* According to Airbnb, nearly two-thirds of Millennials globally say that regular travel is an important part of their lives, and, much like food, prioritize spending on travel over buying a home or paying off debt.[8] And, indeed, Millennials spend more money on travel than members of other generations.[9] But how people travel, and the activities they engage in while abroad, are markedly different than in the past, altered by this unfed hunger for IRL human connection.

"People don't want to be tourists. They want to be travelers," twentysomething Eatwith co-owner Camille Rumani told me. Young globetrotters seek to "live as the locals do": eat local food, stay in local homes, and visit sites that the locals—not the tourists—frequent.[10] Eatwith is a community dinner company that has worked with over twenty-five thousand hosts in 130 countries to create meal experiences in the hosts' homes. Eatwith derives most of their business from travelers on the hunt for more personal and off-the-beaten-path culinary experiences. They also serve as a meeting point for those traveling, and often eating, alone.

In fact, many young jetsetters travel alone, finding that solo travel can bring opportunities to meet more local residents. A solitary adventure encourages one to talk with strangers and say yes to new, unplanned experiences. For many Millennial and Gen Z globetrotters,

---

* *US News and World Report*'s 2014 U.S. News Market Insights "Millennial Report" reveals that Millennials are the most common readers of the travel section, far surpassing Gen Xers and Baby Boomers.

travel is not about museums and monuments; it's about the immersive cultural journey.

This drive for "authentic" experiences has catapulted Airbnb, the home-sharing site, to success as a hospitality industry powerhouse. With a valuation at well over $30 billion, Airbnb far exceeds the worth of long-established hotel chains like Hyatt or Marriott, all without owning any actual property. The company has hosted over four hundred million guests in over 191 countries, and garnered fanfare worldwide by meeting the consumer demand for personal and nontraditional travel experiences. (HVS, a hospitality consultancy, estimates that hotels lose approximately $450 million in direct revenues per year to Airbnb.[11]) Airbnb has also launched an "Experiences" portal, where travelers can find local classes and tours to attend. The days of boarding a tour bus are long gone. People want to be given a tuk-tuk, a camel, or a moped instead, and led to a secret underground restaurant, hidden waterfall, religious ceremony, or local artisan class. Travelers want to be immersed and to bond with those around them.

This desire for more shared in-person experiences is even influencing our working environments back at home, in our day-to-day lives. Around the world, dozens of companies rent out desks and offices in shared spaces that come with perks like community kitchens, group yoga classes, and calendars brimming with events. As of January 2019, co-working company WeWork boasted four hundred thousand members in 425 locations in twenty-seven countries.[*] [12] At nearly every WeWork location—from Lima to Jakarta—people can enjoy coffee and kombucha on tap, partake in organized fitness classes, and attend holiday parties. ("You're not building work space," WeWork co-founder Miguel McKelvey is quoted telling his staff. "You're here building a new infrastructure to rebuild social fabric and rebuild up the potential for human connection."[13])

Of late, WeWork has decided to extend their business beyond the 9-to-5 to cover "after hours" at home through their concept WeLive, which capitalizes on a growing trend called co-living. All around the world, co-living concepts that offer shared apartments or homes

---

[*] It should be noted that, in September of 2019, WeWork's initial public offering collapsed and the company was bailed out by their largest investor, SoftBank.

are reeling in community-starved individuals. In China, a variety of companies (like Mofang Gongyu, Harbour Apartments, and YOU+ International Youth Community) are quickly filling up with young professionals in Tier 1 and Tier 2 cities. In London, some five hundred people live in the Collective, where they can enjoy organized clubs and outings, communal kitchens, dining rooms, lounges, and gyms. From residents of Iyf in Singapore to tenants at Quarters in Berlin, Germany, many are shunning the solo lifestyle for one with roommates, book clubs, and potlucks.

Even if some of our relatedness needs are met through influencer culture, "likes," and loose affiliations such as diet tribes, there remains a greater need for intimacy and connectedness, for building up one's self-esteem and defining one's identity, that can be fulfilled only in person. As more and more people begin to recognize the hunger inside them for living IRL, immersive experiences are luring people outside their "Netflix and binge," smartphone-anchored lifestyles for moments of communal exploration, excitement, and fun. The businesses of the experience economy offer conduits to meet these belonging needs, be it around the dinner table . . . or atop a stationary bicycle.

Sweat Tribes

When I lived in New York City, I often felt tribeless—that is, until I laced up my sneakers and walked into the gym where everyone knew my name. There, only a handful of classes were offered each day, and the same crowd showed up every week, myself included. Between burpees, mountain climbers, and box jumps, we would offer high fives, yell out encouragements, and catch up on each other's latest career changes or vacations. I hugged the instructors hello and high-fived them goodbye.

I am one of many people participating in the booming boutique gym industry. While the early 2000s were glory years for big-box gyms like Barry's Bootcamp, Crunch Fitness, and Life Time, the 2010s saw memberships shift from mega-gyms with pools, rock walls, and personal training staff to smaller gyms with intimate class sizes and personable instructors. The new boutique gym culture emphasizes the relationships built both among attendees and between clients and instructors. People show up to work alongside the same group of people, week after week. Instructors learn your particular strengths, weaknesses, and goals.

Between 2010 and 2014, boutique fitness studios became the fastest-growing part of the US health club industry. By 2015, the industry was generating $25.8 billion in revenue annually, up from $20.4 billion in 2010, largely thanks to the growing popularity of specialty gyms like CrossFit, Pure Barre, and Orangetheory. During that same time, membership at cycling studios, such as Flywheel and SoulCycle, exploded by 70 percent, according to the International Health, Racquet, and Sportsclub Association.[14]

Many modish gyms supply attendees with little more than the necessary equipment—be it a stationary bike or a treadmill—and a cheerleader. Indeed, nearly all classes offer routines one could do at home, with one's own equipment (if any, at all, is actually required), in front of the television, a la Richard Simmons or Jane Fonda. Still, these gyms command fees of around $35 per class, a steep fare for a weekly, if not daily, habit.

Why do people shell out all that cash to pedal in a dark room with forty other people? The answer seems to be as simple as: to pedal with forty other people. Many of us sign up to run alongside a stranger, or grunt in unison as we lift a barbell above our heads, because there is something viscerally satisfying about a real-life shared experience, especially one that pushes us to our physical limits.

At many of these trendy gyms, a feeling of collective effervescence is conjured through shared pain. Often, as soon as class begins, the previously friendly trainers suddenly morph into drill instructors. I recall my first visit to a barre class in New York City, where I was stunned by the difficulty and intensity of a class that had required the purchase of $15 padded socks. (Contrary to what one may think, barre is not a dance class; it is a move-as-little-as-possible class where isometric exercises ever so slightly, twist by agonizing twist, turn your muscles into fit, flauntable trophies.) There, on the carpeted floor, I faced an instructor who screamed into a microphone looped around her head like a pop star in an arena. A nightclub soundtrack blasted in the room and hammered against my eardrums. My heart vibrated with the bass rhythms. As the class progressed, the women around me winced and sweated and lifted their three-pound weights, following the commands of the feath-erweight instructor. I could see their muscles quivering.

Many people thrive on the intense culture around these popular workouts. Boot camp instructors yell, clap, and stomp their feet as they demand one, no two, more burpees. Spin instructors order you to push harder as you pedal your way to Bella Hadid form. Be it a one-hour P90X class or a day-long Tough Mudder obstacle course, people revel in the struggle, the chance that they may not make it to the end. Throwing up or passing out, or potentially both, are completely viable options in many of today's boutique gym experiences.*

A population of privileged, warless Millennials without actual bat-tles to fight are creating the proxy of war for themselves: the inten-sity, the physical strain, a sergeant in fluorescent spandex demanding that they try harder, go faster. Many are proud of their perseverance and dedication. They set themselves up for battle and made it through. Oorah! And in that shared struggle, the quivering, sweating people pull closer not just to victory, but to one another.

Collective Effervescence

Many of the most successful experience economy concepts—in and out-side the fitness world—are those that conjure collective effervescence by placing people in situations that are unique and thrilling. In dining, some seek out shared experiences that push them far past their com-fort zones by stripping away elements like gravity, light, or clothing. At various Dinner in the Sky locations worldwide, up to twenty-two diners are strapped into their seats and hoisted 150 feet in the air for a culi-nary afternoon during which they are served a meal by chefs who bal-ance on a center platform. At Dinner in the Dark events, which also run in locations around the globe, patrons are forced to forgo their sense of sight and rely solely on smell, sound, taste, and touch to experience their meals and absorb their surroundings (not to mention find their forks).

---

* I've actually had someone throw up next to me during a hot yoga class, perhaps the perfect example of today's fitness ferocity. I mean, really . . . puking during *yoga*?

In London, a naked dinner pop-up commanded a waitlist of forty-six thousand people who wished to eat in the nude.

"I'm in a candlelit London restaurant, sitting opposite a total stranger on a workday afternoon, and we're both completely naked," writes Barry Neild for CNN of his experience at the nudist pop-up.[15] "But what should be an awkward moment, getting unclothed with a complete stranger, proves to be anything but. Unable to resort to looking at our phones, we chat unreservedly."

One can imagine that dining with people in the air, in the dark, or in the nude may be more memorable, and create more immediate connections between us, than a kitchen table meal. Right away, you feel a shared energy linking you with those around you, as you each throw yourselves into a shared experience in a novel environment.

Meanwhile, as several of the most popular fitness fads do, dozens of unique business concepts are tapping into friendly competition as a means of forging collective effervescence. Some of these establishments hark back to the "good ol' days" of our pre-digital childhoods and require that groups work together, thereby expediting bonding. Friends, co-workers, or even strangers gather for Escape the Room challenges where they have to work as a team to find clues and de-riddle codes to MacGyver their grand release from a locked room. In recent years, an axe-throwing bar, rock-climbing gym, skateboard park, fencing gym, bocce court, indoor shuffleboard court, and karaoke bar all opened up shop around my home in Brooklyn—business concepts that require some digital detachment and are targeted at my neighborhood's twenty- and thirtysomething matcha latte–drinking, man-bunned, Uber-taking residents.

Many of these modish enterprises aim to bring out the kid inside each of us. Some fitness trends capitalized on obstacle courses that borrow from gym class classics like climbing rope. Various social clubs require dressing up in themed costumes, completing scavenger hunts, or taking part in truth-or-dare challenges. Some twenty- and thirtysomethings are even attending weekend-long adult camps where they can indulge their inner "kidult" with tug-of-war, archery, and lanyard weaving.

Board games are also making a comeback.[16] In 2017, games and puzzles represented over 40 percent of total toy industry gains, with adult games leading the growth.[17] And globally, board game and jigsaw puzzle sales grew by 8 percent in 2016 to become the world's fastest-growing toy category.[18] That year, the bestselling adult game was Speak Out, a wacky board game that asks players to say certain phrases after inserting a plastic mouth expander that makes you look a bit like a cartoon rendition of Batman's toothy Joker. Teammates then have to guess what it is their companions are saying through their Cheshire Cat grins. The game generates experiences that will later conjure the phrase, "You had to be there."

"Individually, then collectively, we realized the virtual world could never provide us with enough bandwidth to associate with each other the way we want," Bernie De Koven, a computer game designer and "fun theorist," tells journalist David Sax in *The Revenge of Analog: Real Things and Why They Matter*, as he explains the resurgence of analog community games. "There's never going to be a virtual environment as completely engaging as the physical environment is. It is so much more engaging to play a game of chess face to face than it is online. Online is a good substitute when we can't meet. The ultimate contest is when you see each other face to face; see each other sweat and squirm."[19]

As in Dr. Brian Primack's comparisons of Apple Jacks to apples and Wii skiing to a real downhill slope, a virtual game can certainly entertain but will never create the same belly laughs, fierce competition, and endorphin-triggering smiles that an in-person game of Cards Against Humanity, Charades, or Twister can.

Many of the group experiences discussed in this chapter help create that intangible connective energy between people that Durkheim described. At a dinner club, it's the secret, unique experience partaken in by only the very few in the room. At a meditation class, it's thirty people exhaling in unison. At a barre class, it's the shared anguish of every little thigh squeeze. Collective effervescence is ignited through a shared goal, shared pain, or shared novel experience. Yet, through these energetic experiences, another belonging need is met: By challenging ourselves within a group, we're able to build up our own self-esteem and sense of worth.

Self-Worth

One of the major benefits of belonging is the ability to conjure feelings of worth by contributing to others. This sense of competence builds our self-esteem and sense of purpose. "We have what we may call the desire for reputation or prestige . . . recognition, attention, importance or appreciation," writes Maslow. "Satisfaction of the self-esteem need leads to feelings of self confidence, worth, strength, capability and adequacy of being useful and necessary in the world."[20] In many of these classes, people support their teammates and often rely on one another to achieve their ultimate goal.

At CrossFit, peer encouragement plays a key role in the success of the business model. "No one's finished until everyone is finished," my sister tells me of her CrossFit experience. "If someone is doing something really difficult and it's taking them longer to complete a set, the rest of us cheer that person on until they make it through."

CrossFit describes itself not as a gym, but as a "lifestyle" marked by high-intensity weight and interval training paired with a Paleo-like diet that shuns sugar and most starches. The business was founded by former gymnast Greg Glassman, who opened his first gym in 1995. Today, there are over fifteen thousand CrossFit "boxes" in over 160 countries. (The second most popular gym is Planet Fitness, which has just over 1,600 locations worldwide.)

As a franchise, each CrossFit location is tailored to the local clientele, but the basic model stays consistent: challenging workouts with a positive but militaristic intensity. Members keep track of their achievements and future goals on gym chalkboards. Participants rally each other through the pain of ten more squats or five more pull-ups and ring bells when they've surpassed a personal record. The comradeship and positive spirit keep people coming back for more.

"The two most striking things about CrossFitters are their evangelical enthusiasm and the way they hold one another to account . . . CrossFit expects members to call each other out if they don't appear at their usual time and let each other know if they're out of town," write Harvard Divinity School Ministry Innovation Fellows Angie Thurston and Casper ter Kuile in a paper titled "How We Gather" that reviews the Millennial attraction to "powerful, surprising, and perhaps even religious"[21] nontraditional communities. Unlike nearly all other environments today, CrossFit is all about supporting one another's goals—whatever they may be—with a fervor that overrides competition. (That is, outside the annual CrossFit Games, where thousands of participants face off—as individuals and as teams—for the title of "Fittest on Earth.")

Those who make it through the gut-shaking, muscle-bending workouts are damn proud and want you to know what they have accomplished. In fact, the vegan joke from the previous chapter could be replicated with CrossFit: *How do you know someone does CrossFit? Don't worry, they'll tell you.* Just as people identify themselves through their diets, it's common for people to mention their CrossFit practice as a way to tell you more about them—their devotion to personal health, interest in clean eating, willingness to work as a team member.

Perhaps CrossFit's success is due to the fact that it hits on all three aspects of belonging: self-esteem, identity, and self-worth. It allows for the in-person interactions we all crave, offers the opportunity to prove our worth to ourselves and others through clear-cut group-centric goals, and provides a frame of identity—much like today's diets do.

These in-person experiences aren't just about forging connections with others, but also with oneself. Many of these immersive programs challenge folks to push themselves mentally and physically to, along the way, find their true selves.

Finding Your True Self

There is an overarching theme found in gym culture worldwide: We're here to help you find who you are. Gyms pitch themselves as conduits to exploring new parts of oneself, providing personal challenges that serve as metaphors for all of life's hardships. At many of these gyms, you do not attend to burn calories; you attend to find yourself.

For example, "At SoulCycle, our riders feed off the group's shared energy and motivation to push themselves to their greatest potential," reads a line in SoulCycle's IPO filing.[22] "We don't just change bodies, we change lives," the stationary-bike mecca states on their website. Classes are called "journeys" and riders are encouraged to "find your soul."

Similarly, Spartan Race is far more than a race; the brand claims it is "a way of life." Spartan Race's company mission is "to change 100 million lives by motivating people to get out of their comfort zones and learn about, experience, and embrace the Spartan lifestyle." They aim to accomplish this self-discovery through obstacle courses where people form teams and wriggle through mud, climb up rope courses, and flip tires. The races are meant to help people bond with one another. With two hundred events each year in thirty different countries, the brand is quickly building a whole community of Spartans.

Other wellness programs blatantly blur the lines between fitness and self-healing by combining sport with motivational speakers and meditation. A global festival culture has taken root to help attendees connect with themselves through group fitness, well-being workshops, and immersive art engagements. These platforms utilize the same language as many wellness influencers, but urge self discovery not just through Instagram posts and diet choices, but through group interactions and challenges.

The US-based events company Wanderlust wants you to "Find Your True North" and offers a menu of pathways to get you there: a 5K run, DJ-powered yoga, guided meditation, musical performances, and conferences with thought leaders who speak on various aspects of well-being. Wanderlust promises to help attendees cultivate their "best self," and achieves this large task in part, Wanderlust co-founder Sean Hoess told me, through one small tactic: bringing people together IRL. They integrate the personal exertion of fitness, the reflection of meditation, and the insights of thought leaders who speak on topics as wide-ranging as finding one's intention to global warming, all in an environment that cultivates a sense of belonging and collaboration. Part of the subtext of Wanderlust, Hoess said, is to show people that they're not alone by introducing them to their tribe: those "trying to live consciously."

"There's no doubt that perhaps in a different age, the need for a large-scale festival built around yoga and mindfulness and wellness and outdoor activities and all that stuff might have been less compelling," Hoess noted of his company's success, citing the influence of Digital

Age loneliness on people's desire for real-world connection and their inability to find a sense of belonging in their day-to-day lives. The overwhelming attendance at Wanderlust events is a testament to the hunger for a greater community of like-minded individuals.

Wellness festivals now make up a significant chunk of the $4.2 trillion global wellness market,[23] and the Global Wellness Institute estimates that wellness tourism, a $639 billion global market in 2017, has been growing more than twice as fast as general tourism.[24] Travelers engaging in practices such as yoga, meditation, and clean eating made 830 million wellness trips in 2017, which is 139 million more than in 2015. In Thailand, over ten thousand "wonderers" attend the annual Wonderfruit festival, a "cross-cultural celebration of art, music and life."[25] Meanwhile, in Indonesia, thousands flock to Ubud, Bali, for the BaliSpirit Festival to attend seminars and yoga classes. A subset of wellness festivals, like A Fest—described as a "global tribe of brilliant minds that come together like family" for "4 days of accelerated growth" to "bring out the most of your capabilities as a human being"—and Summit, which "connects and fosters a global community of today's brightest creators," borrow the DSSC strategy of exclusivity and invite only a particular cohort of individuals to participate.[26] Often, these programs promote concepts akin to "finding oneself" and "setting intentions" that all lead back to the question: *Who am I?*

Even dinner clubs are playing a role in this new era of inner contemplation. Some use dinner programs to curate a safe space for deep conversation and gather people who wish to discuss intimate, personal, or controversial topics. The Dinner Party gathers attendees for potluck meals to talk about grief. Death Over Dinner provides a guide on how to host a dinner party to talk about death. At Make America Dinner Again, guests engage in a guided conversation among folks of differing political views. At an Eat with Muslims dinner in Seattle, you'll share a Middle Eastern meal with people of various faiths. Each of these settings is meant to help people discover new parts of themselves by opening up to a supportive group of strangers.

Others simply curate events that will push attendees intellectually and open the doors to controversial or provocative topics not often broached at an evening soiree. Raman Frey is the founder of Good

People Dinners. Several times a month, Frey hosts thirty to forty people for a family-style meal, prepared by a professional chef, with a guest speaker and guided conversation. "Good People is about inspiration, community, and friendships," the email invitation reads. "Who are good people? They're our best selves, when we rise above tribalism and explore big ideas."

The purpose of each event is to cultivate "meaningful substantive civil discourse," which, Frey told me, can make people uncomfortable in certain situations. But this taboo-breaking is what keeps people coming back time and again. "The essence of the Good People community is meaningful conversations. It's a gesture of vulnerability with a stranger." People show up for thought-provoking exchanges with others who will teach them something new and broaden their minds. Diners are encouraged to shed their assumptions and "embrace highly dynamic, mutable identities, which people experience as an unburdening." This, Frey said, allows people to explore their own beliefs and sit without judgment. It forces attendees to show up as their whole self, not a curated avatar.

"We're social beings. You need to be able to interact with people to figure out what's meaningful to you," Jonathan Kalan, co-founder of Unsettled, said to me as we sipped our coffee in the Fort Greene neighborhood of Brooklyn. "In a new environment, you're able to see yourself differently, you're able to experience things differently, you're able to challenge yourself."

Unsettled offers month-long co-working journeys to countries around the globe. Attendees are of all ages—from twenty to seventy—and so far have hailed from over eighty far-flung countries. Unsettled weaves together many of today's most prominent community-centric businesses: It provides an all-inclusive trip with a bit of co-working, curated tourist events, social club events, and time for self-reflection.

First and foremost, Unsettled aims to create new communities, said Kalan. "The more we move into the digital realm, the more we have to seek out community in a way that we didn't have to before. Community was inherently tied to where we lived, what we did. Now that we are becoming more mobile, becoming more digital, it takes greater effort to seek those communities, but there's also greater opportunities because you can access more communities than ever before. Now it's seven-point-whatever billion people around the world I can consider my friends, so how do I relate to them? How do I share with them? How do I connect with them?"

Many arrive on Unsettled trips hoping that their new connections will lead to a personal aha moment. By connecting with others, reasoned Kalan, people can explore their own personal purpose. The opportunity to live with others who are from entirely different backgrounds gives people the chance to, without guardrails, reassess "who I am authentically to myself," as Kalan put it.

The program "gives you an opportunity to be whoever you want to be for a month," he told me. "We give people a chance to experiment with and explore who they want to be."

At the end of the day, Kalan noted, the people who sign up for Unsettled are "looking for people who think like them, who relate to them. They're looking for that sense of belonging." And—with the help of a new community—they are able to dig into aspects of their personalities and passions that have gone unexplored.

"In the last two centuries, the intimate communities have withered, leaving imagined communities to fill the emotional vacuum," writes historian Yuval Noah Harari in *Sapiens: A Brief History of Humankind*. With more and more of us living alone, trading time spent with others in person for texts, "likes," and Snaps, and often going without the traditional community foundations of strong neighborhood ties or religious congregations, we are each left to our own devices to find a sense of belonging and worth and to define our identities—who we are and where we fit in. But accomplishing this on our own is quite difficult, hence the loneliness epidemic ravaging cultures worldwide. Still, many are searching for opportunities to connect wherever they can—be it in a vegan chat room or on a meditation mat. We fold into downward dog alongside thousands of others under the open morning sky, seek out dinners with strangers in order to dive into intimate topics usually relegated to bosom buddies, drop by speed dating events in the hopes of finding a like-minded partner, and travel abroad on our own, aiming to find others to bond with. With each class, game, and mukbang stream, we're creating communities for ourselves, sometimes imagined, some-times real.

This Digital Generation is not just a bunch of stressed-out, food-obsessed individuals; we are a generation desperately in search of sup-port, love, and self-esteem. Our communities help us define not just who we are, but our purpose in life. Without these solid community foundations, the Digital Generation is left searching for meaning.

PART III

purpose

Urban dwellers never have the chance to see
the Milky Way, or a night radiant with stars, or
even a truly blue sky. They never experience the
subtle fragrances peculiar to each season; they
lose the exhilaration of early spring and the
delightful melancholy of autumn. The loss of these
experiences is more than an aesthetic affliction;
it corresponds to a deprivation of needs which are
essential to physical and mental sanity, because
they were indelibly woven in man's fabric during
his evolutionary past.

—Dr. René Dubos, *Scientist and Citizen*, 1968

CHAPTER EIGHT

DIY & eudaimonia

The city of Los Angeles is asleep, but the hum of the oven and murmur of music keep Andy Kadin company until the sun peeks above the horizon. As he opens the walk-in refrigerator, the rush of cold air causes his face to blush with chill. He pulls out racks of round woven baskets. Inside, hiding behind the basket edges, are plump rounds of pale dough that have proofed overnight. He brings them over to the gargantuan oven and turns the linen-lined baskets over, one by one, onto the gurney-like loader. The heat from the oven immediately melts away any of his remaining shivers. He attaches a new razor blade to his baker's lame and, with strokes going from front to back, scores each loaf. With a dozen set, he pulls the loader back and watches as the mounds gently lower onto the oven's stone deck. He closes the door and soon sees the steam accumulating in moist droplets on the surface of the still pallid loaves. Then, he returns the empty baskets to a drying rack so they can be refilled later in the day with fresh, yeasty dough.

It is three thirty in the morning, and he has seven more decks to load. In twenty minutes or so, the first loaves will begin to brown and he'll start the process of venting each deck. In a few hours, his employees will arrive and add the morning's boules and baguettes into a truck, to be hand-delivered to restaurants around the LA area. As those breads depart the warehouse, new dough will be mixed, weighed, folded, and shaped for the following day's delivery.

This is how Kadin, thirty-seven, spends every morning. Just a few years earlier he was winning awards at the Cannes Lions International

Festival of Creativity for advertising copywriting, and writing a show for Comedy Central. Now, his lanky, six-foot-plus frame and chestnut hair are often dusted in sandy flour and he is up before 3 a.m. every day to prep and conduct his orchestra of bakers and delivery drivers from his California wholesale bakery, Bub and Grandma's Bread. He says he has never felt more fulfilled.

"It's intoxicating," Kadin told me. "The whole process of making bread . . . It just doesn't make any sense that you put this goop into this thing that's hot and it turns it into this thing with a huge ear"—baker talk for that piece of the crust that pokes up in the oven like an envelope fold—"and looks really beautiful and tastes really good. It's confusing every time it happens, and even though you know the science and you know the way it works, it's just miraculous."

After a typical upper-middle-class upbringing on the East Coast, and with a degree in philosophy from Bates College in hand, the young Kadin had little idea where his career was heading. He bounced from local politics to music marketing and eventually found a foothold in advertising, where he rose through the ranks to become a creative director at big-name agencies like Havas and Saatchi & Saatchi. He bounced from New York to Boston and eventually Los Angeles. And while he was finding immense success, as measured in awards and client approvals, he began to experience a persistent knot in his throat that he couldn't clear.

"I remember going to the doctor and complaining about chest pains," Kadin recalled. "I was having such intense anxiety that I would take walks around the block midday just to try and cool myself down, and I was really starting to recognize that I was ashamed to be doing my job. I would go hang out with friends, who were either in or not in the ad industry, and I would complain. I didn't like myself and who I was. I was just not happy." Eventually, he quit.

Kadin and I sat in his sparse office at Bub and Grandma's as we reviewed his early career. He wore a loose, dark-blue sweater and brown leather shoes. His hair, flecked with gray, shot from his head at all angles as he leaned back in his chair behind a wide iron desk. Brown laminate floors ran throughout the room, and a forlorn blue couch was tucked against the back wall. A scattering of wine bottles, proofing baskets, and scales were set out on a mostly empty shelving unit. Bub and

Grandma's had just moved into the space a few weeks earlier, upgrading from a baking space of just over six hundred square feet to one nearly ten times the size, at the edge of the Silver Lake neighborhood. He admitted that the new elbow room was quite welcome, though it meant that no one knew where anything was anymore.

As we talked about his career in advertising, I could see the tension rise in Kadin's shoulders. His face looked pinched. "I was disgusted by what advertising is doing, in general. It's basically manipulating human emotion in order to control people and get them to buy things they don't need that are made cheaper every year," he reflected. "What I think advertising needs to get back to is convincing brands that they need to make better products, and then you just show the product."

(Though he maintains unease about branding and marketing his own bread business, he knows that the product he's selling is, at the very least, worth buying. "We try and make the absolute best product in an earnest way. And our marketing should be people getting that product in their mouths and recognizing that it's better.")

With a clear-headed recognition of his own unhappiness, Kadin was left with a daunting question: What to do next? "I always talked about opening a restaurant," he recalled. Specifically, he daydreamed about opening a sandwich shop.

Why sandwiches? I asked.

It all came from the allure of lunch, he explained—the time when he could escape from work. At one East Coast agency, his co-workers nicknamed him "Lunch" because he would arrive in the morning and habitually ask: "What are we doing for lunch?" Kadin oversaw organizing the daily outings, which often led to a local haunt serving chacarero, a Chilean beef and green bean sandwich, or a falafel shop with chicken kebab pitas.

Yet, his love of sandwiches stretched beyond workdays. He cited a lunchtime pit stop during a trip to Morocco in which he came upon a sandwich housed in a "combo French boule/pita." Kadin's eyes widened as he recalled the experience, and he sat up tall in his chair. This particular bread, he told me, is "rounded, but it's flat on the bottom and curved on the top and it's got a baguette-esque kind of dough inside." By this point, he was leaning toward me, holding up his hands in an "O" shape to demonstrate the pouf. "It's not like a pocket, but they make it a pocket. They cut it in half this way," he said, making the motions in the air, "across the top, and then turn it sideways so it's like a pita pocket, peel open the center of the bread, take that soft French cheese with the cow on it—I can't remember what it's called, in a little tin packaging—spread it along the bottom of the opening; and then they put this relish in there that's argan oil, olive oil, celery, carrot, onion or shallot, and garlic and spread that along the bottom; and then they put a hard-boiled egg, smash it across the bottom; and then boiled, slightly spiced potato on the top, drizzle of olive oil, and that's the whole thing." My stomach began to gurgle as I listened. His excitement was infectious. "It's amazing," he concluded.

Recognizing both his interest in sandwiches and his complete lack of knowledge of either bread or the food industry, Kadin apprenticed at a sandwich shop in Hollywood for nearly a year while also beginning to experiment at home with baking. He started with ciabatta. The first few months, he recalls, were a struggle, but as he baked every day, the loaves improved. Even when his attempts failed, he felt proud.

"I had never been proud of anything that I made," he explained. "There was satisfaction in this, and it was something that no one else was a part of. It was just me. I was the only one who could make it succeed or fail. And when it succeeded—the rare times that it did succeed—it was the most pride I had ever felt." Eventually, he was making so much bread that he was distributing it to anyone who would take it, and one day a restaurant owner asked if Kadin would be their wholesale bread producer. He said yes; the rest, as they say, is history.

There are many elements to the baker's life that, from the outside, appear no easier than a corporate job. Bakes go wrong, shipments go missing, the hours are brutal. But it is the process and the tangibility of the product that make it worth it to Kadin.

"The process of bread baking in general is very Zen," he said, noting the repetition of movements and cadence of each step. "The fact that we are doing one thing and focusing on one thing and trying to perfect that one thing" creates a forced meditative state.

He views many of his days as a persistent pursuit of perfection. "Every single time that I'm scoring loaves, I want them to look exactly the same. You get attempts every single day to try and get there. I'm trying to get somewhere." This process, he says, creates unending opportunity to improve. And he's rewarded with visible edible signs of mastery.

"Bread," Kaden stated succinctly, "brings me happiness."

The Science of Well-Being

In January 2018, Yale psychology professor Laurie Santos debuted a new course on a topic that she thought Yale undergraduates would be interested in; little did she know that it would become the most popular class in Yale's three-hundred-plus-year history. A few days after registration opened, one-fourth of the university's undergraduates—approximately 1,200 students—had enrolled in PSYCH 157: Psychology and the Good Life, which, according to the syllabus, was set to cover scientifically validated strategies for leading a satisfying life. The class had to be held in a concert hall.

Through her role as head of one of Yale's residential colleges, and thus an on-campus resident, Santos was able to observe the anxieties and stresses afflicting the student body in and outside the classroom, and was inspired to stretch beyond her expertise of comparative cognition to craft a course on positive psychology. She decided the course would focus on widely accepted psychological theories on human flourishing. She also wanted to give students ways to directly apply the concepts discussed in the twice-weekly lectures, so she incorporated applied practices into the curriculum. (Her course instructions include some basic directions such as *delete your social media accounts, get exercise every day, take time to do nothing at all, create a gratitude practice,* and *meditate.*)

The class, she told me, quickly "became a phenomenon," not just among students but also with staff, friends, and family. Santos soon rebranded the class, now titled "The Science of Well-Being," for Coursera, an online education platform. From the course's debut in March 2018 to my conversation with her in May 2018, over one hundred thousand learners from 160 countries had already signed up.

While thrilled by the popularity, Santos is also cognizant of the fact that this topic would not be resonating so broadly if more people felt as though they were already leading a life of well-being. People are "so unhappy that they need to take a course on happiness," she affirmed.

She mentioned the high rates of mental health issues on campus, including depression and anxiety, and said she believes that these symptoms explain the course's success. In the wider community, she has observed a hunger for meaning.

While a sense of safety and belonging, the subjects of this book's first two parts, are essential aspects of human well-being, there remains one last theme in need of addressing: a sense of purpose. What do each of us need in our lives to feel that we are flourishing and that our existence has meaning?

Today, many of us are searching for meaning. According to Google Trends, the phrase *what is the meaning to life*, along with the related searches *how to find meaning in life* and *how to find life purpose*, are being entered into Google Search twice as often in 2020 as they were in 2010, and the inquiries span the globe. People living in the Philippines, Nepal, Ghana, Nigeria, and Pakistan top the list of inquisitive meaning-seekers. In the Hungry Study, we found that over three-quarters of Gen Z and Millennial respondents agreed with the statements *I am always searching for something that makes my life feel significant* and *I am seeking a purpose or mission for my life.*

The question of what gives our lives meaning is a conundrum that philosophers have been debating since at least the time of Aristotle. But why is the subject of meaning finding such relevance in today's culture?

In 1950, Abraham Maslow set out to determine what characteristics, beyond achieving safety and belonging, help an individual lead a fulfilled life. Maslow wanted to know what causes some people to "become everything one is capable of becoming" and thus reach their full potential as individuals, a state of being he called "self-actualization."[1]

Ultimately, Maslow identified a number of characteristics he felt were shared by those who achieve "self-actualization": acceptance of the things one cannot control, an ego-less outlook on life that facilitates a view of the world as much larger than the self, a clear set of broad goals that benefit those beyond oneself, a devotion to close relationships, the ability to throw oneself into projects with great concentration, and the ability to not feel bound by cultural or social expectations. These characteristics circle several themes: independence, connectedness to others, and a strong sense of self-efficacy. To reach self-actualization, he asserts, we must continue to challenge ourselves, acquire new talents, and push ourselves to realize our highest potential.

As we saw at the very beginning of this book, Richard Ryan and Edward Deci's more modern take on well-being, Self-Determination Theory (SDT), also emphasizes the importance of autonomy, connectedness, and competence. Together, these theorists seem to agree that those of us searching for meaning in our lives benefit most from engaging in activities that put us in control, provide a feeling of connectedness to others or nature, and offer a true sense of personal accomplishment through personal skill-building and proving our own self-efficacy.

A key part of both Maslow's and Deci and Ryan's theories relies on the concept of constant personal improvement through accomplishing personal goals, big and small. But in today's world, our points of success are becoming increasingly amorphous. What does progress look like? Is it an empty inbox? A finalized PowerPoint? Another client sale? And so, there's a counterbalancing movement of folks like Kadin looking not to gamified stickers or points, but to the crackle of a crust, the aroma of a beer, or a new set of hand-crafted mugs as their tangible, indisputable signs of triumph.

Do-It-Yourself Culture

If you're not already fermenting kombucha; mixing custom batches of slime; learning to weld, paint, or knit; constructing a dining table; shaping clay bowls; or baking sourdough, then it's time for you to jump on the DIY ("Do It Yourself") bandwagon. Everyone else in the world is waiting for you.

Hands-on creative projects are tickling the fancy of folks around the world. Though e-commerce sites like Amazon, Rakuten, and Alibaba now allow us to purchase nearly any product we can imagine, a growing number of global citizens are forgoing clicking and opting instead to make things themselves. According to Google Trends, searches for do-it-yourself topics such as *how to make soap*, *DIY floating shelves*, and *how to pickle* have all risen significantly over the last decade. Interest in sourdough starter has spread beyond wheat-producing countries and is picking up steam in Singapore, South Africa, and Hong Kong. Meanwhile, make-your-own slime is all the rage in Australia, the United States, and Qatar. DIY craft ideas are of particular interest to those in the Philippines, Mauritius, Trinidad and Tobago, and Sri Lanka.[2]

These maker fads are, of course, in direct opposition to many of the other behaviors analyzed in this book: time spent staring at screens, clicking, and scrolling. But technology-fettered young people are the same population driving revolutions in baking, home cooking, gardening, and beyond. In fact, much of the time, the same people who spend their days answering emails and sending Snaps are also the ones logging off and dropping by their local ceramic studio.[3]

Evidence of this Millennial and Gen Z DIY obsession is all over social media. The DIY section of Reddit has over fifteen million subscribers who show off their handmade guitars, jewelry, and crown molding installations. People have applied the hashtag #homemade nearly sixty million times on Instagram, while over 1.2 million posts carry the boastful hashtag #imadethis. Pinterest reports that interest in handcrafted soap made from raw goat milk and acrylic pours was up by 231 percent and 660 percent, respectively, from 2017 to 2018.[4] Meanwhile, subscription boxes that offer monthly craft kits for building things like terrariums, bird houses, and dream catchers have found an enthusiastic audience. Today, plant shops, art stores, adult coloring book publishers, ceramic studios, and edible seed companies are flourishing as the Digital Generation seeks new opportunities to build skill sets and throw themselves deeply into hands-on projects.

My own household is far from immune to this trend. My husband spends weekends working on sourdough loaves (with a sourdough starter he has lovingly named Joseph Gordon Levain). I pickle radishes and cucumbers and grow a bounty of produce in our outdoor garden beds, and take the time to cook dinner nearly every evening. We constructed our own backyard patio, not because it was too expensive to hire help, but because we wanted to do it ourselves. We desired the physical labor, the calloused hands, the sweat-soaked shirts, and, most of all, the immense pride we now feel whenever we look out the window and think to ourselves, "We did that." My husband is also interested in taking a butchering course. He has no plans to ever begin hunting, or to haul a whole cow back to our city apartment; he just wants to know how it all works. And he is far from alone.*

Some, like Andy Kadin, are taking these passions out of their kitchens, basements, and backyards and into their professional lives. Kadin's trajectory from office to bakery resembles a common journey today. We can call it the Maker Archetype, and it's a tale that has become common enough for the mainstream media to mock. In 2017, the *New Yorker* published a cartoon by illustrator Amy Hwang in which two women stand at a table wearing toques and chef coats. One whisks a mystery ingredient in a bowl and says to the other, who is poised to flatten a ball of dough with her rolling pin, "You're the first person I've met who didn't become a pastry chef after suffering a nervous breakdown working in a corporate job."

For the first time since the 1930s, and the division of jobs into white collar and blue collar, throngs of white-collar workers are giving up their desk jobs for more physical gigs in woodshops, fields, or kitchens. In 2017, Richard Ocejo, associate professor of sociology at John Jay College, published a book documenting this shift, titled *Masters of Craft: Odd Jobs in the New Urban Economy*. In it, Ocejo looks specifically into the rising interest in bartending, distilling, barbering, and butchering employment, which runs counter to the career trends of the last few decades. Between 1980 and 2015, the number of US jobs requiring social and analytical skills typical of an office increased by 94 per cent, while jobs requiring physical skills went up by just 12 percent. In contrast, the US Department of Labor now projects that between 2014 and 2024, hands-on occupations like barbering, masonry, pipe laying, makeup artistry, and plumbing will grow at a rate nearly twice

---

* Seventy-three percent of British Millennial viewers of *The Great British Bake Off* say they have been inspired to bake from watching the show, and sales of flour and butter reflect as much; spending on baking ingredients rose by about thirty-one million British pounds during the first few seasons of the show's airing, according to the food marketing agency Kindred. "Millennials are responsible for over 594,000 additional loaves, cakes, pies, biscuits and other baked delicacies every single week during the GBBO series run," *British Baker* reports, also noting that twenty- and thirtysomethings are strapping on aprons and picking up rolling pins in greater numbers than any other generation.

the average—numbers that reflect economic demand as well as antici-pated public interest.[5] Often, it's college-educated individuals who are expected to fill these roles.[6]

While some of the fastest-growing jobs, like solar panel and wind turbine installation, are clearly the result of a shifting energy system, and the demand for healthcare workers is a direct response to aging Baby Boomers, there is no similarly straightforward reason for the expected increase in bike repair specialists, makeup artists, and massage therapists.* So, here's my simple explanation: Young adults are gravitat-ing toward hands-on hobbies and work environments over screen-based employment because these tasks are more likely to deliver the essential elements for well-being: competence, autonomy, and connectedness.

Today, many of us are looking beyond the "likes" and leaderboards to new avenues of self-fulfillment, searching for experiences that allow us to feel in control, connected to others or nature, and increasingly skilled and competent.

Competence, Autonomy, and Connectedness

"When I walk into a place selling our products, I look at them and I'm like, 'I did that!' I can even tell which chocolate croissants I scored," Liza Patriana told me as we dug into two vegetarian sandwiches (on Bub and Grandma's salty focaccia) at All Time, a small neighborhood café in Los Feliz, California. On the table were also two items of Patriana's own creation: a Rueben-themed round croissant crusted with sesame and caraway seeds, and stuffed with pastrami, whole-grain mustard, and Gruyère, and an eye-shaped croissant that oozed mild, semi-melted cream cheese and sour guava jam. Patriana watched with anticipation as I bit into each item, eager to know my review. (They were stunning.)

A former account executive in the music industry, Patriana's move to the pastry world followed a similar plot arc as Andy Kadin's. In fact,

---

* According to the Bureau of Labor Statistics' Occupational Outlook Handbook, jobs in bike repairs are expected to climb by 29 percent, while massage therapy is antici-pated to see a 26 percent boost. Meanwhile, employment in arts and culture contin-ues to rise every year, notes Jeannine Aversa at the Bureau of Economic Analysis.

Patriana apprenticed at Bub and Grandma's Bread while transition-
ing from one career to the next, before landing at Bakers Kneaded, a
small wholesale bakery specializing in pastries, cookies, and breads. We
talked about the differences between working in an office and working
with active yeast.

Success, she explained, is defined differently. "A lot of what I'm
doing every day is repetitive," she said. Her eyes wandered behind her
thick, black-framed glasses, which sat right below her blunt-cut bangs.
"I have mental goals for myself, like I want to shave off two minutes
from doing something. I'm trying to beat my previous day's accomplishments." She is constantly challenging herself to incrementally improve
her own skills.

The process of achieving that success is different from that of her
previous desk job. Instead of clicking her way to an empty inbox, Patriana has to sense her way to the desired end product. "I'm actually feeling
the dough," she notes. "Does it need to be tighter or looser? Five degrees
warmer? The butter feels different today, or looks more yellow. Why is
that? There is this tactile element to it. I'm even aware of which hand is
stronger, my right or left."

The next morning, I met her at ten o'clock at the Bakers Kneaded
workspace, tucked into a larger building shared with other food companies. Patriana had draped her dainty frame in a white T-shirt, dark
jeans, and work clogs, and her straight, jet-black hair was pulled back
with a red bandana. Upon arrival, she tied an apron around her waist.
The work room was no more than 250 square feet and the temperature
was set to a chilly 60 degrees. Taking up most of the windowless white-
and-gray-tiled space was a countertop and large machine that works like
an automatic rolling pin, flattening dough as it cycles through on a con-
veyor belt. That morning, Patriana was working on lamination: creating
copious folded layers of butter and dough for croissants. I followed her
as she traveled back and forth from the workspace to the walk-in refrigerator across the hall to collect racks of butter and pastry sheets, and
watched as she tested the temperature of each rectangular stack before
running it through the machine.

Test, pat, roll, fold, roll, fold, roll, fold, cut, roll, re-rack. She continued the process for hours.

I couldn't help thinking to myself, *Doesn't she get bored?* before remembering our prior conversations. Her days are filled with small goals: Reduce the number of times she walks from workspace to walk-in; increase the number of folds; finish a few minutes sooner. The repetition allows for incremental improvements, obvious and palpable successes that she can attribute to herself and herself alone. And with each small win, she feels more competent.

In an earlier phone call, I asked Patriana if her job satisfaction is greater now than in her music industry days. Yes, she said. At the bakery, she can see her accomplishments clearly in the rows of croissants or baguettes, or in the minutes reclaimed by more fluid motions. Before, she would wake up, check her email, hop on the phone, and then check more emails and make more phone calls. The list of to-dos never ended. The finish line was a constantly moving target. Now, there is a clear endpoint, a time when she can declare: *I have completed this goal.*

Further, in her new job, she feels a part of a community that includes her co-workers as well as the farmers whose flour she uses. There is a camaraderie that she finds comfort in. "If I'm running behind, my co-worker is going to help me," she notes. In her former job, she never felt secure asking a co-worker for assistance. She also feels connected to those who consume her products, something I later witnessed first-hand as she watched with a wide smile as I bit into the guava and cream cheese croissant while flakes of pastry crumbled onto the table.

And finally, Patriana feels more connected to herself. "I am more cognizant of my body, how I handle things with my hands," she remarked. Simple things like an intense focus on pressure and temperature require that she give full attention to bodily senses she had once given no notice to.

Patriana's comments were strikingly similar to the sentiments I heard from Kadin. The first time he successfully made a loaf that "resembled bread," he remembers feeling "swollen" with emotion. As he bit into the yeasted bulk-retarded ciabatta, the piquancy and superiority of the flavor shocked him. The laborious three-day bread-making process, he said, only made the joy at the end that much more thrilling.

"I was working toward something where there was an end product that I could hold and taste," he reflected. Still, he recalled of his early days baking in his home kitchen, "it was never good enough." This mantra of *I could do it better* fueled him to try and try again. And over time, he experienced his incremental successes through his physical senses: hearing the crackle of the crust, looking at the pockets of air within the dough, smelling the fragrant aroma, tasting his creation. With each small improvement, his feelings of proficiency and efficacy ballooned, and his confidence in his own abilities solidified. And, once he was on a roll (pun intended), he was bringing loaves of bread everywhere he went. "I gave it away to everybody. People loved it," he recalled. For both himself and his recipients, "it was the best gift ever," because he could watch others revel in his artisanship.

These sentiments of labor, creation, and joy are, of course, not limited to bakeries. "I never ceased to take pleasure in the moment, at the end of a job, when I would flip the switch. 'And there was light,'" writes philosopher and motorcycle mechanic Matthew Crawford in his book *Shop Class as Soulcraft: An Inquiry into the Value of Work*, where he documents his own satisfaction in manual labor.[7] The ability to physically transform objects, to fix machines and create new ones, is "an experience of agency and competence," he writes. Unlike his work in philosophy—at the time of writing, he is a senior fellow at the University of Virginia's Institute for Advanced Studies in Culture—the results of his work in the motorcycle shop "were visible for all to see, so my competence was real for others as well; it had a social currency."

We can also find competence, autonomy, and connection by creating things virtually—say, scoring music, building a website, or writing a piece of online content. But the creation itself has to be iterative, self-driven, and shareable. By building a skill set over time and through repeated actions, we can observe our growing capabilities and, eventually, develop a secure confidence in ourselves and our talents—then reap the rewards of sharing this new expertise with others.

Still, many makers find satisfaction in their work not only because they can build a sense of competence, but because they are motivated by their personal desires to improve their skill sets rather than just by their employer or revenue sheets. For them, the process of reaching their goals is rewarding in and of itself. This makes them far more prone to finding, in their work, that meaning and satisfaction we are all in search of.

Intrinsic and Extrinsic Motivation

No matter what kind of task we set out to do, our well-being is boosted by accomplishing it.[8] But some achievements feel more fulfilling than others.

"Not all goals are created equal," write Ryan and Deci, along with their colleagues Kennon Sheldon and Tim Kasser, in a 1996 article.[9] Indeed, there are plenty of folks who work in creative jobs who do not find the same personal satisfaction or feel the same motivation for persistent improvement that Patriana, Kadin, and Crawford do.

The makers we have talked about so far are largely *intrinsically* motivated (motivated by their own inner desires). The journey to completing an intrinsic goal is a rewarding activity in and of itself. (Philosophers and psychologists call this an *autotelic experience*, a term derived from the Greek *auto* [self] and *telos* [goal].) But there are plenty of people who code phone applications, plant gardens, or knead dough not because they harbor a personal desire to, but solely because they're seeking an outside reward, be it a paycheck, a student work credit, or approval from a happy spouse. These folks are *extrinsically* motivated. When working toward an extrinsic goal, the process of completing a task can become more of a chore, a means to an end, as you focus on the promise of a future benefit.

"The greater relative importance people place on extrinsic goals, the less their satisfaction of basic psychological needs, and thus the less they experience well-being," Ryan and Deci summarize in another article.[10] "In contrast, placing greater importance on intrinsic goals such as growth and community has been associated with greater satisfaction of basic psychological needs, and enhanced well-being."*

On campus back at Yale, Dr. Santos sees her students striving toward a multitude of extrinsically motivated goals that, she fears, will never fulfill their esteem and self-efficacy needs. The ambitions of Baby

---

* Maslow addresses the dichotomy between these two forms of motivation as well. Honors and prestige awarded by others are "less important than self-development and inner growth," he writes. By focusing on personal progress, individuals can view setbacks as a part of their continued learning experience, and avoid common frustrations.

Boomer and Gen X offspring—especially those who enroll at Yale—include things like high test scores, completed homework, and Instagram validations. These types of goals, Santos told me, "are about things that empirically wouldn't predict happiness," as they are not driven by personal interest, but societal expectations or practical need. Focusing on these external goals therefore inevitably leads to the same contradiction that afflicted Andy Kadin: Although his income and accolades rose, an emotional emptiness persisted. Santos credits this gap, in part, for the popularity of her course on happiness.

All this said, extrinsic rewards are not inherently bad. Sometimes, the promise of a reward increases our internal motivations. The difference lies in one's sense of control, note Ryan and Deci. If you're completing a task that you have full creative authority over and that you'll receive a reward for (think: compensation or a gold star sticker), then you may become even more intrinsically motivated; the task itself is already fulfilling, and the outside reward is an added benefit or even a validation of one's efforts. But if a loss of control accompanies the reward, intrinsic motivation will decrease. For example, if someone says, "You'll be paid only if you do it the way I want you to," one's enjoyment of the activity will plummet. Suddenly, the work is no longer for yourself; it is being done to fulfill someone else's expectations.[11]

But, you may wonder, what about when you are challenged to do something by someone else and you succeed? Doesn't that make you feel good? Of course it does, but not to the same extent that it would have were the exercise purely intrinsically motivated. Succeeding at a project while feeling pressured to do well can still result in a sense of satisfaction—but it's a different form of happiness than that triggered by a personally driven success.

Just as our motivation can come from two different sources, we can also experience pleasure two different ways: *hedonically* and *eudaimonically*. Both are enjoyable, but only one is correlated with improved well-being.

The ancient Greek philosopher Aristippus said the goal of life is to experience the maximum amount of pleasure, and that happiness is found in life's hedonic moments. Others of the time took issue with this notion, considering the concept too selfish and indulgent. Happiness, countered Aristotle, is not achieved by collecting moments of pleasure, but through living in accordance with one's true self, in a way that leads us to realize our full personal potential. This, he asserted, is living eudaimonically.[12]

Time and science have sided with Aristotle's theory over Aristippus's. Though receiving rewards or eating a great meal may provide a pleasurable moment, we know that over time these small wins do not add up to a happy life. Instead, aspects of the eudaimonic lifestyle— such as self-acceptance, openness to new experiences, and a focus on personal growth—have proven to be more closely tied to well-being.[13]

Further, living eudaimonically—by pursuing things that truly matter to you—is far more likely to lead to a state of mind now commonly known as *flow*. Flow is the sense of losing oneself in an experience. It is the moment when you realize you've entirely lost track of time while immersed in a game, an assignment, or a creative endeavor, and it is experiences like these that have been shown to improve one's life satisfaction.[14]

"We all have experienced times when . . . we do feel in control of our actions, masters of our own fate," writes psychologist Mihaly Csikszentmihalyi, who coined the term *flow*.[15] "On the rare occasions that it happens, we feel a sense of exhilaration, a deep sense of enjoyment that is long cherished and that becomes a landmark in memory for what life should be like." The fulfillment brought by money, power, status, and possessions, Csikszentmihalyi argues, dulls in intensity and impact over time, compared to the autotelic experiences of flow.

These "optimal moments," Csikszentmihalyi writes, "usually occur when a person's body or mind is stretched to its limits in a voluntary effort to accomplish something difficult and worthwhile. Optimal experience is thus something that we *make* happen."

During *flow*, Dr. Santos explains in her "Science of Well-Being" course, "Your skills are at their max pushing level to accomplish something that you really dig, that you find intrinsically rewarding."[16]

Engaging in physical acts like playing sports or music, having sex, or fasting can trigger flow, as can moments that challenge our minds like reading, solving puzzles, or writing complicated computer code. Fiddling with ideas can put us into a flow state, as can forms of communication, like writing, storytelling, or intense conversation.

To find flow, says Csikszentmihalyi, we must ride a careful line between the gutters of anxiety and boredom. The task cannot be too difficult for us to complete, and it must require concentration and clear aims. It should provide immediate feedback—be it pages turned or the response of attentive listeners—and remove our awareness of the "worries and frustrations of everyday life." And of course, we must feel a sense of control and autonomy over the task.

With that medley, a "concern for the self disappears, yet paradoxically the sense of self emerges stronger after the flow experience is over."*

Though the term had not yet been coined in Maslow's time, he nods to the concept of flow in his work. The self-actualized individual, he says, is appreciative of solitude and privacy and able to concentrate on tasks for a long period of time. At some point, the individual enjoys a "mystic experience": the feeling of limitless horizons opening up, intense enjoyment, and loss of self.

"When I cook and create something from scratch, I am my original self," Bangalorean chef Nikhil Malhotra explained to me of his work. "If I feel happy, it is pure. If the dish didn't come out as expected, the disappointment is pure. It resonates with my being. I stand for eighteen hours a day sometimes and I don't even know it until I sit down somewhere. I am lost in creating. The same thing happens when I am playing guitar, when I eat my mother's chicken curry, when I am chilling with my dogs, when I look at the woman I love. My original self resonates and I feel alive." Prior to becoming a chef, Mahotra worked in the tech world of Bangalore for sixteen years, bouncing from Google to IBM, before deciding to leave it all behind. "I realized that I wasn't happy doing any of this," he told me. "I couldn't keep working on someone else's dream just to get some salary. I couldn't be a worker bee."

Much of today's white-collar work is less than ideal for finding flow. Interruptions such as notifications make sustained focus nearly impossible. And societal goals like salaries and promotions can undermine our own internal motivations.

---

* During flow, the parts of the brain responsible for self-criticism and fear, the prefrontal cortex and amygdala, are deactivated, notes Daniel Levitin in his book *The Organized Mind: Thinking Straight in the Age of Information Overload.*

Some former white-collar workers, like Kadin, Patriana, and Malhotra, are reorganizing their lives for careers conducive to flow. Others are looking to hobbies as a way to engage in self-motivated tasks.

The creative and challenging DIY tasks that litter message boards and social media pages are ideal conduits to a flow state; they're projects that demand sustained concentration, that because they're offline don't open you up to a barrage of distracting notifications, and that offer the opportunity to develop a new skill set.

Still, flow and intrinsic motivation alone do not explain the transformative DIY lifestyle trends. These theories don't explain why my husband returns home from a day of teaching ninety third-graders to stick his hand in a bowl of bread dough, or why painting classes are all the rage in Shanghai, or why DIY-themed television shows are taking over networks. After all, one can feel masterful and even enter a flow state while executing Excel spreadsheets, playing a video game, managing a classroom, or writing JavaScript.[17] Yet, these forms of work are not what people are flocking to. Instead, they are seeking a respite from these tangible tasks by turning to things made with physical objects—things that can be held in one's own two hands.

The Need for Touch

As our days move into virtual realms and away from hands-on work, we may find ourselves asking: *Is writing an e-document as fulfilling as penning a handwritten note?*

While one can certainly find a sense of meaning by creating an intangible product, there's growing evidence that producing something physical is of greater importance than once thought.

Let's take this very book as an example. I certainly feel accomplished after a productive day of writing, and I know that I'll be mightily relieved when I have the manuscript completed. And I do, routinely, enter a flow state while writing. But there is a saying among writers: Just wait until you hold the book in your hands. It is this physical incarnation of a writer's work—the weight, the scent of fresh print, the texture against your thumb as you flip through the pages—that seems to bring all the previous efforts home. That, many authors attest, is when you really feel like you have written a book.

The physicality of creation is an aspect of fulfillment that often goes overlooked. When people "actively create things, they imbue them with more value than if they just possess them," associate professor of psychology Joshua Ackerman explained to me from his office at the University of Michigan. There, Ackerman runs the Evolutionary Social Psychology Lab, where students investigate how our ancestral histories influence modern human behaviors. Ackerman said that the intensity of an experience can be amplified by sensory triggers: "not just from vision, but through the aroma of things, the taste, the touch." We are not evolutionarily designed for experiences like texting, which evoke mainly visual stimulation; we're designed for experiences like foraging that include all our bodily senses.

Projects in which we can see, feel, hear, and taste not only our successes but also our failures are the ones that often mean the most. While performance reviews and grades can mark progress, it is undeniable that tasting, smelling, or feeling one's success is more intense than viewing a completed PowerPoint or an empty email inbox.

"On a typical day, how much time, on average, do you spend every day making something with your hands (such as cooking a meal, completing an art project, or building something tangible)?" we asked Hungry Study participants. Two-thirds of respondents reported that these tactile moments added up to no more than sixty minutes a day. Compare this to the lives we evolved for: a persistently challenging existence of crafting tools, hunting or foraging for food, and building shelters. When there wasn't something survival-related to keep hands busy, our long-ago ancestors turned to the arts—sculpting, painting, and etching.

"Most of the brain's real estate is devoted to movement," writes University of Richmond biopsychologist and professor of behavioral neuroscience Kelly Lambert, including the motor cortex, striatum, and cerebellum, which control muscle movement and coordination. Given that fact, "it is interesting to consider the impact of our increasingly sedentary lifestyles on these pervasive neural circuits."[18] What, she wonders, is the impact of using our hands so little in today's modern environment? "Hands," she argues, are "one of the most potent activators of the brain's circuits."

Touch is one of the most powerful senses we have. Before we can hear or see, we can feel. Our sense of touch is the first sense to develop in utero.[19] Our skin, essentially a shell of receptors, is the largest of our sensory organs.[20]

"Touch is one of the few senses connected to the limbic parts of our brains," Dr. Adrian David Cheok relayed to me from his office at the Imagineering Institute research lab in the city of Iskandar Puteri, in Johor, Malaysia, just across the Johor Strait from Singapore. "Touch can subconsciously trigger an emotion. Vision can, of course, trigger your emotion, but it goes to the logical part of our brains. Touch goes to emotion." Taste and smell, Cheok noted with enthusiasm, are also more potent than visuals.

"Even in 2018, when we have amazing virtual reality and computer graphics that have become so real, even so, people want to do the same things we always did: go out to have a meal together or get a coffee," Cheok observed. "We somehow still crave the tangible experiences."

Cheok is using this insight to make our online experiences more sensorial. He crafts multisensory virtual realities that often dominate headlines for their quirkiness. For example, he built an app that—through an attachment on one's phone—allows a viewer to both hear and smell a dish being made in a restaurant halfway around the world. He engineered a machine that stimulates olfactory receptors in one's nose through electrical signals. He created a phone attachment that sends haptic touch data of a finger being squeezed or lips kissing over the Internet. (Yes, through the cheekily named Kissenger mobile device, you can feel someone halfway around the world kiss you through a bilateral haptic app.)

Still, many of us are not looking to technology to provide these essential sensory inputs—we are looking to reality.

Human beings use our hands for two main purposes: to gather and share information and to manipulate our environments.[21] These actions help us communicate, develop relationships, absorb key insights, focus, and create pleasurable experiences.

"The satisfactions of manifesting oneself concretely in the world through manual competence have been known to make a man quiet and easy," writes Crawford in *Shop Class as Soulcraft*. And that's because manual, sensorial experiences have been proven to soothe us. We can trigger the release of hormones like serotonin by using our hands, dopamine by accomplishing a goal, and oxytocin when we share that new talent with friends.[22]

In our anxiety-ridden culture, tactile creation is serving a new role: therapy. Today, phrases like "stitch away stress" and "knit therapy" are entering headlines and mental health campaigns, and Google's 2019 Year in Search revealed that "learn to knit" was one of the top ten trending "how to" searches of the year.[23] Some studies show a direct connection between the repetitive, creative practice of knitting and entering a flow state, and one investigation found positive correlations between knitting and relaxation, stress relief, creativity, feelings of calm, happiness, and higher cognitive functioning.[24]

Cooking can have similar benefits, and culinary therapy is an emerging trend. Teen rehabilitation center Newport Academy integrates both cooking courses and farm work into their therapy programs.* When participating in these modes of therapy, the teens "are using their hands, using their ears, their bodies, sight, and smell," the center's founder, Jamison Monroe, told me.

On a warm spring afternoon, I visited a Newport Academy location just outside of Los Angeles. I spoke with counselors who described the power of baking cookies as a way to soothe their enrollees and encourage them to open up. "When you're elbow deep in dough, it's amazing the stuff that comes up," an employee relayed.

Tactile, physical, sensorial inputs are core to the human experience. But over the last century, we have lessened the role of physical labor and even physical play in our lives. Scientists like Dr. Lambert believe that the loss of these experiences is partly responsible for the rising rates of depression, particularly among screen-devoted Millennials and Gen

---

* I visited one of the residential house's chicken coops and learned the proper way to pick up and hold a chicken, something taught to any Newport Academy patient who is interested. As I stood in the hay-covered hen house, I cradled a rust-colored chicken and hugged it close to my chest. I could feel its heart beating against my skin. As I petted its soft feathers, I realized I didn't need anyone to explain why holding a chicken might be a way to treat anxiety.

Zers. She explains that depression symptoms involve compromised levels of dopamine. Repetitive tasks, such as knitting, chopping wood, or kneading dough, "activate the serotonergic system, the system targeted by antidepressants that is involved in mood regulation and many other functions."[25] Meanwhile, the anticipation of a final product and the resulting sense of accomplishment engages the dopaminergic system. Put together, Lambert argues, "crafting and meaningful work may ultimately have a significant impact on preventing and treating depression."

While I could go into more scientific data on why physical touch is so important to human beings, one need not look further than the rising number of book stores and vinyl record stores, and the DIY movement in general, as evidence that many people consider physical reality to be best. Once thought to be the end of print publishing, sales of ebooks are now on the decline, while physical book sales are rebounding.[*][26] (Even digital native, Generation Alpha children "overwhelmingly" prefer paper over digital reading material, according to findings from Common Sense Media.[27]) Physical retail grocery stores, no longer necessary in the world of online delivery, still receive touch-hungry visitors.[28] (The biggest obstacle to online food shopping, some surveys show, is consumers' desire to see and hold their produce before buying it.[29]) In 2017, vinyl record sales in the US rose for the twelfth straight year, according to Nielsen Music.[30] Instant cameras that produce a physical photo, like the bygone Polaroid camera, are finding financial success, and several competing models are now on the market.

All these trends, one can argue, are the result of a "touch hungry" Digital Age society.[31] While the Digital Generation is often thought of as overstimulated—rocked by news alerts, fast-moving videos, and a cacophony of sounds—there is growing evidence that, in fact, we are

---

* As Alberto Gallace and Charles Spence write in their book *In Touch with the Future*: "If you still remain unconvinced of the importance of touch then just try lying down for a few seconds with your eyes closed. If you concentrate, you should soon be able to feel the distinct perception of your body, as a separate entity from the surface on which you happen to be resting . . . the sense of touch plays a major role in terms of contributing to differentiating ourselves from the external world; 'Where touch begins, we are' (or at least, we 'perceive' ourselves to be), if one can put it that way."

sensory *deprived*, from trading in moments of physical interaction for online visuals.

Increasingly, I crave experiences that stimulate my senses, agreed 72 percent of American and British Millennials in a JWT survey. *In today's digital world, I feel more and more disconnected from the physical world*, half of Gen Xers and Millennials said.[32]

I sometimes daydream about leaving my job to do something tangible, like farm or build a home, agreed well over half of our Generation Z and Millennial Hungry Study respondents, far above the total population average. On a separate question, our Gen Z respondents—those whose lives have been most significantly altered by the Digital Age—were the least likely to say they feel in tune with their own bodies.

A craving for sensory immersion can help us understand many mainstream trends—like painting classes, pottery courses, and obsessions with baking—and also throws light on the more perplexing interests of the last few years, like the rising popularity of ASMR (autonomous sensory meridian response), oddly satisfying videos of people performing mundane tasks, food porn, slime, and sound bathing.

There are now over ten million ASMR videos on YouTube that show people making soft sounds by whispering, turning book pages, chewing gum, nibbling food, or tapping their fingernails. For some, these sounds elicit a physical tingling sensation that many find to be soothing. Some watch ASMR content to help with anxiety and insomnia; indeed, these videos have been found to alter a viewer's heart rate and increase skin conductance.[33]

Similar physical sensations are reported by those who watch "oddly satisfying" videos that show people power-washing decks, folding laundry, mixing paint, and completing other innocuous tasks that many voyeurs say create a sensation of calm and pleasure. Food porn also elicits feelings of pleasure. Think: images and videos of unctuous brisket dripping translucent juices as a knife plows back and forth through the muscle; the liquid center of a molten chocolate cake slowly oozing as the sharp edge of a cold spoon cracks the cake's spongy surface; caramel that percolates to form a stiff crust atop a luscious crème as it's bruléed. (In fact, food imagery can alter insulin and ghrelin levels while stimulating our olfactory and gustatory cortexes.[34]) Meanwhile, engaging physically with slime stimulates our sense of touch, smell, and sound with every whack, fold, and stretch of the gooey, scented substance. The rhythm and vibrations of the gongs, Tibetan singing bowls, crystal bowls, and tuning forks used in sound bathing have been shown to shift electrical impulses in the brain and induce physical relaxation.[35]

What ties these trends together is their sensorial impacts. For many, watching videos of a grilled cheese being pulled apart or tile being scrubbed clean, or listening to a person's gentle whispers are ways of triggering physical sensations that are increasingly rare in our screen-based worlds. All around us, lifestyle trends showcase the human need for sensory stimulation.

Some technology companies deliberately try to accommodate our innate desires for sensorial experiences. For example, rumor has it that the original iPhone's home button was designed with a ridge around the edge not because it was required for functionality, but because of our need for touch—a craving so intense that a number of studies, conducted with varying populations around the world, have shown that it is exacerbating smartphone addiction.[36] For those craving a tactile experience, they need to do nothing more than reach in their pockets and feel the pleasurable vibrations and pressure against their fingertips.

Ultimately, people like Liza Patriana and Andy Kadin are not just benefiting from intrinsic motivation, the ability to incrementally improve their skills and see their own accomplishments, or the ability to share those accomplishments with others. They are also benefiting from the sensorial inputs coloring their days—the chill of the walk-in, the heat of the oven, the hollow sound of well-baked crust, the soft pull of the dough—which trigger feel-good neurochemicals and sensations.

In the Hungry Study, we found that the Tech-Tethered Cohort (those who are most anxious about being without their smartphones) consistently agreed with the following statements more than the average survey taker: *I am uncertain about my goals in life, I am looking for something that makes my life feel meaningful, I am always searching for something that makes my life feel significant,* and *I am seeking a purpose or mission for my life.*[37]

Opposing sentiments such as *My life has meaning, I feel I am living up to my potential, I feel in tune with my body, In most ways my life is close to my ideal*, and *I am satisfied with my life* all garnered agreement at a higher rate from a different group of respondents: the IRL Cohort.[38]

To qualify for the IRL Cohort, a respondent had to spend forty-five minutes or more outdoors every day, spend three or more hours a day making things with their hands, or be able to name three or more plants in their neighborhoods. As a good comparator, the IRL Cohort was more likely than average to say their hobbies include outdoor recreation like hiking or bird-watching, and to participate in sports or exercise activities. Meanwhile, the Tech-Tethered Cohort was more likely than average to say their hobbies include playing and/or watching video games and observing (rather than playing) sports.

According to our findings, the folks who spend more time outdoors, more time making things, and more time engaging their bodies are also those who are most likely to feel that their lives have meaning. Perhaps, this analog trend of do-it-yourself is the sensory-packed antidote to our modern environments.

Yet, you don't need to build a bird house, weave a wall tapestry, or bake a pie to find a sense of self and a sense of purpose. In fact, there is one other trend that may be larger than all these DIY and sensorial therapies combined, and it is highlighted in our Hungry Study findings. It's a way to stimulate one's senses, experiment creatively, reduce stress, reconnect with one's body, and re-center the concept of the self as a single actor in a much bigger story. And all it requires is that you step outside.

CHAPTER NINE

nature & well-being

I need your help with something," Chris Melançon said as he led me into the northwest fields of his Sonoma, California, farm. He was wearing a green-and-white plaid collared shirt and faded baggy jeans. A dark green raincoat, baseball cap, and thick salt-and-pepper beard kept him warm on the damp spring afternoon as a rain shower passed through. We were both in tall rubber boots that made satisfying splashes as we stomped across the muddy field.

An apiary soon came into view, with white pallet hives of varying heights and widths lined up in a row. A few bees floated above the wooden boxes, their black bodies stark against the pure blue sky.

"What can I help with?" I asked with curiosity and a bit of fear. Dharma, the herding dog, ran behind me, while the milky-white guard dogs, Khai and Khan, sat out in the soaked hog field. Air gusts rippled through my hair and the farm was silent except for intermittent clucks, oinks, and baas carried on the wind from the hen house, pigpen, and goat sheds nearby.

As we faced the apiary, Melançon stopped. "Put your ear to each box," he instructed, "and tell me what you hear. Which one is the least loud?"

A few days earlier some bees had swarmed and left their nest, having reproduced in numbers that made them unable to all fit inside their cozy home any longer. Melançon was able to direct the swarm into a new box, but he needed to figure out which home had been evacuated, leaving half of the original colony behind.

With some apprehension—for my safety and about my ability to hear anything useful—I bent over and, as instructed, pressed my ear against the dry wooden frame. The sound that bounced back nearly took my breath away. What I heard was not a buzz, as one associates with bees, but a melodic hum, like an orchestra strumming violins in unison. It was as though I was hearing the ocean or blood rushing through veins. I imagined hundreds of bees dancing inside, their wings fluttering against the air, generating the song that was beginning to reverberate through my own body.

My eyes went wide and Melançon smiled. "OK, try the next one," he instructed, waving me along. I did as he said and, one by one, listened in on the wild and unique symphonies playing inside each pallet.

"I think it's this one," I said, pointing to the third box in the row.

He nodded. "I think so, too."

With that, I had completed my farmer assistance for the afternoon. Disappointed there were not more bee arias to hear, I moseyed back toward the farmhouse as Melançon remained in the field to complete more farm chores.

Just a few years earlier, in their early forties, Chris and Lori Melançon were deciding whether to purchase their apartment in San Francisco. The idea of spending over a thousand dollars per square foot, they later told me, just did not seem reasonable, so instead the couple decided to look outside the city they had called home for twenty years. While scouring a home-search website, they zeroed in on a small four-acre parcel of land—with another eight acres adjacent—just outside the wine town of Sonoma in California's Napa Valley, less than an hour north of the city. There was a small farmhouse and soil ripe for wine groves. With no farming experience, but an itch to make a change, they put in an offer.

"We didn't really have a master plan, other than we wanted to have a space that could allow us to connect with the earth a little more, in a more meaningful way," Chris reflected as we talked on the phone prior to my visit. After the purchase finalized, they secured the eight acres next door and began the transition from urban life to farm life.

The couple met at work in the biotechnology industry, where Chris focused on biosecurity and Lori on public relations. Throughout their biotech careers, they dedicated their talents to companies that aligned with their own personal passions: cancer research, human genome research, vaccinations.

"Although it may not seem like a natural evolution to go from the pharmaceutical industry to wanting to be a farmer, to me it does seem like there's a common thread," Chris said, "which is having a positive impact and creating change."

"We're trying to have that same sort of impact," agreed Lori, "but on a day-to-day basis through how people react and learn about food and interact with food."

It took a few years for them to move to Sonoma full-time, and still, Lori and Chris integrate consulting work into their income stream, with Lori picking up the most office hours of the two of them. Sometimes, their two worlds collide. On a recent trip into the city for a lunch meeting on venture capital opportunities for an influenza vaccine company, Chris says he found himself in the restaurant kitchen selling his hogs to the chef.

On the farm, Chris handles the animal care and beekeeping while Lori spearheads gardening and soil initiatives. On the week I visited Lola Sonoma, the farm had just welcomed multiple litters of baby goats and piglets, bringing their farm family to ninety-four animals (not counting the bees).

"I was not an animal person," Chris admits. Now, "I'm a total convert." Neither he nor Lori ever imagined they would be raising livestock. But one thing led to another, and here they are, with a flock of animals they treat as family.

The bees were the first addition to the farm, after which they welcomed the dairy goats so Lori could make cheese. Next, they brought in dogs to help herd the goats and protect them from local coyotes and foxes. Soon, they learned about Kunekune pigs, a breed of stout grazing pigs with short hair, gold-and-cream spotted hides, and comical small wattles that sway from their lower jaws.* The Melançons picked

---

* The name *kunekune* means "fat and round" in the Maori language. They are, in fact, just that, and so mild-mannered that some keep Kunekune pigs as house pets. It's easy to see why. As I walked through the pen on the day of my visit, several of the pigs sidled up and pushed themselves against my leg to ask for a belly rub, a request I happily obliged.

up thirty-five of them from a local breeder, and soon added chickens for eggs. At each step along the way, they used mostly salvaged materials to build the animals' shelters.

The produce side of the farm has been slower to develop. The clay-filled soil is best for growing grapes, but they are not interested in wine. Instead, Lori is working to cultivate the ground for a more biodiverse fruit and vegetable farm, though it is a battle. They use the grazing pigs, whose waste reintroduces carbon to the land, and practice cover cropping as well, in order to build up nutrient-rich soil that can support several plants. "I really want to do compost teas," Lori told me one evening as she prepared dinner, and explained the process of steeping compost and collecting the concentrated nutrients that run off, which can later be used as a natural fertilizer for crops.

Because they have no experience to rely on as they build their business, they have hired a full-time farmer, Les, to both assist them and teach them the ins and outs of raising plants and animals. Other times, they rely on YouTube, Facebook, and fellow farmers to help them manage livestock that are ill, teach them the best way to construct a pigpen, or learn how to milk goats.

"We've made a lot of mistakes," Lori admitted. "But I'm learning to forgive myself."

"We're learning how to stay calm when things go wrong," Chris later told me.

There is a big difference between messing up in an office job and messing up when dealing with living things, noted Lori. "If I mess up, like I sent an email to the wrong person or something, maybe I embarrass myself. If we mess up now, we lose an animal or a plant." But, she pointed out, that's nature. "Nothing makes the circle of life clearer than being on a farm. I remember the first full year where I was here on the farm all the time: watching the seasons change, what blooms first and in what order spring comes, and then through summer and then what starts to die off first into the winter. To be able to witness that was just such a powerful thing," she reflected wistfully.

Losing a baby goat in the labor process, Lori recalled, had thus far been her most difficult experience, while Chris's was slaughtering his first pig. The pig was Bubbles, a 250-pound breeder who was "part of the family." She had injured her leg and could not get up to eat. After some time trying to help her heal, they realized that the next step was harvesting.

While life on the farm can prove stressful, the benefit, Chris and Lori agreed, is that it forces them to slow down and pay attention. Staying in the moment, Chris admitted, is difficult for him. "I grew up with a mom who had task lists all the time: 'Here's all the things we need to do.'" But, he said, he knows that true meaning in life is found in "what you're experiencing right now." The demands of the farm are training him to live in the present. Distraction is not an option; if you do not notice that an animal has a cut or is not eating or has a limp, it could cost that animal its life.

"Through innovation and technology, we've inadvertently become disconnected," Chris said—and not just from each other but also from nature. "Balancing out the digital world with analog experiences, a lot of that really drove us to commit to this lifestyle."

Most folks are not trading in their urban lives to become homesteaders or farmers. But other lifestyle trends point to an active desire to incorporate more bits of nature into our lives—be it with houseplants or routine camping trips with friends. Even these muted nature immersions can produce many of the same benefits that the Melançons told me about: the opportunity to slow down, observe, and offset a screen-filled week with something tangible, sensorial, and alive.

The Plant Economy

One of the most abundant trends of the last few years is not something you can eat or attend; it's a cactus—or, to be specific, a category of plant that includes cacti, called succulents. "Consider the Cactus: How Succulents Took Over Instagram—and Then the World," reads an article on the sports and pop culture site The Ringer.[1] Pinterest reports that searches for cactus arrangements were up by 235 percent in 2019.[2] A *Garden Center* survey of independent retailers found that cactus and succulent sales rose 64 percent between 2012 and 2017 in the US.[3] Just over one-fifth of those surveyed said that succulents were the "hottest trend" in their garden centers for 2017. All over the world, people are integrating a bit of prickly, low-maintenance nature into their homes.[4]

Globally, Millennials are the ones driving this trend forward, as well as expressing their succulent obsession in the fashion and food markets. People are dying their hair to mimic the ombre green-to-pink shades of the newly popular perennials (see #succulenthair for examples). Bakeries are celebrating the striking geometric fractal designs and varied greens, blues, and purples of succulents on cupcake and cake decorations. Succulent bouquets and centerpieces are trending on bridal blogs.

Yet succulents are not the only houseplant receiving fanfare of late; we're in the middle of a full-fledged houseplant bonanza. In the United States, Millennials are said to account for one-third of all houseplant purchases, filling their homes with cascading ferns and shady philodendrons.[5] People have uploaded a whopping 3.4 million boastful images of indoor greenery to Instagram and tagged them #plantsofinstagram. The plant mania is celebrated on home renovation shows, where designers routinely tuck large fig trees along bay windows, and in the hospitality industry as hotels install mammoth monstera and moss grow walls behind check-in desks, and restaurants pin up wallpaper prints that mix Millennial pink with graphic shapes of cacti and wide tropical leaves.

The plant infatuation has also spurred a new category of event programming: plant parties. In Australia, the Jungle Collective hosts pop-up plant parties in Sydney, Melbourne, and Perth, where they sell hundreds of "on-trend" blossoms. Jungle Collective events each have an on-site horticulturalist, like a sommelier at a wine bar, to explain the characteristics of the vegetation throughout the nursery. They regularly sell out events with a cap of five thousand attendees, most of whom—judging by event photos—are Millennials. Each verdant soiree has a different theme, like "Springtime Splendor" or "Rumble in the Jungle," and some offer half-off admission if you show up in wacky attire like all denim or dress up as an animal—"We're talking face paint, fun outfits, hats," the company notes on one event invitation.[6] The concept of a plant party has become so common that, if this sounds alluring to you, chances are you can find a plant store in a city near you that hosts them.

The foliation fad has spurred platitude headlines that mock plant-adoring Millennials: "They don't own homes. They don't have kids. Why Millennials are plant addicts," from the *Los Angeles Times*; "Why more Millennials are buying into 'plant parenthood,'" from NBC News;

"Millennials are filling their homes—and the void in their hearts—with houseplants," from the *Washington Post*.[7] Loneliness, childlessness, and a lack of square footage are cited as the main incentives of plant ownership. A seedling is easier, many journalists argue, than a pet or a child, and you still get to care for something.

It turns out that houseplants are just the tip of the iceberg when it comes to lifestyle trends that integrate a bit of nature into our otherwise indoor and largely soil-less lives. Some are digging deeper than hanging ferns and turning to edible plant gardens, nature walks, camping, and farming as conduits to well-being.

Rooted in Nature

Throughout human history, we have spent most of our existence relying on, living among, and attempting to survive in nature. The human body is innately tied to the earth. Our existence quite literally depends on it. When we eat any food, we are soaking up nutrients once found within the soil to fuel our own corporality.

In our cement-paved, headphone-plugged, and artificially lit modern world, it is easy to forget the environment from which, and for which, our bodies evolved. Inside each of us are talents that, now, most often go untapped. For example, the human nose can detect geosmin, a chemical produced by soil-dwelling bacteria, at concentrations of 5 parts per trillion.[8] It's this sensitivity that allows us to detect healthy versus damaged soils entirely by scent. We can also smell plant oils aerated through raindrops, which create that warm, musky, just-after-a-rainstorm scent. Our noses are so attuned to these compounds that we can actually note differences between the just-after-a-rainstorm-scent of, say, Madrid and the just-after-a-rainstorm-scent in Miami.[9]

The vestigial remnants of our hunter-gatherer talents influence our experiences at the farmers' market or grocery store, or on adventures out foraging. Millennial architect Ben Ezinga spent most of his adult life as a real estate developer in the Midwest, but recently purchased a sixty-two-acre old dairy farm meandering alongside the Claverack Creek, near Hudson, New York. Though raised on a farm in the Hudson, much of Ezinga's outdoor living experience had become a faint memory. His return to the land as an adult, he told me, was punctuated by revelations of his own ancestral ties to the earth.

Soon after the purchase of his land, Ezinga set out one afternoon in search of wild ramps, asparagus, and chanterelles. He noticed that with just one foraging walk around his property, his mind had created a thorough mental map of the edible plants' locations. "Even though the field is covered in snow now," he told me months after his initial foray, "I bet I could go where the ramps are or where the asparagus is. I could find my way back with my eyes closed." How, I asked? "Oh, this is tapping into something evolutionary," he replied. "Something in my brain lit up." Something in his brain he did not know existed.

While it may have felt like a superpower, this mental acuity in locating food sources is not unique. Researchers have found that humans have a keen ability to accurately remember locations of foods with a high caloric density at local farmers' markets.[10] We also have a preference for glossy objects that appear reminiscent of flowing water, essential for hydration and growing vegetation.[11]

All of this is to say: Whether we are aware of it or not, we have sophisticated survival skills ready to be put to use the moment we step outdoors. It's just that in today's screen-saturated settings, we often don't give ourselves the chance to use them.

Nature Deficit

Though we are designed for lives lived in nature, human beings spend less time outdoors today than ever before. A 2014 survey of over five thousand Canadians, both urban and rural, found that the average person spends a whopping 94.2 percent of the day indoors or in a vehicle.[12] Very similar habits have been identified around the world.[13] Globally, people are spending less and less time engaging in outdoor recreation, such as visiting national parks and camping, and folks continue to migrate from rural settings to urban areas.[14] (The United Nations predicts that two-thirds of all people on Earth will live in an urban area by 2050.[15]) Already, over 80 percent of people in North America, Latin America, and the Caribbean call cities their home.

Even the time that kids spend outside is not quite the same as in generations past. A close look at the most comprehensive analyses reveals that most of the time kids spend outside is while hanging out with friends, playing sports, and using electronic devices outdoors, such as listening to music and watching movies. While none of those things are bad, per se, they are *different* from hiking, camping, fishing, or bird-watching, which require one to focus on the natural surroundings, in much the way both Chris Melançon and Ben Ezinga described having to do. Kids are participating in activities that *happen* to be outdoors, not activities that *have* to be in, and involve, the outdoors.

My mother fondly recalls a childhood without toys, where most of her time was spent outside the house dreaming up stories and novel games and exploring her neighborhood with her sisters. These intimate and exploratory forms of outdoor recreation are out of favor among young kids and teens. General outdoor play is on the decline among three- to twelve-year-olds in the United States, while time spent engaging with electronic entertainment continues to rise.[16] A survey of 1,450 American children ages six to nineteen found that only 5.4 percent of the kids surveyed listed nature-based activities as their primary pastime.[17] (A number of parents say they have forgotten how to play without devices, and thus are unable to guide their children. Some are hiring screen-free play coaches to introduce their children to the pleasures of drawing on the sidewalk with chalk, setting up a lemonade stand, and playing catch.[18] Yes, really.)

In his 2005 book, *Last Child in the Woods*, journalist Richard Louv argues that all this time indoors is causing something called nature deficit disorder, defined as the human costs of alienation from nature. Louv points to decreasing time in nature as the cause of rising rates of anxiety and waning concentration, among other modern ailments. Louv's argument is basic: We evolved to live outdoors, and now we are living indoors. How could that *not* impact our well-being?

"For most of human history, people chased things or were chased themselves," writes *New York Times* opinion writer Timothy Egan on the topic of nature deficit disorder. "They turned dirt over and planted seeds and saplings. They took in vitamin D from the sun, and learned to tell a crow from a raven (ravens are larger; crows have a more nasal call;

so say the birders). And then, in less than a generation's time, millions of people completely decoupled themselves from nature."[19]

People are not just spending less time hiking and camping; they are spending far less time communing with nature overall. Many people are unfamiliar with seasonality and how things grow, unaware of natural remedies, dangers, and animal behaviors. In the Hungry Study, more than three-quarters of all survey takers report spending, on average, forty-five minutes or less outdoors each day, and one-third of respondents said they could not identify a single plant that grows outdoors in their local regions. The migration indoors has caused us to become disassociated with the very environment in which we evolved.

So, is Louv right? Can less time outdoors have a detrimental impact on one's well-being?

The Nature Nostrum

In 2010, George MacKerron, senior lecturer in economics at the University of Sussex, and Susana Mourato, professor of environmental economics at the London School of Economics, launched the "Mappiness Project," in which self-selected participants recorded their happiness at random moments during the day.*,[20] Alerted through a free Mappiness app, participants also recorded who they were with, where they were, and what activities they were partaking in at the moment of their happiness recordings. Over six months, MacKerron and Mourato received more than 1.1 million responses from over twenty thousand Brits.

After analyzing the data, MacKerron and Mourato landed on a rather straightforward finding: People are most happy while in nature. "On average, study participants are significantly and substantially happier outdoors in all green or natural habitat types than they are in urban environments," they summarize in their paper, succinctly titled "Happiness Is Greater in Natural Environments."

---

* Due to this self-selection, the study's participants were more likely than the general population to be middle- to high-income earners, employed, and under the age of thirty-five.

The researchers interpret the findings three ways: First, the coast, wetlands, mountains, grasslands, and wooded areas are likely to be without irritants such as traffic noise and air pollution, urban features known to cause higher stress levels, along with cardiovascular problems.[21] Second, when in these outdoor environments, we are more likely to engage our bodies and senses in activities such as gardening, birdwatching, or hiking (which, as we've seen in the Hungry Study, correlates with improved well-being). Third, the researchers point to the biophilia hypothesis: that humans have an innate emotional affiliation with nature and living organisms that contributes to elevated feelings of contentment.[*, 22]

Philosophers have talked about the restorative benefits of nature for thousands of years. In Buddhism, it is believed that Siddhartha Gautama reached enlightenment under the Bodhi tree sometime between 500 and 400 BCE, and Buddha's teachings revolved around humans' inherent connection to nature and oneness with everything. "There is no spot on the ground where men had not died and therefore every part of nature will be endowed with a spirit, these will be the spirits of the trees, the mountains and the water," Buddha is said to have preached.[23]

In *National Geographic*, nature journalist Florence Williams reviews the long history of people who stepped outdoors in search of nature's panacea: "It went back at least to Cyrus the Great, who some 2,500 years ago built gardens for relaxation in the busy capital of Persia. Paracelsus, the sixteenth-century German-Swiss physician, gave voice to that same intuition when he wrote, 'The art of healing comes from nature, not from the physician.'" Odes to the nostrum of nature undulate through the stanzas and sentences of William Wordsworth, Johann Wolfgang von Goethe, Ralph Waldo Emerson, John Muir, Walt Whitman, Henry David Thoreau, and Frederick Law Olmsted. These cultural references "built the spiritual and emotional case for creating the world's first national parks by claiming that nature had healing powers," Williams writes.[24]

---

* The biophilia hypothesis was introduced in the 1980s by Edward Wilson; since then, the concept has spurred several studies and artistic philosophies that look at the benefits of being in nature.

Nowadays we have more than theories, religious teachings, and poems to convince us of nature's healing effects; we have decades of scientific research. Multiple studies, conducted in various countries, have found that being around nature quells feelings of stress, depression, and anxiety, while inducing feelings of happiness and facilitating a sense of calm.[25] Sometimes, a short walk through a park or listening to nature sounds—like running water or birds chirping—is enough to induce these benefits, lessening stress as well as feelings of anger and frustration.[26] Being in nature has been shown to reduce heart rate, blood pressure, and stress hormones, while dampening activity in the sympathetic nervous system, which directs the body's rapid involuntary responses to dangerous or stressful situations.[27]

It should come as no surprise that time spent among trees, flowers, and animals plays an important role in our well-being, given our intricate relationship to nature. "Air, water, earth, fire, the subtle forces of the cosmos, the natural rhythms and diversity of life have shaped man's nature during the evolutionary past and have created deep-rooted sensual and emotional needs that cannot be eradicated," writes French-American microbiologist René Dubos.[28]

This innate connection to our surroundings, and our increasing separation from natural surroundings, may be a factor in some of today's most pressing social issues—including crime and violence. In a landmark 2001 study on the connection between green spaces and well-being, Dr. Frances E. Kuo and Dr. William Sullivan, co-directors of the Human-Environment Research Laboratory at the University of Illinois, Urbana-Champaign, examined the impact of green space on crime rates at Ida B. Wells, which was, at the time, a large public housing development in Chicago.[29] Kuo and Sullivan analyzed both Chicago Police Department crime reports and the amount of greenery, such as grass and trees, around the Ida B. Wells buildings. Characteristics such as resident income, education, and life circumstances remained homogeneous across the study sample; the only variation was the amount of vegetation surrounding each housing unit.

Much like MacKerron and Mourato, Kuo and Sullivan landed on a simple finding: Crime was lower in areas with more greenery. "Analyses revealed consistent, systematically negative relationships between the density of trees and grass around the buildings and the number of crimes per building reported to the police," Kuo and Sullivan write in their often-cited study. "The greener a building's surroundings are, the fewer total crimes; moreover, this relationship extended to both property crimes and violent crimes." The pair attribute the findings to two things: the impact of perceived informal surveillance (people assume there will be other people in green spaces) and the possibility that greenery mitigates the psychological precursors to violence, such as irritability and impulsivity—a hypothesis now with greater scientific backing.

Exposure to the outdoors does not just make us feel happier; it makes us nicer to one another. Several unrelated studies have found that time in nature correlates with prosocial behaviors such as generosity and kindness.[30] Nature alters one's salient life values and aspirations; after exposure to images of natural environments or live plants, participants in one study listed more communal, less selfish life aspirations than those exposed to urban environments.[31] Other experiments have found that those with some form of nature immersion—be it a walk in the park or viewing a nature video—are more likely to help strangers and act cooperatively.[32]

Some studies have focused specifically on the connection between prosocial behavior and the power of nature to induce a state of awe in people.[33] One experiment found that behaviors such as cooperation and generosity are strengthened after exposure to beautiful and awe-inspiring nature scenery, and another found that "a naturalistic induction of awe in which participants looked up at a grove of towering trees led to increased helpfulness, greater ethicality, and decreased entitlement."[34] An experience of wonder conjured by nature can elicit a sense that there is something greater than the self.[35] This, then, can have a ripple effect, reducing feelings of loneliness and stress and thereby facilitating the emotional space for people to be more trusting, generous, and helpful.[36]

Engagements with the outdoors also improve our physical well-being. Those who live in areas of greater greenery exhibit lower rates of cardiovascular disease, musculoskeletal issues, respiratory infections, and migraines, and even lower mortality rates.[37] Researchers have also found that a single interlude in the woods can catalyze one's cancer-fighting "natural killer" cells, an indicator of the strength of the immune function.[38]

Other studies suggest that houseplants also trigger these health windfalls, a finding that brings additional context to the current plant craze. For example, surgery patients who are surrounded by foliage or flowers, or whose hospital rooms feature a scenic window view, recover from surgery faster than the average patient.[39] Being surrounded by nature, be it an indoor hanging plant or a forest preserve, is also shown to have a significant impact on our ability to concentrate. A number of studies show that exposure to water, wind-like air ventilation, and any form of plant life can improve cognitive performance and productivity and calm stressed-out workers.[40] A simple glimpse of the color green, exposure to nature-like ambient noise, or a short walk in the park can enhance creativity and problem-solving skills and improve one's ability to focus (even among those with ADHD).[41] If you are having trouble concentrating at work, or are stuck on a creative problem, a new desk plant may be the solution.

The impact of time spent in nature on one's physical and mental health is so profound that a number of countries are now encouraging their citizens to partake in something called forest bathing. In Japan, the practice is known as shinrin-yoku, a term inspired by ancient Shinto and Buddhist practices that refers to using all five of the body's senses to engage and commune with nature. Japan now boasts over sixty government-certified forest therapy bases, and millions of citizens walk the trails each year.[42] Meanwhile, at the University of California, San Francisco, Benioff Children's Hospital, Dr. Nooshin Razani prescribes time in nature as a clinical treatment for chronic illness, citing the benefits on cortisol levels and mood. In 2009, Razani partnered with the regional park district to run a park prescription program.[43] "We have hiked, fished, sung songs around a campfire, and explored tide pools—all for health. Through the process, we have created some of the first-ever validated protocols for physicians and health systems to integrate nature-based interventions into practice, and recently completed the first randomized trial of a park prescription program," Razani documents on a blog for outdoor retail company REI.[44]

Likewise, South Korea's government has invested millions of dollars in a National Forest Healing Center. There, the forest therapy program utilizes four distinct practices: forest trekking; aquatic therapy, which uses water flow and pressure as curative techniques; relax therapy, which works to awaken the body through meditation, massage, aroma-therapy, and tea tastings; and DIY therapy, where participants combine the pleasure of learning handicrafts with aromatherapy.[45] Finland is also attempting to engage their citizens in forest therapy. They encourage people to hike along "power trails" for a minimum of five hours a month to ward off symptoms of depression.*

The Japanese physical anthropologist Yoshifumi Miyazaki believes that human beings, whether we are aware of it or not, are most comfort-able in nature. Being among the natural outdoor world, he avers, is the only time in which we are engaging all our senses and thus, he says, the only space in which we are fully alive.[46]

You may be wondering at this point how this all works. Why would going outside, seeing green, or feeling wind on your skin have any impact on your cognitive abilities, mood, or immune system? So far, science has provided answers to some of these questions, while others remain unresolved.

When it comes to immune system function, Dr. Qing Li is the Sher-lock Holmes of researchers, working to unravel the links between forest bathing and its killer cell activation.[47] An immunologist at Tokyo's Nip-pon Medical School and a founding member and chairman of the Japa-nese Society for Forest Medicine, Li is known as one of the world's top forest medicine experts. Around 2005, Li began to investigate the poten-tial role of phytoncides in human health. Phytoncides are natural tree oils that serve as a tree's defense system against bacteria, insects, and fungi.†[48]

---

* Of course, this concept is now being commoditized. "Imagine sitting on a deserted beach," encourages writer Ashley Mateo in the *Condé Nast Traveler* article "Thanks to Forest Bathing, We Now Have Island Bathing." "All you can hear is the gentle sway of palm trees in the wind, the lapping of ocean waves on the sand, and the soft instructions of your private meditation instructor: breathe in, breathe out. Sounds pretty damn peaceful, right? This isn't some New-Age nirvana; it's island bathing, an exclusive, two-hour guided excursion for one to two people offered by Carlisle Bay, a five-star resort tucked in a remote inlet along Antigua's shores."

† Concentrations of these oils change based on weather and tree species. The largest producers of phytoncides are evergreen trees, like pine, cedar, spruce, and conifers. The human nose can detect the difference between varying phytoncides; some smell lemony, others piney or herby, still others like turpentine. Phytoncides are also used as a communication mechanism between trees.

For Li's first experiment, he incubated human natural killer (NK) lymphocyte cells critical to our immune system with phytoncides and ultimately found an increase in NK cell activity along with the presence of other anti-cancer proteins.[49] In a subsequent study, Li sequestered twelve middle-aged men at a Tokyo hotel for three nights and, using a humidifier, diffused phytoncide essential oil into their rooms while they slept. Blood and urine samples were collected each day. At the end of the experiment, Li and his colleagues measured a significant increase in NK cells and natural killer activity, paired with a decrease in stress hormones, among other findings.[50]

"It's like a miracle drug," Li has said of the tree-derived oils.[51] In the winter, Li keeps a humidifier with phytoncide oil in his room. In the summer, he uses the oil for aromatherapy.[52]

Simultaneously, scientists in Korea have been unraveling hints as to why nature could cause amicable behaviors such as cooperation and generosity, as well as feelings of happiness. In one study in which subjects' brains were mapped using an fMRI machine, researchers found that viewing images and video of urban settings causes more blood to flow to the amygdala, our fear and anxiety center, as well as the anterior temporal pole, which is associated with feelings of anger and depression. Meanwhile, media of nature landscapes lit up the anterior cingulate and insula of subjects' brains—regions associated with empathy, emotional stability, positive mental outlooks, and feelings of love—as well as the basal ganglia, an area of the brain also activated by happy memories and friendly faces.[53] Somehow, nature cues the deepest recesses of our brains.

Phytoncides are not the only feel-good triggers found in nature. Some scientists credit a creature found in the soil beneath our feet for nature's nostrum-like effects.

"It's a full sensory experience putting your hands into some really fertile dirt," Ben Ezinga said as he reflected on gardening on his new farmland. He told me how surprised he was by just how good it makes him feel to hold fecund soil or traipse around barefoot. On a pleasure scale, he compares it to getting a massage or sunbathing.

The delight Ezinga experiences as he weaves his toes through grass or scoops out holes for tree roots is not an anomaly; our bodies derive pleasure from a very particular soil compound found in fertile humus called *Mycobacterium vaccae*, colloquially known as nature's Prozac. Absorbed through inhalation or ingestion, *M. vaccae* is a living bacterium that is known to boost levels of serotonin and norepinephrine, functioning quite similarly to common antidepressant pharmaceuticals.[54] In multiple studies, *M. vaccae* has been shown to reduce stress, improve mood and concentration, and boost one's immune system.[55] In summary: Nature rewards us for interacting with it.

At the moment, there are several theories as to why mental acuity improves outdoors, beyond the potential impacts of *M. vaccae*. One of them, attention restoration theory (ART), proposed by University of Michigan professors Rachel Kaplan and Stephen Kaplan, suggests that nature exposure has restorative effects on low-level modules of the executive attention system, which is involved in the regulation of thoughts, emotions, memories, and responses. This restoration can improve one's ability to concentrate.[56] The theory rests on the idea that nature is neither cognitively overwhelming nor boring; being in nature allows the mind to wander yet also provides ample opportunity for moments of awe. A number of studies have provided support for this theory and even expanded upon it.[57]

Some suggest that nature aids concentration because being reminded of the great expanse of nature can calm us and refocus the mind.[58] This concept is not new: In 1865, famed landscape architect Frederick Law Olmsted penned a report to document his experience in Yosemite and the Mariposa Grove, in which he writes: "The enjoyment of scenery employs the mind without fatigue and yet exercises it, tranquilizes it and yet enlivens it; and thus, through the influence of the mind over the body, gives the effect of refreshing rest and reinvigoration to the whole system."[59] This sweet spot between bored and overwhelmed is also what Mihaly Csikszentmihalyi identified as the ideal setting for flow.

Today, most of us live in a world of split attention, content inundation, and persistent interruptions, all of which hinder our ability to concentrate. Meanwhile, an environment that benefits our cognition lies just outside. Some, motivated by these learnings, are weaving nature into our indoor environments in more dramatic ways than just adding a houseplant or two.

Biophilic Design

The positive impacts of nature on cognition, stress, happiness, and generosity have inspired an entirely new practice called biophilic design. The tenets of biophilic design include the integration of nature-related visual, auditory, haptic, olfactory, or gustatory stimuli—such as water features, grow walls, changes in air flow that mimic natural wind patterns, building materials with nature-inspired patterns and textures, or the integration of lights with nature-like variations in brightness and shadow—into building architecture and interior design.[60]

Airports and hospitals are employing biophilic design to soothe stressed travelers and patients. Hotels like the forthcoming Rosemont Hotel and Residences in Dubai are incorporating nature features to draw in travelers. The Rosemont's much-anticipated fifty-three-story building is still under construction as of this writing but has earned ample buzz by promoting its plans for robotic luggage handlers, an on-site laser tag arena, and, most anticipated of all, seventy-five thousand square feet of synthetic indoor rain forest. Design renderings illustrate walkways flanked by waterfalls, dangling verdant vines, towering trees, and a blue marsh made all the more convincing with a sensory rain system that will, according to reports, spray recycled rainwater to mimic a rain forest's humidity.

Other companies are embracing biophilic design to improve the employee experience. Somewhat ironically, the big technology companies are leading the way when it comes to biophilic workplace design. The Facebook campus in Menlo Park, California, now features two buildings designed by Frank Gehry that boast features like a nine-acre green rooftop with a half-mile walking trail, an outdoor sunken courtyard filled with forty-foot redwood trees, and a tiered outdoor amphitheater for co-working and meals.

Meanwhile, Google has unveiled plans for a one-million-square-foot campus in nearby Sunnyvale, California, with a structure inspired by hillsides. Early renderings of the building show zigzagging wildflower terraces that climb several stories up, like switchbacks on a mountainside. The terraces support one long, weaving trail that will allow employees to enter the building at multiple access points, on foot, bike, or even in-line skates (should one wish to literally roll into work).

Just a hop, skip, and jump away in Cupertino, California, Apple has erected a circular spaceship-like office that was originally conceived by the late Steve Jobs. Back in 2009, architect Norman Foster recalls that Jobs specifically requested that glass, steel, stone, and trees be used as the main building blocks for Apple's new home base. Jobs insisted that the campus be swarming with trees to "inspire" employees, and he even tracked down an arborist to help bring his vision to life. Ultimately, the campus featured nine thousand trees.[61]

Microsoft took a less high-tech approach to their biophilic aspirations and hired *Treehouse Masters* host Pete Nelson to craft three co-working treehouses for employees at their headquarters in Redmond, Washington, which they outfitted with rocking chairs, sunroofs, the aroma of fresh red cedar, and, of course, Wi-Fi. "These treehouses bring employees into nature for improved focus and creativity," Nelson writes on his own website.[62]

Not one to be left out of any trend, Amazon began designing their own biophilic workspaces back in 2012, dreaming up the glass-enclosed, futuristic jungle spheres that would eventually become a forty-thousand-square-foot facility on the company's Denny Triangle campus in Seattle. The expansive urban gardens, now dubbed the Spheres, feature a waterfall, a fifty-foot ficus tree, and four thousand square feet of vertical vegetative surface decorated with forty thousand species of ferns and tropical plants cultivated in a custom greenhouse set a half hour's drive from the company's headquarters.

"We wanted to create a unique environment for employees to collaborate and innovate," explained John Schoettler, Amazon's vice president of global real estate and facilities, to the *Washington Post* regarding the initial idea to transform the newly acquired downtown plots. "We also asked ourselves what was missing from the modern office, and we discovered that that missing element was a link to nature."[63] Amazon horticulturist Ben Eiben directly credits biophilia as the theory that inspired the initial concept of the Spheres.[64]

While many are incorporating the positive powers of nature into their urban, mainly indoor lifestyles—with houseplants, forest bathing, camping trips, and biophilic design—others are going much further. They're sowing new roots and spurring a new cliché of the hipster farmer.

A Return to the Land

"What is your favorite thing to do on the farm?" I asked Bebe and Carmen, two college-age farm interns at Lola Sonoma. Thanks to a program called World Wide Opportunities on Organic Farms (aka WWOOF), Bebe and Carmen were assisting Lori and Chris Melançon with planting, animal care, and many other tasks around the property for a few weeks. At dinner, the two sat with me as Lori prepared the meal. I leaned on the square kitchen table with a glass of red wine set near my notebook.

"I think shoveling manure and soil into the vegetable beds, because it's probably the most laborious work, aside from moving heavy equipment," Bebe replied, providing me with a very unexpected answer. Twenty-one-year-old Bebe wore baggy pants and a loose, long-sleeve shirt. Her long, wavy hair dangled far past her shoulders. She sat at the table with one knee propped up on the chair.

"Going through high school felt like I was put in an incubator of intellectualism," she reflected. "Having to grow my mind at a really rapid pace and not really ever having enough time to connect to my body was hard. I just felt very disassociated a lot of the time, and so I started to desire doing something more physically laborious." Bebe shrugged and pushed her tangled blond hair back from her face. Her second favorite farm activity, she said, was interacting with the animals. The next morning, I watched Bebe scoop up a piglet and burrow her face in the nape of its little pink body, pushing kisses against its fuzzy skin.

This was Bebe's third two-week-long WWOOF visit to Lola Sonoma. She had bounced from the rigors of a competitive high school outside Los Angeles to the bluestocking environment of Sarah Lawrence University in New York, then back to California to attend community college, and now to the pigpens of Sonoma County. Carmen, also originally from the Los Angeles suburbs, nodded along as Bebe outlined her personal history. This was Carmen's second farm visit on a gap semester from the Rhode Island School of Design. She told me that she wanted to volunteer on the farm in order to learn how to grow her own food, an interest buoyed by her devotion to veganism.

While taking time off from college to farm may sound odd, it is a practice growing in popularity among American youth. "There has been a big increase in the number of people interested in learning first-hand about where their food comes from, being connected to it," Sarah Potenza, executive director of WWOOF-USA, told me. "And most of that interest has come from people ages eighteen to twenty-four." Many WWOOF participants use the weeks- to months-long undertaking as a restorative digital detox, tapping into the benefits about which Henry David Thoreau and others waxed poetic. Today, WWOOF runs programs in over a hundred countries worldwide.

Plenty of Millennials and Gen Zers are not just interning on farms but opting out of common career narratives by choosing to parlay their middle- or upper-class educations into farm work. For only the second time in the last hundred years, the number of farmers under thirty-five years old is increasing, according to the US Department of Agriculture's 2012 Census of Agriculture.[65] According to the USDA, these young farmers are more likely to be college-educated and female, and are more ethnically and racially diverse than most American farmers.[66] In addition, a survey conducted by the National Young Farmers Coalition shows that most of today's young farmers did not grow up in agricultural families, a detail that marks a significant shift in the history of farming, in which farmers have traditionally handed down land from generation to generation.[67] Now, the children of rural farmers are heading to urban centers, while kids with suburban and urban upbringings are leasing land in the country, renting tractors, and learning how to subdue weeds organically.

While the number of young farmers entering the field is still drastically lower than the number of retiring farmers overall, some states are seeing a bigger youth boom than others. Nationally, the number of farmers ages twenty-five to thirty-four grew 2.2 percent between 2007 and 2012, but in California, Nebraska, and South Dakota, the number of newbie farmers has blossomed by 20 percent, if not more.[68] Meanwhile, in Maine, the number of farmers under the age of thirty-five has increased by 40 percent over the same period.[69]

To many, choosing to devote one's life to growing organic produce or raising goats seems outright perplexing, especially when you consider the other career paths open to many of these college-educated farmers. Money, certainly, is not the motivator. For most farmers, income from farming is so minimal that it has to be supplemented with outside work, and most American farmers are responsible for purchasing their own health insurance, a barrier that, for some, is too burdensome to overcome.[70] Additionally, many young American farmers are suffering under the weight of student loan debt. And just to make things a bit trickier, the cost of farmland has been rising steadily since the mid 1980s—again, most of these new farmers are not, as in generations past, inheriting their land; they need to rent or buy their plots.[71] Furthermore, these twenty- and thirtysomething farmers are far more likely than the general farming population to use organic practices on their farms, and they tend to operate small farms of less than fifty acres—two aspects that disqualify many of them from the most common government farm assistance programs, which, in the US, favor large, commodity crop farming.[72] With all these disincentives, why be a farmer? The succinct answer: eudaimonia.

Much like the hands-on trends of the DIY movement, farming—especially small-scale, sustainable farming—lends itself to the tenets of autonomy, competence, and connectedness. As I spoke with new farmers around the world, from Thailand to Maine, I heard familiar stories of feeling independent and of gaining a sense of mastery through constant learning. Much of farm work lends itself to the satisfying processes of producing something with one's own hands and provides the opportunity to repeat and improve upon tactics season after season. In addition, it taps into our most basic safety needs by giving individuals full power over, and knowledge of, their food sources.

The emotional and physical benefits of farm work are so significant that people are implementing farming and other forms of horticulture as forms of therapy for addicts, veterans, and prisoners.[73] In a 2011 Justice Department report, 30 percent of all correctional systems reported adding new green education and training programs. Teaching prisoners how to garden, the report outlines, can provide practical skills, buoy self-esteem, teach the ethics of caring for a living product, and provide other therapeutic remedies.[74] It's been proven to reduce recidivism rates and improve inmates' mental health. Nelson Mandela writes in his autobiography that during his time in prison in South Africa, "A garden was one of the few things in prison that one could control. To plant a seed, watch it grow, to tend it and then harvest it, offered a simple but enduring satisfaction. The sense of being the custodian of this small patch of earth offered a taste of freedom."[75] He goes on to use the process of tending, cultivating, and harvesting as a metaphor for qualities important in leadership.

Of course, not all nature-yearning young people are giving up their dreams of being doctors, journalists, or coders to go buy a farm, or even spend a few weeks on a farm. Many, many more are utilizing backyard and community gardens to satisfy their green thumb urges.

According to multiple sources, the fastest growing population of gardeners in the US are Millennials. Five million of the six million Americans who took up gardening in 2015 were Millennials, according to the 2016 National Gardening Survey, and sales of edible plants to Millennials have grown at nine times the rate of sales to Baby Boomers, claims the Scotts Miracle-Gro Company.[76] This interest in growing food at home has spurred a $1 billion increase in lawn and garden sales over the five years leading up to 2017, as reported by GardenResearch.com.[77] The market for lawn and garden spending for growing vegetables, fruit, berries, and herbs reached a reported $36.1 billion in 2015, surpassing the market for flower gardening.[78]

While some of this new generation of gardeners are doing their growing outdoors in raised beds, plenty of others are storing their plants inside. Remember, Millennials are a generation lagging in home ownership. Plenty of these hungry harvesters do not have outdoor space to work with. Those who are not lucky enough to own land or be able to rent rooftop garden space are looking to indoor hydroponic, aeroponic, and even aquaponic growing systems.* Searches for "vertical gardens" rose by nearly 300 percent between 2017 and 2018 on Pinterest, and the site expects that number to continue to grow.[79] A flood of indoor grow kit startups are now competing for consumer dollars, particularly those of twenty- and thirtysomethings.[80]

Nikhil Arora, CEO of Back to the Roots, has enjoyed watching this trend go from "hippie fad" to something more mainstream, he told me from his office in San Francisco. Back to the Roots sells several home growing systems, such as a mushroom-growing kit, kitchen herb

---

* None of these systems use soil to grow plants. Hydroponics uses water, and aeroponics uses a nutrient-rich water mist. In aquaponics, fish provide nutrients, through their excrement, to the water growing the plants.

garden, and mini aquaponics system with which you can both raise a fish and grow your salad greens in a unit small enough to fit on your windowsill. "We're nationwide now, at Home Depot, Target, Whole Foods, but also in a thousand schools," Arora told me back in 2017. "Seeing kids' eyes light up" as they say "Whoa, that's how it grows?" is one of Arora's favorite moments on the job. "That changes a mindset about how you look at food." And a sense of ownership can make a child more likely to eat a food once it is harvested.[81]

In the housing industry, gardening trends are encouraging urban builders to integrate outdoor growing spaces into their plans, an idea that is already being commoditized. In 2018, Brooklyn welcomed its first luxury condominium building to offer rentable rooftop "garden plots" as one of the many building amenities.[82] Others are making agriculture the centerpiece of their architectural and urban planning designs.

Introducing: the agrihood. Some are calling it the new golf course, but it's not nearly as highbrow, nor exclusive, and there is a lot more dirt on people's knees. All around the world, real-estate developers are designing neighborhoods where the home owners association fees go to the town farmer instead of eighteen-hole maintenance. According to the Urban Land Institute, about two hundred agriculture-centered housing developments have been built or are under construction in the United States; the vast majority have been constructed since 2000. Many of these planned communities include on-site farms, community-supported agriculture shares or farmers' markets, community gardens, and cooking classes.

Agrihoods span the world, from Willowsford just outside Washington, DC, in Virginia, to Sweden's Drömgården on the island of Muskö in Stockholm's archipelago, to the upcoming Witchcliffe Ecovillage outside Perth, Australia. There are even plans for an agrihood in the Pudong District in Shanghai, China. There, amidst the polluted city, 250 acres have been set aside for an agricultural district called Sunqiao. The development will offer produce farms, hydroponic greenhouses, algae farms, and seed vaults, along with public plazas, parks, housing, stores, restaurants, and a science museum.[83]

While farming remains a distant concept for most, we can see, all around us, a desire to reconnect with the land, especially among technology-raised twenty- and thirtysomethings. Be it through a pot of succulents on a sill, a planter of herbs blooming on a fire escape, forest bathing, or community gardens and walking trails, people are experiencing the benefits of integrating a bit of nature into their lives—for direct exposure to the elixirs of nature as well as a space to cultivate autonomy and competence.

Communion with Nature

Another aspect of the nature experience that has significant relevance to well-being: a feeling of connectedness. While many DIYers cite the sense of relatedness formed when they share their products with others and an increased awareness of their bodies, those who work among nature talked to me about a different kind of connectedness that arises on the farm or in a forest or garden. There, the connection expands past one's own body, past the pleasure of feeding others, to a communal relationship with all the living things one is surrounded by every single day.

"The soil, the plants, they really do have ways of telling the farmer what they need and when a plant wants to go to seeding, when it wants to be left alone, when it doesn't want to be harvested anymore. It shows you, and you have to listen," Bebe told me during dinner in the quaint Lola Sonoma farmhouse. "The environment knows what it wants and knows what it needs."

As the cultivator of plants, she said, "you do have to have sort of a conversational relationship to [the land], which I think is very spiritual in a way, because it's a nonhuman. It's still sentient, but it's a nonhuman existence. In our culture, and especially in the industrial culture, we don't think about nature as having feelings or having any kind of brain, I guess, or consciousness." She thinks that this mentality is misleading. She believes plant consciousness exists, though "it's different than the human one.* The soil is always in conversation with itself and so, as a farmer, you have to be able to, in a way, speak its language."

---

* There are, believe it or not, several studies that show evidence of plants having memories and the ability to not just communicate but also strategize amongst themselves for survival and nutrient distribution. See *The Language of Plants: Science, Philosophy, Literature*; "Inside the Vegetal Mind: On the Cognitive Abilities of Plants" in *Memory and Learning in Plants* by Monica Gagliano; and *From Tree to Shining Tree* on Radiolab.

"Sure," Chris Melançon chimed in, as he assisted Lori with the cooking. "There's an intelligence in all of it. If you can speak [the plant's] language," he said, you can see and hear "what it's trying to tell you and feel what it's trying to tell you."

Earlier that day, while out feeding the rambunctious goats, Chris had relayed a similar sentiment about the animals; he talked to me about managing his emotions around them, because they can sense how he is feeling and will react in much the same way human beings will to one another's moods. "The animals pick up on your energies, and I really have to be conscious of it. When you start getting anxious," he told me, peering over the gate to the pigs next door, "the animals pick up on it, and then everything just amplifies from there, right, because the animals get upset, and then that makes you more anxious."

It is this intimate connection, Chris believes, that keeps people like Bebe and Carmen coming to the farm to lend a hand. "There's a general theme," he said of the eight WWOOFers he and Lori had hosted up to that point, of "wanting to get connected with nature, hands that want to get dirty." The opportunity to commune with the land was a significant motivator for Chris and Lori to make the move to a rural lifestyle as well. But you don't need a whole farm. Even caring for a single seedling can allow for that same sense of human–plant connectedness (I talk to my houseplants—don't you?).

We are not alone in this world. As the original nature documentarian Alexander von Humboldt writes in *Personal Narrative*: "A confused noise issues from every bush, from the decayed trunks of trees, from the clefts of the rock, and from the ground undermined by the lizards, millepedes, and cecilias. There are so many voices proclaiming to us, that all nature breathes; and that, under a thousand different forms, life is diffused throughout the cracked and dusty soil, as well as in the bosom of the waters, and in the air that circulates around us."

During my interviews for this book, time and again I met individuals who, in one way or another, felt as though their lives were growing untenable, that their existences were becoming unhinged, chaotic, and steeped in skepticism, anxiety, and loneliness; at times, I have wondered whether these Digital Age ailments are exacerbated by our growing disconnect with the species that coexist with us—whose existence, in fact, we rely on.* Be it a houseplant leaning toward the sunlight, birds whose behavior hints at a coming storm, or a dog who somehow knows you need a hug, paying attention to the lives of plants and animals around us can bring a sense of rootedness. No matter the chaos we feel in this era, a wider ecosystem of life surrounds us. And if we choose to, we can escape the selfies, filters, and alerts to reconnect with the things that truly bring us a sense of joy, awe, and well-being.

News organizations and venture capitalists alike often speak of some soon-to-come technological innovation that will further improve human existence—whether by saving us time grocery shopping or helping us access the secrets within our DNA—yet many raised in this Digital Age are beginning to show hints of technology fatigue.

Who, in the dot-com era, would have predicted the rebounding success of paper book sales or the public demand for in-person immersive events, or could have anticipated that Millennials—the generation exposed to smartphones, social media, and email in young adulthood—would grow up to drive the blossoming food culture, wellness festivals, and gardening markets?

As we move further into this digital era, where new technologies launch by the day, it's important to remind ourselves that beyond the latest gadget, delivery system, or AI innovation is a persistent and unwavering desire for the pleasures that we have always had at our fingertips: the scent of spring rain, the satisfaction of patting an animal's belly, the awe of looking out at a landscape that reminds us that we are simply a small part of a vast ecosystem.

Sometimes, the most transformative and pleasurable experiences of all are right beneath our feet, under our fingertips, on our lips, below our noses, and just outside the front door.

---

* "Shall I not have intelligence with the earth? Am I not partly leaves and vegetable mould myself?" asks Henry David Thoreau in *Walden*.

conclusion

It is easy to view new trends as passing fads, flavors of the moment enjoying their fifteen minutes of fame. But often, trends are signs of yearning—of needs that, if left unmet, will only grow stronger as time goes on. What if these "fads" are signals of where culture is heading, or where it needs to be directed in order to better our societal well-being?

Our "foodie" culture, devotion to tribal fitness groups, and restrictive diets are small symptoms of a much larger societal tidal wave, one that extends far beyond the Millennial generation. These passions are not feckless fancies but a form of self-care, emblems of people choosing to spend their discretionary time and money on activities that fill in the gaps where life is otherwise leaving them famished. By fully grasping the emotional underbelly of these hungers, we are better able to address our own well-being needs, as well as, perhaps, those of our children, students, or customers.

With today's trends in mind, it is important to look ahead: How will our time-crunched, content-overloaded schedules impact the products we're most drawn to? What is the next immersive experience that will help us combat loneliness? As people lean toward digital detoxes, will the same fanfare accompany new technologies in the future? And, of course, what will we be eating?

I am no more an augur than anyone else, but I do believe that a deep understanding of human nature and modern stressors can lead us to well-informed hypotheses. So, I will provide my best guesses. Some of my forecasts are already percolating at the edges of culture, and others are hiding around the corner.

Food will continue to blend itself into the health and beauty industries. Already, there are products that may make you wonder: Is this something I eat or something I rub onto my skin? As long as anxiety and stress levels remain high and skepticism of Big Pharma and

Big Food hold strong, people will continue to search for nontraditional means to conjure the digestive health, glowing skin, and deep sleep they so ardently desire. Be ready to see more labels promoting ingredients like turmeric, collagen, and ashwagandha root, both in food and skincare, as an emphasis on food and beauty products as medicine continues to gain traction.

The introduction of powerful spectrometers and blockchain technologies will reinforce current biohacking tendencies. Already, products have hit the market that scan for pesticides, gluten, and even nutritional density, along with antioxidant concentrations. Not long from now, you'll be able to literally compare apples to oranges to see which was picked most recently, how far it traveled, the health of the soil it was grown in, and which fruit has retained the most nutrients along its journey. You'll be able to track the quality of the air you're breathing and the water you're drinking, and measure the vitamin D your skin is absorbing each day from the sun.

Each of these new technologies will fuel a rebirth of high-tech fitness, beauty, and general health trackers for a new era of personalization. Wearable biophysical trackers and sophisticated new home technologies (I have heard rumors of toilets that will scan individual human waste for daily microbiome panels) will allow innovations like personalized 3D-printed home vitamins, AI-generated nutrition and fitness prescriptions, and even person-specific restaurant menus to become not just possible but probable. Already, we see several companies claiming to deliver personalized meals and workout routines; talk with scientists reveals the nascent science behind these startups. Several years down the road, this arena will be a far cry from its rudimentary beginnings.

It is also possible that these new scanners and personalized insights will further increase consumer interest in soil and farming. Though it may seem counterintuitive, the more that people learn about the nutrients and microbes that live within their foods, the more they will seek to understand why one bin of apples or one bunch of spinach is so different in nutritional quality from another right beside it. Here, consumers will begin to uncover the profound problems with our global supply chain: soil degradation, pesticide use, and extensive storage time, all practices that make our foods less flavorful and less nutritious, and can significantly impair the climate as well (but more on that in a bit).

Along these lines, I remain hopeful that advances in technology will help people reconnect with reality. Our ability to easily communicate with others anywhere in the world has cultivated a globalist and humanistic sensibility among Millennials and Generation Z. These generations share the novel perspective that they are not national citizens first, but rather global citizens.* They are more likely than prior generations to view social and economic inequality as a top political issue, and share values of equality and human rights across races, genders, and ethnicities.[†,1]

This humanistic perspective is a catalyst for the astounding interest in global travel we already see among this Digital Age generation. According to research by Enso, a creative impact agency, 77 percent of Millennials say experiencing other cultures is important to them; meanwhile, only 64 percent of Baby Boomers say the same.[2] And a fascination with global flavors may be related: The World Food Travel Association found that 81 percent of their survey participants believe that food and beverage travel experiences help them better understand local cultures.[3] In many cases, the desire to strap on a backpack, buy a plane ticket, and rent out someone's home is all about exploring someone else's reality.

Other current trends point to a future lighter on the "virtual" and heavier on the "reality." Boomerang IRL economies are blossoming; in-person events are selling out. Even Moleskine notebooks are flying off shelves, thanks to people wanting to put actual pen to actual paper. The

---

* A 2016 survey of one thousand young Americans ages eighteen to twenty-six conducted by Ipsos found that 35 percent of this age group defines themselves as Citizens of the World rather than Citizens of America. "This is a radical departure from what their parents and grandparents think about America and the world," say the authors of a report titled "The Attitudes and Priorities of the Snapchat Generation."

† Moving forward, I predict that we will see a cultural divide between those who adhere to this humanistic view of the world and those who do not. This division will not be drawn along the lines of racial, religious, or sexual orientation, but between those who stress the common needs and desires among all people of the world, and those who consider some of us to be more worthy or valuable than others. One group will travel the world and communicate online with those of varying backgrounds in an effort to understand and cultivate new relationships, while the other will utilize these same networks to find like-minded individuals who will reinforce their ingroup/outgroup theories.

latest must-have items include fig trees, outing-friendly fanny packs, and Instant Pots, things that connect us to the outdoors and real-life creative endeavors.

Further, we are seeing the percolation of a digital detox economy, led by Generation Z. One-third of Gen Zers say they have abandoned or deleted a social media account for good, while another two-thirds have taken social media breaks, according to a 2017 survey of one thousand US eighteen- to twenty-four-year-olds.[4] In the survey, conducted by advertising agency Hill Holliday's in-house research arm, Origin, teens and twentysomethings cite wasted time, online negativity, lack of interest in content, worries of privacy, and damage to self-esteem as reasons for kicking social media to the curb.

Many families are implementing screen-management rules into their households. Some abide by a digital curfew, such as "No screens after 9 p.m.," or digital sabbaths, where families put away all devices from sundown on Friday to sundown on Saturday, opting for family excursions, board games, or art projects instead. Other people make the digital separation into a competition: The phone stack game requires that all diners pile their phones in the center of the restaurant table, and whoever reaches for their phone first foots the bill. Screen-addicted South Koreans attend the Space Out Competition, where attendees compete to see who can stay the most "zoned out"—no talking, sleeping, singing, dancing, or using any electronic devices—for the ninety-minute event duration. Winners are chosen by audience vote and via heart rate monitoring—contestants with the most stable heart rates win. The first Space Out Competition received 1,500 applicants for the 150 spots. It has remained so popular that it is now held at several locales around South Korea, and Space Out Competitions have spread to China, the Netherlands, Taiwan, and Hong Kong.

The value of living in the moment is also slowly infiltrating the entertainment industry. Restaurants encourage patrons to put away their phones by adding signs to walls or notes to menus. Others go beyond polite requests and implement no-phone rules. Musicians like Jack White, Alicia Keys, the Lumineers, and Guns N' Roses have all asked their fans to stash their devices away in Yondr pouches for the duration of their sets. The branded Yondr case securely locks a phone inside and can be freed only by tapping the case against a Yondr unlocking base, usually placed in the venue lobby. Comedians Chris Rock, Dave Chappelle, and Aziz Ansari have asked the same of their audiences.

Of course, businesses are capitalizing on people's desire to separate themselves from their screens. Digital detox retreats in the US, UK, and Hong Kong advocate screen-free meditative, creative, and group-based activities. The German spa hotel Villa Stéphanie purposefully blocks Wi-Fi and cellular signals from all guest bedrooms. And phone companies are releasing limited-feature cell phones that allow users to regress back to the days before apps.

This desire to unplug from our devices and mindfully plug back in to reality has spurred the global adoption of the Danish trend hygge (pronounced *hoo-guh*), defined as a feeling of coziness and conviviality that creates contentment and well-being.* Those wishing to incorporate hygge into their lives are encouraged to create spaces conducive to group gatherings and to incorporate tactile, sensory-stimulating items into their surroundings, like fluffy rugs, crackling fires, and cups of herbal tea. Hygge became so popular that both the Collins and Oxford dictionaries named it the 2016 "word of the year." More than thirty books were published on the topic between 2016 and 2019.

What's interesting about hygge is not the focus on relaxation, but the emphasis on getting cozy with company. "It's possible to hygge alone, wrapped in a flannel blanket with a cup of tea, but the true expression of hygge is joining with loved ones in a relaxed and intimate atmosphere," explains Anna Altman for the *New Yorker*.[5] Here, we see the true impact of disconnecting: It allows us to reconnect with people in real life, which ultimately leads to greater well-being. Some of the most successful technologies of the future are likely to be those that facilitate group meetups, help us organize IRL experiences, and exchange ideas face-to-face.

Some, however, see our future as starkly individual. In a world with virtual reality and "all these other mediums to interact in," technologist and product designer Jinsoo An predicts, people will have to

---

* The word *hygge* has no direct translation in English, though *cozy* is often used as a succinct interpretation. The word comes from the sixteenth-century Norwegian term *hugga*, which means "to comfort" or "to console" and is a cousin to the English word *hug*.

"choose to be here," in actual reality, he told me. "We're going to have these wormholes that allow us to go to different places." He foresees a world in which each of us logs into our own universes, coming up for doses of analog air only when the fancy strikes us, much like the gamers in the fictionalized future world of *Ready Player One*. While he sees this potential existence as "incredibly amazing" thanks to the sensorial experiences and adventures awaiting us in the virtual world, many signs point to VR's opposite use: people using these technologies not to burrow in their own wormholes but to share an immersive experience with others and better connect with nature and food, right here in reality.

The immersive yet communal potential of virtual reality has been most clearly demonstrated in dining, where chefs are using these new technologies as a novel storytelling medium. Belgian artists Filip Sterckx and Antoon Beeck created a projected animated story titled *Le Petit Chef* that uses 3D software to create an optical illusion directly on the table around diners' plates. In the animation, a thumb-sized chef crafts each course by yanking tubers out of the table, sawing down a "tree" of broccoli, and rolling up a ball of snow into a lump of vanilla ice cream. The whimsical, Pixar-like tale does not require headsets or goggles; the entire story is emitted through overhead projectors and speakers. And rather than isolating us from one another, this medium allows for conversation and shared experience among diners as they laugh, gasp, and eat together.

Meanwhile, some restaurants are employing VR headsets to connect patrons with the origins of their food and drink. At the Lobby Bar of London's One Aldwych Hotel, a cocktail dubbed the Origin is served with a garnish of VR. "When someone orders it, we give the guest virtual reality goggles and a headset and explain we are taking you to the origin of the drink. You fly to the distillery where the whisky in the drink is aged, and then to the fields of barley and to the water source," the drink's creator, bar manager Pedro Paulo, explains in *Condé Nast Traveler*.[6] After soaring above the Scottish Highlands distillery, the film brings patrons back to the Lobby Bar, where they are told to remove their goggles. There, their drink is waiting for them on the bar.

Brands are using VR to bring customers into coffee plantations, cheese caves, and dairy farms. "I think [virtual reality] really has massive implications if we combine the technology with human being, touchy-feely senses," British chef Heston Blumenthal tells marketing magazine the *Drum*.[7] Virtual reality allows people to be transported to environments and locations otherwise out of reach, be it a chicken pasture, the top of Yosemite, or a street corner in Tehran. And projects like Shared_Studios' portals make it possible to share a meal with people halfway around the world in real time by using large projection screens and coordinated menus. Participants report feeling like they're in the very same room as others halfway around the world.

Still, An sees a future of individual eating worlds as somewhat inevitable because, as he asserts, "Mankind doesn't have a whole lot of time left on Earth" (thanks to the global climate crisis). And in the time we have, he says, our eating habits will have to change. Maybe, he posits, "we can use tech to open people's minds and allow people to eat things that we're not used to today," like insects, algae, yeast, and other climate-neutral or beneficial ingredients. Through An's own interactive VR creation, titled Project Nourished, diners are served a 3D-printed cube of food while wearing a virtual reality headset and a "bone conduction transducer" that looks like orthodontia headgear and mimics chewing sounds. Diners hold a gyroscopic fork while an aroma diffuser sits nearby. When all those elements are put together, a Project Nourished participant chewing on that printed cube in a lab may feel as though they're eating a T-bone steak on the Amalfi Coast.

While this may seem outrageous, An is convinced that we, as a human race, will need new ways to eat, considering the likely reduction of our future food sources. Technology like Project Nourished can "be used to preserve foods for the future generations by creating chemical and digital carbon copies . . . in case of overfishing or natural disaster," the website explains. And while we could debate the assertion that mankind's doom is imminent, the likelihood of a future with limited food sources is growing.

As we fawn over items like avocado toast and unicorn cakes, we often avoid acknowledging a massively important caveat: Climate breakdown will, likely forever, change the plants and animals we so eagerly devour and photograph. This is a sociological, anthropological, and environmental tidal wave we must consider, because it is likely to influence every industry, and every individual, in the years to come.

The Be-All-End-All Hurdle to Well-Being

The most influential trend of all—the one that will, without question, sway markets for all foreseeable decades—has very little to do with the virtual world and everything to do with the earth beneath our feet. As many companies continue to focus on their quarterly earnings, and individuals obsess over "likes" and food photos, we are failing to address the issue that, if left unchecked, will render nearly all these metrics of success moot: the climate crisis.

The statistics about climate breakdown are jarring, so dark that they are difficult to wrap one's mind around, and many are feeling fatalistic about the future of human life. Over three-quarters of US Millennials say they are "somewhat to extremely concerned about the impact climate change will have on their quality of life during their lifetimes," according to a 2017 survey by sustainability marketing firm Shelton Group, and 82 percent of Millennial parents say they're worried about the impact of climate change on their children's quality of life.[8] A 2019 survey of two thousand Americans by OnePoll, commissioned by the Recycling Partnership, shows that a startling one in five Millennials believes that global warming will lead to the extinction of humanity within their lifetimes, while 38 percent believe human extinction due to climate breakdown will happen within two hundred years.[9]

Most news about the climate crisis puts us into a state of paralysis. We see terrifying data on soil health, animal species extinction, and pending super diseases, but are not shown any concrete way to combat this apocalyptic future.*

Yet, there is a delicious, nutritious, and yes, even Instagrammable solution to climate change.

Soil is among the planet's largest reservoirs of carbon and holds the potential to become a key mechanism for removing excess carbon from the atmosphere and returning it to the ground, where it belongs.[10]

---

* A common trope among climate crisis deniers is this: The environment of the earth has always been changing. And on this point, they are right. The problem is, human beings weren't around when the climate was remarkably warmer or dryer, or when our oceans more acidic. Saying "Save the Planet" is misguided. Mother Earth will be just fine. It's the human race that won't be able to survive.

Recent data from farming systems and pasture trials around the world suggest that we could sequester more than all the world's current carbon emissions through the earth's soil, making agriculture a carbon-negative industry. (Now is the time to pause and say, *Wow, really?!*) All it takes is a shift in farming practices. Essentially, farmers and foodies can be the superheroes of the future.

So how do we get there? Keep obsessing over food.

Seventy-five percent of the world's food comes from only twelve plants and five animal species.[11] How boring is that? "Of the 250,000 to 300,000 known edible plant species, only 150 to 200 are used by humans," reports the Food and Agriculture Organization of the United Nations (FAO). "Only three—rice, maize, and wheat—contribute nearly 60 percent of calories and proteins obtained by humans from plants." After the Green Revolution in the mid-1900s, industrial agriculture focused on high-yield (instead of high-flavor or high-nutrition) crop varietals to "feed the world." In this process, three-quarters of plant genetic diversity was lost to uniform crops with a long supermarket shelf life.[12] This reality is not just a culinary bummer; it also poses an immense threat to food security.* But eaters today are demanding more: unique flavors, vibrant colors, intriguing textures.

The vegetable, fruit, legume, and grain markets are becoming more diverse and more flavorful. Once-forgotten varietals are finding homes on high-end menus and in farmers' market bins. The food industry is facing a new customer, one who doesn't want industrialized white bread, but rather stone-milled bread made from local wheat varietals. They

---

* The Food and Agriculture Organization of the United Nations and World Wildlife Fund note that a changing climate, monoculture farming practices, pollution, illicit poaching, and overharvesting threaten our future food sources. If our eating and farming habits do not change, by the year 2050, the Americas will have 15 percent fewer plants and animals than we do now, which would be 40 percent fewer plants and animals than in the early 1700s. In Asia, there will be no fish stocks for commercial fishing by 2048, and nearly all the coral reefs on the planet will be gone. More than a quarter of the European plant and animal species are already threatened. Africa could lose half of its bird and mammal species by 2100. The earth has lost half of its wildlife just in the last forty years, and the pace of insect extinction surpasses that of vertebrates by a large margin.

don't want only black beans and chickpeas; they're eager to try drought-resistant, speckled tepary beans, native to the southwestern United States and Mexico. Bulk bins of grains like teff, amaranth, and millet are attracting curious shoppers on the hunt for a new twist on their usual rice side dish. A renewed interest in heritage crops is introducing people to types of produce they've never heard of and to new varietals, some grown right in their backyards.

Over recent decades, customers became accustomed to a global marketplace where bananas are available year-round and halibut is always at the market, along with ripe tomatoes. And processed food trained us to expect consistent products no matter the season. Now, many eaters are paying attention to seasonality, learning—and accepting—the natural annual rotation of goods. Just look at the success of seasonal "limited-time-offer" items. (Pumpkin spice latte, anyone?) In addition, an interest in handmade, small-batch products is awakening an appreciation for increased variation.

Similarly, decades of reliance on only a few types and cuts of fish, poultry, and red meat put immense pressure on a select few water and land species while ignoring the plethora of alternative protein sources out there. But today, diners are curious about new proteins, be it the invasive lionfish or insects.

Each of these food trends lends itself to supporting a more biodiverse agricultural system. Healthy ecosystems—ones made up of a diverse array of plants, animals, fungi, and microorganisms—include self-regulating webs of organisms that share resources and care for one another; one crop may protect the soil from erosion and provide a habitat to another organism that, in turn, provides protection from pests. Overall, diverse ecosystems buoy the health of freshwater systems, cultivate topsoil, protect coasts from storm surges, store carbon, provide homes to species, mitigate catastrophic disease outbreaks, and protect pollinators essential to our food system. Just as human beings thrive among communities of support, all living things require a diverse ecosystem—and without it, the health of the environment begins to collapse. But our current agricultural system is far from diverse.

Today, most of the world's agricultural land is used for monoculture farming—meaning, farmers produce one or two crops on the same patch of land, over and over.*, [13] And the tools often used for managing monoculture land—like artificial fertilizers, tilling, and pesticides— damage soils. Thanks to monoculture industrial farming methods, the world's soil is becoming dangerously depleted of carbon (yes, the same carbon we have too much of in the air. See where I am going with this?). Since the advent of industrial farming, most agricultural soils have lost anywhere from 30 to 75 percent of their organic soil carbon.[14] About 40 percent of agricultural soils around the globe are degraded, meaning the topsoil (the rich top layer of soil in which plants grow, known to farmers as "black gold") is gone, its carbon released into the atmosphere, where it contributes to a warming climate and changing weather patterns.[15]

The United Nations warns that without dramatic changes in agriculture (and eating habits), all the world's topsoil could be gone in just a few decades. Without soil carbon, we can't grow food, and even the foods that we're growing today are showing signs of lower nutritional density (which also means less flavor) than in decades prior.[16] Biodiversity at every level, from microbial to ecosystem-wide, is a key tool in the battle against climate breakdown.

Thankfully, the latest foodie fads are already moving us in the direction of greater biodiversity. And this obsession with new flavors, new textures, and new types of grains, legumes, and plants can literally cure the planet. A more biodiverse agriculture system that allows plants to draw down carbon from the atmosphere and back into the ground could ensure a flavorful, nutritious food secure world.

Vanguard farmers are diversifying their land to grow new varietals of local, heirloom, and organic produce. In doing so, many are employing practices that allow crops to take excess carbon out of the atmosphere and store it in the soil, where it will fuel the growth of nutritious

---

* According to the United States Department of Agriculture's Farm Service Agency, corn and soy make up half of all harvested acres in the US. Meanwhile, a study published in the *Proceedings of the National Academy of Sciences* by Christopher Wright and Michael Wimberly from South Dakota State University shows that roughly 1.3 million acres of grassland and prairie were converted to corn and other uses in the western Corn Belt between 2006 and 2011, threatening the health of waterways, wetlands, and species.

and flavorful crops. These farmers let plants naturally decompose, do not use tilling practices, and utilize cover cropping and crop rotations, which transform a farm from monoculture to polyculture.* "With the use of cover crops, compost, crop rotation, and reduced tillage, we can actually sequester more carbon than is currently emitted," summarizes a report by Rodale Institute, a nonprofit that supports research into organic farming.[17]

So, the question becomes: How do we create an economy that rewards those who are farming with climate-friendly methods?

It all starts with the consumer, you and me. As the author and activist Michael Pollan says, we vote three times a day with every meal. We can solve climate change through the foods we choose to buy and those we leave behind on the shelves. Just in the last decade, consumer spending has upended the food system. Organic produce is now sold throughout the world, and organic farming methods are beginning to wriggle their way into the mainstream. We have an entirely new plant-based food culture that celebrates eating root-to-stem with meat as the garnish, not the center of the plate.

"Earthy" flavors and products dominate all future-of-food trend predictions. Google search data shows items like kombucha; matcha, oolong, chamomile, and green teas; turmeric; ginger; and hibiscus topping search lists in the US.[18] Meals loaded with plants continue to take

---

* Tilling is a weed management tactic where farmers break up the soil. This can disturb soil microbes and release carbon into the atmosphere. Crop rotation is the practice of growing different crops in the same area, in sequence, where a diverse array of plants and microbes work together to build soil health and also become natural pest and weed deterrents. For example, clover and kidney beans bring nitrogen into the soil. Brassicas like kale, Brussels sprouts, and collards naturally buffer bacteria, fungi, insects, and weeds. Meanwhile, crops like buckwheat grow so thick that they're called "smother crops" that "outcompete" weeds. Scientists at the University of Illinois recently provided further evidence that rotating crops increases yield and lowers greenhouse gas emissions compared to continuous corn or soybean rotation. This process also helps prevent against soil erosion and enhances biodiversity. For more information, see "Long-Term Crop Rotation and Tillage Effects on Soil Greenhouse Gas Emissions and Crop Production in Illinois, USA," published in *Agriculture, Ecosystems & Environment*, and "Soil Organic Carbon Sequestration Rates by Tillage and Crop Rotation," in *Soil Science Society of America Journal*.

over grocery aisles and restaurant menus, even at fast-casual chains. In 2016, fast-casual restaurant Pret a Manger launched a pop-up no-meat Veggie Pret in London as a prototype to test demand. The company expected sales to dip by 30 percent. Instead, sales surged over 70 percent, and the company decided to make the store permanent as well as open additional Veggie Prets around the world. "Clearly, the move towards a plant-based diet is gathering momentum, especially among Millennials," CEO Clive Schlee wrote on Pret's blog.

The world is moving toward diets less reliant on meat, which is essential for our battle against climate breakdown. "If cattle were their own nation, they would be the world's third-largest emitter of greenhouse gases," writes environmental activist Paul Hawken in his book *Drawdown*, which outlines the most effective tactics for combating climate change. "Plant-rich diets reduce emissions and tend to be healthier, leading to lower rates of chronic disease. According to a 2016 study, business-as-usual emissions could be reduced by as much as 70 percent through adopting a vegan diet and 63 percent for a vegetarian diet, which includes cheese, milk, and eggs. $1 trillion in annual healthcare costs and lost productivity would be saved."[19]

This is not to say that animals do not have a part in the future of food—in fact, they can play a key role in regenerative agriculture and help reduce food waste.* Still, we can't continue consuming meat at our current rates. If each of us limits our daily meat intake to 1.5 ounces, which works out to approximately three hamburgers' worth of meat a week, it would help the world cut emissions by over 50 percent.[20] In fact, some say that substituting mushrooms for even a third of the beef in the 10 billion burgers we eat annually would be like taking 2.3 million cars off the roads.[21] This is a realistic goal—because it's already happening.

---

* The FAO's "The State of the World's Biodiversity for Food and Agriculture" report notes that grazing animals can mitigate fire risk and help control pests and invasive species. Often, carbon farmers use animals in their crop rotation to help fertilize soil. On no-till farmland, some farmers send in cattle, sheep, hogs, or chickens to trample the field to both seed and add manure. In Japan, hogs are used as a vessel for food waste consumption—what people do not eat is sent to the pigs as slop. As they consume the waste, they become yet another nutritious food source for people.

More and more people are forgoing meat and seafood for meals brimming with vegetables, fruits, grains, nuts, and legumes. A 2015 report by NPD Group, Midan Marketing, and trade publication *Meatingplace* found that nearly three-quarters of American consumers who eat meat are substituting a nonmeat protein in their meal at least once a week. And of that group, 22 percent said they are using nonmeat proteins more often than the year before. Consulting firm Technomic reports that two-thirds of Americans think a vegetarian meal can be as satisfying as one with meat.[22]

To support this trend, the marketplace for meat alternatives is growing. Nuts, legumes, and kelp are being integrated into animal-free forms of burgers, yogurts, jerky, ice cream, and cheese. Yeasts are being genetically modified to produce milk and meat through cellular agriculture. These forms of product innovation and synthetic biology hope to make meat and meat-like products available to the masses with a fraction of the environmental impact of their real-meat alternatives.

Many farmers are utilizing new technologies to grow food—both plant and animal—in ways that use fewer resources like water and are impervious to changing climate patterns. And unlike with GMO products, shoppers appear to be open and interested in novel farming practices that are less taxing on our overall environment. Underground bunker greenhouses, pink-light vertical farms, cellular agriculture, hydroponic and aquaponic warehouse farms, rooftop gardens, and home grow boxes all allow the cultivation of produce, fish, and dairy products that are shielded from unpredictable weather patterns. While not an aid to topsoil health, indoor farming is attracting urban customers eager for year-round, high-quality produce, grown with limited water and chemical inputs. AeroFarms, America's largest indoor vertical farm, can produce up to 390 times more per square foot annually than a traditional field farm, through use of advanced tracking technologies. And some believe indoor farming could produce more nutrient-dense—and customizable—crops, with unique flavor profiles augmented by water and nutrient application.

Nearly two decades ago, the Dutch committed to finding a way to produce "twice as much food using half as many resources." Today, they're global leaders in indoor agriculture and have reduced reliance on water for key crops by as much as 90 percent, as well as eliminated the use of chemical pesticides on plants in greenhouses. The Netherlands now produces more tomatoes per square mile than anywhere else in the world and is the second largest global exporter of food based on dollar value after the US, a feat achieved using only a fraction of the land available to other countries.[23] Singapore and China are among other nations currently implementing plans for large vertical farms in order to offset their current produce imports and mitigate use of water and chemicals.

These innovations, of course, are possible only through investment in agriculture technologies, an area of venture capitalism that has blossomed over the last five years. The year 2018 was considered a record-breaker for the industry, with $16.9 billion in funding spread across 1,450 investments in things like drones, sensors, microbial probiotics, and harvesting robotics.[24]

By pairing new food and agriculture technologies with the climate benefits of diversified, soil-based farming, we can have not just a food-secure future, but one filled with a bevy of creative potential for creating the next "it" veggie, dish, or image.

Here we are in a world of eaters hungry for something new, something local, something nutritious, something beautiful, and an environment urging us to indulge these instincts. Many scientists estimate that we can reverse climate breakdown by simply diversifying our diets—which means that a food-obsessed global culture with a passion for unique flavors and nutrient-rich foods may be good for more than health food stores and wellness gurus. It may be the environmental savior we've been looking for.

It is only by celebrating and embracing these food trends that we can replenish topsoil, sequester carbon, filter our air and water, and protect our lands against weather stressors, all while feeding people with foods that are healthier, more colorful, more flavorful, and downright more exciting. So, the next time someone mocks your seaweed snack, fava bean risotto, nopales taco in a teff tortilla, or your interest in foraging wild herbs and mushrooms, just let them know that you're saving the planet, one meal at a time.

Final Thoughts

Here, at the end of this journey, it's easy to see that doing what's best for human health, what's best for well-being, is also what's best for our larger environment.

People are demanding a sense of safety through their food. Let's increase transparency by making our food system more localized, and employ technologies such as blockchain and spectrometers to put a sense of autonomy and authority back in the hands of the buyer. Perhaps with greater knowledge of the time, energy, water, and labor embedded in every piece of food, we will waste less and appreciate more.

People want to connect with others in real life, to feel supported and validated. Let us regenerate a pride in regional cuisine that, just like college sports teams, ignites locals' passions. We should broaden the palette of colors, textures, and flavors on our plates to generate awe-worthy culinary creations. We should show off the crops that grow only where we live, and how these crops change with the seasons.

And people are looking for a sense of purpose, often relying on nature as a guide. The UN Food and Agriculture Organization encourages home gardening, and notes that by converting your lawn into a garden, you could be providing a home for threatened wild and native species as well as food for local pollinators, all while sequestering carbon.[25] Meanwhile, you will reap the personal benefits of time in nature: the emotional, creative, and physical enhancements our bodies reward us with when we dig our hands in the dirt.

Biodynamic agriculture relies on the concept of the farm as a self-sufficient, integrated ecosystem—a living organism unto itself. Each and every aspect of the farm—from the air to the microbes to the plant species—affects and is affected by one another. Perhaps the best approach to well-being is to see ourselves and the entire planet as one biodynamic entity.

"All nature is linked together by invisible bonds and every organic creature . . . is necessary to the well-being of some other among the myriad forms of life," wrote diplomat and conservationist George Perkins Marsh in 1864.[26] He warned that humankind was, through agricultural practices like deforestation, "breaking up the floor and wainscoting and doors and window frames of our dwelling."

In this Digital Age, we have untethered ourselves from communities and land we once intimately relied on and understood. We've severed the bonds of eye-to-eye contact, of touch, of time spent in real life with one another; we have cut from our lives the deeply satisfying elements of manual competence and cohabitation with nature. When we remove our ability to know and understand the very things our lives rely on, we become anxious, and in our efforts to soothe that anxiety, can find ourselves looking to experts and products that hinder our well-being rather than support it. When we decrease time spent engaging with others, we become lonely, question our self-worth, and waste precious moments of time attempting to gain validation through exercises that will always leave us unsatisfied. When we remove our bodies from the physical process of creation, of seeing a project through from start to finish, of proving our own capabilities and self-sufficiencies, we burn to find a deeper purpose. And when we extract ourselves from the intricate web of nature itself, we starve ourselves of the pleasures resting just beneath our toes. We cannot thrive without the essential ingredients of safety, community, and purpose, and our path to fulfilling each of these needs can be found by weaving ourselves back into the biodynamic fabric of human existence, closer to the sources of our food, to one another, and to the wider world around us.

In his bestselling book *Sapiens*, historian Yuval Noah Harari posits that *Homo sapiens* did not cultivate wheat; instead, wheat cultivated us. "Rather than heralding a new era of easy living, the Agricultural Revolution left farmers with lives generally more difficult and less satisfying than those of foragers," he writes. In short, "There is absolutely no proof that human well-being inevitably improves as history rolls along."

Today, in the Digital Age, I sometimes wonder whether we have cultivated our digital world or whether it is cultivating us. Are we using these new technologies in ways that improve our way of life? Or are they using us, keeping us addicted, fearful, and mindlessly engaged?

It is certainly possible to find well-being of the body, mind, and planet in this ever-shifting era of innovation. All it takes is a bit of unplugging, and mindfulness of the hungers that lie within each of us for something a bit more real.

acknowledgments

I am forever indebted to my husband, Jason, for the countless hours of brainstorming and editing, and for the sacrifices that allowed me to galivant around the globe for this project. Thank you to my agent, Wendy Levinson, for your excitement about this book, your willingness to get in the weeds of the text, and your constant positivity, which helped me manage this giant task. To my editor, Leah Wilson, for being a sounding board throughout this process, and for your feedback and flexibility. And to the rest of the BenBella team, for your ongoing contributions to the life of *Hungry*. I appreciate all the hours put in by my research assistants, interns, translators, interpreters, and transcribers, including Kirby Barth, Elizabeth Buchwald, and Hyunjee Cho, among others.

There aren't many projects that call for interviews with farmers, evolutionary psychologists, technologists, and mukbang BJs. Thank you to each of my interviewees for sharing your expertise, your time, your stories, and sometimes your homes. To the researchers who patiently walked me through everything from haptic touch to content overload to gluten sensitivity: Robin Dunbar, Larry Rosen, Brian Primack, Paul Rozin, Daniel Levitin, Ethan Bromberg-Martin, Jon Kaas, Adrian David Cheok, Laurie Santos, Peter Green, Josh Ackerman, Qian Xu, Guido Nicolosi, Klive Oh, Alexandra Boutopoulou, Daniel Rosenfeld, James Ehrlich, Tim Squirrel, and the stellar team at Datassential. To the industry professionals, fervent foodies, and devoted farmers around the world who offered their personal stories and theories: Chris Melançon, Lori Melançon, Maggie Meador, Hardy McQueen, Matt Maloney, Echo Huang Yinyin, Nikhil Malhotra, Nikhil Arora, Jinsoo An, Jenny Gao, Amit Patnaik, Hendrik Haase, Kunal Chandra, Piengor Fai, Adam Tichauer, Juliana Loh, Mark Tanner, Mike Donovan, Andy Tew, Sarah Smith, Tiffany Senin, Jonathan Bernard, Nicole Centeno, Bryan Hugill, Dominc Deustachio, Dov Deustachio, Michelle

Tam, Shreya Soni, Nancy Chen, Guatum Gupta, Della Mbaya, Sanjhi Rajgarhia, Vedant Kanoi, Raman Frey, Jeffrey Zurofsky, Jamison Monroe, Ted Guastello, Asha Carroll, Gena Hamshaw, Anmao Sun, Ashley Dudarenok, Brad Hargreaves, Christopher Bledsoe, Sean Hoess, Megan Bruneau, Julia Bainbridge, Estefania Acuña, David Yeung, Karine Charbonneau, Andy Brighten, Jonathan Kalan, Greg Shewmaker, Sohn JiAe, Jyoti Balani, and *many* more.

Endless thanks to Hahna Yoon, Boon Young Lee, Joe McPherson, Steven Borowiec, and Haeryun Kang for showing me the best of Seoul. Rachel Brujis, thank you for the stellar guide to Hong Kong's vegan and vegetarian establishments and its fabulous food scene. Tianle Chang, thank you for being my mentor on the organic food movement in Beijing. Mia Lu and Yimi Zhang, our delicious Shanghai eats and adventures on the farm were highlights of my trip. To the staff at New Trier High School, thank you for helping me find students to shadow and for welcoming me into classrooms. My thanks to the students who opened up to me and let me pester them with questions over several days and phone calls. Ben Ezinga, our exchanges were some of the most illuminating—thank you for our many hours of conversation. Liza Patriana, Andy Kadin, and Roe Sie, I'm grateful for all our chats about lamination, milling, and flow. Bobby Whisnant and Margaret Partlow, thank you for lending me couches to sleep on and ears to listen as I traveled around California. And of course, thank you to my family and friends for continuing to cheer me on. Special thanks to those who read early drafts and provided feedback: my parents, Annette and Scott Turow; Diana Mahoney; Jessy Grossman; and Ben Marcus.

There are so many others who have, over the past several years, told me about their passions, fears, and anxieties. This book project became a global exploration that left me in awe of our commonalities, the basic needs we each have, and our shared journeys to satisfying these hungers in this unique, chaotic, and beautiful world we're living in. I am grateful to each and every person who expanded my understanding, challenged my assumptions, and gave me something new to chew on (literally and figuratively).

I hope to see each of you some time soon, in person, with something delicious on the table.

notes

INTRODUCTION

1. Mintel Press. "US Millennials Twice as Likely as Non-Millennials to Distrust Large Food Manufacturers." *Mintel*, October 29, 2015. http://www.mintel.com/press-centre/food-and-drink/us-millennials-twice-as-likely-as-non-millennials-to-distrust-large-food-manufacturers.

2. "The Richest and Poorest Countries of Southeast Asia." WorldAtlas. Accessed April 8, 2019. https://www.worldatlas.com/articles/the-richest-and-poorest-countries-of-southeast-asia.html.

3. BabyCenter. "BabyCenter Reveals Top Baby Names Of 2018, Announces New Baby Names App." *PR Newswire*, November 27, 2018. https://www.prnewswire.com/news-releases/babycenter-reveals-top-baby-names-of-2018-announces-new-baby-names-app-300755530.html.

4. "A Tough Road to Growth." *The 2015 Mid-Year Review: How the Top 100 CPG Brands Performed*. Catalina, 2015. https://assets.ctfassets.net/oyvkhyupj8l5/2ZYjJLIB2gsMyaOgmQC2WW/8ece3950dea3f20122cf71ea80229c1a/2015-Mid-Year-Review.pdf.

    Ringquist, Jack, Tom Philips, Barb Renner, Rod Sides, Kristen Stuart, Mark Baum, and Jim Flannery. "Capitalizing on the Shifting Consumer Food Value Equation." *Deloitte*, 2015. https://www2.deloitte.com/content/dam/Deloitte/us/Documents/consumer-business/us-fmi-gma-report.pdf.

5. Mi-hyun, Lee. "Asian Millennials: The New Big Spenders in Global Consumer Market." *HuffPost*, November 13, 2016. https://www.huffpost.com/entry/asian-millennials-the-new_b_12937942.

6. "ASEAN Organic Cosmetics Market | Industry Analysis, Size and Forecast 2014-2024." Future Market Insights, December 31, 2014. https://www.futuremarketinsights.com/reports/asean-organic-cosmetics-market.

    Gleason-Allured, Jeb. "Organic Beauty Market to Reach $66.1 Billion by 2020." Global Cosmetic Industry, October 21, 2015. https://www.gcimagazine.com/marketstrends/segments/natural/Organic-Beauty-Market-to-Reach-661-Billion-by-2020-335331911.html.

7. "2018 IHRSA Health Club Consumer Report." International Health, Racquet and Sportsclub Association, 2018. https://www.ihrsa.org/publications/the-2018-ihrsa-health-club-consumer-report/.

8. Purcell, Denise. "Today's Specialty Food Consumer 2016." Specialty Food Association, September 22, 2016. https://www.specialtyfood.com/media/filer_public/46/3d/463d6863-d249-45c7-9772-f2494e0da6e7/2016consumerreport_8pgs.pdf.

9. Bowerman, Mary. "Spending More on Coffee than Investing? You're Not Alone." *USA Today*, January 11, 2017. https://www.usatoday.com/story/money /nation-now/2017/01/11/spending-more-coffee-than-investing-youre-not-alone /96385882/?fbclid=IwAR0D_aX_JaiILreGtd1OZsrBpngBA1g_tQPx4qJL _RYeWguaSewApZ6Eizw.

10. Barton, Christine, Lara Koslow, Jeff Fromm, and Chris Egan. "Millennial Passions: Food, Fashion, and Friends." Boston Consulting Group, 2012.

Campos, Rolf, Pin Arboledas, and José Ramón. "IESE Insight How Has the Crisis Affected Consumer Spending in Spain?" *IESE Insight*, 2015. https://www .ieseinsight.com/doc.aspx?id=1730&ar=6.

Dsouza Prabhu, Ruth. "Restaurant Trends That Will Change the Way India Eats Out in 2017." *HuffPost India*, January 12, 2017. https://www.huffingtonpost .in/ruth-dsouza-prabhu/restaurant-trends-that-will-change-the-way-india-eats -out-in-201_a_21653409/.

"Global Generational Lifestyles: How We Live, Eat, Play, Work and Save for Our Futures." *Nielsen*, November 2015. https://www.nielsen.com/content/dam /corporate/us/en/reports-downloads/2015-reports/global-generational-report -november.pdf.

"USDA ERS: Food Expenditure Series." *Food Expenditure Series*. United States Department of Agriculture: Economic Research Service, 2018. https:// www.ers.usda.gov/data-products/food-expenditure-series/.

11. "Millennials Are Fueling the Rise of Fine Dining in Asia Pacific." *MasterCard Social Newsroom*, December 22, 2015. https://newsroom.mastercard.com/asia-pacific /press-releases/millennials-are-fuelling-the-rise-of-fine-dining-in-asia -pacific/.

12. "Connecting with the Millennials: A Visa Study." Visa, July 2011. http://www .visa-asia.com/ap/sea/mediacenter/pressrelease/includes/uploads/Visa_Gen_Y _Report_2012_LR.pdf.

13. Taylor, Kate. "Buffalo Wild Wings CEO Hits Back at Activist Investor and Blames Chain's Problems on Millennials." *Business Insider*, May 30, 2017. https://www.businessinsider.com/buffalo-wild-wings-ceo-on-why-restaurants -struggle-2017-5.

14. "Taking Stock with Teens: Spring 2016." Piper Jaffray, 2016. http://www.piper jaffray.com/3col.aspx?id=4035.

15. Khalil, Shireen. "This Is the One Thing We're Happy to Splurge On." *News .Com.Au*, August 30, 2018. https://www.news.com.au/finance/business/aussie -households-spend-big-on-restaurant-and-takeaway-meals/news-story/37d30f7c c7fef71e1db2c339249634b7#.3ag1t.

16. "U.S. Student Loan Debt Statistics for 2019." *Student Loan Hero*. Accessed April 10, 2019. https://studentloanhero.com/student-loan-debt-statistics/.

17. Fry, Richard. "For First Time in Modern Era, Living with Parents Edges Out Other Living Arrangements for 18- to 34-Year-Olds." *Pew Research Center's Social & Demographic Trends*, May 24, 2016. https://www.pewsocialtrends .org/2016/05/24/for-first-time-in-modern-era-living-with-parents-edges-out -other-living-arrangements-for-18-to-34-year-olds/.

18. Laudicina, Paul. "Wages Have Fallen 43% for Millennials. No Wonder They've Lost Hope." World Economic Forum, January 15, 2017. https://www.weforum .org/agenda/2017/01/wages-have-fallen-43-for-millennials-no-wonder-they-ve -lost-hope/.

19. Lee, Claire. "Youth Unemployment Reaches 19-Year High in South Korea." *Korea Herald*, August 22, 2018, sec. National. http://www.koreaherald.com/view .php?ud=20180822000767.

20. Arenge, Andrew, Stephanie Perry, and Ashley Tallevi. "Poll: Majority of Millennials Are in Debt, Hitting Pause on Major Life Events." NBC News, April 4, 2018. https://www.nbcnews.com/news/us-news/poll-majority-millennials-are -debt-hitting-pause-major-life-events-n862376.

    "NBC News/Gen Forward Survey: March 2018 Toplines." NBC News/ University of Chicago, March 2018. https://genforwardsurvey.com/assets /uploads/2018/04/NBC-GenForward-March-2018-Toplines.pdf.

21. Frotman, Seth, and Rich Williams. "New Data Documents a Disturbing Cycle of Defaults for Struggling Student Loan Borrowers." Consumer Financial Protection Bureau, May 15, 2017. https://www.consumerfinance.gov/about-us/blog/new -data-documents-disturbing-cycle-defaults-struggling-student-loan-borrowers/.

22. Laudicina, "Wages Have Fallen 43% for Millennials."

23. COUNTRY Financial. "COUNTRY Financial Security Index." Accessed April 9, 2019. https://www.countryfinancial.com/content/cfin/en/about-us/newsroom /year2018/Failure-to-Launch-Americans-Still-Rely-on-Parents-to-Help-with -Mobile-Phones-Gas-Groceries-and-Health-Insurance.html.

    Head Solutions Group. "Millennial Parents Research and the Support Received from Their Parents." TD Ameritrade, 2017. https://s1.q4cdn .com/959385532/files/doc_downloads/research/2017/Millennial-Parents-Survey -Key-Findings.pdf.

    "PSID Transition into Adulthood Supplement 2013 User Guide." Institute for Social Research, 2013. https://psidonline.isr.umich.edu/CDS/TAS13_User Guide.pdf.

24. Herron, Janna. "Survey: Student Loan Debt Forces Many to Put Life on Hold." Bankrate, August 5, 2015. https://www.bankrate.com/finance/consumer-index /money-pulse-0815.aspx.

    "NBC News/Gen Forward Survey: March 2018 Toplines." NBC News/ University of Chicago, March 2018. https://genforwardsurvey.com/assets /uploads/2018/04/NBC-GenForward-March-2018-Toplines.pdf.

25. "USDA ERS: Food Prices and Spending." Accessed November 28, 2018. https:// www.ers.usda.gov/data-products/ag-and-food-statistics-charting-the-essentials /food-prices-and-spending/.

26. Faw, Larissa. "Millennials Are Redefining Food Culture." Viva Lifestyle and Travel. March 29, 2016. http://vivalifestyleandtravel.com/how-millennials-are -redefining-fine-dining.

27. Haefele, Mark, Simon Smiles, and Matthew Carter. "Millennials—the Global Guardians of Capital." UBS Chief Investment Office Americas Wealth Management. UBS, June 22, 2017.

28. Bradbury, Rurik. "The Digital Lives of Millennials and Gen Z." LivePerson, n.d. https://liveperson.docsend.com/view/tm8j45m; Dorsey, Jason. "IGen Tech Disruption." The Center for Generational Kinetics, 2016. http://genhq.wpengine .com/wp-content/uploads/2016/01/iGen-Gen-Z-Tech-Disruption-Research -White-Paper-c-2016-Center-for-Generational-Kinetics.pdf.

    Williams, Florence. *The Nature Fix: Why Nature Makes Us Happier, Healthier, and More Creative* (New York: Norton, 2017).

29. Bajarin, Ben. "Apple's Penchant for Consumer Security." *Tech.pinions*, April 18, 2016. https://techpinions.com/apples-penchant-for-consumer-security/45122.

30. Wilford, John Noble. "When Humans Became Human." *New York Times*, February 26, 2002, sec. Science. https://www.nytimes.com/2002/02/26/science/when -humans-became-human.html.

31. Tooby, John, and Leda Cosmides. "The Psychological Foundations of Culture." In *The Adapted Mind: Evolutionary Psychology Generation of Culture* (New York: Oxford University Press, 1992).

32. "Cigna U.S. Loneliness Index." Cigna, 2018. https://www.multivu.com/players /English/8294451-cigna-us-loneliness-survey/docs/IndexReport_152406937 1598-173525450.pdf.

    McPherson, Miller, Lynn Smith-Lovin, and Matthew E. Brashears. "Social Isolation in America: Changes in Core Discussion Networks over Two Decades." *American Sociological Review* 71, no. 3 (June 1, 2006): 353–75. https://doi.org/1 .1177/000312240607100301.

    Noack, Rick. "Isolation Is Rising in Europe. Can Loneliness Ministers Help Change That?" *Washington Post*, February 2, 2018. https://www.washington post.com/news/worldviews/wp/2018/02/02/isolation-is-rising-in-europe-can -loneliness-ministers-help-change-that/.

    Stepanikova, Irena, Norman H. Nie, and Xiaobin He. "Time on the Internet at Home, Loneliness, and Life Satisfaction: Evidence from Panel Time-Diary Data." *Computers in Human Behavior* 26, no. 3 (May 1, 2010): 329–38. https://doi .org/10.1016/j.chb.2009.11.002.

    WGSN Insider. "Generation Z: The Lonely Ones?" *WGSN Insider*, January 15, 2016. https://www.wgsn.com/blogs/generation-z-the-young-lonely-ones/.

33. Jayson, Sharon. "Who's Feeling Stressed? Young Adults, New Survey Shows." *USA Today*, February 7, 2013. https://www.usatoday.com/story/news/nation /2013/02/06/stress-psychology-millennials-depression/1878295/.

34. Dove, Rachael. "Anxiety: The Epidemic Sweeping through Generation Y." *Telegraph*, April 20, 2015. https://www.telegraph.co.uk/health-fitness/body/anxiety -the-epidemic-sweeping-through-generation-y/.

35. CDC. "More than a Mental Health Problem." Centers for Disease Control and Prevention, November 27, 2018. https://www.cdc.gov/vitalsigns/suicide/index.html.

    Curtin, Sally, Margaret Warner, and Holly Hedegaard. "Increase in Suicide in the United States, 1999–2014." NCHS Data Brief. Centers for Disease Control and Prevention, April 2016. https://www.cdc.gov/nchs/products/databriefs /db241.htm.

Hedegaard, Holly, Sally Curtin, and Margaret Warner. "Suicide Rates in the United States Continue to Increase." NCHS Data Brief. Centers for Disease Control and Prevention, June 2018. https://www.cdc.gov/nchs/products /databriefs/db309.htm.

Mojtabai, Ramin, Mark Olfson, and Beth Han. "National Trends in the Prevalence and Treatment of Depression in Adolescents and Young Adults." *Pediatrics* 138, no. 6 (December 1, 2016): e20161878. https://doi.org/10.1542/peds .2016-1878.

Twenge, Jean M., Thomas E. Joiner, Megan L. Rogers, and Gabrielle N. Martin. "Increases in Depressive Symptoms, Suicide-Related Outcomes, and Suicide Rates Among U.S. Adolescents after 2010 and Links to Increased New Media Screen Time." *Clinical Psychological Science* 6, no. 1 (January 2018): 3–17. https:// doi.org/10.1177/2167702617723376.

Vuchnich, Allison, and Carmen Chai. "Young Minds: Stress, Anxiety Plaguing Canadian Youth." *Global News*, May 6, 2013. https://globalnews.ca /news/530141/young-minds-stress-anxiety-plaguing-canadian-youth/.

Part I: Control

1. Toffler, Alvin. *Future Shock*. (New York: Penguin Random House LLC, 1970).

   Raymont, Henry. "'Future Shock': The Stress of Great, Rapid Change." *The New York Times*, July 24, 1970, sec. Archives. https://www.nytimes .com/1970/07/24/archives/future-shock-the-stress-of-great-rapid-change.html.

CHAPTER 1: TRANSPARENCY & ANXIETY

1. "盒马宝贝详情." Accessed August 22, 2018. https://m.hemaos.com/page/ share/itemdetail?userid=7fdd44ae33082c96789e67340deffd832ed703004c7 38299459ab9f21dfea1f67f966f5c88df5e27dde1ce477afe648f246295dbe293 ff6eb3e7eeabcc11da171b9c6f55dc0d64b306c606681f3e72c9f7b121925628 916ba19d6e598c9e8e9a7d79319bf9a9ff955fa505ca93cd9c85b7a49c67301fcb 1e985c51b9937c58811c79ea0ea422343a&itemId=544561002664&shopIds =155127129&ut_sk=Page_Detail.b4f94b6431f6a91b09f9c3bd15cd1e69 .Wx3wNpeNOE8DANl%252FZvDg03LA.Friends&spm=a313p.3.1tls747.95 1906977784&short_name=x.ePIr9Z&from=singlemessage&isappinstalled=0 &app=weixin.

2. "Hema Fresh Eyes 2000 Stores by 2022." Inside Retail Hong Kong. July 4, 2019. https://insideretail.hk/2019/07/04/hema-fresh-eyes-2000-stores-by-2022/.

   "Online Retailers Go Offline in China." *The Economist*. April 7, 2018. https:// www.economist.com/business/2018/04/07/online-retailers-go-offline-in-china.

3. Leotti, Lauren A., Sheena S. Iyengar, and Kevin N. Ochsner. "Born to Choose: The Origins and Value of the Need for Control." *Trends in Cognitive Sciences* 14, no. 10 (October 2010): 457–63. https://doi.org/10.1016/j.tics.2010.08.001.

Narisada, Atsushi, and Scott Schieman. "'A Quintessentially American Thing?': The Unexpected Link Between Individualistic Values and the Sense of Personal Control." *Society and Mental Health* 6, no. 3 (November 2016): 147–67. https://doi.org/10.1177/2156869316667448.

Stocks, Alexandra, Kurt April, and Nandani Lynton. "Locus of Control and Subjective Well-Being: A Cross-Cultural Study." *Problems and Perspectives in Management* 10, no. 1 (2012). https://pdfs.semanticscholar.org/73c5/e7d872bcb 7198d15086e1789a87df82d0b6c.pdf.

Wang, Cynthia S., Jennifer A. Whitson, and Tanya Menon. "Culture, Control, and Illusory Pattern Perception." *Social Psychological and Personality Science* 3, no. 5 (September 2012): 630–38. https://doi.org/10.1177/1948550611433056.

Whitson, Jennifer, and Adam D Galinsky. "Lacking Control Increases Illusory Patter Perception." *Science* 322 (November 1, 2008): 115–17. https://doi .org/10.1126/science.1159845.

4. Bromberg-Martin, Ethan S., and Okihide Hikosaka. "Midbrain Dopamine Neurons Signal Preference for Advance Information about Upcoming Rewards." *Neuron* 63, no. 1 (July 16, 2009): 119–26. https://doi.org/10.1016/j.neuron.2009 .06.009.

5. Bromberg-Martin, Ethan S., and Okihide Hikosaka. "Midbrain Dopamine Neurons Signal Preference for Advance Information about Upcoming Rewards." *Neuron* 63, no. 1 (July 16, 2009): 119–26. https://doi.org/10.1016/j.neuron.2009 .06.009.

Gruber, Matthias J., Bernard D. Gelman, and Charan Ranganath. "States of Curiosity Modulate Hippocampus-Dependent Learning via the Dopaminergic Circuit." *Neuron* 84, no. 2 (October 2014): 486–96. https://doi.org/10.1016/j .neuron.2014.08.060.

6. Hemmelder, Vivian, and Tommy Blanchard. "Why Humans Are Hard-Wired for Curiosity." *Footnote*, September 8, 2016. http://footnote.co/why-humans-are -hard-wired-for-curiosity/.

7. Birch, L. L. "Effects of Peer Models' Food Choices and Eating Behaviors on Preschoolers' Food Preference." *Child Development* 51 (1980): 489–96.

DeCosta, Patricia, Per Møller, Michael Bom Frøst, and Annemarie Olsen. "Changing Children's Eating Behaviour: A Review of Experimental Research." *Appetite* 113 (June 2017): 327–57. https://doi.org/10.1016/j.appet.2017.03.004.

Salvy, Sarah-Jeanne, Lenny R. Vartanian, Jennifer S. Coelho, Denise Jarrin, and Patricia P. Pliner. "The Role of Familiarity on Modeling of Eating and Food Consumption in Children." *Appetite* 50, no. 2–3 (March 2008): 514–18. https:// doi.org/10.1016/j.appet.2007.10.009.

Young, E. M, S. W. Fors, and D. M. Hayes. "Associations Between Perceived Parent Behaviors and Middle School Student Fruit and Vegetable Consumption." *Journal of Nutrition Education Behavior* 36, no. 1 (January–February 2004): 2–8.

8. Andersen, B. V., G. Hyldig, and B. M. Jørgensen. *Sensory Factors in Food Satisfaction: An Understanding of the Satisfaction Term and a Measurement of Factors Involved in Sensory- and Food Satisfaction.* (Kgs. Lyngby: Technical University of Denmark, 2014).

9. Stefani, Gianluca, Donato Romano, and Alessio Cavicchi. "Consumer Expectations, Liking and Willingness to Pay for Specialty Foods: Do Sensory Characteristics Tell the Whole Story?" *Food Quality and Preference* 17, no. 1–2 (January 2006): 53–62. https://doi.org/10.1016/j.foodqual.2005.07.010.

   Van der Lans, I. A., K. Van Ittersum, A. De Cicco, and M. Loseby. "The Role of the Region of Origin and EU Certificates of Origin in Consumer Evaluation of Food Products." *European Review of Agricultural Economics* 28, no. 4 (2001): 451–77.

10. Andersen, Barbara Vad, and Grethe Hyldig. "Consumers' View on Determinants to Food Satisfaction: A Qualitative Approach." *Appetite* 95 (December 2015): 9–16. https://doi.org/10.1016/j.appet.2015.06.011.

    Verlegh, P. W. J., and J. B. Steenkamp. "A Review and Meta-analysis of Country of Origin Research." *Journal of Economic Psychology* 20 (1999): 521–46.

    Verlegh, P. W. J., and K. Van Ittersum. "The Origin of Spices: The Impact of Geographic Product Origin on Consumer Decision Making." In L. Frewer, E. Risvik, and H. Schifferstein (eds.), *Food, People and Society* (Berlin: Springer, 2001): 267–80.

11. Andersen, "Consumers' View on Determinants to Food Satisfaction."

12. Van Ittersum, K., M. Candel, and M. Meulemberg. "The Influence of the Image of a Product's Region of Origin on Product Evaluation." *Journal of Business Research* 56 (2003): 215–26.

13. Harris, Doug. "Study Shows Why the Clean Label Trend Is Worth Pursuing." Food Dive, December 22, 2016. https://www.fooddive.com/news/study-shows-why-the-clean-label-trend-is-worth-pursuing/432575/.

14. "Consumer Food Beliefs and Behaviors: The James Beard Foundation Consumer Research Project Executive Summary." Karen Karp & Partners. October 18, 2017. https://jbf-media.s3.amazonaws.com/production/page/2017/10/22/101617_FS_CONSUMER_SURVEY.pdf.

15. United States Department of Agriculture: Economic Research Service. "USDA ERS—Newly Updated ERS Data Show 2016 Production, Trade Volume, and Per Capita Availability of Vegetables and Pulses," August 7, 2017. https://www.ers.usda.gov/amber-waves/2017/august/newly-updated-ers-data-show-2016-production-trade-volume-and-per-capita-availability-of-vegetables-and-pulses/.

16. Karp, David. "Most of America's Fruit Is Now Imported. Is That a Bad Thing?" *The New York Times*, March 13, 2018, sec. Food. https://www.nytimes.com/2018/03/13/dining/fruit-vegetables-imports.html.

17. "The Global Picture: FishWatch." Accessed March 26, 2018. https://www.fishwatch.gov/sustainable-seafood/the-global-picture.

18. "Nationwide Surveys Reveal Disconnect Between Americans and Their Food." *PR Newswire*. September 22, 2011. Accessed August 2, 2018. https://www.prnewswire.com/news-releases/nationwide-surveys-reveal-disconnect-between-americans-and-their-food-130336143.html.

19. Hess, Alexander J., and Cary J. Trexler. "A Qualitative Study of Agricultural Literacy in Urban Youth: What Do Elementary Students Understand about

the Agri-Food System?" *Journal of Agricultural Education* 52, no. 4 (2011): 1–12. http://www.jae-online.org/attachments/article/1575/52.4.1%20Hess%20and%20 Trexler.pdf.

20. Birkenholz, Robert H., et al. "Pilot Study of Agricultural Literacy: Final Report." December 1993. https://files.eric.ed.gov/fulltext/ED369890.pdf.

21. "Survey Finds One in Five Children Aren't Aware that Bacon Comes from Pigs." DJS Research. August 5, 2015. https://www.djsresearch.co.uk/FoodMarket ResearchInsightsAndFindings/article/Survey-finds-one-in-five-children-arent -aware-that-bacon-comes-from-pigs-02415.

22. Maslow, Abraham H. *Motivation and Personality*, 3rd edition. Edited by Robert Frager, James Fadiman, Cynthia McReynolds, and Ruth Cox (New York: Longman, 1987).

23. Davison, Nicola. "Rivers of Blood: The Dead Pigs Rotting in China's Water Supply." *Guardian*, March 29, 2013, sec. World News. https://www.theguardian.com /world/2013/mar/29/dead-pigs-china-water-supply.

24. Watts, Jonathan. "Exploding Watermelons Put Spotlight on Chinese Farming Practices." *Guardian*, May 17, 2011, sec. Environment. https://www.theguardian .com/world/2011/may/17/exploding-watermelons-chinese-farming.

25. LaFraniere, Sharon. "Despite Government Efforts, Tainted Food Widespread in China." *New York Times*, May 7, 2011, sec. Asia Pacific. https://www.nytimes .com/2011/05/08/world/asia/08food.html.

26. Levin, Dan, and Crystal Tse. "In China, Stomachs Turn at News of 40-Year -Old Meat Peddled by Traders." *New York Times*, December 21, 2017, sec. World. https://www.nytimes.com/2015/06/25/world/in-china-stomachs-turn-at-news -of-traders-peddling-40-year-old-meat.html.

27. Zipser, Daniel, Youngang Chen, and Fang Gong. "The Modernization of the Chinese Consumer." *2016 China Consumer Report*. Consumer & Retail Practice. McKinsey & Company, March 2016.

28. Regnier-Davies, Jenelle. "'Fake Meat and Cabbageworms': Connecting Perceptions of Food Safety and Household Level Food Security in Urban China." University of Waterloo, 2015. https://uwspace.uwaterloo.ca/bitstream/handle /10012/9641/Regnier-Davies_Jenelle.pdf.

29. Chao, Sunny. "VIP Treatment: Chinese Top Officials Get Special Food Supplies Delivered to Them." *Epoch Times*, May 3, 2018. https://www.theepochtimes.com/ vip-treatment-chinese-top-officials-get-special-food-supplies-delivered-to-them _2513491.html.

30. Osnos, Evan. *Age of Ambition: Chasing Fortune, Truth, and Faith in the New China* (New York: Farrar, Straus and Giroux, 2014).

31. Ng, Marie, Tom Fleming, Margaret Robinson, Blake Thomson, Nicholas Graetz, Christopher Margono, Erin C Mullany, et al. "Global, Regional, and National Prevalence of Overweight and Obesity in Children and Adults during 1980–2013: A Systematic Analysis for the Global Burden of Disease Study 2013." *The Lancet* 384, no. 9945 (August 2014): 766–81. https://doi.org/10.1016 /S0140-6736(14)60460-8.

32. Abarca-Gómez, Leandra, Ziad A. Abdeen, Zargar Abdul Hamid, Niveen M. Abu-Rmeileh, Benjamin Acosta-Cazares, Cecilia Acuin, Robert J. Adams, et al. "Worldwide Trends in Body-Mass Index, Underweight, Overweight, and Obesity from 1975 to 2016: A Pooled Analysis of 2416 Population-Based Measurement Studies in 128.9 Million Children, Adolescents, and Adults." *Lancet* 390, no. 10113 (December 2017): 2627–42. https://doi.org/10.1016/S0140-6736(17)32129-3.

33. "High Blood Pressure Puts One in Four Nigerians at Risk, Study Says." *ScienceDaily*. Accessed August 27, 2018. https://www.sciencedaily.com/releases/2014/11/141112102642.htm.

     Searcey, Dionne, and Matt Richtel. "Obesity Was Rising as Ghana Embraced Fast Food. Then Came KFC." *New York Times*, October 2, 2017, sec. Health. https://www.nytimes.com/2017/10/02/health/ghana-kfc-obesity.html.

34. Centers for Disease Control and Prevention. "Mortality in the United States, 2015." Accessed August 16, 2018. https://www.cdc.gov/nchs/data/databriefs/db267.pdf.

35. Centers for Disease Control and Prevention. "Division for Heart Disease and Stroke Prevention at a Glance." Accessed August 16, 2018. https://www.cdc.gov/chronicdisease/resources/publications/aag/heart-disease-stroke.htm.

36. World Health Organization. "Global Report on Diabetes." Accessed August 16, 2018. http://apps.who.int/iris/bitstream/handle/10665/204871/9789241565257_eng.pdf?sequence=1.

37. "CDC Press Releases." Centers for Disease Control and Prevention, January 1, 2016. https://www.cdc.gov/media/releases/2017/p0718-diabetes-report.html.

38. Haspel, Tamar. "The Surprising Truth about the 'Food Movement.'" *Washington Post*. Accessed August 27, 2018. https://www.washingtonpost.com/lifestyle/food/the-surprising-truth-about-the-food-movement/2016/01/25/42bed508-bfcf-11e5-9443-7074c3645405_story.html.

39. "It's Clear: Transparency Is Winning In the U.S. Retail Market." Nielsen, 2017. https://www.nielsen.com/wp-content/uploads/sites/3/2019/04/nielsen-clean-label-report-aug-2017.pdf.

40. "Food + Drink: Trends and Futures." J. Walter Thompson Intelligence, September 2015.

41. Mintel Press Team. "US Millennials Twice as Likely as Non-Millennials to Distrust Large Food Manufacturers." Mintel, October 29, 2015. http://www.mintel.com/press-centre/food-and-drink/us-millennials-twice-as-likely-as-non-millennials-to-distrust-large-food-manufacturers.

42. Howard, Alexia. "The Changing Landscape and Growth Opportunities in Packaged Food." Bernstein Research, September 2013. https://www.greenhassonjanks.com/wp-content/uploads/2016/12/Alexia_Presentation.pdf.

     Howard, Alexia. "Inform Your Instinct." Bernstein, 2016. https://www.dwt.com/files/Uploads/Documents/Events/AlexiaHoward2016F2L.pdf.

43. "Marketing Sustainability: What's the Right Message?" Hartman Group. Accessed August 30, 2018. https://www.hartman-group.com/acumenPdfs/sustainability-making-it-personal-2017-03-30.pdf.

44. "Who's Buying Clean Label Products?" Nielsen. Accessed September 6, 2018. http://www.nielsen.com/us/en/insights/news/2017/whos-buying-clean-label-products.

45. "A Tough Road to Growth. The 2015 Mid-Year Review: How the Top 100 CPG Brands Performed." Catalina, 2015. https://assets.ctfassets.net/oyvkhyupj8l5/2Z YjJLIB2gsMyaOgmQC2WW/8ece3950dea3f20122cf71ea80229c1a/2015-Mid-Year-Review.pdf.

46. "The Transparency Imperative: Product Labeling from the Consumer Perspective." Food Marketing Institute, 2018. https://www.fmi.org/forms/store/ProductFormPublic/the-transparency-imperative-product-labeling-from-the-consumer-perspective.

47. Response Media. "Transparency Content and the Consumer Journey." 2017 Transparency Study, 2017. http://www.responsemedia.com/wp-content/uploads/2017/07/RM_Transparency_Survey_Final.pdf.

48. Karen Karp & Partners, Radius Global Market Research, and Good Housekeeping Institute. "Consumer Food Beliefs and Behaviors: The James Beard Foundation Consumer Research Project." The James Beard Foundation, 2017. https://jbf-media.s3.amazonaws.com/production/page/2017/10/22/101617_FS_CONSUMER_SURVEY.pdf.

49. "WP Engine U.S. Crosstabs (2018) Data from Reality Bytes: The Digital Experience Is the Human Experience." WP Engine & The Center for Generational Kinetics, August 31, 2018.

50. Drake, Bruce. "6 New Findings about Millennials." *Pew Research Center*, March 7, 2014. http://www.pewresearch.org/fact-tank/2014/03/07/6-new-findings-about-millennials/.

51. World Economic Forum. "Survey Results 2015." Accessed August 14, 2018. http://www3.weforum.org/docs/Media/GSC/GSC_AnnualSurvey15.pdf.

52. "2017 Edelman Trust Barometer Reveals Global Implosion of Trust." Edelman, January 15, 2017. https://www.edelman.com/news/2017-edelman-trust-barometer-reveals-global-implosion/.

53. "What's In Our Food and On Our Mind: Ingredient and Dining-Out Trends Around the World." Nielsen, August 2016. https://www.nielsen.com/content/dam/nielsenglobal/eu/docs/pdf/Global%20Ingredient%20and%20Out-of-Home%20Dining%20Trends%20Report.pdf.

54. Funk, Cary, and Lee Rainie. "Chapter 6: Public Opinion About Food." *Pew Research Center: Internet, Science & Tech*, July 1, 2015. http://www.pewinternet.org/2015/07/01/chapter-6-public-opinion-about-food/.

55. "107 Nobel Laureates Sign Letter Blasting Greenpeace over GMOs." *Washington Post*. Accessed February 5, 2017. https://www.washingtonpost.com/news/speaking-of-science/wp/2016/06/29/more-than-100-nobel-laureates-take-on-greenpeace-over-gmo-stance/.

56. Li, J. "When GM Foods Are Placed on Your Dinner Table, Do You Eat It or Not?" *China Youth Daily*. February 3, 2015. Retrieved from http://zqb.cyol.com/html/2015-02/13/nw.D110000zgqnb_20150213_4-08.htm.

57. "Food Literacy and Engagement Poll: Wave I." *Food@MSU*. Accessed September 1, 2018. https://www.canr.msu.edu/news/msu-food-literacy-and-engagement-poll.

58. Yu, Nan, and Qian Xu. "Public Discourse on Genetically Modified Foods in the Mobile Sphere: Framing Risks, Opportunities, and Responsibilities in Mobile Social Media in China." In *Mobile Media, Political Participation, and Civic Activism in Asia*, edited by Ran Wei, 81–102 (Dordrecht: Springer Netherlands, 2016). https://doi.org/10.1007/978-94-024-0917-8_5.

59. CBS News. December 14, 2009. "AP: Monsanto Strong-Arms Seed Industry." Accessed February 5, 2017. http://www.cbsnews.com/news/ap-monsanto-strong-arms-seed-industry/.

60. "Demographics of Mobile Device Ownership and Adoption in the United States." *Pew Research Center: Internet, Science & Tech*, June 12, 2019. https://www.pewinternet.org/fact-sheet/mobile/.

61. Wei, Ran. "Mobile Media, Political Participation, and Civic Activism in Asia: Private Chat to Public Communication." Springer, 2016.

62. Shen, Alice. "WeChat, QQ and Weibo Ban Changes to Users' Profiles." *South China Morning Post*, October 18, 2017. http://www.scmp.com/news/china/society/article/2115913/china-cyber-lockdown-wechat-qq-and-weibo-ban-changes-users.

63. "The 2016 WeChat Rumor Analysis Report R." Accessed March 13, 2018. https://www.digitaling.com/articles/24179.html.

64. Price, John Scott. "An Evolutionary Perspective on Anxiety and Anxiety Disorders." *New Insights into Anxiety Disorders*, March 20, 2013. https://doi.org/10.5772/52902.

65. Ibid.

66. Klein, Ezra. "How Technology Is Designed to Bring Out the Worst in Us." *Vox*, February 19, 2018. https://www.vox.com/technology/2018/2/19/17020310/tristan-harris-facebook-twitter-humane-tech-time.

67. Ibid.

68. "18 People Arrested in China for Spreading False Information about 'Plastic Seaweed.'" Accessed August 3, 2018. http://en.people.cn/n3/2017/0607/c90000-9225531.html.

69. "塑料紫菜' 网络谣言波及至少五省市，公安重拳出击抓18人_一号专案_澎湃新闻." Accessed August 3, 2018. https://www.thepaper.cn/newsDetail_forward_1702481.

70. Huang, Echo. "In China, Consumers Have to Be on Guard Not Just against Fake Food, but Also Fake News about Food." *Quartz*. Accessed August 27, 2018. https://qz.com/934038/in-china-fake-news-about-food-goes-viral-because-people-find-it-hard-to-trust-anyone/.

71. Wells, Katie. "Is Soy Healthy or Not?" *Wellness Mama*. Accessed April 11, 2019. https://wellnessmama.com/3684/is-soy-healthy/.

72. Fischler, Claude. "The Nutritional Cacophony May Be Detrimental to Your Health." *Progress in Nutrition* 13 (2011): 217–21; Skrabanek, Petr. *The Death of Humane Medicine and the Rise of Coercive Healthism* (Suffolk, UK: Social Affairs Unit, 1994).

73. Rangel, Cristian, Steven Dukeshire, and Letitia MacDonald. "Diet and Anxiety: An Exploration into the Orthorexic Society." *Appetite* 58, no. 1 (February 2012): 124–32. https://doi.org/10.1016/j.appet.2011.08.024.. https://doi.org/10.1016/j.appet.2011.08.024.

74. Williams, Alex. "Prozac Nation Is Now the United States of Xanax." *New York Times,* June 10, 2017, sec. Style. https://www.nytimes.com/2017/06/10/style/anxiety-is-the-new-depression-xanax.html.

75. Reetz, David, Carolyn Bershad, Peter LeViness, and Monica Whitlock. "The Association for University and College Counseling Center Directors Annual Survey." Association for University and College Counseling Center Directors, September 1, 2015. https://www.aucccd.org/assets/documents/aucccd%202016%20monograph%20-%20public.pdf.

76. "Is Anxiety about Physical Safety Impacting Millennials?" Accessed August 6, 2018. http://media.corporate-ir.net/media_files/IROL/25/254250/adt_anxiety_millennials_FINAL2.pdf.

77. Astor, Maggie. "No Children Because of Climate Change? Some People Are Considering It." *New York Times,* July 18, 2018, sec. Climate. https://www.nytimes.com/2018/02/05/climate/climate-change-children.html.

78. Jones, Lily. "Destress the Classroom: Bringing Mindfulness to Students & Teachers." *Forbes.* Accessed October 26, 2018. https://www.forbes.com/sites/lilyjones/2018/10/26/destress-the-classroom-bringing-mindfulness-to-students-teachers/.

    Kim, Hannah. "The Meditation Industry." *SAGE BusinessResearcher,* January 29, 2018.

79. "2018GWIResearch_BuildWelltoLiveWellReport.pdf." Accessed October 29, 2018. https://static1.squarespace.com/static/54306a8ee4b07ea66ea32cc0/t/5a5fd37c0d9297ee43f742bd/1516229551173/2018GWIResearch_BuildWelltoLiveWellReport.pdf.

80. He, Laura. "Insurtech Giant ZhongAn Plans to Use Facial Recognition, Blockchain to Monitor Chickens." *China Morning Post,* December 10, 2017. https://www.scmp.com/business/companies/article/2123567/blockchain-and-facial-recognition-zhongan-techs-recipe-changing.

81. Sullivan, Naamua. "Just When It Seemed People Were Growing More Detached from Farming, 'Generation Yum' Delivers a Surprise." Cargill, January 8, 2019. https://www.cargill.com/2019/just-when-it-seemed-people-were-growing-more-detached-from-farmi.

CHAPTER 2: DELIVERY & DISTRACTION

1. "A Perspective on Online Food Aggregators—OND16," RedSeer, December 2016. https://redseer.com/articles/a-perspective-on-online-food-aggregators-ond16/.

2. "ALDI Household Expenditure Report: How Economic Pressures and Societal Trends Are Impacting Grocery Spending." Deloitte Access Economics. *Deloitte,* November 2017. https://www2.deloitte.com/content/dam/Deloitte

/au/Documents/Economics/deloitte-au-economics-aldi-household-expenditure -071117.pdf.

   Carey, Alexis. "Australia's Shocking Food Delivery Bill Revealed by New Research." *News.Com.Au*, February 6, 2018. https://www.news.com.au/finance /business/retail/australias-shocking-food-delivery-bill-revealed-by-new-research /news-story/169772bd58ae0f3bd923b390c75b5769#.5jexc.

   Chung, Frank. "Aussies Would Rather Cut Back on Grocery Spend than Give up Netflix, Spotify and Takeaway." *News.Com.Au*, November 13, 2017. https:// www.news.com.au/finance/business/retail/aussies-would-rather-cut-back-on -grocery-spend-than-give-up-netflix-spotify-and-takeaway/news-story/82d8c48 2e85bbebc5f751dae23e77e24#.dmop5.

3. "Blue Apron Holdings, Inc. Reports Fourth Quarter and Full Year 2017 Results." Blue Apron, n.d. https://investors.blueapron.com/~/media/Files/B/BlueApron -IR/press-release/q4-earnings-press-release.pdf.

4. Topper, Amanda. "Salty Snacks," *Mintel*, April 2016. http://reports.mintel.com /display/768765/?highlight#hit1.

5. Hartman Group. "The Future of Snacking: When a Suitcase Full of Snacks Predicted the Demise of Traditional Mealtime." Accessed March 5, 2019. https:// www.hartman-group.com/newsletters/701220295/the-future-of-snacking-when -a-suitcase-full-of-snacks-predicted-the-demise-of-traditional-mealtime

6. Severson, Kim. "Cereal, a Taste of Nostalgia, Looks for Its Next Chapter." *New York Times*, February 22, 2016, sec. Food. https://www.nytimes.com/2016/02/24 /dining/breakfast-cereal.html.

7. Ferdman, Roberto. "The Baffling Reason Many Millennials Don't Eat Cereal." *Washington Post*, February 23, 2016. https://www.washingtonpost.com/news /wonk/wp/2016/02/23/this-is-the-height-of-laziness/.

   Peyser, Eve. "Millennials Literally Too Lazy to Eat Cereal." *The Cut*, February 23, 2016. https://www.thecut.com/2016/02/millennials-literally-too-lazy-to -eat-cereal.html.

   Snyder, Benjamin. "Millennials Think Eating Cereal Is Way Too Difficult." *Fortune*, February 25, 2016. https://fortune.com/2016/02/25/millennials-cereal -sales/.

   Swerdloff, Alex. "Millennials Don't Like Cereal Because They Hate Doing Dishes." *Vice*, February 26, 2016. https://www.vice.com/en_us/article/bm3aem /millennials-dont-like-cereal-because-they-hate-doing-dishes.

8. Darby, Luke. "The Real Reason Millennials Aren't Eating Cereal for Breakfast." *GQ*, March 21, 2016. https://www.gq.com/story/the-real-reason-millennials -arent-eating-cereal-for-breakfast.

9. "Parenting in America." Pew Research Center, December 17, 2015. http://www .pewsocialtrends.org/2015/12/17/2-satisfaction-time-and-support/.

   "Stress and Sleep," American Psychological Association, 2013. http://www .apa.org/news/press/releases/stress/2013/sleep.aspx.

10. "Eaters Digest: The Future of Food." Prosumer Report. Havas Worldwide, 2016.

11. Hartman Group. "Changing Meal Routines." Accessed October 25, 2018. https:// www.hartman-group.com/acumenPdfs/changes-in-meals-10_25_18.pdf.

12. Rubin, Alissa J. "France Lets Workers Turn Off, Tune Out and Live Life." *New York Times*, January 2, 2017, sec. World. https://www.nytimes.com/2017/01/02/world/europe/france-work-email.html.

13. "Demographics of Mobile Device Ownership and Adoption in the United States." *Pew Research Center: Internet, Science & Tech*, June 12, 2019. https://www.pewInternet.org/fact-sheet/mobile/.

14. Petersen, Anne Helen. "How Millennials Became the Burnout Generation." *BuzzFeed News,* January 5, 2019. https://www.buzzfeednews.com/article/annehelenpetersen/millennials-burnout-generation-debt-work.

15. "Burn-Out an 'Occupational Phenomenon': International Classification of Diseases." World Health Organization, May 28, 2019. http://www.who.int/mental_health/evidence/burn-out/en/.

16. Feintzeig, Rachel. "Feeling Burned Out at Work? Join the Club." *Wall Street Journal,* February 28, 2017, sec. Business. https://www.wsj.com/articles/feeling-burned-out-at-work-join-the-club-1488286801.

17. Gallup. "Employee Burnout, Part 1: The 5 Main Causes." Accessed October 25, 2018. https://www.gallup.com/workplace/237059/employee-burnout-part-main-causes.aspx.

18. Workplace Trends. "The 2015 Workplace Flexibility Study." Accessed October 30, 2018. http://workplacetrends.com/the-2015-workplace-flexibility-study/.

19. Deal, Jennifer J. "Always On, Never Done?" Center for Creative Leadership. Accessed October 30, 2018. https://www.ccl.org/wp-content/uploads/2015/04/AlwaysOn.pdf.

20. Fryar, Cheryl, Jeffrey Hughes, Kirsten Herrick, and Namanjeet Ahluwalia. "Fast Food Consumption Among Adults in the United States, 2013–2016." NCHS Data Brief. US Department of Health and Human Services, Centers for Disease Control and Prevention, National Center for Health Statistics, October 2018. https://www.cdc.gov/nchs/data/databriefs/db322-h.pdf.

21. "The North American Workplace Survey: Americans Are Overworked and Burnt Out, But Surprisingly Happy at Work," Workplace Trends, June 29, 2015. https://workplacetrends.com/north-american-workplace-survey/.

22. "Americans Waste Record-Setting 658 Million Vacation Days." Project: Time Off, June 14, 2016. https://projecttimeoff.com/press-releases/americans-waste-record-setting-658-million-vacation-days /.

23. Greenwood, Chelsea. "How Paid Vacation Time Is Different around the World." *Business Insider,* July 19, 2018. https://www.businessinsider.com/how-paid-vacation-time-is-different-around-the-world-2018-7.

24. Mark, Gloria, Shamsi T. Iqbal, Mary Czerwinski, Paul Johns, Akane Sano, and Yuliya Lutchyn. "Email Duration, Batching and Self-Interruption: Patterns of Email Use on Productivity and Stress." In *Proceedings of the 2016 CHI Conference on Human Factors in Computing Systems* 16, 1717–28. Santa Clara, CA: ACM Press, 2016. https://doi.org/10.1145/2858036.2858262.

25. Brod, Craig. *Technostress: The Human Cost of the Computer Revolution* (Reading, MA: Addison-Wesley, 1984); Ragu-Nathan, T. S., M. Tarafdar, B. S.

Ragu-Nathan, and Q. Tu. "The Consequences of Technostress for End Users in Organizations: Conceptual Development and Empirical Validation." *Information Systems Research* 19, no. 4 (2008): 417–33.

26. Turner, Zeke. "How Grocery Giant Aldi Plans to Conquer America: Limit Choice." *Wall Street Journal*, September 21, 2017, sec. Business. https://www.wsj.com/articles /how-grocery-giant-aldi-plans-to-conquer-america-limit-choice-1506004169.

27. Shapiro, Aaron. "The Next Big Thing in Design? Less Choice." *Fast Company*, April 15, 2015. https://www.fastcompany.com/3045039/the-next-big-thing-in -design-fewer-choices.

28. Pattison, Kermit. "Worker, Interrupted: The Cost of Task Switching." *Fast Company*, July 28, 2008. https://www.fastcompany.com/944128/worker-inter-rupted-cost-task-switching; Mark, Gloria, Victor Gonzalez, and Justin Harris. "No Task Left Behind? Examining the Nature of Fragmented Work." In *Take a Number, Stand in Line*. (Portland, OR: 2005). https://www.ics.uci.edu/~gmark /CHI2005.pdf.

29. Leroy, Sophie. "Why Is It So Hard to Do My Work? The Challenge of Attention Residue When Switching Between Work Tasks." *Organizational Behavior and Human Decision Processes* 109, no. 2 (July 1, 2009): 168–81. https://doi .org/10.1016/j.obhdp.2009.04.002.

30. Gazzaley, Adam, and Larry D. Rosen. *The Distracted Mind: Ancient Brains in a High-Tech World* (Cambridge, MA: MIT Press, 2016).

Loh, Kep Kee, and Ryota Kanai. "Higher Media Multi-Tasking Activity Is Associated with Smaller Gray-Matter Density in the Anterior Cingulate Cortex." Edited by Katsumi Watanabe. *PLOS ONE* 9, no. 9 (September 24, 2014): e106698. https://doi.org/10.1371/journal.pone.0106698.

Montag, Christian, Alexander Markowetz, Konrad Blaszkiewicz, Ionut Andone, Bernd Lachmann, Rayna Sariyska, Boris Trendafilov, et al. "Facebook Usage on Smartphones and Gray Matter Volume of the Nucleus Accumbens." *Behavioural Brain Research* 329 (June 2017): 221–28. https://doi.org/10.1016/j .bbr.2017.04.035.

Montag, Christian, Zhiying Zhao, Cornelia Sindermann, Lei Xu, Meina Fu, Jialin Li, Xiaoxiao Zheng, et al. "Internet Communication Disorder and the Structure of the Human Brain: Initial Insights on WeChat Addiction." *Scientific Reports* 8, no. 1 (December 2018): 2155. https://doi.org/10.1038 /s41598-018-19904-y.

31. Hölzel, Britta K., James Carmody, Mark Vangel, Christina Congleton, Sita M. Yerramsetti, Tim Gard, and Sara W. Lazar. "Mindfulness Practice Leads to Increases in Regional Brain Gray Matter Density." *Psychiatry Research: Neuroimaging* 191, no. 1 (January 2011): 36–43. https://doi.org/10.1016/j .pscychresns.2010.08.006.

Zeidan, Fadel, Katherine T. Martucci, Robert A. Kraft, John G. McHaffie, and Robert C. Coghill. "Neural Correlates of Mindfulness Meditation-Related Anxiety Relief." *Social Cognitive and Affective Neuroscience* 9, no. 6 (June 2014): 751–59. https://doi.org/10.1093/scan/nst041.

32. Baker, Wayne. "Cell Phones Are Involved in an Estimated 27 Percent of All Car Crashes, Says National Safety Council." National Safety Council, June 17, 2015. https://www.nsc.org/in-the-newsroom/cell-phones-are-involved-in-an -estimated-27-percent-of-all-car-crashes-says-national-safety-council.

  Hall, Jeffrey A., and Nancy K. Baym. "Calling and Texting (Too Much): Mobile Maintenance Expectations, (over)Dependence, Entrapment, and Friendship Satisfaction." *New Media & Society* 14, no. 2 (March 2012): 316–31. https://doi.org/10.1177/1461444811415047.

  Nasar, Jack L., and Derek Troyer. "Pedestrian Injuries Due to Mobile Phone Use in Public Places." *Accident Analysis & Prevention* 57 (August 2013): 91–95. https://doi.org/10.1016/j.aap.2013.03.021.

33. "NSC Releases Latest Injury and Fatality Statistics and Trends." National Safety Council, March 24, 2014. https://www.nsc.org/Portals/0/Documents/News Documents/2014-Press-Release-Archive/3-25-2014-Injury-Facts-release.pdf.

34. Perlow, Leslie, and Jessica L. Porter. "Making Time Off Predictable—and Required." *Harvard Business Review* 87, no. 10 (October 2009).

35. Levitin, Daniel J. *The Organized Mind: Thinking Straight in the Age of Information Overload* (New York: Dutton, 2015).

36. Stothart, Cary, Ainsley Mitchum, and Courtney Yehnert. "The Attentional Cost of Receiving a Cell Phone Notification." *Journal of Experimental Psychology: Human Perception and Performance* 41, no. 4 (August 2015): 893–97. https://doi .org/10.1037/xhp0000100.

37. Clayton, Russell B., Glenn Leshner, and Anthony Almond. "The Extended iSelf: The Impact of iPhone Separation on Cognition, Emotion, and Physiology." *Journal of Computer-Mediated Communication* 20, no. 2 (March 1, 2015): 119–35. https://doi.org/10.1111/jcc4.12109.

38. American Psychological Association. "Stress in America 2017: Technology and Social Media." *Part 2. Stress in America: Coping with Change.* American Psychological Association, 2017.

39. Mark, G., S. T. Iqbal, M. Czerwinski, P. Johns, A. Sano, and Y. Lutchyn. "Email Duration, Batching, and Self-Interruption." *Proceedings of the 2016 CHI Conference on Human Factors in Computing Systems* (2016). https://doi.org/10 .1145/2858036.2858262.

40. Coxon, Rebecca. "Overwhelming Technology Disrupting Life and Causing Stress New Study Shows." *Mental Healthy.* Accessed November 2, 2018. http:// www.mentalhealthy.co.uk/news/568-overwhelming-technology-disrupting-life -and-causing-stress-new-study-shows.html.

41. "1 in 3 Adults Don't Get Enough Sleep." Centers for Disease Control and Prevention, January 1, 2016. https://www.cdc.gov/media/releases/2016/p0215-enough -sleep.html.

42. Alter, Adam. *Irresistible: The Rise of Addictive Technology and the Business of Keeping Us Hooked* (New York: Penguin Press, 2017); Underhill, Justine. "The 100 Hour Work Week in Japan." Yahoo! Finance, August 20, 2015. http://finance.yahoo .com/news/working-towards-death-in-japan-140758364.html.

Fuertes, Joannas. "How the World Forgot to Sleep." *Esquire*, November 21, 2017. http://www.esquire.co.uk/life/fitness-wellbeing/a18577/sleep-loss-epidemic-insomnia-treatment/.

43. "Demographics of Mobile Device Ownership and Adoption in the United States." Accessed November 2, 2018. http://www.pewInternet.org/fact-sheet/mobile/.

"More Teens Than Ever Aren't Getting Enough Sleep: A New Study Finds Young People Are Likely Sacrificing Sleep to Spend More Time on Their Phones and Tablets." *ScienceDaily*. Accessed October 30, 2018. https://www.sciencedaily.com/releases/2017/10/171019100416.htm.

44. Twenge, Jean M., Zlatan Krizan, and Garrett Hisler. "Decreases in Self-Reported Sleep Duration Among U.S. Adolescents 2009–2015 and Links to New Media Screen Time." *Sleep Medicine*, 2017; https://doi.org/10.1016/j.sleep.2017.08.013.

45. Fortune Business Insights. "Ready-to-Drink (RTD) Coffee Market to Exhibit a CAGR of 8.5%, Recent Mergers and Acquisitions to Enable Growth, Says Fortune Business Insights." *GlobeNewswire News Room*, June 27, 2019. http://www.globenewswire.com/news-release/2019/06/27/1875164/0/en/Ready-to-drink-RTD-Coffee-Market-to-Exhibit-a-CAGR-of-8-5-Recent-Mergers-and-Acquisitions-to-Enable-Growth-says-Fortune-Business-Insights.html.

46. Ibid.

47. "Caffeine Kick." *Early Bird*, September 14, 2018. https://www.amerisleep.com/blog/caffeine-kick/.

48. Bivin, J. B., P. Mathew, P. C. Thulasi, and J. Philip. "Nomophobia: Do We Really Need to Worry About?" *Reviews of Progress* 1 (2013). http://www.indianjournals.com/ijor.aspx?target=ijor:jnt&volume=5&issue=3&article=003.

Sharma, N., P. Sharma, N. Sharma, and R. Wavare. "Rising Concern of Nomophobia Amongst Indian Medical Students." *International Journal of Research in Medical Sciences* 3, no. 3 (2015): 705. http://dx.doi.org/10.5455/2320-6012.ijrms20150333.

49. Chóliz M. *Mobile Phone Addiction in Adolescence: Evaluation and Prevention of Mobile Addiction in Teenagers*. (Saarbrücken, Germany: Lambert Academic Publishing; 2010).

Oksman, V., and J. Turtiainen. "Mobile Communication as a Social Stage: The Meanings of Mobile Communication Among Teenagers in Finland." *New Media and Society* 6 (2004): 319–39.

Krajewska-Kułak, E, W. Kułak, A. Stryzhak, A. Szpakow, W. Prokopowicz, and J. T. Marcinkowski. "Problematic Mobile Phone Using Among the Polish and Belarusian University Students: A Comparative Study." *Progress in Health Sciences* 2, no. 1 (2012): 45–50.

Toda, M., K. Monden, K. Kubo, and K. Morimoto. "Mobile Phone Dependence and Health-Related Life-Style of University Students." *Social Behavior and Personality* 34 (2006):1277–84.

50. Yildirim, C., and A. Correia. "Exploring the Dimensions of Nomophobia: Development and Validation of a Self-Reported Questionnaire." *Computers in Human Behavior* 49 (2015): 130–37.

51. McCann Worldgroup. "The Truth About Youth." Accessed November 6, 2018. https://www.scribd.com/doc/56263899/McCann-Worldgroup-Truth-About-Youth.

52. Ibid.

53. Haefele, Mark, Simon Smiles, and Matthew Carter. "Millennials—the Global Guardians of Capital."

54. Richtel, Matt. "Are Teenagers Replacing Drugs with Smartphones?" *New York Times,* December 22, 2017, sec. Health. https://www.nytimes.com/2017/03/13/health/teenagers-drugs-smartphones.html.

55. Przybylski, Andrew K., Kou Murayama, Cody R. DeHaan, and Valerie Gladwell. "Motivational, Emotional, and Behavioral Correlates of Fear of Missing Out." *Computers in Human Behavior* 29, no. 4 (July 2013): 1841–48. https://doi.org/10.1016/j.chb.2013.02.014.

56. Bayindir, Nisa, and Duncan Kavanagh. "Social: GlobalWebIndex's Flagship Report on the Latest Trends in Social Media." *GlobalWebIndex*, 2018. https://www.globalwebindex.com/hubfs/Downloads/Social-H2-2018-report.pdf.

57. Alt, Dorit, and Meyran Boniel-Nissim. "Links Between Adolescents' Deep and Surface Learning Approaches, Problematic Internet Use, and Fear of Missing Out (FoMO)." *Internet Interventions* 13 (September 2018): 30–39. https://doi.org/10.1016/j.invent.2018.05.002.

    Blackwell, David, Carrie Leaman, Rose Tramposch, Ciera Osborne, and Miriam Liss. "Extraversion, Neuroticism, Attachment Style and Fear of Missing out as Predictors of Social Media Use and Addiction." *Personality and Individual Differences* 116 (October 1, 2017): 69–72. https://doi.org/10.1016/j.paid.2017.04.039.

    Carbonell, Xavier, Ursula Oberst, and Marta Beranuy. "The Cell Phone in the Twenty-First Century." In *Principles of Addiction,* ed. by Peter M. Miller. (Amsterdam: Elsevier, 2013): 901–9. https://doi.org/10.1016/B978-0-12-398336-7.00091-7.

    Elhai, Jon D., Jason C. Levine, Robert D. Dvorak, and Brian J. Hall. "Fear of Missing Out, Need for Touch, Anxiety and Depression Are Related to Problematic Smartphone Use." *Computers in Human Behavior* 63 (October 1, 2016): 509–16. https://doi.org/10.1016/j.chb.2016.05.079.

58. Susan M. Snyder, Wen Li, Jennifer E. O'Brien and Matthew O. Howard, "The Effect of U.S. University Students' Problematic Internet Use on Family Relationships: A Mixed-Methods Investigation." *PLOS One* (December 11, 2015).

59. "A Quarter of Americans Are Online Almost Constantly." *Pew Research Center.* Accessed November 6, 2018. http://www.pewresearch.org/fact-tank/2018/03/14/about-a-quarter-of-americans-report-going-online-almost-constantly/.

60. "Reality Bytes: The Digital Experience Is the Human Experience." WP Engine and the Center for Generational Kinetics, LLC, 2018. https://wpengine.com/wp-content/uploads/2019/01/GenZ_RealityBytes_EbookUS.pdf.

61. Haefele, Mark, Simon Smiles, and Matthew Carter. "Millennials—The Global Guardians of Capital."

62. Curtin, Melanie. "Are You On Your Phone Too Much? The Average Person Spends This Many Hours On It Every Day." *Inc.com*, October 30, 2018. https://www.inc.com/melanie-curtin/are-you-on-your-phone-too-much-average-person-spends-this-many-hours-on-it-every-day.html.

63. Deloitte. "Americans Look at Their Smartphones More Than 12 Billion Times Daily, Even as Usage Habits Mature and Device Growth Plateaus." Accessed December 12, 2018. https://www.prnewswire.com/news-releases/deloitte-americans-look-at-their-smartphones-more-than-12-billion-times-daily-even-as-usage-habits-mature-and-device-growth-plateaus-300555703.html.

CHAPTER 3: DIETS & ORDER

1. The Vegan Society. "Statistics." Accessed December 25, 2019. https://www.vegansociety.com/news/media/statistics.
   "Veganism Booms by 350%." Vegan Life. May 18, 2016. https://www.veganlifemag.com/veganism-booms/.

2. Parker, John. "The Year of the Vegan." The Economist. Accessed September 12, 2019. https://worldin2019.economist.com/theyearofthevegan?utm_source=412&utm_medium=COM.
   Plant Based Foods Association. "2018 U.S. Retail Sales Data for Plant-Based Foods." Accessed September 12, 2019. https://plantbasedfoods.org/consumer-access/nielsen-data-release-2018/.

3. Parker, John. "The Year of the Vegan." *The Economist*. Accessed September 12, 2019. https://worldin2019.economist.com/theyearofthevegan?utm_source=412&utm_medium=COM.

4. Shirvell, Bridget. "More Than 50% of Millennials Trying to Incorporate Plant-Based Foods into Their Diet." *Forbes*, September 9, 2019. https://www.forbes.com/sites/bridgetshirvell/2019/09/09/more-than-50-of-millennials-trying-to-incorporate-plant-based-foods-into-their-diet.

5. Chan, Bernice. "The Meat-Free Impossible Burger 2.0 Has Arrived. We Give It a Taste." *South China Morning Post*, March 24, 2019. https://www.scmp.com/lifestyle/food-drink/article/3002803/plant-based-impossible-burger-20-now-hong-kong-we-give-it-taste.

6. Taylor, Derrick Bryson. "What Sandwich War? KFC Sells Out of Plant-Based 'Chicken' in Atlanta." *The New York Times*, August 28, 2019, sec. Business. https://www.nytimes.com/2019/08/28/business/kfc-beyond-meat-vegan-chicken.html.

7. News Desk. "US Non-Dairy Milk Sales Rise to $2.11bn in 2017—Mintel." *FoodBev Media*, January 5, 2018. https://www.foodbev.com/news/non-dairy-milk-sales-mintel/.

8. Bernstein, Joshua M. "Dairy Farms Find a Lifeline: Beer." *The New York Times*, June 11, 2018, sec. Food. https://www.nytimes.com/2018/06/11/dining/dairy-farm-beer-craft-brewery.html.

9. Bruno, Audrey. "What Gena Hamshaw Of the Vegan Blog 'The Full Helping' Eats in a Day." *SELF*, September 23, 2016. Accessed November 19, 2018. https://www.self.com/story/what-gena-hamshaw-of-the-vegan-blog-the-full-helping-eats-in-a-day.

Romero, Melissa. "Food Diaries: How Nutritionist Gena Hamshaw Eats for a Day." *Washingtonian,* November 12, 2013. Accessed November 19, 2018. https://www.washingtonian.com/2013/11/12/food-diaries-how-nutritionist-gena-hershaw-eats-for-a-day/.

10. Bardone-Cone, Anna M., Ellen E. Fitzsimmons-Craft, Megan B. Harney, Christine R. Maldonado, Melissa A. Lawson, Roma Smith, and D. Paul Robinson. "The Inter-Relationships between Vegetarianism and Eating Disorders among Females." *Journal of the Academy of Nutrition and Dietetics* 112, no. 8 (August 2012): 1247–52. https://doi.org/10.1016/j.jand.2012.05.007.

Barnett, Michaela J., Weston R. Dripps, and Kerstin K. Blomquist. "Organivore or Organorexic? Examining the Relationship between Alternative Food Network Engagement, Disordered Eating, and Special Diets." *Appetite* 105 (October 1, 2016): 713–20. https://doi.org/10.1016/j.appet.2016.07.008.

Klopp, Sheree A., Cynthia J. Heiss, and Heather S. Smith. "Self-Reported Vegetarianism May Be a Marker for College Women at Risk for Disordered Eating." *Journal of the American Dietetic Association* 103, no. 6 (June 2003): 745–47. https://doi.org/10.1053/jada.2003.50139.

Lindeman, Marjaana, Katariina Stark, and Krista Latvala. "Vegetarianism and Eating-Disordered Thinking." *Eating Disorders* 8 (June 13, 2007): 157–65. https://doi.org/10.1080/10640260008251222.

Martins, Y., P. Pliner, and R. O'Connor. "Restrained Eating among Vegetarians: Does a Vegetarian Eating Style Mask Concerns about Weight?" *Appetite* 32, no. 1 (February 1999): 145–54. https://doi.org/10.1006/appe.1998.0185.

Sassaroli, Sandra, Marcello Gallucci, and Giovanni Maria Ruggiero. "Low Perception of Control as a Cognitive Factor of Eating Disorders. Its Independent Effects on Measures of Eating Disorders and Its Interactive Effects with Perfectionism and Self-Esteem." *Journal of Behavior Therapy and Experimental Psychiatry* 39, no. 4 (December 2008): 467–88. https://doi.org/10.1016/j.jbtep.2007.11.005.

Trautmann, J., S. Rau, M. Wilson, and C. Walters. "Vegetarian Students in Their First Year of College. Are They at Risk for Restrictive or Disordered Eating Behavior?" *College Student Journal* 42 (January 1, 2008): 340–47.

Zuromski, Kelly L., Tracy K. Witte, April R. Smith, Natalie Goodwin, Lindsay P. Bodell, Mary Bartlett, and Nicole Siegfried. "Increased Prevalence of Vegetarianism among Women with Eating Pathology." *Eating Behaviors* 19 (December 2015): 24–27. https://doi.org/10.1016/j.eatbeh.2015.06.017.

11. Centers for Disease Control and Prevention. "National Health Interview Survey." Accessed April 20, 2017. https://www.cdc.gov/nchs/nhis/.

12. Cramer, Holger, Christian S. Kessler, Tobias Sundberg, Matthew J. Leach, Dania Schumann, Jon Adams, and Romy Lauche. "Characteristics of Americans Choosing Vegetarian and Vegan Diets for Health Reasons." *Journal of Nutrition Education and Behavior* 49, no. 7 (July 1, 2017): 561–567. https://doi.org/10.1016/j.jneb.2017.04.011.

13. Belluz, Julia. "The Most Googled Diets in Every City." *Vox*, November 10, 2015. Accessed September 5, 2017. https://www.vox.com/2015/11/10/9704544/most -populardiet.

Choung, R. S., et al. "Less Hidden Celiac Disease but Increased Gluten Avoidance Without a Diagnosis in the United States: Findings from the National Health and Nutrition Examination Surveys From 2009 to 2014." *Mayo Clinic Proceedings* 1, no. 92 (January 2017): 30-38. https://doi.org/10.1016/j .mayocp.2016.10.012.

Choung, R. S., I. C. Ditah, A. M. Nadeau, et al. "Trends and racial/ethnic disparities in gluten-sensitive problems in the United States: findings from the National Health and Nutrition Examination Surveys from 1988 to 2012." *The American Journal of Gastroenterology* 110, no. 3 (February 2015): 455–461. https:// www.ncbi.nlm.nih.gov/pubmed/25665935.

Kim, H. S., et al. "Time Trends in the Prevalence of Celiac Disease and Gluten-Free Diet in the US Population: Results from the National Health and Nutrition Examination Surveys 2009–2014." *JAMA Internal Medicine* 176, no. 11 (2016): 1716–1717. https://doi.org/10.1001/jamainternmed.2016.5254.

Rubio-Tapia, A., J. F. Ludvigsson, T. L. Brantner, et al. "The Prevalence of Celiac Disease in the United States." *American Journal of Gastroenterology* 107, no. 10 (October 2012): 1538–1544, quiz 1537, 1545. https://www.ncbi.nlm.nih.gov /pubmed/22850429.

14. Terazono, Emiko. "Healthy Appetites Drive Jump in Sales of Gluten-Free Foods." *Financial Times*, April 30, 2017. https://www.ft.com/content/4ec0f2f2 -2c0a-11e7-9ec8-168383da43b7.

15. Terazono, Emiko. "Gluten Free: One of 3 Trends Shaking up Commodities." *Financial Times*, April 7, 2017. https://www.ft.com/content/5348432e-1a13-11e7 -bcac-6d03d067f81f.

16. Team, Mintel Press. "Italy's Love of Pasta Goes off the Boil as Sales Fall by 2%." *Mintel*, May 25, 2017. Accessed November 16, 2018. http://www.mintel.com /press-centre/food-and-drink/italys-love-of-pasta-goes-off-the-boil.

17. "Pomeroy, Ross. "Non-Celiac Gluten Sensitivity May Not Exist." *Real Clear Science*, May 13, 2014. Accessed November 29, 2018. https://www.realclearscience .com/blog/2014/05/gluten_sensitivity_may_not_exist.html.

18. Biesiekierski, Jessica R., Simone L. Peters, Evan D. Newnham, Ourania Rosella, Jane G. Muir, and Peter R. Gibson. "No Effects of Gluten in Patients with Self-Reported Non-Celiac Gluten Sensitivity After Dietary Reduction of Fermentable, Poorly Absorbed, Short-Chain Carbohydrates." *Gastroenterology* 145, no. 2 (August 2013): 320–328.e3. https://doi.org/10.1053/j.gastro.2013.04.051.

19. Blackett, John W., Meghana Shamsunder, Norelle R. Reilly, Peter H. R. Green, and Benjamin Lebwohl. "Characteristics and Comorbidities of Inpatients Without Celiac Disease on a Gluten-Free Diet." *European Journal of Gastroenterology & Hepatology* 30, no. 4 (April 2018): 477–83. https://doi.org/10.1097/ MEG.0000000000001071.

Laszkowska, Monika, Henna Shiwani, Julia Belluz, Jonas F. Ludvigsson, Peter H. R. Green, Daniel Sheehan, Andrew Rundle, and Benjamin Lebwohl.

"Socioeconomic vs Health-Related Factors Associated with Google Searches for Gluten-Free Diet." *Clinical Gastroenterology and Hepatology* 16, no. 2 (February 2018): 295–97. https://doi.org/10.1016/j.cgh.2017.07.042.

20. Brogan, Kelly, MD. "Where Do Vaccines Fit into a Paleo Lifestyle?" *Kelly Brogan MD*, March 10, 2014. https://kellybroganmd.com/vaccines-fit-paleo-lifestyle/.

    Kresser, Chris. "RHR: CoQ10, Vaccination, and Natural Treatment for Migraines." Revolution Health Radio. Accessed November 29, 2018. https://www.mixcloud.com/revolutionhealthradio/rhr-coq10-vaccination-and-natural-treatment-for-migraines/.

21. "Public Opinion about Genetically Modified Foods and Trust in Scientists." *Pew Research Center*, December 1, 2016. http://www.pewInternet.org/2016/12/01/public-opinion-about-genetically-modified-foods-and-trust-in-scientists-connected-with-these-foods/.

22. Stackpole, Thomas. "You Call It Starvation. I Call It Biohacking." *New York Times*, July 11, 2019, sec. Opinion. https://www.nytimes.com/2019/07/11/opinion/sunday/men-extreme-diets.html.

23. Whitson, Jennifer, and Adam D. Galinsky. "Lacking Control Increases Illusory Patter Perception." *Science* 322, no. 5898 (October 3, 2008): 115–17. https://doi.org/10.1126/science.1159845.

24. Whitson, Jennifer A., Adam D. Galinsky, and Aaron Kay. "The Emotional Roots of Conspiratorial Perceptions, System Justification, and Belief in the Paranormal." *Journal of Experimental Social Psychology* 56 (January 2015): 89–95. https://doi.org/10.1016/j.jesp.2014.09.002.

25. Kay, Aaron C., Danielle Gaucher, Jaime Napier, Mitchell Callan, and Kristin Laurin. "God and the Government: Testing a Compensatory Control Mechanism for the Support of External Systems." *Journal of Personality and Social Psychology* 95 (August 1, 2008): 18–35. https://doi.org/10.1037/0022-3514.95.1.18.

26. Sales, S. M. "Economic Threat as a Determinant of Conversion Rates in Authoritarian and Nonauthoritarian Churches." *Journal of Personality and Social Psychology* 23, no. 3 (1972): 420–28. http://dx.doi.org/10.1037/h0033157.

27. Sales, S. M. "Threat as a Factor in Authoritarianism: An Analysis of Archival Data." *Journal of Personality and Social Psychology* 28, no. 1 (1973): 44–57. https://doi.org/10.1037/h0035588.

28. Atran, Scott, and Joseph Henrich. "The Evolution of Religion: How Cognitive By-Products, Adaptive Learning Heuristics, Ritual Displays, and Group Competition Generate Deep Commitments to Prosocial Religions." *Biological Theory* 5, no. 1 (March 2010): 18–30. https://doi.org/10.1162/BIOT_a_00018.

    Azar, Beth. "A Reason to Believe." *American Psychological Association* 41, no. 11 (December 2010): 52. https://www.apa.org/monitor/2010/12/believe.

29. Drake, Bruce. "6 New Findings about Millennials." *Pew Research Center*, March 7, 2014. http://www.pewresearch.org/fact-tank/2014/03/07/6-new-findings-about-millennials/.

30. Kramer, Stephanie, and Dalia Fahmy. "Younger People Are Less Religious Than Older Ones in Many Countries." Pew Research Center, June 13, 2018. Accessed

November 20, 2018. http://www.pewresearch.org/fact-tank/2018/06/13/younger
-people-are-less-religious-than-older-ones-in-many-countries-especially-in-the
-u-s-and-europe/.

31. Hays, Brooke. "Majority of Young Adults Think Astrology Is a Science."
UPI, February 11, 2014. Accessed November 20, 2018. https://www.upi.com
/Science_News/2014/02/11/Majority-of-young-adults-think-astrology-is-a
-science/5201392135954/.

    "Psychic Services in the US—Marketing Research Report." *IBISWORLD*,
September 2018. Accessed November 20, 2018. https://www.ibisworld.com
/industry-trends/specialized-market-research-reports/consumer-goods-services
/personal/psychic-services.html.

32. Paul, Kari. "Why Millennials Are Ditching Religion for Witchcraft and Astrology." *MarketWatch*, October 31, 2018. Accessed November 20, 2018. https://www
.marketwatch.com/story/why-millennials-are-ditching-religion-for-witchcraft
-and-astrology-2017-10-20.

33. "Astrology by Bite Amuse Bouche Lipstick Virgo." Accessed November 20,
2018. https://www.bitebeauty.com/astrology-by-bite-amuse-bouche-lipstick
-virgo/2082204.html.

34. Lipsky, Laura van Dernoot (2018). *The Age of Overwhelm: Strategies for the Long
Haul*. (San Francisco: Berrett-Koehler Publishers, 2018).

35. Denizet-Lewis, Benoit. "Why Are More American Teenagers Than Ever Suffering
from Severe Anxiety?" *New York Times*, October 11, 2017, sec. Magazine. https://
www.nytimes.com/2017/10/11/magazine/why-are-more-american-teenagers
-than-ever-suffering-from-severe-anxiety.html.

    Lee, Yu-Kang, Chun-Tuan Chang, You Lin, and Zhao-Hong Cheng. "The
Dark Side of Smartphone Usage: Psychological Traits, Compulsive Behavior
and Technostress." *Computers in Human Behavior* 31 (February 1, 2014): 373–83.
https://doi.org/10.1016/j.chb.2013.10.047.

36. Jeffries, Stuart. "Interview: Stuart Jeffries Meets Sociologist Ulrich Beck." *The
Guardian*, February 11, 2006. http://www.theguardian.com/books/2006/feb/11
/society.politics.

37. Cerroni, Andrea, Marco D'Addario, Andrea Pozzali, and Paola Truglia. "Biotec-
nologie e opinione pubblica. Una ricerca sulla percezione della scienza in Italia."
Sociologia e ricerca sociale 67 (2002): 117-140.

    Cerroni, Andrea. *Homo Transgenicus: Sociologia e Comunicazione Delle Biotec-
nologie*. Confini Sociologici 5. Milano: F. Angeli, 2003.

38. "Forecasted market size of the natural and organic beauty industry in 2016 and
2024 (in billion U.S. dollars)." *Statista*. Accessed November 30, 2018. https://
www.statista.com/statistics/750779/natural-organic-beauty-market-worldwide/.

39. "Clean at Sephora." *Sephora*. http://www.sephora.com/natural.

40. "Nielsen Global Health and Wellness Report." Accessed September 6, 2018.
https://www.nielsen.com/wp-content/uploads/sites/3/2019/04/Nielsen20Global
20Health20and20Wellness20Report20-20January202015-1.pdf.

41. Ibid.

42. "The Meaning of 'Natural': Process More Important Than Content." *Association for Psychological Science*, August 1, 2005. Accessed September 15, 2018. http://journals.sagepub.com/doi/pdf/10.1111/j.1467-9280.2005.01589.x.

43. Abouab, Nathalie, and Pierrick Gomez. "Human Contact Imagined During the Production Process Increases Food Naturalness Perceptions." *Appetite* 91 (August 2015): 273–77. https://doi.org/10.1016/j.appet.2015.04.002.

44. Gray, Kurt. "The Power of Good Intentions: Perceived Benevolence Soothes Pain, Increases Pleasure, and Improves Taste." *Social Psychological and Personality Science* 3, no. 5 (September 2012): 639–45. https://doi.org/10.1177/1948550611433470.

45. Smith, Tyler, Kimberly Kawa, Veronica Eckl, Claire Morton, and Ryan Stredney. "Herbal Supplement Sales in US Increased 8.5% in 2017, Topping $8 Billion." *The Journal of the American Botanical Council*, no. 119 (2018): 62–71. http://cms.herbalgram.org/herbalgram/issue119/hg119-herbmktrpt.html?ts=1575875473&signature=8e60ad58be68f94b58651dc6eaf76600.

46. Sumner, William. "Natural and Specialty Retail Hemp-Derived CBD Sales Projected to Grow by More Than 600% by 2022." *Hemp Business Journal*, August 24, 2018. https://www.hempbizjournal.com/natural-specialty-retail-hemp-cbd-sales/.

47. Devinsky, Orrin, Eric Marsh, Daniel Friedman, Elizabeth Thiele, Linda Laux, Joseph Sullivan, Ian Miller, et al. "Cannabidiol in Patients with Treatment-Resistant Epilepsy: An Open-Label Interventional Trial." *The Lancet Neurology* 15, no. 3 (March 2016): 270–78. https://www.ncbi.nlm.nih.gov/pubmed/26724101.

    McGuire, Philip, Philip Robson, Wieslaw Jerzy Cubala, Daniel Vasile, Paul Dugald Morrison, Rachel Barron, Adam Taylor, and Stephen Wright. "Cannabidiol (CBD) as an Adjunctive Therapy in Schizophrenia: A Multicenter Randomized Controlled Trial." *American Journal of Psychiatry* 175, no. 3 (March 2018): 225–31. https://doi.org/10.1176/appi.ajp.2017.17030325.

    O'Brien, Melissa, and Jason J. McDougall. "Cannabis and Joints: Scientific Evidence for the Alleviation of Osteoarthritis Pain by Cannabinoids." *Current Opinions in Pharmacology* 40 (June 1, 2018): 104–9. https://doi.org/10.1016/j.coph.2018.03.012.

48. "Brain Dust." *Moon Juice*. Accessed November 30, 2018. https://moonjuice.com/products/brain-dust.

Part II: Belonging

CHAPTER 4: INFLUENCERS & LONELINESS

1. "10dae ch'ŏngsonyun midiŏ yiyongchosa" [Survey of media usage of teenagers]. Korea Press Foundation, 2016. Retrieved from https://www.kpf.or.kr/site/kpf/research/selectMedia PdsView.do?seq=573958.

2. "Rethinking Mukbang: Does Watching People Eat Help or Hurt Us?" *Korea JoongAng Daily*, November 12, 2018. Accessed January 10, 2019. http://mengnews.joins.com/view.aspx?aId=3055454.

3. Moon, Young Eun, Ji Soo Shim, and Dong Sook Park. "'My Favorite Broadcasting Jockey Is. . .' Interpretive Analysis on the 'Mukbang' Viewing Experience." *Media & Society* 25, no. 2 (May 2017): 58–101. http://www.riss.kr/search/detail /DetailView.do?p_mat_type=1a0202e37d52c72d&control_no=4ea33df677dd57 d3c85d2949c297615a.

4. Maslow, Abraham H. *Motivation and Personality.*

5. 최수향. "Number of One-Person Households in S. Korea Hits 7.39 Mln Mark." *Yonhap News Agency,* October 6, 2016. https://en.yna.co.kr/view /AEN20161006009400315.

6. "South Korea's Fertility Rate Is the Lowest in the World." *The Economist,* June 30, 2018. https://www.economist.com/asia/2018/06/30/south-koreas-fertility-rate-is -the-lowest-in-the-world.

7. Borowiec, Steven. "Honbap: Eating Alone Is a New Norm." *KOREA EXPOSÉ* (blog), May 29, 2017. https://www.koreaexpose.com/honbap-eating -alone-new-norm-korea/.

8. Buck, Stephanie. "Japan Has Perfected the Art of Eating Alone, and You Can Too." *Timeline,* November 4, 2016. https://timeline.com/japan-eating-alone -56c5fafe89ee.

9. "'배달음식' 의존도 높은 소비자들, '배달료' 부과 움직임에 촉각 곤두세워 [Consumers highly dependent on 'delivery food' are keen on the move to charge delivery]." Food & Drink. Trend Monitor. Embrain, 2018. http://www.trendmonitor .co.kr/tmweb/trend/allTrend/detail.do?bIdx=1672&code=0301&trendType =CKOREA.

10. Jang, Y. "Koreans Choose Which TV Shows They Are Enjoying The Most In June." Soompi, June 25. 2018. Accessed January 10, 2019. https://www.soompi .com/article/1190413wpp/koreans-choose-tv-shows-enjoying-june.
    Sohn, Ji Ae. "Being Alone Is Full of Fun." *Korea.net,* January 10, 2017. http:// www.korea.net/NewsFocus/Travel/view?articleId=143184.

11. "Figure HH-4, The Rise of Living Alone." *United States Census Bureau,* n.d. https://www.census.gov/content/dam/Census/library/visualizations/time-series /demo/families-and-households/hh-4.pdf.

12. "Going It Alone: Solo Dwellers Will Account for 40% of Japan's Households by 2040, Forecast Says." *The Japan Times Online,* January 13, 2018. https:// www.japantimes.co.jp/news/2018/01/13/national/social-issues/going-alone-solo -dwellers-will-account-40-japans-households-2040-forecast-says/.

13. "Lonely Beijing Nights Inspire $273 Million Home-Cooking Startup." *Bloomberg News,* December 15, 2016. https://www.bloombergquint.com/technology /lonely-beijing-nights-inspire-273-million-home-cooking-startup.

14. Putnam, Robert D. *Bowling Alone: The Collapse and Revival of American Community.* (Simon and Schuster, 2001).

15. McPherson, Miller, Lynn Smith-Lovin, and Matthew E. Brashears. "Social Isolation in America: Changes in Core Discussion Networks over Two Decades." *American Sociological Review* 71, no. 3 (2006): 353–75. www.jstor.org /stable/30038995.

16. Kingman, David. "2018 IF Index: How Does the Well-Being of Today's Twentysomethings Compare to Previous Cohorts?" *The Intergenerational Foundation*, August 2018. https://www.iser.essex.ac.uk/research/publications/525540.

17. Wallsten, Scott. "What Are We Not Doing When We're Online." National Bureau of Economic Research, Working Paper Series 19549, October 2013. https://www.nber.org/papers/w19549.pdf.

18. "Table A-1. Time Spent in Detailed Primary Activities 1 and Percent of the Civilian Population Engaging in Each Detailed Primary Activity Category, Averages per Day by Sex, 2011 Annual Averages." Bureau of Labor Statistics, 2011. https://www.bls.gov/tus/tables/a1_2011.pdf.

   "Table A-1. Time Spent in Detailed Primary Activities and Percent of the Civilian Population Engaging in Each Activity, Averages per Day by Sex, 2016 Annual Averages." Bureau of Labor Statistics, 2016. https://www.bls.gov/tus/a1_2016.pdf.

   "Table A-1. Time Spent in Detailed Primary Activities and Percent of the Civilian Population Engaging in Each Activity, Averages per Day by Sex, 2018 Annual Averages." Bureau of Labor Statistics, 2018. https://www.bls.gov/tus/a1-2018.pdf.

19. Kliff, Sarah, Soo Oh, and Sarah Frostenson. "Today's Teens Are Better than You, and We Can Prove It." *Vox*, June 9, 2016. Accessed December 12, 2018. https://www.vox.com/a/teens.

20. "New Report Finds Teens Feel Addicted to Their Phones, Causing Tension at Home." *Common Sense Media*, May 3, 2016. Accessed December 25, 2018. https://www.commonsensemedia.org/about-us/news/press-releases/new-report-finds-teens-feel-addicted-to-their-phones-causing-tension-at.

21. Johnson, Chandra. "Growing up Digital: How the Internet Affects Teen Identity." *DeseretNews*, May 28, 2014. https://www.deseretnews.com/article/865603981/Growing-up-digital-How-the-Internet-affects-teen-identity.html.

22. Shrum, Wesley, Antony Palackal, Dan-Bright S. Dzorgbo, Paul Mbatia, Mark Schafer, Paige Miller, and Heather Rackin. "Network Decline in the Internet Era: Evidence from Ghana, Kenya, and India, 1994–2010." *International Review of Social Research* 6, no. 4 (October 1, 2016): 163–71. https://doi.org/10.1515/irsr-2016-0019.

23. Kingman, David. "2018 IF Index: How Does the Well-Being of Today's Twentysomethings Compare to Previous Cohorts?"

24. Ballard, Jamie. "Millennials Are the Loneliest Generation." *YouGov*, July 30, 2019. https://today.yougov.com/topics/lifestyle/articles-reports/2019/07/30/loneliness-friendship-new-friends-poll-survey.

25. Murthy, Vivek. "Work and the Loneliness Epidemic." *Harvard Business Review*, September 26, 2017. https://hbr.org/2017/09/work-and-the-loneliness-epidemic.

26. "Cigna U.S. Loneliness Index." *Cigna*, 2018. https://www.multivu.com/players/English/8294451-cigna-us-loneliness-survey/docs/IndexReport_1524069371598-173525450.pdf.

27. Wahlquist, Calla. "Eighty-Two Per Cent of Australians Say Loneliness Is Increasing, Lifeline Survey Finds." *The Guardian*, September 26, 2016, sec.

Society. https://www.theguardian.com/society/2016/sep/27/eighty-two-per-cent-of-australians-say-loneliness-is-increasing-lifeline-survey-finds.

28. Noack, Rick. "Isolation Is Rising in Europe. Can Loneliness Ministers Help Change That?" *Washington Post*, February 2, 2018. https://www.washington post.com/news/worldviews/wp/2018/02/02/isolation-is-rising-in-europe-can -loneliness-ministers-help-change-that/.

29. Ballard, Jamie. "Millennials Are the Loneliest Generation."

30. Seppälä, Emma. "Connect to Thrive: Social Connection Improves Health, Well-Being, and Longevity." *Emma Seppälä, Ph.D* (blog), August 26, 2012. https:// emmaseppala.com/connect-to-thrive-social-connection-improves-health-well -being-longevity/.

31. Schawbel, Dan. "Vivek Murthy: How to Solve the Work Loneliness Epidemic." *Forbes*, October 7, 2017. https://www.forbes.com/sites/danschawbel /2017/10/07/vivek-murthy-how-to-solve-the-work-loneliness-epidemic-at-work /#6c2646917172.

32. Pantell, Matthew, David Rehkopf, Douglas Jutte, S. Leonard Syme, John Balmes, and Nancy Adler. "Social Isolation: A Predictor of Mortality Comparable to Traditional Clinical Risk Factors." *American Journal of Public Health* 103, no. 11 (October 9, 2013): 2056–62. https://doi.org/10.2105/AJPH.2013.301261.

33. Jang, Yoon Jae et al. "Need for Interaction or Pursuit of Information and Entertainment?: The Relationship among Viewing Motivation, Presence, Parasocial Interaction, and Satisfaction of Eating and Cooking Broadcasts." *Korean Journal of Broadcasting and Telecommunication Studies* 30, no 4 (2016): 152–185. http:// www.dbpia.co.kr/Article/NODE06735346.

34. Borowiec, Steven. "Honbap: Eating Alone Is a New Norm." *KOREA EXPOSÉ*, May 29, 2017. https://www.koreaexpose.com/honbap-eating-alone-new-norm-korea/.

35. Borowiec, Steven. "Eating for an Online Audience in South Korea." *Al Jazeera*, 2015. https://interactive.aljazeera.com/aje/2015/what-food-means-to-me-around -the-world-ajeats/index.html.

36. 창현거리노래방KPOP COVER. BJ창현[동대문 엽기떡볶이+주먹밥 먹방] 160319 *Changhyun Mukbang Eating Show*. Accessed January 17, 2019. https:// www.youtube.com/channel/UCPJmHR4CG_lRuVwKCo0kjjg.

37. Evans, Stephen. "The Koreans Who Televise Themselves Eating Dinner." *BBC News*, February 5, 2015. https://www.bbc.com/news/magazine-31130947.

38. Oh, Soo Kwang, and Hyun Ju Choi. "Broadcasting upon a Shooting Star: Investigating the Success of Afreeca TV's Livestream Personal Broadcast Model." *International Journal of Web Based Communities* 13, no. 2 (2017): 193. https://doi .org/10.1504/IJWBC.2017.084414.

39. Moon, Young Eun, Ji Soo Shim, and Dong Sook Park. "'My Favorite Broadcasting Jockey Is . . .'—Interpretive Analysis on the 'Mukbang' Viewing Experience."

40. Hertz, Noreena. "Think the Millennials Have It Tough? For Generation K Life's Even Harsher." *The Guardian*, March 19, 2016. https://www.theguardian .com/world/2016/mar/19/think-millennials-have-it-tough-for-generation-k-life -is-even-harsher.

41. Dunbar, R. I. M. "Breaking Bread: The Functions of Social Eating." *Adaptive Human Behavior and Physiology* 3, no. 3 (September 2017): 198–211. https://doi .org/10.1007/s40750-017-0061-4.

CHAPTER 5: "LIKES" & SELF-ESTEEM

1. Bradbury, Rurik. "The Digital Lives of Millennials and Gen Z." *LivePerson*, n.d. https://liveperson.docsend.com/view/tm8j45m.

2. "Landmark Report: U.S. Teens Use an Average of Nine Hours of Media Per Day, Tweens Use Six Hours." *Common Sense Media,* November 3, 2015. https://www .commonsensemedia.org/about-us/news/press-releases/landmark-report-us-teens -use-an-average-of-nine-hours-of-media-per-day.

3. Jiang, Jingjing, and Monica Anderson. "Teens, Social Media & Technology 2018." *Pew Research Center* (blog), May 31, 2018. https://www.pewinternet .org/2018/05/31/teens-social-media-technology-2018/.

4. "How Much Time Do We Spend on Social Media? [Infographic]." *Mediakix*. Accessed April 21, 2019. http://mediakix.com/how-much-time-is-spent-on -social-media-lifetime/.

5. Cole, Jeffrey, Michael Suman, Phoebe Schramm, and Liuning Zhou. "Surveying the Digital Future." *2017 Digital Future Project*, 2017. https://www.digitalcenter .org/wp-content/uploads/2013/10/2017-Digital-Future-Report.pdf.

6. Dorsey, Jason. "iGen Tech Disruption." *The Center for Generational Kinetics*, 2016. http://genhq.wpengine.com/wp-content/uploads/2016/01/iGen-Gen-Z-Tech -Disruption-Research-White-Paper-c-2016-Center-for-Generational-Kinetics .pdf.

7. Ellison, Nicole B., Charles Steinfield, and Cliff Lampe. "The Benefits of Face-book 'Friends:' Social Capital and College Students' Use of Online Social Net-work Sites." *Journal of Computer-Mediated Communication* 12, no. 4 (July 2007): 1143–68. https://doi.org/10.1111/j.1083-6101.2007.00367.x.

   Valkenburg, Patti M., Jochen Peter, and Alexander P. Schouten. "Friend Net-working Sites and Their Relationship to Adolescents' Well-Being and Social Self-Esteem." *CyberPsychology & Behavior* 9, no. 5 (October 11, 2006): 584–90. https:// doi.org/10.1089/cpb.2006.9.584.

8. "#FoodPorn: The Growing Influence of Social Food." *Ypulse*, May 18, 2015. Accessed December 10, 2018. https://www.ypulse.com/post/view/foodporn-the -growing-influence-of-social-food.

   "Chinas Digital Powered Foodie Revolution." *Labbrand*. Accessed Decem-ber 10, 2018. http://www.labbrand.com/brandsource/china%E2%80%99s-digital -powered-foodie-revolution.

9. "Two Fifths of Millennials Choose Their Holiday Destination Based on How 'Instagrammable' the Holiday Pics Will Be." *Schofields Insurance*, April 3, 2017. https://www.schofields.ltd.uk/blog/5123/two-fifths-of-millennials-choose-their -holiday-destination-based-on-how-instagrammable-the-holiday-pics-will-be/.

10. Kozlowska, Hanna. "Swiss Hotels Are Hiring Instagram 'Sitters' to Post Photos for You." *Quartz*, November 27, 2018. Accessed December 20, 2018. https://qz.com/1475378/swiss-hotels-are-hiring-instagram-sitters-to-post-photos-for-you/.

11. Hampton, Keith et al. "Social Media and the 'Spiral of Silence.'" *Pew Research Center*, August 26, 2014. http://www.pewInternet.org/2014/08/26/social-media-and-the-spiral-of-silence/.

12. "Modern Life Is Rubbish." *Sainsbury's*, 2016. https://www.about.sainsburys.co.uk/~/media/Files/S/Sainsburys/documents/modern-life-is-rubbish-food-waste-report.pdf.

13. Mull, Amanda. "Opinion: Instagram Food Is a Sad, Sparkly Lie." *Eater*, July 6, 2017. https://www.eater.com/2017/7/6/15925940/merican-influencers-cronuts-milkshakes-burgers.

14. Kross, Ethan, Philippe Verduyn, Emre Demiralp, Jiyoung Park, David Seungjae Lee, Natalie Lin, Holly Shablack, John Jonides, and Oscar Ybarra. "Facebook Use Predicts Declines in Subjective Well-Being in Young Adults." *PloS ONE* 8, no. 8 (August 14, 2013): https://doi.org/10.1371/journal.pone.0069841/.

   Primack, Brian A., Ariel Shensa, Jaime E. Sidani, Erin O. Whaite, Liu yi Lin, Daniel Rosen, Jason B. Colditz, Ana Radovic, and Elizabeth Miller. "Social Media Use and Perceived Social Isolation Among Young Adults in the U.S." *American Journal of Preventive Medicine* 53, no. 1 (July 2017): 1–8. https://doi.org/10.1016/j.amepre.2017.01.010.

15. Chou, Hui-Tzu Grace, and Nicholas Edge. "'They Are Happier and Having Better Lives than I Am': The Impact of Using Facebook on Perceptions of Others' Lives." *Cyberpsychology, Behavior, and Social Networking* 15, no. 2 (February 2012): 117–21. https://doi.org/10.1089/cyber.2011.0324.

   Faris, Marion K. Underwood and Robert W. "Being 13: Perils of Lurking on Social Media." *CNN*, October 6, 2015. Accessed December 21, 2018. https://www.cnn.com/2015/10/05/opinions/underwood-faris-being-thirteen-lurking-social-media/index.html.

   Krasnova, Hanna, Helena Wenninger, Thomas Widjaja, and Peter Buxmann. "Envy on Facebook: A Hidden Threat to Users' Life Satisfaction?" 11th International Conference on Wirtschaftsinformatik, Leipzig, Germany. March 27, 2013. https://www.ara.cat/2013/01/28/855594433.pdf?hash=b775840d43f9f93b7a9031449f809c388f342291.

   Mehdizadeh, Soraya. "Self-Presentation 2.0: Narcissism and Self-Esteem on Facebook." *Cyberpsychology, Behavior and Social Networking* 13 (August 1, 2010): 357–64. https://doi.org/10.1089/cyber.2009.0257.

   Muise, Amy, Emily Christofides, and Serge Desmarais. "More Information than You Ever Wanted: Does Facebook Bring Out the Green-Eyed Monster of Jealousy?" *CyberPsychology & Behavior* 12, no. 4 (August 2009): 441–44. https://doi.org/10.1089/cpb.2008.0263.

   Smith, Richard H., and Sung Hee Kim. "Comprehending Envy." *Psychological Bulletin* 133, no. 1 (2007): 46–64. https://doi.org/10.1037/0033-2909.133.1.46.

Tandoc, Edson C., Patrick Ferrucci, and Margaret Duffy. "Facebook Use, Envy, and Depression among College Students: Is Facebooking Depressing?" *Computers in Human Behavior* 43 (February 1, 2015): 139–46. https://doi .org/10.1016/j.chb.2014.10.053.

Utz, Sonja, Nicole Muscanell, and Cameran Khalid. "Snapchat Elicits More Jealousy than Facebook: A Comparison of Snapchat and Facebook Use." *Cyberpsychology, Behavior, and Social Networking* 18, no. 3 (March 2015): 141–46. https://doi.org/10.1089/cyber.2014.0479.

Winter, Jennifer. "Selfie-Loathing." *Slate*, July 23, 2013. http://www.slate .com/articles/technology/technology/2013/07/instagram_and_self_esteem_why _the_photo_sharing_network_is_even_more_depressing.html.

16. Smink, Frédérique R. E., Daphne van Hoeken, and Hans W. Hoek. "Epidemiology of Eating Disorders: Incidence, Prevalence and Mortality Rates." *Current Psychiatry Reports* 14, no. 4 (August 2012): 406–14. https://doi.org/10.1007 /s11920-012-0282-y.

17. "American Society of Plastic Surgeons Weighs in On Growing Popularity of Teen Plastic Surgery." American Society of Plastic Surgeons, August 22, 2018. Accessed December 22, 2018. https://www.plasticsurgery.org/news/press-releases/merican-society-of-plastic-surgeons-weighs-in-on-growing-popularity-of-teen-plastic-surgery.

"Going under the Knife in China's Plastic Surgery Stampede." *The Straits Times*, September 25, 2017. https://www.straitstimes.com/asia/east-asia/going -under-the-knife-in-chinas-plastic-surgery-stampede.

Hazlehurst, Beatrice. "If This Is the Age of Body Positivity, Why Are So Many Kiwis Getting Plastic Surgery?" *Vice*, November 10, 2016. https://www .vice.com/en_au/article/gqkd3q/if-this-is-the-age-of-body-positivity-why-are-so -many-young-kiwis-getting-plastic-surgery.

Kekatos, Mary. "Surgeons Warn of the Rise of Teens Who Want 'Back-to-School Surgery.'" *Daily Mail*, June 27, 2018. http://www.dailymail.co.uk/health /article-5888949/Plastic-surgeons-warn-rise-teenagers-want-school-surgery .html.

McDow, Kendra, Duong Nguyen, Kirsten Herrick, and Lara Akinbami. "Attempts to Lose Weight Among Adolescents Aged 16–19 in the United States, 2013–2016." *Centers for Disease Control and Prevention*, July 2019. https://www .cdc.gov/nchs/data/databriefs/db340-h.pdf.

Stone, Zara. "South Korean High Schoolers Get Plastic Surgery for Graduation." *The Atlantic*, June 27, 2013. Accessed December 22, 2018. https:// www.theatlantic.com/international/archive/2013/06/south-korean-high -schoolers-get-plastic-surgery-for-graduation/277255/.

18. Limburg, Karina, Hunna J. Watson, Martin S. Hagger, and Sarah J. Egan. "The Relationship Between Perfectionism and Psychopathology: A Meta-Analysis." *Journal of Clinical Psychology* 73, no. 10 (October 2017): 1301–26. https://doi .org/10.1002/jclp.22435.

19. Morgan, Catharine, Roger T. Webb, Matthew J. Carr, Evangelos Kontopantelis, Jonathan Green, Carolyn A. Chew-Graham, Nav Kapur, and Darren M.

Ashcroft. "Incidence, Clinical Management, and Mortality Risk Following Self Harm among Children and Adolescents: Cohort Study in Primary Care." *BMJ* 359 (October 18, 2017). https://doi.org/10.1136/bmj.j4351.

20. Twenge, Jean M., Thomas E. Joiner, Megan L. Rogers, and Gabrielle N. Martin. "Increases in Depressive Symptoms, Suicide-Related Outcomes, and Suicide Rates Among U.S. Adolescents After 2010 and Links to Increased New Media Screen Time." *Clinical Psychological Science* 6, no. 1 (January 2018): 3–17. https://doi.org/10.1177/2167702617723376.

21. Curtin, Sally, Melonie Heron, Arialdi Miniño, and Margaret Warner. "Recent Increases in Injury Mortality Among Children and Adolescents Aged 10–19 Years in the United States: 1999–2016." *Centers for Disease Control and Prevention* 67, no. 4 (June 1, 2018): 1–16. https://www.cdc.gov/nchs/data/nvsr/nvsr67/nvsr67_04.pdf.

22. Lin, Liu yi, Jaime E. Sidani, Ariel Shensa, Ana Radovic, Elizabeth Miller, Jason B. Colditz, Beth L. Hoffman, Leila M. Giles, and Brian A. Primack. "Association between Social Media Use and Depression among U.S. Young Adults." *Depression and Anxiety* 33, no. 4 (January 19, 2016): 323–31. https://doi.org/10.1002/da.22466.

23. Primack, Brian A., Ariel Shensa, César G. Escobar-Viera, Erica L. Barrett, Jaime E. Sidani, Jason B. Colditz, and A. Everette James. "Use of Multiple Social Media Platforms and Symptoms of Depression and Anxiety: A Nationally-Representative Study among U.S. Young Adults." *Computers in Human Behavior* 69 (April 2017): 1–9. https://doi.org/10.1016/j.chb.2016.11.013.

   Shensa, Ariel, César G. Escobar-Viera, Jaime E. Sidani, Nicholas D. Bowman, Michael P. Marshal, and Brian A. Primack. "Problematic Social Media Use and Depressive Symptoms among U.S. Young Adults: A Nationally-Representative Study." *Social Science & Medicine* 182 (June 2017): 150–57. https://doi.org/10.1016/j.socscimed.2017.03.061.

24. Bayindir, Nisa, and Duncan Kavanagh. "Social: GlobalWebIndex's Flagship Report on the Latest Trends in Social Media." *GlobalWebIndex*, 2018. https://www.globalwebindex.com/hubfs/Downloads/Social-H2-2018-report.pdf.

25. Girl Scout Research Institute. *Who's That Girl? Image and Social Media* (New York: Girl Scouts of the USA, 2010).

26. Nicholson, Nicholas R. "A Review of Social Isolation: An Important but Under-assessed Condition in Older Adults." *The Journal of Primary Prevention* 33, no. 2–3 (June 2012): 137–52. https://doi.org/10.1007/s10935-012-0271-2.

27. Dunbar, R. I. M. "Do Online Social Media Cut through the Constraints that Limit the Size of Offline Social Networks?" *Royal Society Open Science* 3, no. 1 (January 1, 2016). https://doi.org/10.1098/rsos.150292.

28. Frison, Eline, and Steven Eggermont. "The Impact of Daily Stress on Adolescents' Depressed Mood: The Role of Social Support Seeking through Facebook." *Computers in Human Behavior* 44 (March 2015): 315–25. https://doi.org/10.1016/j.chb.2014.11.070.

   Leung, Louis, and Paul S.N. Lee. "Multiple Determinants of Life Quality: The Roles of Internet Activities, Use of New Media, Social Support, and Leisure

Activities." *Telematics and Informatics* 22, no. 3 (August 2005): 161–80. https://doi
.org/10.1016/j.tele.2004.04.003.

Manago, Adriana M., Tamara Taylor, and Patricia M. Greenfield. "Me and
My 400 Friends: The Anatomy of College Students' Facebook Networks, Their
Communication Patterns, and Well-Being." *Developmental Psychology* 48, no. 2
(2012): 369–80. https://doi.org/10.1037/a0026338.

Nabi, Robin L., Abby Prestin, and Jiyeon So. "Facebook Friends with (Health)
Benefits? Exploring Social Network Site Use and Perceptions of Social Support,
Stress, and Well-Being." *Cyberpsychology, Behavior, and Social Networking* 16, no.
10 (October 22, 2013): 721–27. https://doi.org/10.1089/cyber.2012.0521.

Oh, Hyun Jung, Elif Ozkaya, and Robert LaRose. "How Does Online Social
Networking Enhance Life Satisfaction? The Relationships among Online Supportive Interaction, Affect, Perceived Social Support, Sense of Community,
and Life Satisfaction." *Computers in Human Behavior* 30 (January 2014): 69–78.
https://doi.org/10.1016/j.chb.2013.07.053.

29. Shensa, Ariel, Jaime E. Sidani, Mary Amanda Dew, César G. Escobar-Viera, and
Brian A. Primack. "Social Media Use and Depression and Anxiety Symptoms:
A Cluster Analysis." *American Journal of Health Behavior* 42, no. 2 (March 2018):
116–28. https://doi.org/10.5993/AJHB.42.2.11.

30. Shensa, "Social Media Use and Depression and Anxiety Symptoms."

31. Shensa, Ariel, Jaime E. Sidani, Cesar G. Escobar-Viera, and Brian A. Primack.
"Emotional Support from Social Media and In-Person Relationships: Associations
with Depressive Symptoms Among Young Adults." *Journal of Adolescent Health*
64, no. 2 (February 2019): S32. https://doi.org/10.1016/j.jadohealth.2018.10.073.

Wang, Kexin, Eline Frison, Steven Eggermont, and Laura Vandenbosch.
"Active Public Facebook Use and Adolescents' Feelings of Loneliness: Evidence
for a Curvilinear Relationship." *Journal of Adolescence* 67 (August 2018): 35–44.
https://doi.org/10.1016/j.adolescence.2018.05.008.

32. Bonetti, L., M.A. Campbell, and L. Gilmore. "The Relationship of Loneliness
and Social Anxiety with Children's and Adolescents' Online Communication."
Cyberpsychology, Behavior, and Social Networking 13, no. 3 (June 17, 2010): 279–
285. doi:10.1089/cyber.2009.0215.

CHAPTER 6: DIETS & IDENTITY

1. Hogg, Michael A. "Uncertainty–Identity Theory." *Advances in Experimental Social
Psychology* 39, (2007): 69–126. https://doi.org/10.1016/S0065-2601(06)39002-8.

2. "'Nones' on the Rise." *Pew Research Center*, October 9, 2012. https://www.pew
forum.org/2012/10/09/nones-on-the-rise/.

3. Fingerhut, Hannah. "Millennials' Views of News Media, Religious Organizations Grow More Negative." *Pew Research Center*, January 4, 2016. Accessed January 16, 2019. http://www.pewresearch.org/fact-tank/2016/01/04/millennials
-views-of-news-media-religious-organizations-grow-more-negative/.

4. Villacorta, Natalie. "Poll: Half of Millennials Independent." *Politico*, March
7, 2014. Accessed January 11, 2019. https://www.politico.com/story/2014/03
/millennials-independence-poll-104401.html.

5. "Key Takeaways from the Pew Research Survey on Millennials," *Pew Research Center.*

6. Bisogni, Carole A., Margaret Connors, Carol M. Devine, and Jeffery Sobal. "Who We Are and How We Eat: A Qualitative Study of Identities in Food Choice." *Journal of Nutrition Education and Behavior* 34, no. 3 (May 2002): 128–39. https://doi.org/10.1016/S1499-4046(06)60082-1.

7. Ferrell, Casey. "Por qué los millennials están tan obsesionados con las fotos de comida." *Kantar España,* July 28, 2016. https://es.kantar.com/empresas/consumo/2016/julio-2016-qué-significa-la-comida-para-los-millennial-y-por-qué/.

8. Team, Mintel Press. "US Millennials Twice as Likely as Non-Millennials to Distrust Large Food Manufacturers." *Mintel,* October 29, 2015. Accessed January 31, 2019. http://www.mintel.com/press-centre/food-and-drink/us-millennials-twice-as-likely-as-non-millennials-to-distrust-large-food-manufacturers.

9. Xu, Angela. "China's Digital Powered Foodie Revolution." *Labbrand Brand Innovations,* January 6, 2015. http://www.labbrand.com/brandsource/china%E2%80%99s-digital-powered-foodie-revolution.

10. Snyder Bulik, Beth. "Growing Up Foodie: Marketers Turn Kids into Sophisticated Chefs." *AdAge,* August 31, 2015. https://adage.com/article/cmo-strategy/marketers-turn-kids-sophisticated-chefs/300139/.

11. Purcell, Denise. "Today's Specialty Food Consumer 2016." *Specialty Food Association,* September 22, 2016. https://www.specialtyfood.com/media/filer_public/46/3d/463d6863-d249-45c7-9772-f2494e0da6e7/2016consumerreport_8pgs.pdf.

12. Barton, Christine, Lara Koslow, Jeff Fromm, and Chris Egan. "Millennial Passions: Food, Fashion, and Friends." *Boston Consulting Group,* 2012. https://www.bcg.com/documents/file121010.pdf.

13. "Truth About Global Brands 2: Powered by the Streets." McCann Worldgroup, 2016.
    "Study: Millennials to Continue Shaping the Food Industry." *QSR Magazine,* February 2, 2017. https://www.qsrmagazine.com/news/study-millennials-continue-shaping-food-industry.

14. "Local Foods: A Sales Boom on Par with 'Organic'?" *Packaged Facts,* March 3, 2015. Accessed January 31, 2019. https://www.packagedfacts.com/Content/Blog/2015/03/03/Local-foods--A-sales-boom-on-par-with-%E2%80%9Corganic%E2%80%9D.

15. "Drinking Ghana: Meet the Entrepreneurs Competing for Ghana's Drinkers." *Food Tank,* 2017. https://foodtank.com/news/2017/12/cashew-sorghum-sugarcane-ghana/.

16. Rosenfeld, Daniel L., and Anthony L. Burrow. "The Unified Model of Vegetarian Identity: A Conceptual Framework for Understanding Plant-Based Food Choices." *Appetite* 112 (May 1, 2017): 78–95. https://doi.org/10.1016/j.appet.2017.01.017.

17. Lindeman, Marjaana, and Minna Sirelius. "Food Choice Ideologies: The Modern Manifestations of Normative and Humanist Views of the World." *Appetite* 37, no. 3 (December 2001): 175–84. https://doi.org/10.1006/appe.2001.0437.

18. Greenebaum, Jessica B. "Managing Impressions: 'Face-Saving' Strategies of Vegetarians and Vegans." *Humanity & Society* 36, no. 4 (October 10, 2012): 309–25. https://doi.org/10.1177/0160597612458898.

19. Goossaert, Vincent, and David A. Palmer. *The Religious Question in Modern China* (Chicago, London: University of Chicago Press, 2011).

20. Klein, Jakob A. "Buddhist Vegetarian Restaurants and the Changing Meanings of Meat in Urban China." *Journal of Anthropology* 82, no. 2 (2017): 252–76. https://doi.org/10.1080/00141844.2015.1084016.

21. Rosenfeld, Daniel L. "A Comparison of Dietarian Identity Profiles between Vegetarians and Vegans." *Food Quality and Preference* 72 (March 2019): 40–44. https://doi.org/10.1016/j.foodqual.2018.09.008.

22. "Caveman Eats: Paleo Could Hit $4bn by 2020 but It's Never Going to Be Greek Yogurt—IRI, Mintel." *Food Navigator,* July 7, 2017. Accessed January 25, 2019. https://www.foodnavigator-usa.com/Article/2017/07/10/Paleo-foods-market-could-hit-4bn-by-2020-IRI-Mintel.

    Contreras, Tricia. "Restaurants, Food Companies Cater to the Diets Du Jour." *SmartBrief,* July 17, 2018. https://www.smartbrief.com/original/2018/07/restaurants-food-companies-cater-diets-du-jour.

23. "Kris Carr." YouTube. Accessed January 18, 2019. https://www.youtube.com/channel/UCTMXwu4TgF3j9oHiBn_Iaqw.

24. Whitney, Brian. "Melissa Hartwig: From Addict to Whole30 Self-Help Queen." *The Fix*, April 29, 2016. https://www.thefix.com/melissa-hartwig-heroin-addict-self-help-whole30.

25. "Sometimes, It Is Hard." *Whole 30,* April 2, 2012. https://whole30.com/2012/04/sometimes-it-is-hard/.

CHAPTER 7: SHARED EXPERIENCES & RELATEDNESS

1. Dunbar, R. I. M., R. Baron, A. Frangou, E. Pearce, E. J. C. van Leeuwen, J. Stow, G. Partridge, I. MacDonald, V. Barra, and M. van Vugt. "Social Laughter Is Correlated with an Elevated Pain Threshold." *Proceedings of the Royal Society B: Biological Sciences* 279, no. 1731 (September 14, 2011): 1161–67. https://doi.org/10.1098/rspb.2011.1373.

    Machin, A.J., and R.I.M Dunbar. "The Brain Opioid Theory of Social Attachment: A Review of the Evidence." *Behaviour* 148, no. 9–10 (2011): 985–1025. https://doi.org/10.1163/000579511X596624.

    Pearce, Eiluned, Jacques Launay, Max van Duijn, Anna Rotkirch, Tamas David-Barrett, and Robin I. M. Dunbar. "Singing Together or Apart: The Effect of Competitive and Cooperative Singing on Social Bonding within and between Sub-Groups of a University Fraternity." *Psychology of Music* 44, no. 6 (November 2016): 1255–73. https://doi.org/10.1177/0305735616636208.

    Pearce, Eiluned, Jacques Launay, Anna Machin, and Robin I. M. Dunbar. "Is Group Singing Special? Health, Well-Being and Social Bonds in

Community-Based Adult Education Classes: Group Singing, Well-Being and Social Bonds." *Journal of Community & Applied Social Psychology* 26, no. 6 (November 2016): 518–33. https://doi.org/10.1002/casp.2278.

Tarr, Bronwyn, Jacques Launay, Emma Cohen, and Robin Dunbar. "Synchrony and Exertion during Dance Independently Raise Pain Threshold and Encourage Social Bonding." *Biology Letters* 11, no. 10 (October 2015): 20150767. https://doi.org/10.1098/rsbl.2015.0767.

Tarr, Bronwyn, Jacques Launay, and Robin I.M. Dunbar. "Silent Disco: Dancing in Synchrony Leads to Elevated Pain Thresholds and Social Closeness." *Evolution and Human Behavior* 37, no. 5 (September 2016): 343–49. https://doi.org/10.1016/j.evolhumbehav.2016.02.004.

2. Niedenthal, P. M. "Embodying Emotion." *Science* 316, no. 5827 (May 18, 2007): 1002–5. https://doi.org/10.1126/science.1136930.

3. Girl Scout Research Institute. *Who's That Girl? Image and Social Media* (New York: Girl Scouts of the USA, 2010).

4. Hertz, Noreena. "Think the Millennials Have It Tough? For Generation K, Life Is Even Harsher." *The Guardian*, March 19, 2016. https://www.theguardian.com/world/2016/mar/19/think-millennials-have-it-tough-for-generation-k-life-is-even-harsher.

5. McCann Worldgroup. "Truth About Global Brands 2: Powered by the Streets." 2016.

6. "Millennials: Fueling the Experience Economy." Eventbrite, 2014. https://eventbrite-s3.s3.amazonaws.com/marketing/Millennials_Research/Gen_PR_Final.pdf.

7. "Ya Hay Más de 60 Restaurantes a Puertas Cerradas En Capital." *Ciudades,* June 29, 2014. https://www.clarin.com/ciudades/restaurantes-puertas-cerradas-capital_0_rkPehnocwmx.html.

8. "Airbnb and the Rise of Millennial Travel." Airbnb, November 2016. https://2sqy5r1jf93u30kwzc1smfqt-wpengine.netdna-ssl.com/wp-content/uploads/2016/08/MillennialReport.pdf.

9. Turner, Matt. "The State of the U.S. Consumer." *Business Insider,* November 16, 2016. https://www.businessinsider.com/the-state-of-the-us-consumer-2016-11.

10. "Airbnb and the Rise of Millennial Travel." *Airbnb Citizen.*

11. Mahmoud, Ahmed. "The Impact of AirBnb on Hotel and Hospitality Industry." *Hospitality Net,* March 7, 2016. Accessed February 25, 2019. https://www.hospitalitynet.org/opinion/4074708.html.

12. Lewis-Kraus, Gideon. "The Rise of the WeWorking Class." *The New York Times*, February 21, 2019. https://www.nytimes.com/interactive/2019/02/21/magazine/wework-coworking-office-space.html.

13. Ibid.

14. Belluz, Julia. "The Case against Luxury Gyms like SoulCycle." *Vox*, January 4, 2017. https://www.vox.com/science-and-health/2017/1/4/13982272/exercise-inequality-luxury-gyms-cheap-workout-spaces.

15. Neild, Barry. "What It's like to Eat in a Naked Restaurant." *CNN Travel*, June 15, 2016. https://www.cnn.com/travel/article/what-its-like-in-naked-restaurant-bunyadi-london-food/index.html.

16. "From Board Games to Toothbrushes, Five Holiday Hits You'd Never Expect." *NPD*, Accessed February 20, 2019. https://www.npd.com/wps/portal/npd/us/news/tips-trends-takeaways/from-board-games-to-toothbrushes-five-holiday-hits-youd-never-expect/.

17. "Toy Industry Analysis 2017." *NPD*, Accessed February 20, 2019. https://www.npd.com/wps/portal/npd/us/news/press-releases/2017/us-toy-industry-grows-its-sales-by-3-percent-mid-way-through-2017-reports-the-npd-group/.

18. "Games and Puzzles Surpass Construction as Fastest Growing Toy Category Globally in 2016." *Euromonitor International Market Research Blog*, June 12, 2017. https://blog.euromonitor.com/games-and-puzzles-surpass-construction-as-fastest-growing-toy-category-globally-in-2016/.

19. Sax, David. *The Revenge of Analog: Real Things and Why They Matter* (New York, NY: PublicAffairs 1 ed, 2016).

20. Maslow, A. H. *A Theory of Human Motivation* (Kindle Locations 185–187). Start Publishing LLC, 2013. Kindle Edition.

21. Thurston, Angie, and Casper ter Kuile. "How We Gather." *How We Gather*, 2015. https://static1.squarespace.com/static/5a32a872ace8649fe18ae512/t/5a6f3b9bec212de83ac81b77/1517239214228/How_We_Gather_Digital_4.11.17.pdf.

22. "SoulCycle IPO filing, Form S-1." *Securities and Exchange Commission*, July 30, 2015. https://www.sec.gov/Archives/edgar/data/1644874/000119312515270469/d844646ds1.htm.

23. McGroarty, Beth. "Wellness Now a $4.2 Trillion Global Industry." *Global Wellness Institute*, October 6, 2018. https://globalwellnessinstitute.org/press-room/press-releases/wellness-now-a-4-2-trillion-global-industry/.

24. Yeung, Ophelia, and Katherine Johnston. "Global Wellness Tourism Economy." *Global Wellness Institute*, November 2018. https://globalwellnessinstitute.org/wp-content/uploads/2018/11/GWI_GlobalWellnessTourismEconomyReport.pdf.

25. "Wonderfruit Festival 2017." The Confluence Group. Accessed January 24, 2020. http://www.theconfluencegroup.com/Wonderfruit/.

26. "About A-Fest." Accessed January 24, 2020. https://afest.com/about/.
   "Summit." Accessed January 24, 2020. https://summit.co/.

Part III: Purpose

CHAPTER 8: DIY & EUDAIMONIA

1. Maslow, Abraham H. *Motivation and Personality*.

2. "Google Trends." *Google Trends*. Accessed March 13, 2019. https://trends.google.com/trends/explore?date=all&q=make%20soap,DIY%20crafts,Sourdough%20starter,garden%20ideas,acrylic%20painting.

3. Barton, Christine, Lara Koslow, Jeff Fromm, and Chris Egan, "Millennial Passions: Food, Fashion, and Friends." Boston Consulting Group, 2012.

   Cooke, Alice. "Millennial Baking Boom." *British Baker*, October 24, 2016. https://bakeryinfo.co.uk/news/fullstory.php/aid/16944/Millennial_baking _boom.html.

   "Survey: Millennials Cooking at Home More in 2017." *Specialty Food Association*, January 4, 2017. https://www.specialtyfood.com/news/article /survey-millennials-cooking-home-more-2017/.

4. "Pinterest 100: The Top Trends for 2019." *Pinterest Newsroom*, 2019. https:// newsroom.pinterest.com/en/post/pinterest-100-the-top-trends-for-2019.

5. Aversa, Jeannine. "Arts and Culture Grow for Fourth Straight Year." Bureau of Economic Analysis, March 6, 2018.

   "Data for Occupations Not Covered in Detail: Occupational Outlook Handbook: U.S. Bureau of Labor Statistics." Accessed March 13, 2019. https://www .bls.gov/ooh/about/data-for-occupations-not-covered-in-detail.htm#Life,%20 physical,%20and%20social%20science%20occupations.

6. Ocejo, Richard E. *Masters of Craft: Old Jobs in the New Urban Economy* (Princeton, NJ: Princeton University Press, 2017).

7. Crawford, Matthew B. *Shop Class as Soulcraft: An Inquiry into the Value of Work*. Reprint edition. (New York: Penguin Books, 2010).

8. Brunstein, Joachim C. "Personal Goals and Subjective Well-Being: A Longitudinal Study." *Journal of Personality and Social Psychology* 65, no. 5 (1993): 1061–70. https://doi.org/10.1037/0022-3514.65.5.1061.

   McGregor, Ian, and Brian R. Little. "Personal Projects, Happiness, and Meaning: On Doing Well and Being Yourself." *Journal of Personality and Social Psychology* 74, no. 2 (1998): 494–512. https://doi.org/10.1037/0022-3514.74.2.494.

9. Ryan, Richard M., Kennon M. Sheldon, Tim Kasser, and Edward L. Deci. "All Goals Are Not Created Equal: An Organismic Perspective on the Nature of Goals and Their Regulation." *Psychology of Action: Linking Cognition and Motivation Behavior* (1996): 7–26. https://psycnet.apa.org/record/1996-98326-001.

10. Ryan, Richard M., and Edward L. Deci. "Brick by Brick: The Origins, Development, and Future of Self-Determination Theory."

11. Ryan, Richard M., Valerie Mims, and Richard Koestner. "Relation of Reward Contingency and Interpersonal Context to Intrinsic Motivation: A Review and Test Using Cognitive Evaluation Theory." *Journal of Personality and Social Psychology* 45, no. 4 (1983): 736–50. https://doi.org/10.1037/0022-3514.45.4.736.

12. Aristotle. *Aristotle's Nicomachean Ethics*. Translated by Robert C. Bartlett and Susan D. Collins. Reprint edition (Chicago: University of Chicago Press, 2012).

13. Schmutte, Pamela S., and Carol D. Ryff. "Personality and Well-Being: Reexamining Methods and Meanings." *Journal of Personality and Social Psychology* 73, no. 3 (1997): 549–59. https://doi.org/10.1037/0022-3514.73.3.549.

14. Csikszentmihalyi, Mihaly, and Reed Larson. "Validity and Reliability of the Experience-Sampling Method." *The Journal of Nervous and Mental Disease* 175, no. 9 (September 1987): 526–36. https://doi.org/10.1097/00005053-198709000-00004.

15. Csikszentmihalyi, Mihaly. *Flow: The Psychology of Optimal Experience* (New York: Harper Perennial Modern Classics, 2008).

16. Santos, Laurie. "The Science of Well-Being." Coursera. Accessed January 10, 2020. https://www.coursera.org/learn/the-science-of-well-being/home/welcome.

17. Przybylski, Andrew K., C. Scott Rigby, and Richard M. Ryan. "A Motivational Model of Video Game Engagement." *Review of General Psychology* 14, no. 2 (2010): 154–66. https://doi.org/10.1037/a0019440.

18. Lambert, Kelly. "DO OR DIY." *RSA Journal* 161, no. 5561 (2015): 20-23. http://www.jstor.org/stable/26204384.

19. Atkinson, J., O.J. Braddick, E. Pimm-Smith, and K. Durden. "Refractive Screening of Infants." *American Journal of Ophthalmology* 93, no. 3 (March 1982): 372–73. https://doi.org/10.1016/0002-9394(82)90550-5.

    Bremner, Andrew J., David J. Lewkowicz, and Charles Spence. "The Multisensory Approach to Development." *Oxford University Press* (2012): 1-26. https://doi.org/10.1093/acprof:oso/9780199586059.003.0001.

20. Field, Tiffany. *Touch* (Cambridge: MIT Press, 2001).

    Gallace, Alberto, and Charles Spence. *In Touch with the Future: The Sense of Touch from Cognitive Neuroscience to Virtual Reality* (Oxford: Oxford University Press, 2014).

    Montagu, Ashley. *Touching: Human Significance of the Skin* (New York: Columbia University Press, 1971).

21. Ackerman, J. M., C. C. Nocera, and J. A. Bargh. "Incidental Haptic Sensations Influence Social Judgments and Decisions." *Science* 328, no. 5986 (June 25, 2010): 1712–15. https://doi.org/10.1126/science.1189993.

22. Gonzalez, Sasha. "Get a Grip: Why Keeping Your Hands Busy Can Make You Happier." *South China Morning Post*, July 29, 2018. https://www.scmp.com/lifestyle/health-wellness/article/2157207/what-knitting-painting-and-pottery-do-your-brain-and-why.

23. "Year in Search 2019." Google Trends. Accessed January 7, 2020. https://trends.google.com/trends/yis/2019/US/.

24. Lampitt Adey, Kate. "Understanding Why Women Knit: Finding Creativity and 'Flow.'" *TEXTILE* 16, no. 1 (January 2, 2018): 84–97. https://doi.org/10.1080/14759756.2017.1362748.

    Riley, Jill, Betsan Corkhill, and Clare Morris. "The Benefits of Knitting for Personal and Social Well-Being in Adulthood: Findings from an International Survey." *British Journal of Occupational Therapy* 76, no. 2 (February 2013): 50–57. https://doi.org/10.4276/030802213X13603244419077.

25. Lambert, Kelly. "DO OR DIY."

26. Turner, Zeke. "Book Publishers Go Back to Basics." *Wall Street Journal*, October 14, 2017. https://www.wsj.com/articles/book-publishers-go-back-to-basics-1507983856.

27. "The Common Sense Census: Media Use by Kids Age Zero to Eight." *Common Sense Media*, 2017. https://www.commonsensemedia.org/research/the-common-sense-census-media-use-by-kids-age-zero-to-eight-2017.

28. "How Much Do We Spend in Each Sector of the Food Economy?" *Earnest Blog*, August 29, 2017. https://www.earnest.com/blog/food-economy-spending-data/.

29. Alaimo, Dan. "Survey: 80% of Shoppers Prefer Independent Stores to Online." *Food Dive*, February 20, 2018. https://www.fooddive.com/news /survey-80-of-shoppers-prefer-independent-stores-to-online/517157/?mc_eid =5c5014c674&mc_cid=d03999f236.

30. "2017 U.S. Music Year-End Report." *Nielsen*, January 3, 2018. http://www .nielsen.com/us/en/insights/reports/2018/2017-music-us-year-end-report.

31. Field, Tiffany, *Touch*.

   Gallace, Alberto, and Charles Spence. *In Touch with the Future: The Sense of Touch from Cognitive Neuroscience to Virtual Reality*.

32. "Data-Point_012513.Png (532×671)." *JWT Intelligence*. Accessed March 15, 2019. https://www.jwtintelligence.com/wp-content/uploads/2013/01/Data-point _012513.png.

33. Barratt, Emma L., and Nick J. Davis. "Autonomous Sensory Meridian Response (ASMR): A Flow-like Mental State." *PeerJ* 3 (March 26, 2015): e851. https://doi .org/10.7717/peerj.851.

   Poerio, Giulia Lara, Emma Blakey, Thomas J. Hostler, and Theresa Veltri. "More than a Feeling: Autonomous Sensory Meridian Response (ASMR) Is Characterized by Reliable Changes in Affect and Physiology." *PLOS ONE* 13, no. 6 (June 20, 2018): e0196645. https://doi.org/10.1371/journal.pone.0196645.

34. Killgore, William D. S., Ashley D. Young, Lisa A Femia, Piotr Bogorodzki, Jadwiga Rogowska, and Deborah A. Yurgelun-Todd. "Cortical and Limbic Activation during Viewing of High- versus Low-Calorie Foods." *NeuroImage* 19, no. 4 (August 1, 2003): 1381–94. https://doi.org/10.1016/S1053-8119(03)00191-5.

   Schüssler, Petra, Michael Kluge, Alexander Yassouridis, Martin Dresler, Manfred Uhr, and Axel Steiger. "Ghrelin Levels Increase After Pictures Showing Food." *Obesity* 20, no. 6 (2012): 1212–17. https://doi.org/10.1038/oby.2011.385.

   Simmons, W. Kyle, Alex Martin, and Lawrence W. Barsalou. "Pictures of Appetizing Foods Activate Gustatory Cortices for Taste and Reward." *Cerebral Cortex* 15, no. 10 (October 1, 2005): 1602–8. https://doi.org/10.1093/cercor /bhi038.

   Spence, Charles, Katsunori Okajima, Adrian David Cheok, Olivia Petit, and Charles Michel. "Eating with Our Eyes: From Visual Hunger to Digital Satiation." *Brain and Cognition* 110 (December 2016): 53–63. https://doi.org/10.1016/j. bandc.2015.08.006.

   Versace, Francesco, David W. Frank, Elise M. Stevens, Menton M. Deweese, Michele Guindani, and Susan M. Schembre. "The Reality of 'Food Porn': Larger Brain Responses to Food-Related Cues than to Erotic Images Predict Cue-Induced Eating." *Psychophysiology* 56, no. 4 (2019): e13309. https://doi .org/10.1111/psyp.13309.

35. Berger, Jonathan, and Gabe Turow. *Music, Science, and the Rhythmic Brain: Cultural and Clinical Implications* (Philadelphia: Routledge, 2012).

   Padmanabhan, R., A. J. Hildreth, and D. Laws. "A Prospective, Randomised, Controlled Study Examining Binaural Beat Audio and Pre-Operative Anxiety in Patients Undergoing General Anaesthesia for Day Case Surgery." *Anaesthesia* 60, no. 9 (September 2005): 874–77. https://doi.org/10.1111/j.1365-2044.2005 .04287.x.

Saarman, Emily. "Feeling the Beat: Symposium Explores the Therapeutic Effects of Rhythmic Music." *Stanford University*, May 31, 2006. http://news .stanford.edu/news/2006/may31/brainwave-053106.html.

36. Elhai, Jon D., Jason C. Levine, Robert D. Dvorak, and Brian J. Hall. "Fear of Missing Out, Need for Touch, Anxiety and Depression Are Related to Problematic Smartphone Use." *Computers in Human Behavior* 63 (October 1, 2016): 509– 16. https://doi.org/10.1016/j.chb.2016.05.079.

Lee, Yu-Kang, Chun-Tuan Chang, You Lin, and Zhao-Hong Cheng. "The Dark Side of Smartphone Usage: Psychological Traits, Compulsive Behavior and Technostress." *Computers in Human Behavior* 31 (February 1, 2014): 373–83. https://doi.org/10.1016/j.chb.2013.10.047.

Oulasvirta, Antti, Tye Rattenbury, Lingyi Ma, and Eeva Raita. "Habits Make Smartphone Use More Pervasive." *Personal and Ubiquitous Computing* 16, no. 1 (January 2012): 105–14. https://doi.org/10.1007/s00779-011-0412-2.

37. These questionnaire items are borrowed, in part, from the self-actualization section of David Lester's "Needs Satisfaction Inventory" and Michel Steger et al's "Meaning in Life Questionnaire" (MLQ-10).

Lester, David. "Maslow's Hierarchy of Needs and Personality." *Personality and Individual Differences* 11, no. 11 (January 1990): 1187–88. https://doi .org/10.1016/0191-8869(90)90032-M.

Steger, Michael F., Patricia Frazier, Shigehiro Oishi, and Matthew Kaler. "The Meaning in Life Questionnaire: Assessing the Presence of and Search for Meaning in Life." *Journal of Counseling Psychology* 53, no. 1 (January 2006): 80–93. https://doi.org/10.1037/0022-0167.53.1.80.

38. These questions are borrowed from Lester's "Needs Satisfaction Inventory" and Steger et al's MLQ-10, as well as Ed Diener et al's "Satisfaction with Life Scale."

Lester, David. "Maslow's Hierarchy of Needs and Personality."

Steger, Michael F., Patricia Frazier, Shigehiro Oishi, and Matthew Kaler. "The Meaning in Life Questionnaire: Assessing the Presence of and Search for Meaning in Life."

Diener, Ed, Robert A. Emmons, Randy J. Larsen, and Sharon Griffin. "The Satisfaction With Life Scale." *Journal of Personality Assessment* 49, no. 1 (February 1985): 71–75. https://doi.org/10.1207/s15327752jpa4901_13.

CHAPTER 9: NATURE & WELL-BEING

1. Bereznak, Alyssa. "How the Succulent Took Over the World." *The Ringer*, May 22, 2018. https://www.theringer.com/tech/2018/5/22/17374708/consider-the -cactus-how-succulents-took-over-instagram-and-then-the-world.

2. "Pinterest 100 2019." Pinterest, 2019. https://newsroom.pinterest.com/sub /newsroom/assets/pinterest-100-2019.pdf.

3. "2017 State of the Industry Report." *Garden Center*, November 2017. https://www .gardencentermag.com/article/2017-state-of-the-industry-report/.

4. "Google Trends: Succulents." *Google Trends*. Accessed July 25, 2019. https://trends .google.com/trends/explore?date=2013-01-01%202019-07-25&q=succulents.

5. Biggs, Caroline. "Plant-Loving Millennials at Home and at Work." *New York Times*, August 7, 2018. https://www.nytimes.com/2018/03/09/realestate/plant -loving-millennials-at-home-and-at-work.html.

 Hanbury, Mary. "Millennials Are Obsessed with Raising Plants, and One New York-Based Startup Is Poised to Capitalize." *Business Insider*, August 19, 2018. https:// www.businessinsider.com/millennial-plants-lead-the-sill-funding-2018-8.

 "Instead of Houses, Young People Have Houseplants." *The Economist*, August 6, 2018. https://www.economist.com/graphic-detail/2018/08/06/instead-of -houses-young-people-have-houseplants.

6. The Jungle Collective. "Perth—Huge Indoor Plant Warehouse Sale—Rumble in the Jungle." Facebook, May 4, 2019. https://www.facebook.com/events /408267636644735/.

7. Boone, Lisa. "They Don't Own Homes. They Don't Have Kids. Why Millennials Are Plant Addicts." *Los Angeles Times*, July 24, 2018. https://www.latimes.com /home/la-hm-millennials-plant-parents-20180724-story.html.

 Davies, Taylor. "Why More Millennials Are Buying into 'Plant Parenthood.'" *NBC News*, November 19, 2018. https://www.nbcnews.com/better/health/why -more-millennials-are-buying-plant-parenthood-ncna935836.

 Ramanathan, Lavanya. "Millennials Are Filling Their Homes—and the Void in Their Hearts—with Houseplants." *Washington Post*, September 7, 2017, sec. Style. https://www.washingtonpost.com/lifestyle/style/young-urbanites-are -filling-their-homes-and-the-void-in-their-hearts-with-houseplants/2017/09/06 /ec98993c-89c8-11e7-961d-2f373b3977ee_story.html.

8. Polak, E. H., and J. Provasi. "Odor Sensitivity to Geosmin Enantiomers." *Chemical Senses* 17, no. 1 (1992): 23–26. https://doi.org/10.1093/chemse/17.1.23.

9. Stromberg, Joseph. "What Makes Rain Smell So Good?" *Smithsonian*, April 2, 2013. https://www.smithsonianmag.com/science-nature/what-makes-rain -smell-so-good-13806085/.

10. New, Joshua, Max M. Krasnow, Danielle Truxaw, and Steven J.C. Gaulin. "Spatial Adaptations for Plant Foraging: Women Excel and Calories Count." *Proceedings of the Royal Society B: Biological Sciences* 274, no. 1626 (November 7, 2007): 2679–84. https://doi.org/10.1098/rspb.2007.0826.

11. Meert, Katrien, Mario Pandelaere, and Vanessa M. Patrick. "Taking a Shine to It: How the Preference for Glossy Stems from an Innate Need for Water." *Journal of Consumer Psychology* 24, no. 2 (April 2014): 195–206. https://doi.org/10.1016/j .jcps.2013.12.005.

12. Matz, Carlyn, David Stieb, Karelyn Davis, Marika Egyed, Andreas Rose, Benedito Chou, and Orly Brion. "Effects of Age, Season, Gender and Urban-Rural Status on Time-Activity: Canadian Human Activity Pattern Survey 2 (CHAPS 2)." *International Journal of Environmental Research and Public Health* 11, no. 2 (February 19, 2014): 2108–24. https://doi.org/10.3390/ijerph110202108.

13. Diffey, B.L. "An Overview Analysis of the Time People Spend Outdoors: Time Spent Outdoors." *British Journal of Dermatology* 164, no. 4 (April 2011): 848–54. https://doi.org/10.1111/j.1365-2133.2010.10165.x.

    Klepeis, Neil E., William C. Nelson, Wayne R. Ott, John P. Robinson, Andy M. Tsang, Paul Switzer, Joseph V. Behar, Stephen C. Hern, and William H. Engelmann. "The National Human Activity Pattern Survey (NHAPS): A Resource for Assessing Exposure to Environmental Pollutants." *Journal of Exposure Science and Environmental Epidemiology* 11, no. 3 (July 2001): 231–52. https://doi.org/10.1038/sj.jea.7500165.

14. Pergams, O. R. W., and P. A. Zaradic. "Evidence for a Fundamental and Pervasive Shift Away from Nature-Based Recreation." *Proceedings of the National Academy of Sciences* 105, no. 7 (February 19, 2008): 2295–2300. https://doi.org/10.1073/pnas.0709893105.

    Stevens, Thomas H., More, Thomas A. More, and Marla Markowski-Lindsay. "Declining National Park Visitation: An Economic Analysis." *Journal of Leisure Research* 46, no. 2 (2014):153–164. https://www.fs.fed.us/nrs/pubs/jrnl/2014/nrs_2014_stevens_001.pdf.

15. "2018 Revision of World Urbanization Prospects." United Nations Department of Economic and Social Affairs, May 16, 2018. https://www.un.org/development/desa/publications/2018-revision-of-world-urbanization-prospects.html.

16. Bassett, David R., Dinesh John, Scott A. Conger, Eugene C. Fitzhugh, and Dawn P. Coe. "Trends in Physical Activity and Sedentary Behaviors of United States Youth." *Journal of Physical Activity and Health* 12, no. 8 (August 2015): 1102–11. https://doi.org/10.1123/jpah.2014-0050.

17. Larson, Lincoln, H. Ken Cordell, Carter Betz, and Gary Green. "Children's Time Outdoors: Results from a National Survey." University of Massachusetts, 2011. https://scholarworks.umass.edu/cgi/viewcontent.cgi.

18. Bowles, Nellie. "Now Some Families Are Hiring Coaches to Help Them Raise Phone-Free Children." *New York Times*, July 6, 2019. https://www.nytimes.com/2019/07/06/style/parenting-coaches-screen-time-phones.html.

19. Egan, Timothy. "Nature-Deficit Disorder." *The New York Times*, March 29, 2012. https://opinionator.blogs.nytimes.com/2012/03/29/nature-deficit-disorder/.

20. MacKerron, George, and Susana Mourato. "Happiness Is Greater in Natural Environments." *Global Environmental Change* 23, no. 5 (October 2013): 992–1000. https://doi.org/10.1016/j.gloenvcha.2013.03.010.

21. "Air Quality Guidelines: Global Update 2005." *World Health Organization*, 2005: 87–109.

    Gouveia, N. C., M. Maisonet. "Health effects of air pollution: an overview." *World Health Organization*, January 1, 2005: 87–109. https://www.researchgate.net/publication/287103073_Health_effects_of_air_pollution_an_overview.

    Hartig, Terry, Richard Mitchell, Sjerp de Vries, and Howard Frumkin. "Nature and Health." *Annual Review of Public Health* 35, no. 1 (2014): 207–28. https://doi.org/10.1146/annurev-publhealth-032013-182443.

Passchier-Vermeer, W., and W. F. Passchier. "Noise Exposure and Public Health." *Environmental Health Perspectives* 108, no. suppl 1 (March 2000): 123–31. https://doi.org/10.1289/ehp.00108s1123.

22. Wilson, Edward O. *Biophilia*. Reprint edition (Cambridge, MA: Harvard University Press, 1984).

23. Johnson, Laura Kay. "The Buddhist Perception of Nature: Implications for Forest Conservation in Thailand." *Trumpeter: Journal of Ecosophy*, 1992.

24. Williams, Florence. "This Is Your Brain on Nature." *National Geographic*, January 2016. https://www.nationalgeographic.com/magazine/2016/01/call-to-wild.

25. Alvarsson, Jesper J., Stefan Wiens, and Mats E. Nilsson. "Stress Recovery during Exposure to Nature Sound and Environmental Noise." *International Journal of Environmental Research and Public Health* 7, no. 3 (March 11, 2010): 1036–46. https://doi.org/10.3390/ijerph7031036.

Annerstedt, Matilda, Peter Jönsson, Mattias Wallergård, Gerd Johansson, Björn Karlson, Patrik Grahn, Åse Marie Hansen, and Peter Währborg. "Inducing Physiological Stress Recovery with Sounds of Nature in a Virtual Reality Forest—Results from a Pilot Study." *Physiology & Behavior* 118 (June 2013): 240–50. https://doi.org/10.1016/j.physbeh.2013.05.023.

Benfield, Jacob, B. Derrick Taff, Peter Newman, and Joshua Smyth. "Natural Sound Facilitates Mood Recovery." *Ecopsychology* 6, no. 3 (September 2014).

Beyer, Kirsten, Andrea Kaltenbach, Aniko Szabo, Sandra Bogar, F. Nieto, and Kristen Malecki. "Exposure to Neighborhood Green Space and Mental Health: Evidence from the Survey of the Health of Wisconsin." *International Journal of Environmental Research and Public Health* 11, no. 3 (March 21, 2014): 3453–72. https://doi.org/10.3390/ijerph110303453.

Brereton, Finbarr, J. Peter Clinch, and Susana Ferreira. "Happiness, Geography and the Environment." *Ecological Economics* 65, no. 2 (April 2008): 386–96. https://doi.org/10.1016/j.ecolecon.2007.07.008.

Chang, C. Y., Y. H. Lin, and M. T. Chou. "Experiences and Stress Reduction of Viewing Natural Environmental Settings." *Acta Horticulturae*, no. 775 (November 2008): 139–46. https://doi.org/10.17660/ActaHortic.2008.775.16.

Houlden, Victoria, Scott Weich, João Porto de Albuquerque, Stephen Jarvis, and Karen Rees. "The Relationship between Greenspace and the Mental Well-Being of Adults: A Systematic Review." Edited by C. Mary Schooling. *PLOS ONE* 13, no. 9 (September 12, 2018): e0203000. https://doi.org/10.1371/journal.pone.0203000.

Nutsford, D., A. L. Pearson, and S. Kingham. "An Ecological Study Investigating the Association between Access to Urban Green Space and Mental Health." *Public Health* 127, no. 11 (November 2013): 1005–11. https://doi.org/10.1016/j.puhe.2013.08.016.

Roe, Jenny, Catharine Thompson, Peter Aspinall, Mark Brewer, Elizabeth Duff, David Miller, Richard Mitchell, and Angela Clow. "Green Space and Stress: Evidence from Cortisol Measures in Deprived Urban Communities." *International Journal of Environmental Research and Public Health* 10, no. 9 (September 2, 2013): 4086–4103. https://doi.org/10.3390/ijerph10094086.

Stigsdotter, Ulrika K., Ola Ekholm, Jasper Schipperijn, Mette Toftager, Finn Kamper-Jørgensen, and Thomas B. Randrup. "Health Promoting Outdoor Environments—Associations between Green Space, and Health, Health-Related Quality of Life and Stress Based on a Danish National Representative Survey." *Scandinavian Journal of Public Health* 38, no. 4 (April 22, 2010): 411–17. https://doi.org/10.1177/1403494810367468.

Sugiyama, T., E. Leslie, B. Giles-Corti, and N. Owen. "Associations of Neighbourhood Greenness with Physical and Mental Health: Do Walking, Social Coherence and Local Social Interaction Explain the Relationships?" *Journal of Epidemiology & Community Health* 62, no. 5 (May 1, 2008): e9–e9. https://doi.org/10.1136/jech.2007.064287.

Ulrich, Roger S., Robert F. Simons, Barbara D. Losito, Evelyn Fiorito, Mark A. Miles, and Michael Zelson. "Stress Recovery during Exposure to Natural and Urban Environments." *Journal of Environmental Psychology* 11, no. 3 (September 1991): 201–30. https://doi.org/10.1016/S0272-4944(05)80184-7.

Ward Thompson, Catharine, Jenny Roe, Peter Aspinall, Richard Mitchell, Angela Clow, and David Miller. "More Green Space Is Linked to Less Stress in Deprived Communities: Evidence from Salivary Cortisol Patterns." *Landscape and Urban Planning* 105, no. 3 (April 2012): 221–29. https://doi.org/10.1016/j.landurbplan.2011.12.015.

White, Mathew P., Ian Alcock, Benedict W. Wheeler, and Michael H. Depledge. "Would You Be Happier Living in a Greener Urban Area? A Fixed-Effects Analysis of Panel Data." *Psychological Science* 24, no. 6 (June 2013): 920–28. https://doi.org/10.1177/0956797612464659.

26. Alvarsson, Jesper J., Stefan Wiens, and Mats E. Nilsson. "Stress Recovery during Exposure to Nature Sound and Environmental Noise."

Aspinall, Peter, Panagiotis Mavros, Richard Coyne, and Jenny Roe. "The Urban Brain: Analysing Outdoor Physical Activity with Mobile EEG." *British Journal of Sports Medicine* 49, no. 4 (February 2015): 272–76. https://doi.org/10.1136/bjsports-2012-091877.

Hartig, Terry, Gary W. Evans, Larry D. Jamner, Deborah S. Davis, and Tommy Gärling. "Tracking Restoration in Natural and Urban Field Settings." *Journal of Environmental Psychology* 23, no. 2 (June 2003): 109–23. https://doi.org/10.1016/S0272-4944(02)00109-3.

Grahn, Patrik, and Ulrika K. Stigsdotter. "The Relation between Perceived Sensory Dimensions of Urban Green Space and Stress Restoration." *Landscape and Urban Planning* 94, no. 3–4 (March 2010): 264–75. https://doi.org/10.1016/j.landurbplan.2009.10.012.

Zhao, Jingwei, Wenyan Xu, and Li Ye. "Effects of Auditory-Visual Combinations on Perceived Restorative Potential of Urban Green Space." *Applied Acoustics* 141 (December 1, 2018): 169–77. https://doi.org/10.1016/j.apacoust.2018.07.001.

27. Berg, Agnes E. van den, Terry Hartig, and Henk Staats. "Preference for Nature in Urbanized Societies: Stress, Restoration, and the Pursuit of Sustainability." *Journal of Social Issues* 63, no. 1 (March 2007): 79–96. https://doi.org/10.1111/j.1540-4560.2007.00497.x.

Berg, Magdalena van den, Jolanda Maas, Rianne Muller, Anoek Braun, Wendy Kaandorp, René van Lien, Mireille van Poppel, Willem van Mechelen, and Agnes van den Berg. "Autonomic Nervous System Responses to Viewing Green and Built Settings: Differentiating Between Sympathetic and Parasympathetic Activity." *International Journal of Environmental Research and Public Health* 12, no. 12 (December 14, 2015): 15860–74. https://doi.org/10.3390/ijerph121215026.

Brown, Daniel K., Jo L. Barton, and Valerie F. Gladwell. "Viewing Nature Scenes Positively Affects Recovery of Autonomic Function Following Acute-Mental Stress." *Environmental Science & Technology* 47, no. 11 (April 16, 2013): 5562–69. https://doi.org/10.1021/es305019p.

Gladwell, V. F., D. K. Brown, J. L. Barton, M. P. Tarvainen, P. Kuoppa, J. Pretty, J. M. Suddaby, and G. R. H. Sandercock. "The Effects of Views of Nature on Autonomic Control." *European Journal of Applied Physiology* 112, no. 9 (September 2012): 3379–86. https://doi.org/10.1007/s00421-012-2318-8.

Hartig, Evans, Jamner, Davis, and Gärling, "Tracking Restoration in Natural and Urban Field Settings."

Li, Qing. "Effect of Forest Bathing Trips on Human Immune Function." *Environmental Health and Preventive Medicine* 15, no. 1 (January 2010): 9–17. https://doi.org/10.1007/s12199-008-0068-3.

Orsega-Smith, Elizabeth, Andrew J. Mowen, Laura L. Payne, and Geoffrey Godbey. "The Interaction of Stress and Park Use on Psycho-Physiological Health in Older Adults." *Journal of Leisure Research* 36, no. 2 (June 2004): 232–56. https://doi.org/10.1080/00222216.2004.11950021.

Park, Bum-Jin, Yuko Tsunetsugu, Tamami Kasetani, Takeshi Morikawa, Takahide Kagawa, and Yoshifumi Miyazaki. "Physiological Effects of Forest Recreation in a Young Conifer Forest in Hinokage Town, Japan." *Silva Fennica* 43, no. 2 (2009). https://doi.org/10.14214/sf.213.

Tsunetsugu, Yuko, and Yoshifumi Miyazaki. "Measurement of Absolute Hemoglobin Concentrations of Prefrontal Region by Near-Infrared Time Resolved Spectroscopy: Examples of Experiments and Prospects." *Journal of Physiological Anthropology and Applied Human Science* 24, no. 4 (2005): 469–72. https://doi.org/10.2114/jpa.24.469.

Ulrich, Roger S., Robert F. Simons, Barbara D. Losito, Evelyn Fiorito, Mark A. Miles, and Michael Zelson. "Stress Recovery during Exposure to Natural and Urban Environments."

28. Dubos, R. "Man Overadapting." *Psychology Today* 4 (1971c): 50–53.

29. Kuo, F. E., and W. C. Sullivan. "Environment and Crime in the Inner City: Does Vegetation Reduce Crime?" *Environment & Behavior* 33, no. 3 (May 1, 2001): 343–67. https://doi.org/10.1177/00139160121973025.

30. Guéguen, Nicolas, and Jordy Stefan. "'Green Altruism': Short Immersion in Natural Green Environments and Helping Behavior." *Environment and Behavior* 48, no. 2 (February 2016): 324–42. https://doi.org/10.1177/0013916514536576.

Piff, Paul K., Pia Dietze, Matthew Feinberg, Daniel M. Stancato, and Dacher Keltner. "Awe, the Small Self, and Prosocial Behavior." *Journal of Personality and Social Psychology* 108, no. 6 (2015): 883–99. https://doi.org/10.1037/pspi0000018.

Weinstein, Netta, Andrew K. Przybylski, and Richard M. Ryan. "Can Nature Make Us More Caring? Effects of Immersion in Nature on Intrinsic Aspirations and Generosity." *Personality and Social Psychology Bulletin* 35, no. 10 (October 2009): 1315–29. https://doi.org/10.1177/0146167209341649.

   Williams, Florence. *The Nature Fix: Why Nature Makes Us Happier, Healthier, and More Creative* (New York: W. W. Norton & Company, 2017).

   Zelenski, John M., Raelyne L. Dopko, and Colin A. Capaldi. "Cooperation Is in Our Nature: Nature Exposure May Promote Cooperative and Environmentally Sustainable Behavior." *Journal of Environmental Psychology* 42 (June 2015): 24–31. https://doi.org/10.1016/j.jenvp.2015.01.005.

   Zhang, Jia Wei, Paul K. Piff, Ravi Iyer, Spassena Koleva, and Cacher Keltner. "An Occasion for Unselfing: Beautiful Nature Leads to Prosociality." *Journal of Environmental Psychology* 37 (March 2014): 61–72. https://doi.org/10.1016/j.jenvp.2013.11.008.

31. Weinstein, Netta, Andrew K. Przybylski, and Richard M. Ryan. "Can Nature Make Us More Caring? Effects of Immersion in Nature on Intrinsic Aspirations and Generosity."

32. Guéguen, Nicolas, and Jordy Stefan. "'Green Altruism': Short Immersion in Natural Green Environments and Helping Behavior."

   Zelenski, John M., Raelyne L. Dopko, and Colin A. Capaldi. "Cooperation Is in Our Nature: Nature Exposure May Promote Cooperative and Environmentally Sustainable Behavior."

33. Rudd, Melanie, Kathleen D. Vohs, and Jennifer Aaker. "Awe Expands People's Perception of Time, Alters Decision Making, and Enhances Well-Being." *Psychological Science* 23, no. 10 (October 2012): 1130–36. https://doi.org/10.1177/0956797612438731.

34. Piff, Paul K., Pia Dietze, Matthew Feinberg, Daniel M. Stancato, and Dacher Keltner. "Awe, the Small Self, and Prosocial Behavior." *Journal of Personality and Social Psychology* 108, no. 6 (2015): 883–99. https://doi.org/10.1037/pspi0000018.

   Zhang, Jia Wei, Paul K. Piff, Ravi Iyer, Spassena Koleva, and Cacher Keltner. "An Occasion for Unselfing: Beautiful Nature Leads to Prosociality." *Journal of Environmental Psychology* 37 (March 2014): 61–72. https://doi.org/10.1016/j.jenvp.2013.11.008.

35. Piff, Paul K., Pia Dietze, Matthew Feinberg, Daniel M. Stancato, and Dacher Keltner. "Awe, the Small Self, and Prosocial Behavior."

36. Barton, J., and J. Pretty. "What Is the Best Dose of Nature and Green Exercise for Improving Mental Health? A Multi-Study Analysis." *Environmental Science & Technology* 44 (March 25, 2010): 3947–3955. https://pubs.acs.org/doi/abs/10.1021/es903183r.

   Green, Kristophe, and Dacher Keltner. "What Happens When We Reconnect with Nature." *Greater Good*, March 1, 2017. https://greatergood.berkeley.edu/article/item/what_happens_when_we_reconnect_with_nature.

   Rudd, Melanie, Kathleen D. Vohs, and Jennifer Aaker. "Awe Expands People's Perception of Time, Alters Decision Making, and Enhances Well-Being." *Psychological Science* 23, no. 10 (October 2012): 1130–36. https://doi.org/10.1177/0956797612438731.

Velarde, M. D., G. Fry, and M. Tveit. "Health Effects of Viewing Landscapes—Landscape Types in Environmental Psychology." *Urban Forestry & Urban Greening* 6, no. 4 (November 2007): 199–212. https://doi.org/10.1016/j.ufug.2007.07.001.

37. Li, Q., M. Kobayashi, and T. Kawada. "Relationships between Percentage of Forest Coverage and Standardized Mortality Ratios (SMR) of Cancers in All Prefectures in Japan." *Open Public Health Journal,* 1 (2008): 1–7.

Maas, J. "Green Space, Urbanity, and Health: How Strong Is the Relation?" *Journal of Epidemiology & Community Health* 60, no. 7 (July 1, 2006): 587–92. https://doi.org/10.1136/jech.2005.043125.

Maas, J., R. A. Verheij, S. de Vries, P. Spreeuwenberg, F. G. Schellevis, and P. P. Groenewegen. "Morbidity Is Related to a Green Living Environment." *Journal of Epidemiology & Community Health* 63, no. 12 (December 1, 2009): 967–73. https://doi.org/10.1136/jech.2008.079038.

Richard, Mitchell, Ph.D., and Frank Popham, Ph.D. "Effect of Exposure to Natural Environment on Health Inequalities: An Observational Population Study." *The Lancet* 372, no. 9650 (November 8, 2008): 1655–60. https://www.thelancet.com/journals/lancet/article/PIIS0140-6736(08)61689-X/fulltext.

Takano, T., J. Fu, K. Nakamura, K. Uji, Y. Fukuda, M. Watanabe, and H. Nakajima. "Age-Adjusted Mortality and its Association to Variations in Urban Conditions in Shanghai." *Health Policy* 61, no. 3 (September 2002): 239–53. https://www.sciencedirect.com/science/article/pii/S0168851001002342.

Takano, T., K. Nakamura, and M. Watanabe. "Urban Residential Environments and Senior Citizens' Longevity in Megacity Areas: The Importance of Walkable Green Spaces." *Journal of Epidemiology Community Health* 56, no. 12 (December 2002): 913–8. https://jech.bmj.com/content/56/12/913.

Villeneuve, P. J., M. Jerrett, J. G. Su, R. T. Burnett, H. Chen, A. J. Wheeler, and M. S. Goldberg. "A Cohort Study Relating Urban Green Space with Mortality in Ontario, Canada." *Environmental Research* 115 (May 2012): 51–8. https://www.ncbi.nlm.nih.gov/pubmed/22483437.

Zhiyong, Hu, John Liebens, and K. Ranga Rao. "Linking Stroke Mortality with Air Pollution, Income, and Greenness in Northwest Florida: An Ecological Geographical Study." *International Journal of Health Geographics* 7, no. 20 (2008). https://doi.org/10.1186/1476-072X-7-20.

38. Horiuchi, M., J. Endo, S. Akatsuka, T. Uno, T. Hasegaw, and Y. Seko. "Influence of Forest Walking on Blood Pressure, Profile of Mood States, and Stress Markers from the Viewpoint of Aging." *Journal of Aging and Gerontology* 1 (January 2013): 9–17. http://savvysciencepublisher.com/downloads/jagv1n1a2/.

Mao, G. X., X. G. Lan, Y. B. Cao, Z. M. Chen, Z. H. He, Y. D. Lv, et al. "Effects of Short-Term Forest Bathing on Human Health in a Broad-Leaved Evergreen Forest in Zhejiang Province, China." *Biomedical and Environmental Sciences* 25, no. 3 (June 2012): 317–24. https://www.sciencedirect.com/science/article/pii/S0895398812600610.

Mao, G. X., Y. B. Cao, X. G. Lan, Z. H. He, Z. M. Chen, Y. Z. Wang, et al. "Therapeutic Effect of Forest Bathing on Human Hypertension in the Elderly."

Journal of Cardiology 60, no. 6 (December 2012): 495–502. https://www.science
direct.com/science/article/pii/S0914508712001852.

Miyazaki, Yoshifumi, Juyoung Lee, Bum-Jin Park, Yuko Tsunetsugu, and
Keiko Matsunaga. "Preventive Medical Effects of Nature Therapy." *Japanese Journal of Hygiene* 66, no. 4 (2011): 651–56. https://doi.org/10.1265/jjh.66.651.

Park, B. J., Y. Tsunetsugu, T. Kasetani, T. Kagawa, and Y. Miyazaki. "The
Physiological Effects of Shinrin-yoku (Taking in the Forest Atmosphere or Forest
Bathing): Evidence from Field Experiments in 24 Forests across Japan." *Environmental Health and Preventive Medicine* 15, no. 1 (June 2009): 18–26. https://www
.ncbi.nlm.nih.gov/pubmed/19568835.

Song, C., H. Ikei, J. Lee, B. J. Park, T. Kagawa, and Y. Miyazaki. "Individual
Differences in the Physiological Effects of Forest Therapy Based on Type A and
Type B Behavior Patterns." *Journal of Physiological Anthropology* 32, no. 1 (October
2, 2013). https://www.ncbi.nlm.nih.gov/pmc/articles/PMC3851594/.

Song, C., D. Joung, H. Ikei, M. Igarashi, M. Aga, B. J. Park, et al. "Physiological and Psychological Effects of Walking on Young Males in Urban Parks in
Winter." *Journal of Physiological Anthropology* 32, no. 1 (October 29, 2013). https://
www.ncbi.nlm.nih.gov/pmc/articles/PMC3817995/.

Song, C., H. Ikei, M. Igarashi, M. Miwa, M. Takagaki, and Y. Miyazaki.
"Physiological and Psychological Responses of Young Males during Springtime
Walks in Urban Parks." *Journal of Physiological Anthropology* 33, no. 8 (May 1,
2018). https://www.ncbi.nlm.nih.gov/pubmed/24887352.

Sung, J., J. M. Woo, W. Kim, S. K. Lim, and E. J. Chung. "The Effect of
Cognitive Behavior Therapy-Based 'Forest Therapy' Program on Blood Pressure,
Salivary Cortisol Level, and Quality of Life in Elderly Hypertensive Patients."
Clinical and Experimental Hypertension 34, no. 1 (2012): 1–7. https://www.ncbi
.nlm.nih.gov/pubmed/22007608.

Takayama, N., K. Korpela, J. Lee, T. Morikawa, Y. Tsunetsugu, B. J. Park,
Q. Li, L. Tyrväinen, Y. Miyazaki, and T. Kagawa. "Emotional, Restorative and
Vitalizing Effects of Forest and Urban Environments at Four Sites in Japan."
International Journal of Environmental Research and Public Health 11, no. 7 (July 15,
2014 11): 7207–30. https://www.ncbi.nlm.nih.gov/pmc/articles/PMC4113871/.

Takayama, N., K. Korpela, J. Lee, T. Morikawa, Y. Tsunetsugu, B. J. Park, et
al, "Emotional, Restorative and Vitalizing Effects of Forest and Urban Environments at Four Sites in Japan."

Toda, M., R. Den, M. Hasegawa-Ohira, and K. Morimoto. "Effects of Wood-
land Walking on Salivary Stress Markers Cortisol and Chromogranin A." *Complementary Therapies in Medicine* 21, no. 1 (February 2013): 29–34. https://www
.ncbi.nlm.nih.gov/pubmed/23374202.

Tsunetsugu, Y., B. J. Park, Y. Miyazaki. "Trends in Research Related to 'Shinrin-yoku' (Taking in the Forest Atmosphere or Forest Bathing) in Japan." *Environmental Health Preventive Medicine* 15, no. 1 (January 2010): 27–37. https://
www.ncbi.nlm.nih.gov/pubmed/19585091.

39. Franklin, Deborah. "How Hospital Gardens Help Patients Heal." *Scientific American*, March 1, 2012. https://www.scientificamerican.com/article/nature-that
-nurtures /.

Park, Seong-Hyun, and Richard H. Mattson. "Effects of Flowering and Foliage Plants in Hospital Rooms on Patients Recovering from Abdominal Surgery." *HortTechnology* 18, no. 4 (January 2008): 563–68. https://doi.org/10.21273/HORTTECH.18.4.563.

Park, Seong-Hyun, and Richard H. Mattson. "Ornamental Indoor Plants in Hospital Rooms Enhanced Health Outcomes of Patients Recovering from Surgery." *The Journal of Alternative and Complementary Medicine* 15, no. 9 (September 2009): 975–80. https://doi.org/10.1089/acm.2009.0075.

Ulrich, R. "View through a Window May Influence Recovery from Surgery." *Science* 224, no. 4647 (April 27, 1984): 420–21. https://doi.org/10.1126/science.6143402.

40. Alvarsson, J., S. Wiens, and M. Nilsson. "Stress Recovery during Exposure to Nature Sound and Environmental Noise."

Chang, Chen-Yen, and Ping-Kun Chen. "Human Response to Window Views and Indoor Plants in the Workplace." *HortScience* 40, no. 5 (August 2005): 1354–59. https://doi.org/10.21273/HORTSCI.40.5.1354.

Hartig, Terry, Marlis Mang, and Gary W. Evans. "Restorative Effects of Natural Environment Experiences." *Environment and Behavior* 23, no. 1 (January 1991): 3–26. https://doi.org/10.1177/0013916591231001.

Kaplan, Rachel, and Stephen Kaplan. "The Experience of Nature: A Psychological Perspective." *University of Michigan*, 1989. http://willsull.net/resources/270 Readings/ExpNature1to5.pdf.

Larsen, Larissa, Jeffrey Adams, Brian Deal, Byoung Suk Kweon, and Elizabeth Tyler. "Plants in the Workplace: The Effects of Plant Density on Productivity, Attitudes, and Perceptions." *Environment and Behavior* 30, no. 3 (May 1998): 261–81. https://doi.org/10.1177/001391659803000301.

Leather, Phil, Mike Pyrgas, Di Beale, and Claire Lawrence. "Windows in the Workplace: Sunlight, View, and Occupational Stress." *Environment and Behavior* 30, no. 6 (November 1998): 739–62. https://doi.org/10.1177/0013916598030 00601.

Lottrup, Lene, Patrik Grahn, and Ulrika K. Stigsdotter. "Workplace Greenery and Perceived Level of Stress: Benefits of Access to a Green Outdoor Environment at the Workplace." *Landscape and Urban Planning* 110 (February 2013): 5–11. https://doi.org/10.1016/j.landurbplan.2012.09.002.

Mehta, Ravi, Rui (Juliet) Zhu, and Amar Cheema. "Is Noise Always Bad? Exploring the Effects of Ambient Noise on Creative Cognition." *Journal of Consumer Research* 39, no. 4 (2012): 784–99. https://doi.org/10.1086/665048.

Nieuwenhuis, Marlon, Craig Knight, Tom Postmes, and S. Alexander Haslam. "The Relative Benefits of Green versus Lean Office Space: Three Field Experiments." *Journal of Experimental Psychology Applied* 20, no. 3 (September 2014): 199–214. https://doi.org/10.1037/xap0000024.

Ryan, Richard M., Netta Weinstein, Jessey Bernstein, Kirk Warren Brown, Louis Mistretta, and Marylène Gagné. "Vitalizing Effects of Being Outdoors and in Nature." *Journal of Environmental Psychology* 30, no. 2 (June 2010): 159–68. https://doi.org/10.1016/j.jenvp.2009.10.009.

Tham, K. W. and H. C. Willem. "Temperature and Ventilation Effects on Performance and Neurobehavioral-Related Symptoms of Tropically Acclimatized Call Center Operators Near Thermal Neutrality." *ASHRAE Transactions* 111 (January 2005): 687–698. https://www.semanticscholar.org/paper/Temperature -and-ventilation-effects-on-performance-Tham-Willem/8485c1ccfde935ee746b 4b6d3a72e625d5a9244f.

Windhager, Sonja, Klaus Atzwanger, Fred L. Bookstein, and Katrin Schaefer. "Fish in a Mall Aquarium—An Ethological Investigation of Biophilia." *Landscape and Urban Planning* 99, no. 1 (January 2011): 23–30. https://doi.org/10.1016/j .landurbplan.2010.08.008.

41. Atchley, Ruth Ann, David L. Strayer, and Paul Atchley. "Creativity in the Wild: Improving Creative Reasoning through Immersion in Natural Settings." Edited by Jan de Fockert. *PLoS ONE* 7, no. 12 (December 12, 2012): e51474. https://doi .org/10.1371/journal.pone.0051474.

Faber Taylor, A. and Kuo, F.E. "Children with Attention Deficits Concentrate Better after Walk in the Park." *Journal of Attention Disorders* 12 (2209): 402–409.

Hartig, Terry, Marlis Mang, and Gary W. Evans. "Restorative Effects of Natural Environment Experiences."

Kaplan, Rachel, and Stephen Kaplan, "The Experience of Nature: A Psychological Perspective."

Lichtenfeld, Stephanie, Andrew J. Elliot, Markus A. Maier, and Reinhard Pekrun. "Fertile Green: Green Facilitates Creative Performance." *Personality and Social Psychology Bulletin* 38, no. 6 (June 2012): 784–97. https://doi .org/10.1177/0146167212436611.

McAnally, Helena Margaret, Lindsay Anne Robertson, and Robert John Hancox. "Effects of an Outdoor Education Programme on Creative Thinking and Well-Being in Adolescent Boys." *New Zealand Journal of Educational Studies* 53, no. 2 (November 2018): 241–55. https://doi.org/10.1007/s40841-018-0111-x

Mehta, Zhu, and Cheema, "Is Noise Always Bad?"

42. 森林セラピー®総合サイト. "全国62の森 | 森林セラピー総合サイト." Accessed March 28, 2019. http://quarter/cn49/62forest_across_japan.html.

43. "Prescribing Nature for Better Kids' Health." *UCSF: The Campaign*. Accessed March 28, 2019. https://campaign.ucsf.edu/stories/prescribing-nature-better-kids -health.

44. Razani, Nooshin. "Prescribing Nature for Health." *REI Co-Op Journal*, November 21, 2016. https://www.rei.com/blog/fitness/prescribing-nature-for-health.

45. "National Forest Healing Center." *Visit Medical Korea*. Accessed March 28, 2019. http://english.visitmedicalkorea.com/eng/wellnessKorea/wellnessKorea_03 /wellnessKorea_03_3.jsp.

46. Williams, Florence. *The Nature Fix: Why Nature Makes Us Happier, Healthier, and More Creative.*

47. Li, Qing, Ari Nakadai, Hiroki Matsushima, Yoshifumi Miyazaki, Alan M. Krensky, Tomoyuki Kawada, and Kanehisa Morimoto. "Phytoncides (Wood Essential Oils) Induce Human Natural Killer Cell Activity."

Immunopharmacology and Immunotoxicology 28, no. 2 (January 2006): 319–33. https://doi.org/10.1080/08923970600809439.

Li, Q., M. Kobayashi, Y. Wakayama, H. Inagaki, M. Katsumata, Y. Hirata, K. Hirata, et al. "Effect of Phytoncide from Trees on Human Natural Killer Cell Function." *International Journal of Immunopathology and Pharmacology* 22, no. 4 (October 2009): 951–59. https://doi.org/10.1177/039463200902200410.

Li, Qing. "Effect of Forest Bathing Trips on Human Immune Function." *Environmental Health and Preventive Medicine* 15, no. 1 (January 2010): 9–17. https://doi.org/10.1007/s12199-008-0068-3.

48. Li, Qing. *Forest Bathing: How Trees Can Help You Find Health and Happiness* (London, England: Penguin, 2018).

49. Li, Nakadai, Matsushima, Miyazaki, Krensky, Kawada, and Morimoto, "Phytoncides (Wood Essential Oils) Induce Human Natural Killer Cell Activity."

50. Li, Q., M. Kobayashi, Y. Wakayama, H. Inagaki, M. Katsumata, Y. Hirata, K. Hirata, et al. "Effect of Phytoncide from Trees on Human Natural Killer Cell Function."

51. Williams, Florence. "Take Two Hours of Pine Forest and Call Me in the Morning." *Outside*, December 2012. https://www.outsideonline.com/1870381/take-two-hours-pine-forest-and-call-me-morning.

52. Li, Qing, *Forest Bathing: How Trees Can Help You Find Health and Happiness*.

53. Kim, Gwang-Won, Gwang-Woo Jeong, Tae Hoon Kim, Han Su Back, Seok-Kyun Oh, Heoung-Keun Kang, Sam-Gyu Lee, Yoon Soo Kim, and Jin-Kyu Song. "Functional Neuroanatomy Associated with Natural and Urban Scenic Views in the Human Brain: 3.0T Functional MR Imaging." *Korean Journal of Radiology* 11, no. 5 (2010): 507. https://doi.org/10.3348/kjr.2010.11.5.507.

Selhub, Eva M., and Alan C. Logan. *Your Brain on Nature: The Science of Nature's Influence on Your Health, Happiness and Vitality.* (Hoboken, NJ: Wiley, 2012).

54. Lowry, C. A., J. H. Hollis, A. de Vries, B. Pan, L. R. Brunet, J. R. F. Hunt, J. F. R. Paton, et al. "Identification of an Immune-Responsive Mesolimbocortical Serotonergic System: Potential Role in Regulation of Emotional Behavior." *Neuroscience* 146, no. 2 (May 2007): 756–72. https://doi.org/10.1016/j.neuroscience.2007.01.067.

55. Frank, Matthew G., Laura K. Fonken, Samuel D. Dolzani, Jessica L. Annis, Philip H. Siebler, Dominic Schmidt, Linda R. Watkins, Steven F. Maier, and Christopher A. Lowry. "Immunization with Mycobacterium Vaccae Induces an Anti-Inflammatory Milieu in the CNS: Attenuation of Stress-Induced Microglial Priming, Alarmins and Anxiety-like Behavior." *Brain, Behavior, and Immunity* 73 (October 2018): 352–63. https://doi.org/10.1016/j.bbi.2018.05.020.

Matthews, Dorothy M., and Susan M. Jenks. "Ingestion of Mycobacterium Vaccae Decreases Anxiety-Related Behavior and Improves Learning in Mice." *Behavioural Processes* 96 (June 2013): 27–35. https://doi.org/10.1016/j.beproc.2013.02.007.

Reber, Stefan O., Philip H. Siebler, Nina C. Donner, James T. Morton, David G. Smith, Jared M. Kopelman, Kenneth R. Lowe, et al. "Immunization with a Heat-Killed Preparation of the Environmental Bacterium Mycobacterium Vaccae Promotes Stress Resilience in Mice." *Proceedings of the National Academy of Sciences* 113, no. 22 (May 31, 2016): E3130–39. https://doi.org/10.1073/pnas.1600324113.

56. Kaplan, Stephen. "The Restorative Benefits of Nature: Toward an Integrative Framework." *Journal of Environmental Psychology* 15, no. 3 (September 1995): 169–82.

Kaplan, Rachel, and Stephen Kaplan. "The Experience of Nature: A Psychological Perspective."

57. Berman, Marc G., John Jonides, and Stephen Kaplan. "The Cognitive Benefits of Interacting with Nature." *Psychological Science* 19, no. 12 (December 2008): 1207–12. https://doi.org/10.1111/j.1467-9280.2008.02225.x.

Berman, Marc G., Ethan Kross, Katherine M. Krpan, Mary K. Askren, Aleah Burson, Patricia J. Deldin, Stephen Kaplan, Lindsey Sherdell, Ian H. Gotlib, and John Jonides. "Interacting with Nature Improves Cognition and Affect for Individuals with Depression." *Journal of Affective Disorders* 140, no. 3 (November 2012): 300–305. https://doi.org/10.1016/j.jad.2012.03.012.

Berto, Rita. "Exposure to Restorative Environments Helps Restore Attentional Capacity." *Journal of Environmental Psychology* 25, no. 3 (September 2005): 249–59. https://doi.org/10.1016/j.jenvp.2005.07.001.

Ohly, Heather, Mathew P. White, Benedict W. Wheeler, Alison Bethel, Obioha C. Ukoumunne, Vasilis Nikolaou, and Ruth Garside. "Attention Restoration Theory: A Systematic Review of the Attention Restoration Potential of Exposure to Natural Environments." *Journal of Toxicology and Environmental Health, Part B* 19, no. 7 (October 2, 2016): 305–43. https://doi.org/10.1080/1093 7404.2016.1196155.

Stevenson, Matt P., Theresa Schilhab, and Peter Bentsen. "Attention Restoration Theory II: A Systematic Review to Clarify Attention Processes Affected by Exposure to Natural Environments." *Journal of Toxicology and Environmental Health,* Part B 21, no. 4 (May 19, 2018): 227–68. https://doi.org/10.1080/10937404 .2018.1505571.

58. Green, Kristophe, and Dacher Keltner. "What Happens When We Reconnect with Nature." *Greater Good*, March 1, 2017. https://greatergood.berkeley.edu /article/item/what_happens_when_we_reconnect_with_nature.

Piff, Paul K., Pia Dietze, Matthew Feinberg, Daniel M. Stancato, and Dacher Keltner. "Awe, the Small Self, and Prosocial Behavior."

Zhang, Jia Wei, Paul K. Piff, Ravi Iyer, Spassena Koleva, and Dacher Keltner. "An Occasion for Unselfing: Beautiful Nature Leads to Prosociality." *Journal of Environmental Psychology* 37 (March 2014): 61–72. https://doi.org/10.1016/j .jenvp.2013.11.008.

59. Olmsted, Frederick Law. "Yosemite and the Mariposa Grove: A Preliminary Report, 1865," 1865. https://www.yosemite.ca.us/library/olmsted/report.html.

60. Browning, William, Catherine Ryan, and Joseph Clancy. "14 Patterns of Biophilic Design: Improving Health & Well-Being in the Built Environment."

Terrapin Bright Green, September 12, 2014. http://www.terrapinbrightgreen.com /reports/14-patterns-of-biophilic-design/.

61. Levy, Steven. "Apple's New Campus: An Exclusive Look Inside the Mothership." *Wired,* May 16, 2017. https://www.wired.com/2017/05/apple-park-new-silicon -valley-campus/.

62. Nelson, Pete. "Techie Treehouses—Microsoft's Treetop Work Spaces." *Nelson Treehouse,* October 27, 2017. https://www.nelsontreehouse.com/blog/2017/10/20 /techie-treehouses-microsoft.

63. McGregor, Jena. "Why Amazon Built Its Workers a Mini Rain Forest inside Three Domes in Downtown Seattle." *The Washington Post,* January 30, 2018. https://www.washingtonpost.com/.

64. Day One Staff. "Inspiring Innovation with Biophilia." *The Amazon Blog,* November 20, 2017. https://blog.aboutamazon.com/amazon-offices/inspiring-innovation -with-biophilia.

65. "USDA ERS—Beginning Farmers and Age Distribution of Farmers." Accessed March 26, 2019. https://www.ers.usda.gov/topics/farm-economy/beginning -disadvantaged-farmers/beginning-farmers-and-age-distribution-of-farmers/.

66. "2012 Census of Agriculture—Beginning Farmers Highlights | USDA— National Agricultural Statistics Service." Accessed March 27, 2019. https://www .nass.usda.gov/Publications/Highlights/2014/Beginning_Farmers/index.php.

    Ahearn, M.C. "Potential Challenges for Beginning Farmers and Ranchers." *Choices,* 2011. http://choicesmagazine.org/choices-magazine/theme-articles /innovations-to-support-beginning-farmers-and-ranchers/potential-challenges -for-beginning-farmers-and-ranchers.

67. Ackoff, Sophie, Andrew Bahrenburg, and Lindsey Shute. "National Young Farmers Coalition | Building a Future with Farmers II." November 27, 2017. *National Young Farmers Coalition,* November 23, 2017. https://youngfarmers.btcsupport. com/resource/building-a-future-with-farmers-ii/.

68. "2012 Census of Agriculture—Farm Demographics Highlights | USDA— National Agricultural Statistics Service." Accessed March 27, 2019. https://www .nass.usda.gov/Publications/Highlights/2014/Farm_Demographics/index.php.

69. Curtis, Abigail. "USDA Farming Census: Maine Has More Young Farmers, More Land in Farms." *Bangor Daily News,* February 23, 2014. Accessed March 27, 2019. https://bangordailynews.com/2014/02/23/business/usda-farming -census-maine-has-more-young-farmers-more-land-in-farms/.

70. Ackoff, Sophie, Andrew Bahrenburg, and Lindsey Shute. "National Young Farmers Coalition | Building a Future with Farmers II."

71. Hansen, Eric, Sophie Ackoff, Lindsey Shute, and Chelsey Simpson. "Farming Is Public Service: A Case to Add Farmers to the Public Service Loan Forgiveness Program." *National Young Farmers Coalition,* 2015. https://bfnmass.org/blog /lets-add-farmers-public-service-loan-forgiveness-program.

72. Ackoff, Sophie, Andrew Bahrenburg, and Lindsey Shute. "National Young Farmers Coalition | Building a Future with Farmers II."

73. Poulsen, Dorthe Varning, Ulrika K. Stigsdotter, Dorthe Djernis, and Ulrik Sidenius. "'Everything Just Seems Much More Right in Nature': How Veterans with Post-Traumatic Stress Disorder Experience Nature-Based Activities in a Forest Therapy Garden." *Health Psychology Open* 3, no. 1 (March 7, 2016): 205510291663709. https://doi.org/10.1177/2055102916637090.

    "Wilderness Therapy for Teens & Young Adults." *Pacific Quest.* https://pacific quest.org/.

74. Feldbaum, Mindy, Frank Greene, Sarah Kirschenbaum, Debbie Mukamal, Megan Welsh, and Raquel Pinderhughes. "The Greening of Corrections: Creating a Sustainable System." *National Institute of Corrections,* March 2011. https://info.nicic.gov/nicrp/system/files/024914.pdf.

75. Mandela, Nelson. *Long Walk to Freedom: The Autobiography of Nelson Mandela* (New York: Little, Brown, 2008).

76. BPT Staff. "Seven Reasons Why Millennials Love Gardening (and You Should, Too)." *Fairfax County Times,* March 30, 2017. http://www.fairfaxtimes.com/articles/seven-reasons-why-millennials-love-gardening-and-you-should-too/article_94b2dee0-1582-11e7-b1e0-db06766bf936.html.

    Byron, Ellen. "America's Retailers Have a New Target Customer: The 26-Year-Old Millennial." *Wall Street Journal,* October 9, 2017. https://www.wsj.com/articles/americas-retailers-have-a-new-target-customer-the-26-year-old-millennial-1507559181.

77. Hartke, Kristen. "Seeds of Change: Mini Gardens Help Drive the Growth of Food at Home." NPR, *The Salt,* May 31, 2017. https://www.npr.org/sections/thesalt/2017/05/31/527069263/seeds-of-change-mini-gardens-help-drive-the-growth-of-food-at-home.

78. Garden Research. "Spending on Lawns and Gardens Jumps, Led by Millennials and Boomers." *Garden Research,* April 27, 2016. https://gardenresearch.com/blog/-spending-on-lawns-and-gardens-jumps-led-by-millennials-and-boomers/.

79. "Pinterest 100 2019."

80. Chaker, Anne Marie. "Love Local Farming? Try Your Living Room." *Wall Street Journal,* February 12, 2018. https://www.wsj.com/articles/love-local-farming-try-your-living-room-1518454522.

81. Evans, Alexandra, Nalini Ranjit, Cori N. Fair, Rose Jennings, and Judith L. Warren. "Previous Gardening Experience and Gardening Enjoyment Is Related to Vegetable Preferences and Consumption among Low-Income Elementary School Children." *Journal of Nutrition Education and Behavior* 48, no. 9 (October 2016): 618–624.e1. https://doi.org/10.1016/j.jneb.2016.06.011.

    Greer, Anna E., Stacey Davis, Cristina Sandolo, Nicole Gaudet, and Brianna Castrogivanni. "Agricultural Experiences Are Positively Associated with High School Students' Fruit and Vegetable Perceptions and Consumption." *Journal of Nutrition Education and Behavior* 50, no. 2 (February 2018): 133–140. https://doi.org/10.1016/j.jneb.2017.08.009.

    Haire-Joshu, Debra, Michael B. Elliott, Nicole M. Caito, Kimberly Hessler, M. S. Nanney, Nancy Hale, Tegan K. Boehmer, Matthew Kreuter, and Ross C. Brownson. "High 5 for Kids: The Impact of a Home Visiting Program on Fruit and Vegetable Intake of Parents and Their Preschool Children." *Preventive Medicine* 47, no. 1 (July 2008): 77–82. https://doi.org/10.1016/j.ypmed.2008.03.016.

Heim, Stephanie, Jamie Stang, and Marjorie Ireland. "A Garden Pilot Project Enhances Fruit and Vegetable Consumption among Children." *Journal of the American Dietetic Association* 109, no. 7 (July 2009): 1220–26. https://doi.org/10.1016/j.jada.2009.04.009.

Nova, Paulo, Elisabete Pinto, Benedita Chaves, and Margarida Silva. "Urban Organic Community Gardening to Promote Environmental Sustainability Practices and Increase Fruit, Vegetables and Organic Food Consumption." *Gaceta Sanitaria*, November 2018, S0213911118302280. https://doi.org/10.1016/j.gaceta.2018.09.001.

Parmer, Sondra M., Jill Salisbury-Glennon, David Shannon, and Barbara Struempler. "School Gardens: An Experiential Learning Approach for a Nutrition Education Program to Increase Fruit and Vegetable Knowledge, Preference, and Consumption among Second-Grade Students." *Journal of Nutrition Education and Behavior* 41, no. 3 (May 2009): 212–17. https://doi.org/10.1016/j.jneb.2008.06.002.

82. "Amenities." 550 Vanderbilt. Accessed March 27, 2019. https://550vanderbilt.com/amenities/.

Pomranz, Mike. "Fancy Brooklyn Condos Come with Rooftop Farmland." *Food & Wine*, May 24, 2017. https://www.foodandwine.com/news/fancy-brooklyn-apartments-come-rooftop-farmland.

83. Garfield, Leanna. "Shanghai Is Getting an Entire 'Farming District' with Towering Vertical Farms and Seed Libraries." *Business Insider*, April 18, 2017. https://www.businessinsider.com/sunqiao-shanghai-farming-district-2017-4.

Pudong Agriculture Development Group. "Sunqiao Urban Agricultural District." *Sasaki*. Accessed March 27, 2019. http://www.sasaki.com/project/417/sunqiao-urban-agricultural-district/.

CONCLUSION

1. Crowcroft, Orlando. "Generation Z Rejects Donald Trump and Brexit with Call to Let in More Migrants and Refugees." *International Business Times UK*, February 8, 2017. https://www.ibtimes.co.uk/generation-z-rejects-donald-trump-brexit-call-let-more-migrants-refugees-1605290.

Luntz, Frank. "The Attitudes and Priorities of the Snapchat Generation." *Politico*, February 18, 2016. http://static.politico.com/bc/7c/c808106e44eaa8855a3a12553bb7/snapchat-generation-release.pdf.

Maniam, Shiva, and Samantha Smith. "Younger, Older Generations Divided in Partisanship and Ideology." *Pew Research Center*, March 20, 2017. https://www.pewresearch.org/fact-tank/2017/03/20/a-wider-partisan-and-ideological-gap-between-younger-older-generations.

"Survey Results 2015: Global Shapers Community." *World Economic Forum*, 2015. http://www3.weforum.org/docs/Media/GSC/GSC_AnnualSurvey15.pdf.

2. "World Value Index: How People Perceive Brands' Purpose." Enso, 2017. https://www.enso.co/wp-content/uploads/2018/09/WorldValueIndex_2017_enso.pdf.

3. "2016 Food Travel Monitor." *World Food Travel Association*, 2016. https://world foodtravel.org/food-travel-research-monitor.

4. "Meet Gen Z: The Social Generation." *Origin*, December 2017. https://genz.hhcc .com/hubfs/Gen%20Z%20-%20The%20Social%20Generation%20%7C%20 Hill%20Holliday-5.pdf.

5. Altman, Anna. "The Year of Hygge, the Danish Obsession with Getting Cozy." *The New Yorker*, December 18, 2016. https://www.newyorker.com/culture/culture -desk/the-year-of-hygge-the-danish-obsession-with-getting-cozy.

6. Adams, Jenny. "London's One Aldwych Hotel Now Serves a Virtual Reality Cocktail." *Condé Nast Traveler*, April 15, 2017. https://www.cntraveler.com/story /londons-one-aldwych-hotel-now-serves-a-virtual-reality-cocktail.

7. "Heston Blumenthal on VR and How It Can Aid Dining and Social Occasions." *The Drum*, May 2, 2017. https://www.thedrum.com/news/2017/05/02/heston -blumenthal-vr-and-how-it-can-aid-dining-and-social-occasions.

8. "Millennials Are Crowdsourcing You: How Companies and Brands Have the Chance to Do What Millennials Think They Can't Do Themselves." *Millennial Pulse 2017 Special Report*. Shelton Group, 2017. https://storage.googleapis.com /shelton-group/Pulse%20Reports/Millennial%20Pulse%20FINAL.pdf.

9. Bauman, Valerie. "20% of Millennials Say Climate Change Will Cause Humans to Die Out." *Daily Mail*, April 23, 2019. https://www.dailymail.co.uk/news /article-6952273/20-Millennials-believe-global-warming-lead-extinction -humanity-lifetimes.html.

10. "Regenerative Organic Agriculture and Climate Change: A Down-to-Earth Solution to Global Warming." *Rodale Institute*, n.d. https://rodaleinstitute.org /wp-content/uploads/rodale-white-paper.pdf.

11. "What Is Agrobiodiversity?" *FAO*. Accessed April 29, 2019. http://www.fao .org/3/y5609e/y5609e02.htm.

12. FAO Commission on Genetic Resources for Food and Agriculture. "The State of the World's Biodiversity for Food and Agriculture." Food and Agriculture Organizations of the United Nations, 2019. http://www.fao.org/3/CA3129EN /CA3129EN.pdf.

13. Foley, Jonathan. "It's Time to Rethink America's Corn System." *Scientific American*. Accessed August 19, 2016. http://www.scientificamerican.com/article/time -to-rethink-corn/.

    "Hidden Costs of Industrial Agriculture." *Union of Concerned Scientists*, July 11, 2008. Accessed August 19, 2016. http://www.ucsusa.org/our-work/food -agriculture/our-failing-food-system/industrial-agriculture.

    Nink, Emily. "Accounting for the Hidden Costs of Monoculture Crops." *Food Tank*, June 4, 2015. http://foodtank.com/news/2015/06/accounting-for-the -hidden-costs-of-monoculture-crops.

14. Lal, R., Follett, R. F., Stewart, B. A., and Kimble, J. M. "Soil carbon sequestration to mitigate climate change and advance food security." *Soil Science* 172, no. 12 (December 2007): 943–956 (2007). https://pubag.nal.usda.gov/catalog/9747.

15. Secretariat of the United Nations Convention to Combat Desertification. "Global Land Outlook, 1st ed." United Nations Convention to Combat Desertification, 2017. https://www.unccd.int/actions/global-land-outlook-glo.

World Economic Forum. "What If the World's Soil Runs Out?" *Time,* December 14, 2012. http://world.time.com/2012/12/14/what-if-the-worlds-soil-runs-out/.

16. Halweil, Brian. "Still No Free Lunch: Nutrient Levels in U.S. Food Supply Eroded by Pursuit of High Yields." *Organic Center,* September 2007. https://www .organic-center.org/reportfiles/YieldsReport.pdf.

Myers, Samuel S., Antonella Zanobetti, Itai Kloog, Peter Huybers, Andrew D. B. Leakey, Arnold J. Bloom, Eli Carlisle, et al. "Increasing CO2 Threatens Human Nutrition." *Nature* 510 (May 7, 2014): 139. https://www.nature.com /articles/nature13179.

Tan, Z. X., R. Lal, and K. D. Wiebe. "Global Soil Nutrient Depletion and Yield Reduction." *Journal of Sustainable* Agriculture 26, no. 1 (June 14, 2005): 123–46. https://doi.org/10.1300/J064v26n01_10.

17. "Regenerative Organic Agriculture and Climate Change: A Down-to-Earth Solution to Global Warming." *Rodale Institute,* n.d. https://rodaleinstitute.org /wp-content/uploads/rodale-white-paper.pdf.

18. Crawford, Elizabeth. "3 Beverage Trends Spotted by Google That Promise Sustained Growth." *Food Navigator,* September 19, 2017. https://www.food navigator-usa.com/Article/2017/09/20/3-beverage-trends-spotted-by-Google -that-promise-sustained-growth.

19. Hawken, Paul. "Plant-Rich Diet." *Drawdown,* February 7, 2017. https://www .drawdown.org/solutions/food/plant-rich-diet.

20. Philpott, Tom. "You Don't Have to Be a Vegan to Be a Climate-Friendly Eater." *Mother Jones.* Accessed April 29, 2019. https://www.motherjones.com /food/2019/04/meat-beef-climate-change-greenhouse-gas-emissions-hamburger -plant-based-impossible-burger-mushrooms-vegetarian-vegan/?mc_cid=bb07 bde9c6&mc_eid=5c5014c674.

21. Waite, Richard, Daniel Vennard, and Gerard Pozzi. "This Flavor-Packed Burger Saves As Many Emissions As Taking 2 Million Cars Off the Road." World Resources Institute, February 22, 2018. https://www.wri.org/blog/2018/02 /flavor-packed-burger-saves-many-emissions-taking-2-million-cars-road.

22. McKean, Ben. "Vegetables Will Replace Meat by 2020—And Millennials Are Driving the Shift." *Observer,* October 10, 2016. https://observer.com/2016/10 /vegetables-will-replace-meat-by-2020-and-millennials-are-driving-the-shift/.

23. Viviano, Frank. "This Tiny Country Feeds the World." *National Geographic,* August 31, 2017. https://www.nationalgeographic.com/magazine/2017/09 /holland-agriculture-sustainable-farming/.

24. "Agfunder Agrifood Tech Investing Report 2018." *AgFunder,* 2018. https://research. agfunder.com/2018/AgFunder-Agrifood-Tech-Investing-Report-2018.pdf.

25. Hemp, A. "The Banana Forests of Kilimanjaro: Biodiversity and Conservation of the Chagga Homegardens." *Biodiversity and Conservation* 15, no. 4 (2006): 1193–1217.

Larios, C., A. Casas, M. Vallejo, A. I. I. Moreno-Calles, and J. Blancas. "Plant Management and Biodiversity Conservation in Náhuatl Homegardens of the Tehuacán Valley, Mexico." *Journal of Ethnobiology and Ethnomedicine* 9, no. 1 (2013): 74–90.

Webb, E. L. and M. E. Kabir. "Home Gardening for Tropical Biodiversity Conservation." *Conservation Biology* 23(6) (2009): 1641–44.

26. Marsh, George Perkins. *Man and Nature* (1864).

index

about the author

Photo credit: Jason Turow-Paul

Eve Turow-Paul is a globally recognized thought leader on youth food culture and the impact of the Digital Age. With her unique blend of investigative reporting and analysis of academic research and lifestyle markets, Turow-Paul identifies the wants and needs that explain today's hottest trends.

Born in Evanston, Illinois, Turow-Paul graduated from Amherst College in 2009, with a major in psychology. She is a frequent keynote speaker, a *Forbes* contributor, and the author of *A Taste of Generation Yum: How the Millennial Generation's Love for Organic Fare, Celebrity Chefs and Microbrews Will Make or Break the Future of Food*. You can see her in the documentary film *WASTED! The Story of Food Waste*. Today, Turow-Paul utilizes her extensive empirical research to advise Fortune 500 companies, startups, and independent entrepreneurs on how to connect with and better serve people in this Digital Age.

After a decade in New York City, she has returned to the Chicagoland area with her family.